LEGAL INSTITUTIONS AND COLLECTIVE MEMORIES

In recent decades the debate among scholars, lawyers, politicians and others about how societies deal with their past has been constant and intensive. *Legal Institutions and Collective Memories* situates the processes of transitional justice at the intersection between legal procedures and the production of collective and shared meanings of the past. Building upon the work of Maurice Halbwachs, this collection of essays emphasises the extended role and active involvement of contemporary law and legal institutions in public discourse about the past, and explores their impact on the shape that collective memories take in the course of time. The authors uncover a complex pattern of searching for truth, negotiating the past and cultivating the art of forgetting. Their contributions explore the ambiguous and intricate links between the production of justice, truth and memory.

The essays cover a broad range of legal institutions, countries and topics. These include transitional trials as 'monumental spectacles' as well as constitutional courts and the restitution of property rights in Central and Eastern Europe and Australia. The authors present biographical accounts of victims and how their voices were repressed, as in the case of Korean 'Comfort Women'. They explore the role of law and legal institutions in linking individual and collective memories in the transitional period through processes of lustration, and they analyse divided memories about the past and their impact on future reconciliation in South Africa. The collection offers a genuinely comparative approach, allied to cutting-edge theoretical accounts.

Oñati International Series in Law and Society

A SERIES PUBLISHED FOR
THE OÑATI INSTITUTE FOR THE SOCIOLOGY OF LAW

General Editors

Judy Fudge   David Nelken

Founding Editors

William LF Felstiner   Eve Darian-Smith

Board of General Editors

Rosemary Hunter, University of Kent, United Kingdom
Carlos Lugo, Hostos Law School, Puerto Rico
David Nelken, Macerata University, Italy
Jacek Kurczewski, Warsaw University, Poland
Marie Claire Foblets, Leuven University, Belgium
Roderick Macdonald, McGill University, Canada

Titles in this Series

Social Dynamics of Crime and Control: New Theories for a World in Transition edited by Susanne Karstedt and Kai Bussmann

Criminal Policy in Transition edited by Andrew Rutherford and Penny Green

Making Law for Families edited by Mavis Maclean

Poverty and the Law edited by Peter Robson and Asbjørn Kjønstad

Adapting Legal Cultures edited by Johannes Feest and David Nelken

Rethinking Law Society and Governance: Foucault's Bequest edited by Gary Wickham and George Pavlich

Rules and Networks edited by Richard Appelbaum, Bill Felstiner and Volkmar Gessner

Women in the World's Legal Professions edited by Ulrike Schultz and Gisela Shaw

Healing the Wounds edited by Marie-Claire Foblets and Trutz von Trotha

Imaginary Boundaries of Justice edited by Ronnie Lippens

Family Law and Family Values edited by Mavis Maclean

Contemporary Issues in the Semiotics of Law
edited by Anne Wagner, Tracey Summerfield and Farid Benavides Vanegas

The Geography of Law: Landscapes, Identity and Regulation
edited by Bill Taylor

Theory and Method in Socio-Legal Research edited by Reza Banakar
and Max Travers

Luhmann on Law and Politics edited by Michael King
and Chris Thornhill

*Precarious Work, Women and the New Economy: The Challenge to
Legal Norms* edited by Judy Fudge and Rosemary Owens

*Juvenile Law Violators, Human Rights and the Development of New
Juvenile Justice Systems* edited by Eric L Jensen and Jørgen Jepsen

*The Language Question in Europe and Diverse Societies: Political, Legal
and Social Perspectives* edited by Dario Castiglione and Chris Longman

European Ways of Law: Towards a European Sociology of Law
edited by Volkmar Gessner and David Nelken

*Crafting Transnational Policing: Police Capacity-Building and Global
Policing Reform* edited by Andrew Goldsmith and James Sheptycki

*Constitutional Politics in the Middle East: With Special Reference to
Turkey, Iraq, Iran and Afghanistan* edited by Saïd Amir Arjomand

Parenting after Partnering: Containing Conflict after Separation
edited by Mavis Maclean

*Responsible Business: Self-Governance and Law in Transnational
Economic* Transactions edited by Olaf Dilling, Martin Herberg
and Gerd Winter

Rethinking Equality Projects in Law edited by Rosemary Hunter

*Women, Crime and Social Harm: Towards a Criminology for the
Global Age* edited by Maureen Cain and Adrian Howe

*Multicultural Jurisprudence: Comparative Perspectives on the Cultural
Defence* Edited by Marie-Claire Foblets and Alison Dundes Renteln

Legal Institutions and Collective Memories

Edited by
Susanne Karstedt

Oñati International Series in Law and Society

A SERIES PUBLISHED FOR
THE OÑATI INSTITUTE FOR THE SOCIOLOGY OF LAW

·HART·
PUBLISHING

OXFORD AND PORTLAND, OREGON
2009

Published in North America (US and Canada)
by Hart Publishing
c/o International Specialized Book Services
920 NE 58th Avenue, Suite 300
Portland, OR 97213-3786
USA
Tel: +1-503-287-3093 or toll-free: 1-800-944-6190
Fax: +1-503-280-8832
Email: orders@isbs.com
Website: www.isbs.com

Hart Publishing, 16c Worcester Place, Oxford, OX1 2JW
Telephone: +44 (0)1865517530
Fax: +44 (0)1865 510710
Email: mail@hartpub.co.uk
Website: www.hartpub.co.uk

British Library Cataloguing in Publication Data
Data Available

ISBN: 978-1-84113-326-3 (hardback)
ISBN: 978-1-84113-327-0 (paperback)

Typeset by Compuscript, Shannon
Printed and bound in Great Britain by
Antony Rowe, Chippenham, Wiltshire

Contents

Part I: 'The Truth and Nothing but the Truth': Truth and Justice between the Past and the Present

Part II: Divided Memories, Contested Truths, Silenced Voices

Part III: Law, Memory and the Politics of Culture and Identity

Acknowledgements

The contributions to this collection were first presented in a workshop entitled 'Legal Institutions and Collective Memories' at the International Institute for the Sociology of Law in Oñati, Spain in 1999. The workshop was supported by the Institute and a generous grant from the Volkswagen Foundation, Germany, as part of their Programme 'Recht und Verhalten' (Law and Behaviour). The Volkswagen Foundation gave further financial support to the publication of this volume. I wish to express my gratitude to both institutions, in particular to Malen Gordoa from the International Institute in Oñati, whose support in organising the workshop was invaluable, and to Dr Hagen Hof from the Volkswagen Foundation, for his encouragement, advice and support throughout the project. I owe a great debt of gratitude to the authors not only for their wonderful contributions but for their patience with the editor. Kirsten Lieps, Nadine Bals and Lena Kruckenberg from the University of Bielefeld helped with the editorial work, and I am grateful to these wonderful young women. A Visiting Fellowship at the Regulatory Institutions Network at the Australian National University and a visit to Oñati finally allowed for the time to put everything together. I wish to thank my colleagues at RegNet for their inspiring ideas, the Australian National University for financial support and the International Institute of the Sociology of Law for a wonderful office.

Susanne Karstedt
Keele University
United Kingdom

Biographical Notes

Maurice Halbwachs (1877–1945) was the first to coin the term and conceptualise the notion of 'collective memory'. As a student and collaborator of Emile Durkheim on the 'L'Année Sociologique' since 1905, his debts to this teacher can be traced throughout his work. Nonetheless, his work on collective memory, though perhaps the most Durkheimian in spirit and in method, is also the most independent from the master as well as the other disciples, who were friends and collaborators. He started his lifelong engagement with the topic as early as 1925 with 'Les Cadres sociaux de la mémoire' (Paris, Alcan, 1925; translated into English as *On Collective Memory*, with an introduction by Lewis A Coser (Chicago, University of Chicago Press, 1992)). He combined his interests in both social morphology and the imprint of social life into social space, and collective memory in his 1941 study on the legends from a book of gospels from rural France (*La Topographie légendaire des Évangiles en Terre Sainte, étude du mémoire collective* (Paris, Presses universitaires de France, 1941). His exploration of the spatial organisation of social life also shaped his last (unfinished) work on collective memory, *La Mémoire collective* that was posthumously published by his sister (Paris, Presses Universitaires de France, 1950; translated into English as *The Collective Memory*, with an introduction by Mary Douglas (New York, Harper, 1950)). The amazing diversity of his work and research is characterised by a continuous engagement with what he saw as 'collective psychology' and the material conditions of social life. Collective psychology, at the core of which is his work on collective memory, is the science of the representation of material conditions in social life, and simultaneously the science of the representation of social life in the individual. His last book on collective memory testifies to this, starting with a chapter on individual memory and dreams, and finishing with a chapter on social space and memory. In 1919, Maurice Halbwachs became Professor of Sociology at the University of Strasbourg. From 1935 to 1944 he held a Chair in Sociology at the Sorbonne. In 1944 he was awarded a Chair in Collective Psychology; but only a month later, he was arrested by the Gestapo and deported to the concentration camp Buchenwald in Germany. He was murdered there in March 1945, only days before the Allies liberated the camp.

Heribert Adam is Professor Emeritus of Sociology and Anthropology at Simon Fraser University, Canada. He won international recognition for his comparative work on transitional justice, politics of memory and Truth and

Reconciliation Commissions. In 2000, he was elected Fellow of the Royal Society of Canada. In 1998 he was awarded with the Konrad Adenauer Research Prize, and he received the Outstanding Contribution Award of the Canadian Sociology and Anthropology Association. He was President of the International Sociological Association's Research Committee on Ethnic, Minority and Race Relations. He has published widely on transitional justice in South Africa and Germany, and in his most recent book, *Seeking Mandela: Peacemaking between Israelis and Palestinians* (with K Moodley, 2005) he takes his expertise to a new area.

Emilios Christodoulidis is Professor of Legal Theory at the University of Glasgow. Prior to that he taught at the University of Edinburgh. His area of research and publishing comprises philosophy and sociology of law, and constitutional theory. He has authored numerous articles on these subjects, and his book *Law and Reflexive Politics* won the European Award for Legal Theory in 1996 and the 1998 SPTL Prize for Outstanding Legal Scholarship. He was visiting Professor at the European Academy for Legal Theory in Brussels and gave the Kobe Lectures in Japan in 2002. Together with Scott Veitch he edited a book entitled *Lethe's Law: Justice, Law and Ethics in Reconciliation* (2001) and has published in particular on the South-African TRC. His most recent book (together with Scott Veitch) is on jurisprudence.

Stanley Cohen is Professor Emeritus of Sociology at the London School of Economics and a member of the Mannheim Centre of Criminology. In 1987, he was elected to the British Academy and is currently on the Board of the International Council on Human Rights. He has published groundbreaking work in criminology, of which he is presently preparing new editions. His book, *States of Denial: Knowing About Atrocities and Suffering* (2001), for which he won the 2002 British Academy Book Prize, deals with public reactions to information, images and appeals about inhumanities. His current work includes follow-up research to *States of Denial;* a study of how Truth Commissions create collective memory; and an international project on 'crime, order and security' as a human rights problem.

Roger Engelmann is Research Fellow and Senior Manager in the Department for Education and Research at the Agency of the Federal Commissioner for Documents of the Secret Service of the former German Democratic Republic. He trained as a historian, and his areas of research and publication comprise the work of the secret service during the 1950s; political prosecution and trials in the former GDR; and the critical edition of documents and sources. In his most recent work he analyses how revolutionary and defining events like 17 June 1953 or the building of the Berlin Wall are reflected in the documents and work of the secret service at that time. His co-authored book *Kommunismus in der Krise: Die Entstalinisierung und die Folgen. Analysen und Dokumente der BStU* was published in 2007.

Carol A Heimer is Professor and Chair of the Department of Sociology at Northwestern University and a Senior Research Fellow at the American Bar Foundation. She was previously Research Fellow at Australian National University and Fellow at the LAPA at Princeton University. Her research focuses on risk and the management of risk, which she has researched in a wide range of settings, from the insurance industry to infant intensive care units. Her recent book *For the Sake of Children* (with Lisa Staffen, 1998) won several awards, amongst them the Theory Prize from the Theory Section of the American Sociological Association and the Eliot Freidson Award from the Medical Sociology Section of the American Sociological Association. With her current research on AIDS treatment across continents she is interweaving the worlds of sociology, medicine and law, and addressing the intersection of normative systems, organisations, and trust, risk and uncertainty.

Ruth G Herz was a Presiding Judge at the Juvenile Court in Cologne. She started numerous initiatives in that position, in particular the first mediation project in Germany in the mid-1980s, for which she was awarded with the Federal Cross in 1998. From 2000 until 2005 she was the judge in a popular TV court room show 'The Juvenile Court'. She has taught at the University of Siegen and Bielefeld, at the University of Toronto and at the Law Faculty of Hebrew University in Jerusalem. She has also been a Fellow at St Anthony's College, Oxford. She has published a text book on juvenile law and numerous articles on juvenile delinquency. Her most recent book *Law Quite Personally: From the Desk of a Juvenile Judge* (in German) was published in 2006.

Susanne Karstedt is Professor of Criminology at the School for Sociology and Criminology at Keele University, UK. She was previously Visiting Fellow at the Law Programme and Regulatory Institutions Network at Australian National University. Her areas of research and publishing comprise transitional justice; democracy, crime and justice; emotions, crime and justice; and contemporary moral economies. In 2005, she was awarded the Christa-Hoffmann-Riehm Prize for contributions to German socio-legal studies, and in 2007 with the Sellin-Glueck Award from the American Society of Criminology. Her current research and most recent publications centre on cross-cultural comparisons.

Kathy Laster is Executive Director at the Institute of Public Administration Australia in Victoria. She has been Associate Professor in the Department of Law at La Trobe University, Melbourne; Executive Director of the Victoria

Law Foundation; and a barrister and solicitor of the Supreme Court of Victoria, Australia. She is a consultant to government agencies, including the Refugee Tribunal and the Review of Post-Arrival Programmes and Services. Her research interests focus on legal culture, the legal profession and multiculturalism and law. Representations of law in film and the role of the culture industry in shaping understandings of justice have been defining strands of her work. Her books, written in collaboration with various colleagues, include, *The Drama of the Courtroom: A Filmography; Law as Culture, Interpreters and the Legal System* and *Domestic Violence: Global Issues*. She is a regular contributor to public debate on immigration, multiculturalism, legal education and ethics, and Australian identity.

Juan E Mendez is President of the International Centre for Transitional Justice. In 2004, he was appointed the first UN Special Adviser on the Prevention of Genocide by UN Secretary General Kofi Annan. He served in this position until 31 March 2007. He was imprisoned twice in Argentina for his political and professional activities. In 1996, he became Executive Director of the Inter-American Institute of Human Rights in Costa Rica and was Professor of Law and Director of the Center for Civil and Human Rights at the University of Notre Dame, Indiana, from 1999 to 2004. He also was a member of the Inter-American Commission on Human Rights of the Organization of American States, and its President in 2002. He has published widely on human rights in Latin America and transitional justice and has won several awards for his human rights activities.

Konstanze Plett is Professor of Gender Law at the Faculty of Law, University of Bremen and was previously Director of the Centre for Feminist Studies at the University of Bremen. She is a member of the Bremen Institute for German, European and International Gender, Labour and Social Welfare Law. Her research interests focus on the interaction between social and legal change, with special emphasis on civic and human rights, access to law, and the legal treatment of gender questions. In her current project she explores the construction of gender through law and the rights of the inter-sexed. She has widely published on gender and law and feminist studies in law, and her most recent publications address the history and contemporary problems of the laws of sexual self-determination, in particular for the inter-sexed.

Kim Lane Scheppele is Laurance S Rockefeller Professor of Public Affairs at the Woodrow Wilson School and the University Center for Human Values, and Director of the Program on Law and Public Affairs at Princeton University. Before joining Princeton University, she was John O'Brien Professor of Comparative Law and Sociology at the Law School of the University of Pennsylvania. She was Visiting Fellow at the Institute for Law and Policy and

Visiting Researcher at the Constitutional Court of the Russian Federation in Moscow (2003) and Co-Director of the Programme on Gender and Culture at the Central European University, Budapest. Her research interests and publications are in the area of comparative constitutional law, in particular post-Soviet constitutional law, constitutional courts and judicial activism in the transition period. Her book-in-progress, *The International State of Emergency*, explores the creation of international security law through UN Security Council resolutions and examines the effect that apparent compliance with these resolutions has had on constitutional integrity.

Young-Hee Shim is Professor of Sociology at Hanyang University, Seoul and Director of the Hanyang Institute for Women. Since 1999, she has been Director of the Korean Women's Association United. She is a member of the Parole Commission and on the Board of numerous organisations for young offenders, women and crime prevention. She is particularly active in promoting the cause of the Korean comfort women and is on the Committee for Distribution of Funds of the Korea Women Foundation. Since 2002, she has been a Co-Representative for the organisation 'Women Making Peace'. Her research and published work mirror her activist role. Her most recent book (in English), *Sexual Violence and Feminism in Korea*, was published in 2002.

Jiřina Šiklová is Professor Emeritus of Social Work at the Faculty of Humanities of Charles University, Prague, where she founded the Department of Social Work. She also founded the Gender Studies Center in Prague in 1991. She was a member of the Czech Helsinki Committee and a signatory of Charter 77, the document of the Czech dissidents, for which she lost her job and was harassed by the authorities. Currently, she publishes on women in Central Europe and is a regular contributor to the daily newspaper *Lidove Noviny* and a frequent guest in nationally televised political and sociological debates. In 2005, she also started an organisation for the promotion of reconciliation between Czechs and Germans who lived in Czechoslovakia during the pre-war period and actively supported the Czech government against Nazi-Germany. In 1999, she was awarded for her work by Vaclav Havel.

Grażyna Skąpska is Professor of Sociology of Law and Norms at the Department of Sociology at Jagiellonian University, Krakow. She is Vice-President of the International Institute of Sociology, the oldest international sociological association. She was Fellow at the Wissenschaftskolleg in Berlin in 2002–03 and has also been at universities in Australia and the US. Her research and numerous publications are in the area of social and economic transitions and transitional justice. Her most recent book in English is *The Moral Fabric in Contemporary Societies* (2003).

Heinz Steinert is Professor Emeritus of Sociology and Social Policy at Johann Wolfgang Goethe-University, Frankfurt. He was founder and until 2002 Director of the Institute for the Sociology of Law and Crime in Vienna. In 2000, he won the Lifetime Achievement Award of the Division of International Criminology of the American Society of Criminology. He has researched and published on a wide range of criminological and socio-legal topics. More recently, his research interests have focused on culture industry and critical theory, in particular the Frankfurt School and the work of Adorno. His recent publications include *Culture Industry* (2003), as well as books on deviancy and social control, citizenship and critical theory.

Arthur L Stinchcombe is Professor Emeritus of Sociology, Political Science and Organizational Behaviour at the Department of Sociology at Northwestern University and has a visiting appointment at the American Bar Foundation. He has authored numerous books on sociological theory and methods, the sociology of organisations and social history. His books include *The Logic of Social Research* (2005), *When Formality Works: Authority and Abstraction in Law and Organizations* (2001) and *Sugar Island Slavery in the Age of Enlightenment* (1995). His awards include the Sorokin Prize of the American Sociological Association for his book *Constructing Social Theories*, the Weber Prize of the American Sociological Association for his book *Information and Organizations*, and the Distinguished Career Prize of the American Sociological Association in 2004. In 2003, he was elected Fellow of the National Academy of Sciences. His most recent book, *The Logic of Social Research* (2005) is the sum of a life in social research. His current research centres on federalism.

Gunnar Theissen is a member of the task force on 'Police Reconstruction and Training in Afghanistan' at the Foreign Office (Auswärtiges Amt) of the Federal Republic of Germany since 2003. He has worked as an academic, academic adviser and member of staff with numerous other organisations in the area of crisis prevention and post-war reconciliation, including the Gesellschaft fuer Technische Zusammenarbeit, the Berghof Center for Constructive Conflict Management, Amnesty International and the German Institute for Human Rights. He has taught on the International Criminal Court at the Free University, Berlin. From 1996–98 he worked for the Centre for the Study of Violence and Reconciliation (CSVR), Johannesburg, on a review of public opinion surveys on the TRC in South Africa and has published widely on his results.

Scott Veitch is Professor of Jurisprudence at the School of Law at the University of Glasgow. Before joining the School of Law he taught at Macquarie University in Sydney. His research focuses on the areas of philosophy and politics of law. He has held visiting positions at the University of Cape Town (1997), the European Academy of Legal Theory, Brussels (1999–2001), the University of Canterbury, NZ (2004) and the University of New South Wales, Sydney (2004). His book *Moral Conflict and Legal Reasoning* (1999) won the European Award for Legal Theory. His most recent books are *Jurisprudence* (with E Christodoulidis, 2007), *Law and the Politics of Reconciliation* (2007) and on Isaiah Berlin. His current research interests focus on the political economy of reconciliation and on complicity and irresponsibility.

Andrzej Zybertowicz is Associate Professor of Sociology and Director of the Institute of Sociology at Nicholas Copernicus University in Torun, Poland. He has been Visiting Fellow at Cambridge University and Visiting Research Scholar in Law at Macquirie University, Sydney. His area of research and publication is the role of the secret service and police in the communist state and after its downfall. His publications include *Between Dogma and a Research Program: In the Grip of Secret Services. The Collapse of Communism and the Post-Nomenklatura Networks* (in Polish) and *Privatizing the Police State: The Case of Poland* (with Maria Los, 2000, in English). Further English publications include a book chapter on 'Hidden Actors, Overlooked Dimensions and Blind Intellectuals' (2006). He has been active in a newly founded institution at the local and regional level, the Regional Social Dialogue Commissions, and has written an extensive report on their work and achievements. From July to November 2007 he was Chief Security Advisor to the Prime Minister of Poland and remains a presidential adviser. He also was an advisor for a book publication that accused Lech Walesa of collaboration with the secret Police.

Introduction

The Legacy of Maurice Halbwachs

SUSANNE KARSTEDT

The mere punishment of the defendants ... can never redress the terrible injuries
the Nazis visited on these unfortunate people. For them it is far more important
that these incredible events be established by clear and public proof, so that no
one can doubt that they were fact and not fable: and that this Court ... stamp
these acts, and the ideas which engendered them, as barbarous and criminal.

> Telford Taylor in his opening statement for the prosecution in the
> Nuremberg trials of Nazi physicians[1]

Father, I am ready to forgive, but I need to know whom to forgive and for
what.

> Woman to a priest in Uruguay when counseled about the
> disappearance of her child[2]

My critics may have the chronicle, but history belongs to me, and that is where
the final verdict will be decided.

> Former Argentina junta commander Emilio Massera[3]

History is only an opinion.

> Defence counsel in the Touvier trial in France, commenting on the
> testimony of a historian[4]

I. MAURICE HALBWACHS AND COLLECTIVE MEMORY

ALL THESE STATEMENTS on facts and history, proof, knowledge and
opinion were with one exception made in the course of criminal trials and legal procedures. They testify to the intricate links between

---

[1] Osiel 1997, 276.
[2] Cohen 1995, 41.
[3] Osiel 1997, 255.
[4] *Ibid*, 218.

legal institutions, memories and history, and raise questions about truth, justice and forgiving. These were, however, 'exceptional procedures' (Karstedt 1998) in every respect: They were intended as 'monumental spectacles' (Osiel 1997, 3) that dramatised the contrast between a totalitarian past and a democratic present and as such represented 'constitutional moments' for the societies in which they took place. They were transformative events that simultaneously involved catastrophes and triumphs. They presented former rulers in prison uniforms and former victims now empowered by the law. They provided narratives of history and simultaneously of morality, tales of what went wrong and how the future should be. They brought history and historians to the court room, and court files became invaluable historical archives and stores of memory for future generations.

As 'monumental spectacles' they were intended to shape and reshape collective memories of society, but they did so not only in their grand narratives, but equally on the more vernacular level of common experiences and memories of people. On this level, they brought to the court room experiences and memories of terror and violence that were attached to cities, streets and houses but had been eradicated from the normal spaces in which memory is exercised and sedimented in society. They (re)created a space for such memories for the first time, even within the restrictive boundaries of the law, legal procedures and court rooms.

Such trials and legal procedures capture the public imagination, and there can be little doubt that they impact on how the events and the period of history that they deal with are collectively remembered. They do so by giving a voice to victims and perpetrators, by selecting what will be remembered and in which way, by judging on guilt and innocence, by selecting a guilty few and thus exonerating the many. Simultaneously, they set the stage for all types of forgetting, for individual denial of guilt and repression of memories, amounting to 'social amnesia' of a terrible past, for amnesties as 'lawful amnesia' stamped by courts and procedures (Osiel 1997, 175), and equally for those kinder versions of forgetting like reconciliation and forgiveness. However, in capturing public and scholarly imagination, criminal trials and procedures as morality narratives usually do more than other legal procedures; they in a way distract attention from other legal institutions and the ways in which these other institutions also shape the collective, ie, the *shared* memories of a group or whole society (Margalit 2000, 35).

Clearly, transitional situations and transitional justice epitomise and in many ways bring to the fore the intricate relationship between legal institutions and collective memories. At the same time, the very situation of transition conceals from our captivated imagination how much and in how many realms of law collective memories are 'legalised' and how much of collective memory and history in modern societies is constructed following 'legal blueprints' (Osiel 1997, 209; see also Markovits 2001). In the same vein, we tend to elide other fields of the law like constitutions, property rights and legal liberties, as well as administrative law, and how these provide mechanisms and channels for collective memories. Finally and critically, the ways that collective memories—their construction and their selective 'loss of memory'—shape and permeate law, and thus the 'legal blueprint', has comparably rarely attracted attention.

Maurice Halbwachs' last manuscript on 'Collective Memory' (1985), which he left behind as a fragment when he was deported and murdered at Buchenwald days before the liberation in 1945 actually provides a much broader perspective on the role of legal institutions in the formation of collective memories of groups, societies and nations.[5] The section on law, 'The Legal Space and the Memory of Law' is part of the last chapter on 'Collective Memory and Space', both demonstrating how Halbwachs developed the concept of collective memory from a discussion on social time and space (Coser 1992). Law in particular, as it defines property rights or relations of domination and subordination within a society and between its different groups, leaves its visible stamp on social space and thus shapes the collective memory of groups and society as a whole. This is, however, a dialectical relationship. Law builds on collective memories about its legitimacy and the justification of the rights it provides; therefore collective memory has to intervene to guarantee the rights which law invests. Both social time and space are represented in legal relationships within society, and conversely, law and its representation in the social time-space produce the sum of individual memories as well as the shared memories of a group. Notably, Halbwachs chooses slavery (and for modern times the worker in the factory) as a relationship of domination and subordination in order to exemplify his argument. For a powerless group and enslaved people, the law that confines them to their position is imprinted in the social space of their lives and thus produces deep and rich layers of collective memories. Terror in modern societies shapes the collective memory in exactly this way, as Halperin writes about the experience of the people of Argentina:

> An experience like that ... turns terror into one of the basic dimensions of collective life. This necessarily redefines the horizon on which the experience of every Argentine is played out. His relation to his country, to his city, to his street cannot remain untouched after having come to see them as places where death always lurks (quoted in Osiel 1997, 76).

---

[5] The following is based on the German translation *Das kollektive Gedächtnis* (Frankfurt, 1985; originally Stuttgart, 1967); the original text with an introduction by Mary Douglas was published in 1950. This was translated by Francis J Ditter and Vida Y Ditter in 1980/1992 under the title *The Collective Memory* (from which the English quotes herein are taken). Halbwachs' work *The Social Frameworks of Memory* was edited and translated by Lewis Coser under the title *On Collective Memory* and published in 1992.

For Maurice Halbwachs, law becomes increasingly important as a mechanism to establish collective memories in modern societies. As a student of Durkheim he ultimately sees law and legal institutions as powerful mechanisms to establish and contribute to the collective conscience and social solidarity within a society. However, in contrast to his teacher, he does not identify collective conscience with collective memories; nor does he contend that collective memory in modern and more diverse societies is unified or uniform. Collective memories are pluralised and multiple, as his example of enslaved people and powerless groups shows: property laws and power relations as they imprint themselves onto the time-space of society produce decisively different collective memories for slaves, factory workers, or their masters and factory owners. This of course is equally the case of apartheid laws and their impact on South African divided society (see Part II of this volume). The ways in which modern societies try to construct a common core of collective memory necessarily become increasingly difficult and diversified, and societies might simultaneously follow different routes, which contradict as well as interact with each other. History (Halbwachs devotes one out of four chapters to the relation between history and collective memory) and legal institutions supersede and replace rituals and traditions; archives (different ones for legal and historical purposes) and bureaucracies provide stores of memory; museums and memorials celebrate the past. Modern societies need a wide range of different institutions that store and construct collective memories, and do so in differing ways. Constructing 'one' collective and shared memory is an increasingly difficult task, and law and legal institutions play an ever more important role, providing finally the 'legal blueprints' (Osiel 1997) for the construction of collective memories.

Establishing collective memories implies both that a shared meaning is given to events of the past, and that there are shared practices of their commemoration. In liberal societies, legal procedures of all types provide shared and institutionalised practices that are at least in theory accessible to all groups of society. Criminal justice procedures in particular give deeply ingrained meanings and interpretations to 'facts' by establishing guilt and innocence and meting out sentences and punishment as moral closure to these events. This might explain their prominent place in transitions as legal or quasi-legal lustration procedures. Stanley Cohen (1995; 2001), though clearly opposing the criminal justice model, points out how important such reconstructions of individual and shared memory are for victims of torture, in whose bodies it was inscribed in the first instance that they were 'outcasts' beyond the boundaries of the collective. Sharing their individual memories even within the confined space of legal procedures is a route towards renewed inclusion.

Criminal justice procedures, however, constitute only one amongst a range of legal institutions that establish shared meanings. Constitutions are powerful landmarks of how a society wishes to define itself and how it wants to relate to its past (see Kim Lane Scheppele in this volume). Habermas (1989) has argued that 'constitutional patriotism' allows liberal societies to define themselves and the legacies of their past not in terms of a nation, but in terms of their achievements as societies that found themselves on human rights and the rule of law.

In modern societies, individual memories are set apart from common and shared memories, notwithstanding that they are shaped by what they share with the memory of a group or even society. Halbwachs draws distinct boundaries between collective and individual memory

> While the collective memory endures and draws strength from its base in a coherent body of people, it is individuals as group members who remember (1985, 28; 1992, 48).

Coser concludes that for Halbwachs, 'there are as many collective memories as there are groups and institutions in a society (1992, 22). Halbwachs argues that individuals share the collective memories of many and different groups, and thus the individual's memory is constitutive of the unique entity—the individual—and is not identical with the shared memories of any of the groups that contribute to it. This applies even more so to larger collectivities like a nation:

> ...[T]he nation is too remote from the individual for him to consider the history of his country as anything else but a very large framework with which his own history makes contact at only a few points (Halbwachs 1992, 77).

Modern societies are thus characterised by 'weak ties' between individual and collective memories. This is of critical importance for the relation between legal institutions and collective memories for a number of reasons.

First, legal institutions and legal relations are precisely what provide those weak ties. They might be less important in shaping and constructing the *content* of collective memories but are channels for the expression of individual memories that link them to those of others. As such they function less as constraints and more as *enabling structures* for the construction of authentical and 'truthful' memories for individuals and groups, for reworking them in contest with other memories, and finally for reaching a core of shared meanings of events (see Osiel 1997 for this argument; see also Arthur L Stinchcombe in this volume).

Second, this capacity as enabling structures contributes to their decisive role (in criminal as well as other procedures) in transitions when the reconstruction of the past and its meaning are at stake. As far as they give space and voice to the countless individual stories, even the most vernacular will contribute to forging new collective memories out of common and shared experiences of the many victims, and thus redraw group boundaries (Karstedt 1998). Common law courts seem to be more 'situation sensitive' (Osiel 1997, 71) than those in civil law traditions and therefore more receptive to such expressions of individual memory. It might be added that they are also better equipped to channel these into collective memories than courts in the European Continental tradition.[6]

Third, the weak ties that exist between individual and collective memory in contemporary society, and the fact that both make contact only in a few areas and at few points, seems to mean that collective memories cannot be easily usurped or totally controlled by those in power. Certainly, memories are suppressed and muted; however, they are rarely totally silenced, and increasingly less so in the global sphere. Victims address themselves and find support outside their countries and nations, as did the Korean comfort women (see Young-Hee Shim in this volume). Legal procedures and courts during transitions seem to emerge as particularly strong institutions when struggles about power are not yet fully resolved, and they are capable of contributing to power shifts by giving voice to hitherto unheard of memories and testimonies. When former Argentina junta commander Emilio Massera exclaimed that 'history belongs to me, and that is where the final verdict will be decided', his appeal to higher orders and a distant future was made from a position of weakness, not strength. Germany's history of coming to terms with its past shows, eg, that courts were consistently more willing to judge in libel suits in favour of those who had revealed facts about the implication of high-level bureaucrats and politicians in the Holocaust and war crimes during the Nazi-Regime and World War II. Collective memories, it seems, are neither suitable to be subjected to disciplinary measures, nor fundamentally and overwhelmingly constructed through the exertion of power, as a Foucauldian approach would suggest (see Osiel 1997, 210; for further arguments, see Emilios Christodoulidis and Scott Veitch in this volume).

Fourth, as much as the collective memories of groups differ within society and in particular in transitional societies, the same events and periods of history affect the collective memories of different nations and societies, which then take a different shape in each. In the wake of World War II, victims and perpetrators were separated into different nations (and by the Iron Curtain), which contributed to a period of collective amnesia in Germany and the selectivity of its collective memory during this long period. International human rights regimes have emerged as mechanisms

---

[6] It is important to note that common law courts can of course also be insensitive to witnesses and the stories they want to tell, as David Hirsh (2003) shows for the Sawoniak trial conducted in Britain. Further, as Fiona Ross (2003) shows for the Truth and Reconciliation Commissions in South Africa, women as victims and witnesses have a crucial role, since their stories relate to families and normally include numerous victims. Legal and quasi-legal procedures tend to ignore this role. (For East Timor, see Charlesworth and Wood 2002).

that are in principle capable of bringing together different sets of collective memories, forcing groups and nations out of collective amnesia. The history and story of the Korean comfort women are most exemplary in this respect. However, as Halbwachs reminds us, collective memory does not exist detached from space and time, and international human rights regimes and legal procedures in the international sphere need to relate to the 'local' in order to function as enabling structures for the construction of collective memory.

Halbwachs acknowledges that there are certain events that alter group life and the collective memories of a nation. These are events 'of such moral magnitude that they become "imbued with the concerns, interests, and passions of a nation"' (Osiel 1997, 76; Halbwachs 1992, 77). The mass atrocities and 'administrative massacres' (Osiel 1997) of the last century constitute traumatic experiences on a collective scale and have become quintessential to the collective memory of many societies. Legal procedures and institutions were and are seminal in the process of reconstructing the basis of a shared understanding of the past and the future. It is here that the legacy of Maurice Halbwachs—his life, his work and his death—resonates most compellingly.

II. INTRODUCTION TO THE VOLUME

The contributions to this volume take a broad perspective on legal institutions and how they shape and are shaped by collective memories. The focus on transitional justice comes as a natural consequence of this task. The links between legal institutions and collective memories seem to be laid bare and open to critical inspection in such transformative periods, and mechanisms are made manifest that under normal conditions would have remained latent. The volume offers an international and thoroughly comparative perspective by covering different historical events, countries and legal institutions. The contributions span the period from the end of World War II until today and include case studies from South Africa, Latin America, Australia, South Korea, Poland, Czechoslovakia and Germany. They cover a range of legal institutions and procedures, from criminal justice and lustration to quasi-legal procedures of Truth and Reconciliation Commissions. They further analyse constitutions, property rights, and liberties in their relations to collective memories and look into international human rights regimes and their role in this process. They explore the ways in which legal institutions are crucial to the rendition of cultural images and the formation of cultural identity.

The warehouses of collective and legal memory, in particular the secret files left behind by the communist regimes of Central Europe, are showcases of how legal procedures shape and reshape the relation between individual and 'collective' biographies and memories. Files are links between the secret and the public, the open and the hidden, and their (unintended) opening becomes decisive in writing and rewriting the past of individuals and collectivities. The past and collective memories of the legal system itself and the judiciary lend themselves to close inspection. In its entirety as well as in its single contributions, this volume offers a comparative perspective that opens up new routes toward our understanding of the principles and mechanisms underlying the relationship between legal institutions and collective memories, and the social and cultural forces that shape this relationship.

The overall comparative perspective of this volume is further achieved by the decisively different approaches the authors take. The contributions vary between in-depth analyses of specific cases and countries, and more sweeping comparative and historical perspectives, between individual biography and collective perceptions. A number of them focus on the 'art of forgetting' to which legal institutions lend themselves. They embed legal institutions into the wider institutional, political and cultural arrangements of society that engender distorted views of the past and consequently distort collective memories. They convey a critical and sceptical view of legal institutions and their role in shaping collective memories. This will help in developing more realistic expectations about this role, as well as legal procedures that are better equipped to deal with individual and collective memories of the past. In the following sections a brief overview of the different parts of the volume is given.

Part I: 'The Truth and Nothing but the Truth': Truth and Justice between the Past and the Present

The pursuit of 'truth' in its many forms—as recovery of what happened, as clarification of its moral content, as a consensual truth—is the central and common focus of legal and quasi-legal procedures, of individual remembrance and collective renderings of the past. It is the core problem of transitional justice: how to realign truth in these various forms with the needs of reconciliation and recovery within post-violence societies. As selective, distorting and restricting as legal institutions and quasi-legal procedures are, likewise are individual and collective memories, and as such, neither the individual sphere nor the institutional or wider social realm differs in principle in rendering distorted, orchestrated or manipulated 'truths'. However, the names given to the legal institutions that were specifically set up during the past two decades to deal with the past and transitions, make perfectly clear that 'truth' *is* at stake, even if they do not directly include the word—like the Truth and Reconciliation Commission in South Africa, which seems to have emerged as their archetype.

Even if not all such procedures do require the 'beyond reasonable doubt' of criminal procedures, and substitute it by a more manageable and adapted requirement, they rely on basic characteristics of legal procedures. In the form of People's Tribunals they retain the legal form and procedural legality and use these morally powerful instruments for assigning criminal liability to individuals and responsibility to states (Chinkin 2001). Postmodern narratives of scepticism, which posit the lack of both truth and sharable memory, question the foundations of the traditional ideal of legal procedures that produce truth as well as the belief that individual moral responsibility is capable of acknowledging 'truth' and guilt. The assumption that there is a core of memories that can be shared is consequently also interrogated by postmodern discourses.

Nonetheless, the fact that we use terms like forgetting, denial, repression and distortion in referring to both individual and collective memory, makes perfectly clear that the 'pursuit' of truth within the universe of legal procedures and institutional arrangements is a 'social fact' (in the Durkheimian sense) that calls for analytical efforts, even destructive ones.

Stanley Cohen's contribution to this volume (see also Cohen 2001) gives an overview to these seminal problems. He describes the dilemmas of 'transitional truth' and juxtaposes truth as 'recovery' of facts with truth as moral 'clarification'. Highly critical of the criminal justice model as a road to 'truth' but not rejecting it outright, he explores different types of truths, from 'forensic truth' to 'restorative truth'. He concludes by outlining a number of meta-problems and paradoxes that highlight the tensions between truth, justice and reconciliation, and the (impossible?) task of legal institutions in recovering individual and collective memory.

Juan Mendez takes a decisively different approach and comes to the opposite conclusion. Drawing on Latin American experiences from over two decades, he distils an unambiguous defence of the criminal justice model from the different routes that Latin American countries took in dealing with their pasts. The criminal justice model, he contends, is the most appropriate institutional form to achieve 'truth', in both its form as recovery of facts and as moral clarification. He acknowledges the important role of legal procedures and in particular of the judiciary (even if highly implicated) in the process of recovering the truth and thus shaping collective memories in these countries. Most important in this respect was the declaration by the Inter-American Commission that proclaimed a justiciable right to 'truth' for individuals and the ensuing obligation for the state to provide those legal procedures that were capable of addressing such claims for truth. He draws attention to the constant impact of international and national human rights organisations and the international legal community on this process, and their role in extending such procedures beyond the narrow timeframes of the imminent transition period. He argues that no other social institutions but legal institutions can muster the moral authority in the search for truth.

Part II: Divided Memories, Contested Truths, Silenced Voices

It is typical of transitions and post-violence societies that collective memories are deeply divided. Finding and establishing even a minimal core of shared truths is the task often assigned to legal and quasi-legal procedures. Group identities are based on deeply ingrained collective memories of such conflicts, which might take on a mythical quality. This became most visible in the conflicts and ethnic cleansing in former Yugoslavia, where the evocation of historical events centuries ago was decisive in fuelling the conflict. (See Arthur L Stinchcombe in this volume). However, as deep as these dividing lines are between the collective memories of groups, and as much as they inhibit a common understanding of the past, they simultaneously implicate all groups in violence and easily blur the lines between victims and perpetrators.

South Africa in many ways epitomises divided societies that seek to establish shared memory, and its Truth and Reconciliation Commission (TRC) has become the exemplary model for quasi-legal procedures and institutions to achieve this objective. Truth seems to be less divisive than justice, and punishment much more prohibitive to the establishment of shared memories across the lines than the recovery of facts. Three contributions in this section focus on the South African transition and the achievements and failures of the TRC in constructing shared memories out of divided memories.

Emilios Christodoulidis and **Scott Veitch** start their exploration of the role of the TRC in the process of constructing collective (instead of merely 'collected') memories by reminding us of memory's disruptive potential and its liberating force in the struggle of one group against hegemonic memories imposed by another. Memory establishes itself as a divisive mechanism rather than an inclusionary one. Collective memories thus can only be constructed at the expense of difference and with acknowledgment of the reality of conflicts; enforcing their construction may cover up deep economic and social conflicts that persist beyond the transition period. Their critique of the TRC focuses on how these procedures glossed over the structure that apartheid imposed and how the complicity of the hegemonic group in the structural arrangements of apartheid was ignored in the TRC process. The pressing quest for reconciliation inherent to the proceedings elided an exhaustive probe into the conflict. The authors illustrate their argument by choosing two crucial features of the TRC process. They show how the judiciary, deeply implicated in the running of the apartheid system, evaded any clarification of its role and thus avoided responsibility. Further, they show how the 'most legal' of all TRC procedures, granting amnesties, ignored the real divisions within the community and between memories, all in the name of an imagined future and undivided community. This became manifest in what was accepted as 'truth' and 'authentic memory', on which the granting of amnesty was based.

Heribert Adam takes this argument further by suggesting ways in which legal procedures can make use of conflicts instead of ignoring or glossing over them. He situates his analysis of the TRC in a comparative analysis of legal procedures that democratic societies use in order to deal with divided memories of the past. He contrasts *progressive memories*, which help societies to understand their past in a liberating way, with *retrogressive memory*, which locks them into vicious cycles. He identifies six forms and provides representative examples: Amnesia (post-war Germany and Japan, Spain, Russia), criminal trials (the Nuremberg trials, International Criminal Tribunals), lustration (Central and Eastern Europe), negotiated restitutions (Germany's reparations to Israel, Canada's and Australia's negotiations about aboriginal land rights), political re-education (post-war Germany), and finally truth commissions (Latin America and South Africa). Reviewing these strategies for creating memory, he argues that truth cannot be brought in from the outside or it will be rejected; instead, he advocates a thoroughly local approach to finding truth and constructing collective (group) memories. The local approach is strengthened when quasi-legal procedures avoid the quest for objectivity by appointing non-partisan members, and rely instead on hardliners from both sides who share interests and memories. These members in particular can subsequently communicate and amplify an even minimal consensus to both sides with the authority that they have in their communities.

Gunnar Theissen provides one of the rare empirical spotlights on divided memories and legal procedures. His analyses a number of public opinion surveys in South Africa that were conducted before and during the TRC process and when the final TRC Report was released. His results clearly show that the public was divided along the lines of apartheid from the start and that the procedures did little to weaken these allegiances; on the contrary, they reinforced them. Whilst members of the African community became increasingly supportive, members of the White Afrikaner community became hardened in their initial negative reaction. However, a new generation might make a difference, as successive generations of post-war Germans did, since young white Afrikaners are significantly more supportive of the TRC than the generation of their parents. In addition, a majority cutting across the dividing lines felt that the TRC was successful in uncovering the truth. Notwithstanding that opinion about amnesties was clearly divided, with half of the population in opposition to this most prominent feature of the TRC, a significant minority still wanted amnesties granted to 'the other side'. The TRC, it seems, was not successful in breaking up past allegiances and promoting a 'common' view of the past, but it at least was supported in the task of uncovering the truth. This and the fact that Theissen finds evidence in his data that in the long run a common core of collective memories might emerge, paint a far more hopeful picture for the future than this spotlight on a divided society provides at a first glance.

Collective memories can be contested only if they are debated in public, including the public sphere of legal institutions. It is therefore crucial to give 'voice' to both victims and perpetrators. However, as Adam reminds us, collective amnesia can easily take over, and worse still, the voices of victims are often suppressed. Nonetheless, during the last decades, victims have gained an ever more prominent role in transitional justice and have often prevented collective amnesia. The Korean 'comfort women', who were forced by the Japanese army into sexual slavery during World War II, were forced into silence by their families, their society and their governments for decades after they had survived their first ordeal. In her study of these women, **Young-Hee Shim** demonstrates the importance of truth as 'voice' from the perspective of individual biographies. Shim's analytically astute and emotionally moving description of the life-course of six comfort women shows how Korean post-war families, communities and society silenced these women and their memories of sexual and violent abuse, making them outcasts. Silencing them and ignoring their fate prevented most of them from ever leading normal lives. The author identifies four stages that lead from silenced individual memories to testimony, and finally to public debate and the recovery of individual and collective memory. In this process, the national and international women's movement and international human rights organisations were crucial in supporting women to break their silence and address courts with their claims. The Women's International Tribunal on Japanese Military Sexual Slavery was finally staged in Japan and impacted on the collective memories in two countries (Piper 2001).

Part III: Law, Memory and the Politics of Culture and Identity

Even their most ardent supporters have described legal procedures of coming to terms with the past as 'political trials' or 'political spectacles'. Mark Osiel (1997, 283) conceptualises them as spectacles corresponding to the dramatic genres of tragedy and morality plays. Without doubt they cannot avoid being political, as they are part of a crucial political process. Their dramatic style and content is pertinent to individual and collective memories, as well as to the political process itself. However, truth and justice are at stake when such legal procedures are captured by the political process of which they are part, and when the quest for shared memories and reconciled communities is pursued at the expense of both. (See also Christodoulidis and Veitch in this volume). In acknowledging political capture and drama, we have to turn our attention to those mechanisms of capture that become manifest in transition periods and might remain more latent, even if similarly powerful, under less contentious conditions.

In the process of coming to terms with the past, legal institutions are thoroughly implicated in the political process and concomitant social and cultural changes. It is exactly their objective of establishing a shared truth and common past that makes them particularly vulnerable to being captured by powerful forces. From the perspective of the wider political and cultural environment in which they operate they might emerge as weak and endangered in comparison to political institutions and vested interests, and seem to be badly equipped to compete with the powerful dramatic images rendered by contemporary culture industry.

Heinz Steinert explores the continuous process of production and obliteration of memories in contemporary societies. He identifies commodification of individual and collective memories as its most decisive characteristic. Culture industry (a concept originally coined by Adorno) has become a powerful player in this process, and memories are 'for sale' in entertainment and education. However, the state has not wielded its power of organising the production of memories and is capable of establishing a particular and 'politicised' common memory. Trials as dramatic and powerful performances are instrumental in the state's efforts to establish its own version of the past, and even if not obsequious, they are subservient to the state's cause and interest in rendering the past. Both the state's interest in a suitable rendition of the past and the commodification of the past by culture industry, make criminal trials a powerful (and immensely useful) instrument for the different players in the process of writing and rewriting the past, and finally instrumental for their causes. This, however, makes the quest for truth utterly futile.

In her analysis of the famous *Mabo* decision, by which the High Court of Australia acknowledged the land rights of the Aboriginal population, **Kathy Laster** critically assesses the impact of this decision and its consequences for the collective identity of Australian society. She scrutinises the political, economic and social environment of this particular decision. The High Court was part of a thorough re-rendering of the past and actively and visibly involved in the process of shaping a new national identity. The author shows how a new nationalism has emerged as a consequence of the *Mabo* decision, ultimately resulting in right-wing populist politics, which mainly address those who feel betrayed and left out by the pace of change. In addition, becoming involved in the political process and cultural politics in the wake of the *Mabo* decision has left the Court and other legal institutions more vulnerable to political influence. The case, which can claim to have changed Australian history and its perception by the public, could, however, only indirectly contribute to the rights of aboriginal people. Powerful economic interests were at stake and impacted on political decisions. Ultimately, interest politics provide a better explanation for thoroughly rewriting the past and reshaping Australian national identity and collective memory than this landmark decision. More important, the constant public discussion of national identity made an issue of what had formerly been mainly ignored in a country populated by immigrants. Laster cautions that the Australian experience shows that the revision of collective memories is inexorably tied to national identity politics, and law as a key player will—even if mostly unintentionally—contribute to nationalist enterprises.

Arthur Stinchcombe steps outside the framework of transitional justice, taking a broader view of law and culture in the sense of a stock of collective memories. He analyses the ways in which legal liberties allow for an 'authentic experience' of culture and tradition. It is not the past but a predictable future that is framed by the institutions of liberal law. Since the experience of authenticity is linked to the field of imagined future action, Stinchcombe argues that legal liberties are crucially involved in its formation. Authentic experiences of culture and traditions are built on constant changes and reinterpretations of the past, as they emerge in the imagined future of individuals and groups. Legal liberties provide the modern institutional framework for the processes through which multiple social and ethnic groups define their identity by linking their past with a specific vision of the future. Freedom of speech and assembly and the ability to petition government allow for the expression of different interests and for authentic expressions of individual experiences. A regime of liberty allows for multiple ethnic and social identities and their differing images of the future. Stinchcombe points out that where these liberties are missing and not provided, ethnic and social groups are locked in mythical renditions of the past, conflicts of the present and narrow images of the future.

Part IV: Creating and Restituting Rights after Abusive Regimes: Bridges between the Past and the Future

Law and legal institutions can have a powerful role only in transitions toward liberal society, democracy and the rule of law. As Osiel argues throughout his seminal book *Mass Atrocity, Collective Memory and the Law*, liberal law and its procedures provide an 'enabling structure' for a diversity of narratives and individual memories, thus—at their best—more passively paving the way toward the reconstruction of collective memories than actively imposing and constructing them. Liberal law with all its shortcomings, which are most visible in the transitional process, allows for the recovery of the truth and backs moral clarification by its authority and the trust invested in it. As such, legal procedures in themselves promote the cause of the rule of law and liberal justice in the transition period, and the more they adhere to their principles the better they serve as models for the future society. (See Karstedt 1998.) As far as they abrogate a claim to a strictly unified and tightly controlled collective memory and subscribe to the more modest cause of establishing a common core of memories that can be agreed upon in the future, they activate public discourse about the past. Thus they provide the backdrop for future processes of remembering and forgetting and acknowledgment of guilt and reconciliation. Liberal law and legal institutions, it seems, are strong in this process because they are modest in the task they can (and want to) achieve. They build bridges between the past and the present in a more general way and with more long-term perspectives than the particular procedures of transitional (criminal) justice. They transcend the urgency and impatience present in transitional justice (Elster 2004) and supply the foundations for writing and rewriting the past over an extended period.

The two authors in Part IV of this volume analyse liberal law and its institutions from a broader perspective in order to explore the mechanisms that link it to the construction of collective memories. Importantly, they focus on legal institutions and procedures other than criminal justice.

The Constitution of the United States is an extraordinarily brief document compared to the constitutions that have been written after transitions from 'regimes of horror'. It has weathered a civil war and reconciliation afterwards, and accommodated a civil rights movement with a number of amendments (see Stinchcombe 1995). In this process, judicial activism played a decisive role in interpreting the Constitution and guaranteeing its flexible adaptation to new social and political problems. In contrast, constitutions that are drafted with vivid collective memories of recent abhorrent pasts reflect a much shorter timeframe. They decidedly epitomise a sense of 'never again', representing in their clauses lessons to be drawn from most recent history. Consequently, they are long, detailed and 'bristling with rights', as **Kim Lane Scheppele** puts it in her chapter. The 1949 constitution of the Federal Republic of Germany was drafted with the objective to erect a number of safeguards to protect the new republic from the fate of its predecessor, the Weimar Republic, which had become an easy prey of the anti-democratic Nazi-movement. A prominent role was assigned to an activist constitutional court that by design acts as a guarantor against backsliding into fascism.

The new constitutions in Central and East Europe reflect a different kind of collective 'constitutional' memory. They are imbued with collective memories of the constitutions of the former authoritarian communist states and the rights they granted, which however were not worth the paper on which they were printed. Authoritarian communist states did not give any role to the judiciary in ensuring these rights, not to speak of any independent legal interpretation. Scheppele explores how these experiences of the public and the judiciary provide the rationale for an extensive judicial activism in the interpretation of constitutions. Such activism gives rights provisions their broadest possible reading against claims of the state. Focusing on post-communist Hungary, she shows how the Constitutional Court in this country used the debate on collective memories to give the new Constitution its broadest possible meaning.

In this process, the post-war constitutional courts in Germany, Italy and Japan and their activism in defence of liberties and rights provided the model for the course on which the Hungarian Constitutional Court embarked. Constitutions written for transitions are decidedly framed as recognition and rejection of former 'regimes of horror' and thus give expression to the ideas that are constitutive for the new democratic regimes and the identity of the citizenry. They try to create a particular and specifically unified collective memory, which lays the foundation for the development of 'constitutional patriotism' in the sense of Habermas (1989). Unsurprisingly, the efforts to create such an unambiguous rendition of the past produce tensions, which arise not only in the process of drafting the constitution but equally when the constitutional courts assume their activist role. Emerging from the constitutional moment of the transition, constitutional courts often see themselves as 'guardians of the transition' and sometimes take their 'interpretive inspiration' more from the evil to be avoided than from the good to be achieved. Scheppele's chapter makes clear that constitutions and constitutional courts emerge as strong links between collective memories and legal institutions, while constitutions seem to be cast in terms of memories of the past.

It may be that such links are easier to achieve in the realm of constitutional interpretation and jurisprudential arguments. However, on the ground of social time-space, property rights provide a crucial and highly contested link between the past and the present. For Halbwachs, they are seminal in the dialectic relationship between collective memory and the law, and represent both the imprint of law on collective memory and the way that collective memory penetrates law. In Part III of this volume, Laster reminds us of the power of moral and political arguments and of the vested interests that are implicated in property rights. In Part IV, **Grażyna Skapska** discusses the problems of the restitution of property rights that Central and Eastern European countries face as a legacy from World War II, German occupation and ethnic cleansing, huge shifts of populations between borders, and finally the nationalisation of property under the communist regimes and their state-run economies. The historical experience of the Polish population provides an outstanding and unique case for Skapska's exploration of the culturally and historically rooted conceptualisations of property and property rights in collective memories. The issue of restitution is intricately linked to images of historical justice and as part of the transformation to a market economy embedded in the discourse on social justice and the moral economy.

Property rights reveal particular features of popular legal cultures and national identity in the domain of private law. For Poland, Skapska shows how they represent a distinct symbolic, communitarian and collectivistic dimension of Polish culture, whereby land ownership has been a guarantor of resistance against foreign oppression through the centuries. Collective memories attached to property rights therefore acted as liberating forces in Polish history. (See also Christodoulidis and Veitch in this volume.) Beyond their collective dimension, property rights embody individual rights, thus linking individual biographies to the collective history. Vested interests and collective emotions produce winners and losers in the process of restitution, in which it seems to be decisive that vested interests are backed by collective memories and sentiments.

Part V: The Stores of Memory: Files, Individual Biographies and Collective Memories

Modern societies and their institutions keep huge and exponentially growing stores of memory. In Part III of this volume, Heinz Steinert terms this the 'anticipatory construction of memory', as such stores are 'organised attempts' to determine what future remembrance of the past will include. The 'selective memory' (Markovits 2001) that is kept in these stores is defined by both the laws and legal institutions that channel recollections of the past. These laws regulate access to historical documents and archives, what is to be preserved and how long; and they balance freedom of information against the protection of individual data. Legal and quasi-legal procedures and in particular criminal trials in transition periods assume a prominent role in collecting documents: both the Nuremberg and the Tokyo Trials were crucial in preserving documents that would likely have been destroyed otherwise. In their unintended role as archives, such legal institutions might actually have the most enduring impact on collective memories. (See Dower 2001, 450 for the Tokyo Trials.) 'Selective memory', as Inga Markovits reminds us, favours particular events, groups and individuals, and mostly not vernacular stories but the great villains. Thus, the narratives it renders are not glossed-over versions of past 'regimes of horror' but ones that tend more toward exaggeration of their horrific features.

Legal procedures in transitional justice play a key role in bringing to light the abhorrent secrets of the past. Regimes of horror plan for 'maximum deniability' (Cohen 2001, 79), and the frantic destruction of files by the Nazi Party bureaucracy during the last days of the war and the similar activities of the Secret Police of the former German Democratic Republic (GDR) in 1989 unambiguously demonstrate that there was knowledge that needed to be denied later. Paradoxically, what is kept secret implies knowledge, both factual and moral. The infamous speech of Heinrich Himmler to the SS in Posen 1943 makes this perfectly clear (see Cohen 2001, 80). However, what is often obsessively and meticulously recorded is equally revealing (see eg Browning 1998).

Modern societies collect huge amounts of biographical information in dossiers, court files and application forms, as well as in the records of patients, pensioners and students. Each of these selectively represents individual biographies, and it is here where the individual biography enters the public domain and memory. The fact that individual existence in modern societies is dependent on an 'existence on paper' in public memory stores has been the topic of literary and satirical comment, but there is a much darker side. Making people disappear without leaving any trace behind, what can be termed 'administrative massacre' (Osiel 1997), and as has happened in Argentina, is a particular strategy of modern regimes of horror.

Not only is the entry of biographical information into the public domain selective according to institutional requirements, but it is in addition a deliberately 'edited' version of the individual's history, which covers up what is undesirable, focusing on those parts of the biography that are exemplary. Authoritarian states knowingly require such biographical information throughout the life course of their citizens (see Jiřina Šiklová in this volume), which then necessarily needs to be complemented by more 'trustworthy' but secretly compiled information. The communist states of Central and Eastern Europe left in the wake of their downfall millions of secret files with biographical information that had been collected and stored by the various branches of the secret police.

The transition toward a democratic and liberal society dramatically changes the relationship between individual biographical information and public memory storage, between what is secret and what is public. As **Carol A Heimer** and **Arthur L Stinchcombe** argue in Part V of this volume, biographical dossiers are turned into court cases, formerly exemplary biographies suddenly provide evidence of involvement in crimes, and secret files enter the public domain, whilst the 'editions' by individuals are eliminated. The intricate linkages between individual biographies, histories and memories, and collective and public memories make these files crucial in the transition period, transforming them into ticking bombs for the new regime.

Rewriting the collective past includes rewriting individual biographies. People want to know why they did not get the job, why they were not admitted to university or who the informer was amongst the group of dissidents that they had joined. Equally, they worry about previous renditions of their biographies and about what kind of new exemplary biography might be requested from them. Secret files can be used for blackmailing by those who feel betrayed by the transition. (See Los and Zybertowicz 2000 for Poland.) The post-communist regimes in Central and Eastern Europe were under pressure to decide in which ways biographical information should be used—secret and public information alike—and how dossiers collected by the Secret Police should be handled. Moreover, it had to be decided in which ways both types of biographical information should be used in procedures of lustration. Czechoslovakia and the former GDR adopted the most far-reaching laws in order to define the legal use of this information, how to make these files accessible for individual inspection and to transfer them to the public domain and memory (see Markovits 2001), whilst Poland refrained nearly totally from such an enterprise (see Andrzej Zybertowicz in this volume).

Communist states collected and requested a huge amount of information, some of which was secretly acquired and other willingly provided by citizens. This confronts individuals and collectivities during the transition period with problems of suitable forgetting rather than with the problem of remembering. Just as in individual lives, oblivion of traumatic experiences helps to overcome these, and to forget negative events is 'normal'; in an analogous way, collectivities not only select memories but also forget about parts of their less than admirable past.

Oblivion is the central theme that runs through the contributions in Part V of this volume. They mainly focus on the transition in Central Europe, where the secret police had infiltrated all realms of society and life. As an introduction to the section, **Heimer** and **Stinchcombe** theoretically and conceptually explore the ways in which lustration procedures and legal rites of passage in transitions transfer individuals and their biographies from the old to the new regime. At the core of their argument is the contrast between *case* and *biographical* information and analysis. If individuals are treated as cases, highly selective and pertinent information is collected in order to compare *across* cases. Biographically grounded information in contrast supplies coherent information within the same case, and 'a key question for biographical analysis is how the behaviour and reactions of a person, assumed to have the usual coherence and continuity of personality, can be expected to vary from one condition to another'.

Biographical information in this sense is time-consuming, whilst case information allows for processing large numbers much more swiftly. However, such procedures need a backdrop of other and comparable cases. For this reason, biographical information turns out to be more useful in turbulent times like transitions, which render comparison across time a more or less useless exercise. Lustration procedures based on the criminal justice model reflect the impatience and urgency of the transition period by transforming biographies into cases. In contrast, legal procedures like the TRC in South Africa, which are ultimately based on models of rites of passage, use biographical information. Whilst lustration procedures in East Germany blocked the route toward a transformed biography, the TRC explicitly encouraged and opened the route towards a transformed biography compatible with the new regime. The TRC approach of biographical information, it seems, is aiming at the future whilst lustration as a case processing procedure is stuck in the past. Moreover, lustration procedures based on the criminal justice model and the case method provide unsound and misleading information on how individuals will react under the new regime. In this sense, previous human rights abuses are not a consistent predictor of behaviour under the new regime, and as a consequence, biographical information needs to be contextualised within the past that shaped this biography. Heimer and Stinchcombe develop four types of moral dispositions that allow us to assess which types of behaviour under the old regime predict problematic, dangerous and unacceptable behaviour under the new one.

Jiřina Šiklová uses her own biography to lead us directly into the Kafka-esque world of questionnaires through which communist states relentlessly collect biographical information and monitor their subjects. In hindsight, Šiklová cannot conceal her astonishment about how perfectly normal this relentless questioning appeared to citizens and how willingly, though very carefully, they supplied again and again the most detailed information. This information concerned relatives (even if deceased), membership in organisations and the party, and their opinion on a number of political events, with the wording of questions clearly implying the expected answers. These biographies had to be carefully edited (a capitalist grandfather might prohibit the admission to university, eg), and thus biographies were twisted towards utmost conformity with the regime, even if they deviated widely.

Moreover, the requirements changed according to the course of political events and their official interpretation. New questions appeared and disappeared, or their wording simply changed. Leading us through such a questionnaire, the author provides us with an experience that borders on the surreal and satirical, but there is a dark side to it. The population was subject to constant police interrogation, and the 'required' biography thus imposed on real life by the communist state amounted to what Šiklová terms a 'rape' of individual (and collective) memory. After the transition, people simply forgot (or preferred to forget) about the earlier renditions of their biographies, but as the author argues, they remain captives of their past, as does the new generation, who now edit their biographical accounts as proper inversions of what had been required from their parents.

The information stored in secret files is highly ambivalent and provides both a truth that can be helpful and knowledge that can be dangerous and disastrous. The Secret Police ('Stasi') in the GDR was a particularly hated institution, and this collective sentiment erupted when in January 1990 Berlin headquarters and local branches were stormed by the population. The 1991 Statute on the Stasi Files allowed individuals to access their own files (see Markovits 2001), thus opening up routes towards rewriting individual biographies and collective memories. In his contribution, **Roger Engelmann** explores the impact that the inspection of their own files had on individual lives and collective memories. He writes, 'the inspection of personal files of the Secret Police on a massive scale is a unique phenomenon in history ... a collectively taken course in political education, based on individual biographies.'

Even after nearly more than a decade, there is a strong interest among citizens of the former GDR in inspecting their files. From his analysis of several surveys conducted among groups that applied for and obtained permission to inspect their files, in which code names had been disclosed, Engelmann concludes that open access to personal files had a twofold impact. It helped those who had been affected to 'make sense' of their experiences and recollections, and it allayed the fears and suspicions that had been nourished around the activities of the Stasi. Both were crucial results for individuals when they discovered (or failed to discover) unofficial informants in their closest social circles. The process of opening up the Stasi files prevents the construction of myths, both individual and collective ones.

Transitions are periods when secrets that have been an undercurrent in social life and society finally surface into the public realm and collective consciousness. Having been surrounded and covered up by official and unofficial lies, such secrets reappear as a particular kind of 'reality' and 'truth', or 'non-reality' and 'non-truth', in both cases making it easy to cover them up again. (See Kuran 1995.) The art of lying, which is so vividly described by Šiklová in this volume seamlessly transforms into the 'art of forgetting', as **Andrzej Zybertowicz** argues in his analysis of how the practices of the Secret Police were denied in Poland after the transition.

The Secret Police had two objectives, both intricately and paradoxically linked. First and foremost, they had to prevent the expression of ideas different from the official ideological line, and second, they subsequently had to uncover the secret reality of thoughts they had prevented from being expressed. Achieving the first of these objectives made the second one extremely difficult but the more necessary, as those in power had themselves cut off from any valuable knowledge of what their subjects actually thought. Importantly, this implied a number of other tasks for the Secret Police, including the regulation of the command economy. The Secret Police achieved these objectives by infiltrating all realms of life and thus establishing a domain of invisible power and control. The highly conspiratorial nature of the communist state, though pervading the life of ordinary citizens and institutions, was neither fully known when it was in operation nor acknowledged after the transition. The process of turning this covert 'reality' into 'unreality' has been driven by rational interests as well as irrational fears. Zybertowicz explores several narratives that push towards social amnesia; they partially emerge as adapted and sophisticated versions of techniques of neutralisation (see Cohen 2001) and partially include some distinctly contextual and historical techniques. Exemplary for the latter is the argument that 'since communism was a fake, the secret police produced artifacts like any other institution in the communist state'.

Powerful interests, implication and fear prohibited the development and implementation of policies and legal procedures that dealt with the files of the secret police. This unsettling postmodern narrative, the author argues, produces a 'political illusion of the present' that captures politicians and citizens alike.

Part VI: Failing Memory: The Law and its Past

Legal institutions, the judiciary and the legal professions seem to be a notorious 'blind spot' in the process of coming to terms with the past. Paradoxically, this is the result of (re)establishing the independence and impartiality of the judiciary in the transition process and extending it backwards into the past regime. Judges who are required to be independent now can hardly deny that they were not previously required to be so. It is obvious that post-war Germany failed in dealing with the everyday complicity of the judiciary and legal professions during the Nazi regime, and also with their direct involvement in outrageous death sentences, mass atrocities, war crimes and the provision of legal underpinnings for the Holocaust (Frei et al 2000). As Dyzenhaus (1999) reports from the TRC process in South Africa, past complicity and responsibility were similarly negated in the hearings into the legal system under apartheid. In Germany, the repressed and denied past has haunted the judiciary and legal professions throughout the decades after the foundation of the Federal Republic. Notwithstanding a number of widely publicised scandals, all efforts at laying criminal charges to any prosecutor or judge were finally not successful (Frei et al 2000). Likewise for individuals, the repression and denial of the past can produce subterranean layers of collective mentalities, which then emerge in new forms and in new disguises, as Adorno argued (1974). Both contributions to Part VI of this volume focus on the legal professions in Germany.

In her essay on juvenile courts in Germany, **Ruth G Herz** takes up Adorno's arguments by tracking down such subterranean layers in crime policies and juvenile courts in the 1990s. She finds traces of the unresolved past in how juvenile court judges deal with young offenders from ethnic minorities. However, this should not be interpreted as a continuous 'stream of unconsciousness'. Paradoxically, the unresolved past shows itself and is part of a general post-unification mood and movement to 'put the Nazi past behind'. German politicians and the public engaged in a discourse on foreigners, immigrants, asylum seekers and 'otherness', in which they felt mainly free from the burden of the past. The criminal justice system was in particular affected by this populist discourse, as well as by the crime policies that were promoted by this discourse.

The failure of the legal professions to address their past includes academic jurisprudence. Legal scholars who in their writings had justified the policies of genocide and euthanasia, as well as the war crimes of the Nazi regime, mainly returned to their positions after the lustration period.[7] The student movement of the 1960s targeted the denial and repression of memory in academia, and of those who at that time were still their teachers. **Konstanze Plett** shows how the silencing of memories had a wider impact on the collective memory of academic jurisprudence. Academic jurisprudence ignored the achievements of their colleagues who had emigrated or perished in the Holocaust, and consequently lost a rich intellectual heritage and important parts of their collective memory as a group.

Such impoverishment of intellectual traditions throws long shadows. Plett uses the form of the biographical narrative to explore these processes in the life course of Magdalene Schoch, the first woman scholar who achieved her Habilitation in jurisprudence (which made her eligible for a chair). She migrated to the United States in the 1930s after the Nazis had seized power and never returned to Germany, despite an offer to do so. Magdalene Schoch had been so utterly eliminated from the collective memory of the profession that it took a research on early female lawyers to find her. Her multiple marginalised position was responsible for her expulsion from collective memory. The fact that she was not affiliated to any group that was persecuted and victimised by the Nazi regime, which might have meant her integration into the collective memory of one of those groups, further contributed to her total loss from collective memory. Plett's use of Schoch's biography shows not only how collective memories are based on processes of exclusion and inclusion, but also how the repression of memory and the male domination of the legal profession interact as powerful exclusionary mechanisms.

REFERENCES

Adorno, Theodor W. 1974. *Minima Moralia: Reflections from Damaged Life*. London: NLB Publishing (partially reprinted as Adorno (1986)).
——. 1986. What does Coming to Terms with the Past Mean? In *Bitburg in Moral and Political Perspective,* edited by Geoffrey Hartmann. Plymbridge: Indiana (partial reprint from Adorno (1974)).
Browning, Christopher. 1998. *Ordinary Men: Reserve Police Battalion 101 and the Final Solution in Poland*. New York: Harper.
Charlesworth, Hilary and Wood, Mary. 2002. Women and Human Rights in the Rebuilding of East Timor. *Nordic Journal of International Law* 71: 325–48.
Chinkin, Christine. 2001. Women's International Tribunal on Japanese Military Sexual Slavery. *American Journal of International Law* 95(2): 335–40.

---

[7] A notable exception is Carl Schmitt who had justified "the law of the Führer" in the 1934 murders of Hitler's rivals in the SA; he never returned to his chair.

Cohen, Stanley. 1995. State Crimes of Previous Regimes: Knowledge, Accountability and the Policing of the Past. *Law & Social Inquiry* 20(1): 7–50.

——. 2001. *States of Denial: Knowing About Atrocities and Suffering*. Cambridge: Polity.

Coser, Lewis A. 1992. Introduction. In Halbwachs, Maurice, *On Collective Memory*. Edited and translated by Lewis A Coser. Chicago: University of Chicago Press.

Dower, John W. 1999. *Embracing Defeat: Japan in the Wake of World War II*. New York: WW Norton & Company.

Dyzenhaus, David. 1999. *Judging the Judges, Judging Ourselves*. Oxford: Hart.

Elster, John. 2004. *Closing the Books: Transitional Justice in Historical Perspective*. Cambridge: Cambridge University Press.

Frei, Norbert, van Laak, Dirk and Stolleis, Michael (eds). 2000. *Geschichte vor Gericht. Historiker, Richter und die Suche nach Gerechtigkeit*. München: Beck.

Habermas, Jürgen.1989. Historical Consciousness and Post-traditional Identity: The Federal Republic's Orientation to the West. In *The New Conservatism: Cultural Criticism and the Historians' Debate*. Edited and translated by Shierry Nicholsen. Cambridge, MA: MIT Press.

Halbwachs, Maurice. 1950. *The Collective Memory*. (French.) New York: Harper.

——. 1980/1992. *The Collective Memory*. Translated by Francis J Ditter and Vida Y Ditter. New York: Harper and Row.

——. 1985. *Das kollektive Gedächtnis*. Frankfurt: Fischer

——. 1992. *On Collective Memory*. Edited and translated by Lewis A Coser. Chicago: University of Chicago Press.

Hirsh, David. 2003. *Law Against Genocide: Cosmopolitan Trials*. London: Glasshouse Press.

Karstedt, Susanne. 1998. Coming to Terms with the Past in Germany after 1945 and 1989: Public Judgment on Procedures and Justice. *Law & Policy* 20(1): 15–56.

Kuran, Timur. 1995. *Private Truths, Public Lies: The Social Consequences of Preference Falsification*. Cambridge, MA: Harvard University Press.

Los, Maria and Zybertowicz, Andrzej. 2000. *Privatizing the Police State: The Case of Poland*. London and New York: Macmillan/St Martin's Press.

Marghalit, Avishai. 2000. *Ethik der Erinnerung*. Frankfurt: Fischer.

Markovits, Inga. 2001. Selective Memory: How the Law Affects What We Remember and Forget about the Past. The Case of East Germany. *Law & Society* 35(3): 513–64.

Osiel, Mark. 1997. *Mass Atrocity, Collective Memory and the Law*. New Brunswick: Transaction Publishers.

Piper, Nicola. 2001. War and Memory: Victim Identity and the Struggle for Compensation in Japan. *War & Society* 19(1): 131–48.

Ross, Fiona. 2003. *Bearing Witness: Women and the Truth and Reconciliation Commission in South Africa*. London: Pluto.

Stinchcombe, Arthur L. 1995. Lustration as a Problem of the Social Basis of Constitutionalism. *Law and Social Inquiry* 20: 245–73.

I

'The Truth and Nothing but the Truth': Truth and Justice between the Past and the Present

1

Unspeakable Memories and Commensurable Laws

STANLEY COHEN

What the Nazis did to the Jews was unspeakable: language has no word for it, since even mass murder would have sounded, in face of its planned, systematic totality, like something from the good old days of the serial killer. And yet a term needed to be found if the victims—in any case too many for their names to be recalled—were to be spared the curse of having no thoughts turned unto them. So in English the concept of genocide was coined. But by being codified, as set down in the International Declaration of Human Rights, the unspeakable was made, for the sake of protest, commensurable. By its elevation to a concept, its possibility is virtually recognised: an institution to be forbidden, rejected, discussed. One day negotiations may take place in the forum of the United Nations on whether some new atrocity comes under the heading of genocide, whether nations have a right to intervene that they do not want to exercise in any case, and whether, in view of the unforeseen difficulty of applying this in practice, the whole concept of genocide should be removed from the statutes. Soon afterwards there are inside-page headlines in journalese: East-Turkestan genocide programme nears completion.

Theodor W Adorno, *Minima Moralia* (1951)

'THE TRUTH, THE whole truth and nothing but the truth'. The phrase still resonates in the real world of criminal trials and the fictional world of courtroom dramas. When these worlds overlap into media events (like the OJ Simpson case) the legal version of truth loses its privileged epistemology, symbolic grandeur and moral imperative. In the real world, verdicts seem to be continually appealed, overturned and rendered 'unsafe'. Meantime, fictional courtroom dramas are becoming more 'realistic': they focus on mundane cases and show that legal outcomes are negotiated, contested and bargained. Anyone can grasp that a plea-bargained truth (the fate of most criminal cases) is neither the truth nor the whole truth; by definition, it is anything but the truth. The brilliant barrister is not playing truth games but wins or loses games. Only cultural dummies would think of reading a legal verdict as a historical record of the event, let alone its context and why it happened.

Postmodern culture generates a casual acceptance that there are truth*s*, not 'the truth', and that legal truths (the 'finding' of not guilty, guilty 'as proven' or wrongful conviction) are partial and misleading. Even a complete mosaic of legal truths cannot create a full or shared knowledge of 'what really happened', let alone *why* it happened. Trials that generate the strongest factual consensus and shared memory are often those that pose the most puzzling causal questions—for example, about the offender's motivations.

Under these circumstances, it is surprising that the notion of a 'historical verdict' on the truth still retains any potency at all. This is especially surprising when leaving the individual, personal and criminal realm for the mass, public and political realms of wars, military dictatorships and genocides. The transmogrification of these massive political conflicts into a series of discrete legal events—with individual defendants, rules of evidence, formal procedure, legal dialect—may be the only fair way to pursue justice and accountability. But it would hardly qualify as a research method for studying offences committed by (or on behalf of) organisations with the ideology, command structure and power of a legitimate state. Ideally, a morally justifiable finding of individual culpability should expose this political context. More often, however, this context is obscured and relegated to social backdrop. The legal doctrine of the 'inadmissibility' of certain evidence is well designed to distort moral judgements and sociological attributions of culpability. The result is a political history without either politics or history.

Recent transitions have unveiled the opposite problems. Too much truth may compromise or threaten other aspirations—for social justice, democracy, reconciliation and social stability. And the political consequences of failure to achieve a shared consensus on the historical verdict can be devastating.

As the moral stakes become higher—a judgement on history that may shape the society's future—so the empirical contest is becoming more open and chaotic. The history of long-distant pasts could always be revised or even completely denied. But this was an elitist game. Old-fashioned history was the monopoly of experts who had access to specialised sources, mastery of other languages and academic credibility. Their currency was the written word: the pasts of an Eichmann, even a Pinochet, a Mobuto or a Ceausescu had to be verbally described. Survivors may talk to the TV camera, but there are few *real-time* photographic images of the offence or perpetrator. The powerful visual iconography of the Holocaust—the faded black and white photos of skeletons piled up in concentration camps—weakens through too much clichéd repetition, even becomes *kitsch*.

Contrast this with the blasé realism of CNN instant history, real time news that is always and democratically available. Ethnic cleansing in Bosnia, children shot in Gaza, bodies hacked in Sierra Leone—scenes all filmed and transmitted *as they happen*. And right there in the frame—a constituent part of the postmodern atrocity picture—are other photographers and reporters, or the Israeli soldier, straight from central casting, putting his hand over the camera. Brechtian proof that it all really happened. And more extraordinarily, there are the arch-perpetrators themselves: General Mladic casually talking about avenging the Serbian 'side's' defeat at the Battle of Kosovo—as if he were a football club manager talking about the next game against a rival team.

I. TRANSITIONAL TRUTHS

The political interest in 'justice in transition'—how societies going through democratic changes should deal with atrocities committed by the previous regime—intersects only uneasily with the theoretical interest in concepts such as 'collective memory'. Far from being a transitory moment, an interval, a mere passage between one important historical phase and the next, the 'transition' is a phase—often long, sometimes endless—in itself. Private mindsets and public discourse are strained in trying to make sense of the visible turmoil: forbidden and permitted, rulers and ruled, heroes and villains, rapidly exchanging positions. This is hardly the best time for a whole society to 'remember' or 'forget' its past. But this is a good time to observe people (alone or together) working hard to figure out what happened or what 'must have happened'. This is not the *same* way as individuals work on their autobiographical past. Is it even a good analogy? Why are private memories of public events (a coup, a war, an assassination) different from authorised versions? When does an event pass from living memory into history or 'pre-history'? When is collective memory gradually constructed as a shared, democratic experience—and when does it result from state-organised memory work: memorial sites, ceremonies, marches and monuments?

Just at the time when establishing a consensual memory cannot possibly be a priority, heavy and audacious demands are made on transitional governments:

— Survivors of torture, trauma and pain want their suffering to be publicly recognised and vindicated. The world must know that they were victimised either for doing nothing or doing (what turns out now to be) the right thing.
— Families, friends and political comrades of the dead—victims of massacres, death squads and disappearances—want all the details: How and when was Maria abducted, how and when was she killed? Who was responsible, where was she buried?
— Historians, local and foreign, want cover-ups to be uncovered, mass graves to be exposed, files to be opened, population registers to be tabulated.

— Cosmopolitan human rights advocates demand not only that pathways to all these truths be opened, but also to see a detailed lexicon of accountability: names of suspected or certain perpetrators, their responsibilities and place in the old hierarchy, lines of command.
— The ordinary public may be interested in all, some or hardly any of this information. But they might be insistent about special information—such as the names of collaborators and informants.

As if this agenda were not heavy enough, it calls for a conclusion far beyond the 'whole truth'. Not just overcoming denial, exposing cover-ups and recovering lost memories, but an interpretation of the facts that is tendentious enough to draw moral lessons about how past horrors should never happen again—but a version not *too* tendentious to be rejected by groups on the edge of the consensus.

The difference between uncovering factual happenings and interpreting their moral meanings might be called *Recovery* and *Clarification*. I take these terms from Guatemala, where the Catholic Church's project Recovery of Historical Memory (REHMI) was followed by the UN-sponsored official enquiry, the Commission on Historical Clarification (known as CEH for its initials in Spanish). Despite its theoretical instability, the distinction between Recovery (especially factual recovery) and Clarification (especially the redrawing of moral and political boundaries) is a useful way to compare political intentions and outcomes.

Recovery works with first-order data—continually reviving, revising and re-recovering them. In some protracted conflicts (as in the Balkans and Middle East) each side has already acknowledged most episodes (massacres, terrorist bombs) and inscribed them into its official history. Memory disputes are more about moral clarification. In some cases of communist state terror, the ideological boundaries have long been clear; the bitter task is to recover specific fears, rumours, false arrests and intimidation. In yet other instances, we need mere recovery of simple repressed memories woven into national myths: contrary to five decades of unshaken historical reputation, we now know that very few Dutch citizens rescued Jews during the War. Furthermore, in all of occupied Europe, the ratio of Jewish victims was highest in the Netherlands (Bouvenkirk 2000). Clarification may refer to values, strategies or messages derived from the historical record (such as 'Never Again') or, these days, something quite different: meta reflections on the foolishness of still believing in the 'whole truth'.

II. TRUTH AS RECOVERY

The many obstacles to recovering the truths of a brutal past have been well documented: official denials and cover-ups (it didn't happen) and individual denial (I wasn't even there) or amnesia (I must have been there, but I can't remember anything). Past landmark criminal trials (Nuremberg, Eichmann) did overcome many of these obstacles. Current models (such as the International Tribunals on Rwanda and the former Yugoslavia) and the future International Criminal Court are far superior in terms of methodological sophistication and procedural justice. But however successful such legal institutions, their discrete findings cannot be patched into a sociological narrative of causation ('This is what really happened in Chile.') without a committed political leadership, a serious intelligentsia and an independent media. Indeed, the more successful the legal model as a mode of recovery, the heavier price it pays as a mode of clarification. This is because it converts a deep political conflict (already misunderstood through constant CNN sound bites) into a series of discrete legal events, the legal dialect and testimonies of individual moral culpability.

Osiel (1997) reviews further problems: the rights of defendants may be sacrificed for the sake of social solidarity. Historical perspective may be lost. Citing faulty precedents or false analogies between past and future controversies may foster delusions of purity and grandeur. Admissions of guilt and repentance required may be too extensive: more people are required to admit more responsibility and to break too strongly with past. Legal blueprints are ill suited to evoke and construct a consensual collective memory. Even if the law can deliberately construct collective memory, this may be done dishonestly (by concealing the deliberate formality from the public).

Such misgivings about the suitability of the legal model have never disappeared. Nor has anyone refuted Arendt's reading of the Eichmann trial: that the criminal law is not well suited to control, understand and certainly not to remember 'administrative massacres'.

The post-Sixties scepticism about legal authority and the search for 'alternatives'—to criminal justice, punishment and prison—trickled down into the human rights discourse. Ideas such as restorative justice and reconciliation just took longer to be heard in a system governed by legal and diplomatic monopolies. By the time of the post-Seventies transitions, many alternative pathways to truth and justice were in place. Some were new (like truth commissions); some were traditional (such as memorialisation); some were adaptations of existing models (such as mass disqualification/decommunisation/lustration or compensation/restitution/redress). A novel use of prohibitive law was to criminalise the denial of the Holocaust and other genocides. Judges in Toronto, Paris, Sydney and London are suddenly appointed as arbiters of historical truths about how many people were killed at a particular concentration camp sixty years ago. They become like external readers—deciding on which manuscripts are worthy of publication in a journal.

The unsuitability of legal procedures to recover such knowledge has been known since Nuremberg. This matters less today simply because there are so many alternative ways of getting at the truth. All these methods together, though, however impeccably they arrive at legal facts, can only generate the type and amount of *contextual* knowledge that they are requested (or allowed to) consider. Understandably, many South Africans criticised the Truth and Reconciliation Commission (TRC) for concentrating only on dramatic major violence (death squads, kidnapping, torture) and not the endless humiliations of everyday life, the laws of 'petty apartheid' and the people who routinely inflicted these pains. There are standard problems in managing such contextual memory:

— *Time*: How far back should we go? For a military junta that lasted for five years after seizing power from a previous democracy, this is less of a problem. But for South Africa, post-communist societies or the Israeli–Palestinian conflict there is no original sin, no consensual year zero, from which to start accountability.
— *Authority and obedience*: Who gave what orders to whom, and who obeyed? The administrative atrocity renders these questions deliberately opaque. Neither adversarial justice nor popular storytelling can easily find individual responsibility in these texts and testimonies of deliberately ambiguous orders, intentional deniability and multiple command structures.
— *Degrees of involvement*: How to identify the different modes of involvement in keeping the old regime going? Occupied Europe is the standard historical precedent: the differences between commission, collaboration and collusion; between active and passive collusion; between deliberate silence and wilful ignorance; variations of the morally repellent but historically accurate idea of collective responsibility. The range runs from the military elite of a Latin American junta to the nuanced involvement, collusion and silence that characterised—in different ways—South Africa and the former communist regimes.

These 'nuances' may have simple empirical indices—Was she paid? Was he blackmailed into informing? Did he harm anybody?—but they carry contested moral meanings. In the German Democratic Republic (GDR), husbands and wives informed on each other—would doing it for money be better or worse than ideological conviction?

III. TRUTH AS CLARIFICATION

The twentieth century has left some stubborn and important cases of atrocities the very existence of which continues to be denied by perpetrator governments—such as the Japanese exploitation of comfort women and the Turkish genocidal massacres of Armenians. Other even more egregious cases—the mass starvation and killings in Mao's China and Stalin's Soviet Union—have slid off the politically convenient list of tragedies to remember. Significantly, the most dramatic attempt at historical accountability regarding any of these four cases took the form of a People's Tribunal. From 8–12 December 2000, the Women's International War Crimes Tribunal 2000 sat in Tokyo, considering the liability of the Japanese state and named high-ranking military and political officials for rape and sexual slavery as crimes against humanity.[1] Popular Tribunals obviously lack either state or international legitimacy and can be easily ridiculed as 'mock trials'. Yet as Chinkin (2001) argues, the legal form, especially the adherence to procedural legality, allows assigning individual criminal liability, state responsibility for violations of international law, and awarding of reparations. At the same time, the populist form of the Tribunal's origin in the women's movement allowed for consciousness raising about gender-based violence, militarism and the inadequate legal protection of women's rights.

Unlike discovery, all modes of *clarification* (consciousness raising, pedagogy, moral education and boundary drawing) are and should be open to dispute. As long as there is no literal denial of the historical record of any group's suffering, disputes about interpretation are essential to democratic discourse. Thus the importance of struggles about memorialisation: should a Holocaust museum refer also to the other simultaneous victims of the Nazi death machine, like Roma and gays? Should the commemoration brochure on the anniversary of Hiroshima admit the possibility that the bombing might not have been justified in military terms? As Young (1993) suggests, we should not just commemorate but do 'memory-work', not just build monuments but argue about them, change them and reinterpret them. This is also Osiel's conclusion (1997) about the classic political trial: despite its defects as a source of shared memory, the liberal model of a criminal trial—at its best—provides a generous arena for contesting the truth about the past. This can happen even in anticipation of a trial. As the Pinochet case showed, the simple opening move of the legal game did more to undermine collective amnesia about the Chilean junta than any number of histories or human rights reports.

Political 'clarification', unfortunately, has some undesirable connotations: Maoist re-education, Stalinist show trials; propaganda, the party

---

[1] Graphic revelations from the late 1980s onwards (initially by the women's movement in the Republic of Korea) had been totally denied by the Japanese government. Later acknowledgement was only limited. The Tribunal used documentary evidence (including diaries of Japanese officials) and the testimonies of some 75 survivors to establish criminal liability. I am grateful to Christine Chinkin for information and her draft for the Tribunal's Board of Editors (Chinkin 2001). See also Young-Hee Shim in this volume.

line and political correctness. But surely the Durkeimian goal of boundary setting also needs some careful stage management: the free and fair rules of a contested and undetermined liberal criminal trial—which must, however, reach the correct verdict—is the only democratically acceptable lesson from this particular history.

As if this were not enough, the new society is instructed to take on a task that is beyond imagination to define, let alone accomplish. This is the quest for 'coming to terms with the past'. Once again, there are some unconvincing transpositions from personal to political life. The concept of 'closure', for example—misleading in itself for personal life (can parents really achieve closure about the kidnapping, torture and killing of their child?)—is even weaker when applied to a whole society 'closing the book' on the past. A more empowering image of how to deal with past horrors is the truth commission. In various permutations—coupled with justice, coupled with reconciliation or staying 'only' with truth—the model has been reproduced in many countries and justifiably captured universal imagination. The South African TRC under Archbishop Tutu's direction has become the archetype: extensively studied and already set in the public mind (misleadingly) as the only competitor to Nuremberg.

In building the 'historic bridge' to the new society, the Commission saw its role as establishing as 'complete a picture as possible' of the injustices committed in the past, coupled with a public, official acknowledgement of the untold suffering that resulted from these injustices (TRC Act 1995). 'Untold' means vast, but it also literally means 'untold'. The public hearings (and the intense media coverage) offered a stage for people to tell stories that had never been told.

The Commission knew that it had to arrive at a version of the past that would achieve some common consent: 'We believe we have provided enough of the truth about our past for there to be a consensus about it.' But whose truth? At this point, the TRC Report finds four versions of truth-telling, each more complicated than the notion of 'consensual truth'.

— *Factual or forensic truth*: legal or scientific information which is factual, accurate and objective and is obtained by impartial procedures. At the individual level this means information about particular events and specific people: what exactly happened to whom, where, when and how. At the societal level, this means recording the context, causes and patterns of violations.
— *Personal and narrative truth*: the stories told by perpetrators and (more extensively) by victims. Personal testimony can be healing in itself; it adds to the collective truth and prepares for reconciliation by validating the memories of people who had previously been silenced or voiceless.

— *Social truth*: the truth generated by interaction, discussion and debate. The hearings alllowed transparency and encouraged participation. Conflicting views about the past could be considered and compared.
— *Healing and restorative truth*: the narratives that face the past in order to go forward. Truth goes beyond a factual record (recovery) towards interpretations (clarification) directed at self-healing, reconciliation and reparation. This requires the acknowledgement that everyone's suffering was real and worthy of attention.

This nuanced classification of types of truth, however, was too subtle to support the advertising jingle of the TRC's slogan 'Truth: The Road to Reconciliation'. As Wilson (2000) sadly records, internal tensions were glossed over and forensic truth privileged. Moreover the criteria and format of the Report's final text became informed by the 'technology of human rights information management'. Narratives of suffering flowed not backwards to their historical sources but sideways into protocols designed to accommodate an 'information flow' that led only to the right managerial source—none other than Infocomm, the Information Management System itself.

But the Report did not abandon its driving metaphors of scars and wounds, opening and healing. The past left 'indelible scars' on the collective consciousness; these scars often concealed 'festering wounds'; these wounds must be 'opened up' for the 'cleansing and eventual healing' of the body politic. It was not enough, however, to open these wounds and then 'sit back for the light of exposure to do the cleansing'.

Let us assume that the 'light of exposure' is just another term for enlightenment or the Enlightenment. By the time that all the planners, members and administrators of the South African TRC had reached their adult lives, this historical light was already shining. The broad contours of the apartheid regime, if not its fine lines, were visible to all. When the entire system of power began to collapse, visionaries like Archbishop Tutu were caught between their traditional (modernist) belief in the self-evident value of truth and their new (postmodernist) wisdom that this astonishing transition needed nurturing by the right amount and type of truth. In his memoirs, Tutu identifies the graded tuning of truth: better amnesty–forgiveness–reconciliation (for some, not all) than a 'society in ashes'; the Commission's careful link between truth and reconciliation as a 'third way' between 'the Nuremberg trial paradigm' and 'national amnesia' (Tutu 1999).

Postmodern culture is curiously more concerned with the past than high modernism ever was. But fragmentation makes this a collected rather than collective history. There will be more wreath-laying ceremonies, theme parks, museums and memorials; more secret files opened and waxwork figures rearranged; history textbooks rewritten and revised; public inquiries and truth commissions established about all sorts of unresolved conflicts, grievances and disputed facts. But the problems behind these complementary projects—creating a shared memory by delving further into the past and constructing the present in order to ensure a future consensus about the past—cannot be solved by sheer political will.

IV. META PROBLEMS

This is because some of these problems result from (but cannot be solved within) the highly developed reflexivity of the discourse:

— The concept of 'collective memory' itself, especially the tangled links between the psychic and political levels, remains both useful and misleading. It is simply not self-evident that whole collectivities ('the Serbs') can remember and forget like individuals. Take the therapeutic notion of catharsis: the emotional release of all hidden, suppressed or repressed truths and the subsequent sense of emotional relief. This connotation is not given to the legal declaration of the 'whole truth', nor the Truth Commission's injunction for full disclosure. The ideal of national catharsis (like social amnesia) may sound vivid, but is difficult to even imagine.

— There is a tension between the absolute truth required by the ideals of legality, justice and personal moral responsibility on the one hand, and today's relativist narratives—the notion that there is neither a single truth nor a sharable memory—on the other hand. Far from being resolved, this tension is heightening. Quasi-legal institutions like the South African TRC explicitly replace the criterion of 'beyond reasonable doubt' by 'balance of probabilities'.

— The tension has long been recognised between truth-telling as an absolute value versus the demands of political expediency and pragmatic social policy. Few if any state-initiated political trials follow the positivist sequence of an open-ended quest for what really happened—and only then stack the recovered truth onto the pile of collective memory. We know in advance the construction best suited for present purposes. 'Victory for the truth' does not necessarily even mean that the empirically most guilty are the most punished. The point is to fit the verdict into the preferred macro-narrative behind public memories: from repression to freedom; end of the nightmare; monsters from the past; beginning of a new dawn. Managers of transitional justice calibrate and then ration the truth. If too much truth is held back, then victims will be dissatisfied and reconciliation impossible: no one will forgive the unknown. The 'whole truth', however, might be too bitter for reconciliation. Nor does legal justice need anything like the 'whole truth' to fulfill its function of preventing revenge. It only has to show that it is doing enough to achieve some measure of legitimacy or—in less benign terms—to re-establish state domination. Memories of the past are reconstructed to fit what the legal system is best suited to do—punish individuals. Judicial truths require a suspension of collective memory and common sense. We are reminded that Corporal K was found guilty, but we have to pinch ourselves to remember that the Corporal's whole organisation was corrupted; that his membership of a racist organisation shows up, but not the racism of many others.

— There is a classic liberal dilemma in knowing where to draw the boundaries beyond which a 'consensual' collective memory is not necessary and some contestation is healthy. Democratic pluralism cannot tolerate all disputes about the past.

A final problem is more paradoxical. The great success of the human rights movement has been the replacement of diverse sets of ethical intuitions and religious commandments with a common, uniform and universal set of standards. This also created a new language to describe the minimum norms of human dignity. The problem though is that legal and human rights talk may erase the concrete and pictorial sensations on which memory depends. Instead of remembering genocidal killings by what happened, we register the debate about whether these events fit the definition of genocide in the United Nations convention. And instead of ordinary people having to struggle with the unpleasant disjunctions between private self-consciousness and public history (Did my fellow citizens, even people whom I knew and thought incapable of this, really do those horrible things? Did I only pretend not to suspect what was happening?) we will soon have Centres for the Study of Justice in Transition to calculate the optimal managerial balance between means and ends. This is what Adorno meant—the unspeakable is made commensurable.

REFERENCES

Adorno, Theodor W. 1951/1974. *Minima Moralia: Reflections from Damaged Life*. London: New Left Books. (Original 1951. *Minima Moralia: Reflexionen aus dem beschädigten Leben*. Frankfurt: Suhrkamp.)

Bouvenkirk, Frank. 2000. The Other Side of the Anne Frank Story. *Crime, Law and Social Change* 34: 237–58.

Chinkin, Christine. 2001. Women's International Tribunal on Japanese Military Sexual Slavery. *American Journal of International Law* 95(2): 335–40.

Osiel, Mark. 1997. *Mass Atrocity, Collective Memory and the Law*. New Brunswick, NJ: Transaction Publishers.

TRC Act. 1995. *Promotion of National Unity and Reconciliation Act*. Act No 34 of 1995.

TRC. 1998. Final Reports, volume I–VII. http://www.doj.gov.za/trc/report/index.htm

Tutu, Desmond M. 1999. *No Future without Forgiveness*. New York: Doubleday.

Wilson, Richard. 2000. From Historical Truths to Legal Facts: The Truth and Reconciliation Commission in South Africa. Paper presented at International Studies Conference on *Justice, Memory and Reconciliation*, University of Toronto.

Young, James E. 1993. *The Texture of Memory: Holocaust Memorials and Meanings*. New Haven: Yale University Press.

2

An Emerging 'Right to Truth': Latin-American Contributions

JUAN E MENDEZ[1]

I. INTRODUCTION

IN RECENT YEARS, the theory and practice of human rights protection has been shaped to a very large extent by the struggle of organisations in civil society to overcome the recurring cycle of impunity for the most egregious crimes committed in the exercise of authority. The detention of General Augusto Pinochet in London, for purposes of extradition to Spain, was a veritable leap forward in the development of tools for human rights protection. This stunning development forced jurists everywhere to reckon again with the proper balance between notions of sovereignty and non-intervention in internal affairs and effective ways to implement fundamental principles of humanity. It also extended the debate about what states and the international community owe to victims beyond the limited circles of the international human rights movement.

Even before the Pinochet case, however, there were important developments in the struggle to overcome impunity, often linked to the transitions from authoritarian rule to democracy. In each society making such a transition, the issue of how to deal with the legacy of past abuses has been high on the agenda. The experiments thus put in practice are examined elsewhere with great interest, as other communities confront similar problems. Only a few countries have attempted to prosecute such crimes, often against very heavy pressure from entrenched military elites. Even without such pressure, invocations of false 'reconciliation' have only very thinly disguised a business-as-usual attitude and a desire to avoid the course of

[1] The author appreciates the invaluable assistance of Javier Mariezcurrena, and of Gastón Chillier of Notre Dame Law School. Parts of this paper have been published in Mendez, Juan E. The Human Right to Truth: Lessons Learned from Latin American Experiences with Truth-telling. In TA Borer (ed), *Telling the Truths: Truth Telling and Peace Building in Post-Conflict Societies*. Notre Dame: Notre Dame University Press, 2006.

justice. Truth commissions have been appointed in many countries, and in each case a profound ethical and political debate has taken place about the value of criminal prosecutions—often, though not necessarily always—as opposed to truth-telling.

In Latin America in the 1980s and 1990s, civil society pushed the extended boundaries of both domestic and international law to an unprecedented point. An explanation of why Latin America has seen more innovation and activity in this regard, in comparison with other parts of the world, exceeds the scope of this essay. The recent history of the region, however, does offer some clues to understanding this phenomenon.

The generation of the 1960s was as rebellious in Latin America as elsewhere. Unlike Europeans and North Americans, however, young Latin Americans of that time created relatively large political movements that were heavily influenced by the Cuban Revolution of 1959. In many countries, strong guerrilla movements emerged to implement forms of 'armed struggle' as a strategy for the attainment of political power. Societies with weak legal institutions reacted to this challenge by giving a free rein to repressive military forces; elsewhere the military simply took over and governed dictatorially. While the social, economic and political establishments cheered them on, the military engaged in 'dirty war' campaigns to eliminate subversion (invariably defined as going far beyond the armed opponent). In country after country, the 1970s and 1980s produced massive, systematic violations of the most fundamental human rights and equally egregious violations of the laws of armed conflict, by both government and insurgent forces.

In a continent with a history of two centuries of political violence and strife, this period was arguably the most tragically repressive. It was also, fortunately, an unstable and ultimately brief period. Even before the end of the bipolar world, Latin American dictatorships were giving way to transitions to democratic rule. This change was necessary, both because of the military's inability to govern and because rapid changes in the world economy tended to link open markets with some need for the rule of law. In any event, the transition occurred everywhere (except in Cuba), although in each country the pace of change and the military's ability to impose conditions differed widely. As to the contents of those conditions, there were obvious variations as well, but one standard demand was common to all: assurances of impunity for crimes against humanity and violations of human rights. Many observers thought at the time that this precluded the possibility of any real inquiry, insisting that it was reckless and detrimental to the cause of democracy. But human rights organisations wisely ignored this advice, and soon the question of how to deal with the legacy of human rights abuses became central to the transition itself.

In no single country was the matter resolved completely to the satisfaction of those seeking truth and justice. Nevertheless, in all of them the debate produced some result, and everywhere it has helped shape the kind of democracy Latin Americans want for the future. Remarkably, and contrary to expectations, the debate on how to overcome impunity has outlived the transitions. Today it figures prominently on political agendas throughout the hemisphere, and its paradigms apply not only to the legacy of the past, but also to the struggle against 'endemic' violations, to corruption and generally to the accountability of elected leaders and officials of state institutions. Latin Americans continue to find new ways to advance the cause of truth and justice in domestic as well as in international law.

II. AN OVERVIEW OF TRANSITIONAL EXPERIENCES

As a result of these struggles, international law is rapidly developing in this field. Such 'emerging principles' are generally not found in the letter of the law of human rights instruments but rather in authoritative interpretations of otherwise binding norms. There may be some discussion as to how firmly 'settled' in international law these emerging principles are. On the other hand, there seems to be remarkable unanimity of opinion among scholars and bodies as to their existence and certainly no *opinio juris* going in a contrary direction (Mendez 1997a; see also Orentlicher 1991, 1994; Roht-Arrazia 1995; and Joinet 1997).

These emerging principles apply to human rights crimes of a particularly severe nature, such as extra-judicial executions, disappearances and torture, when they take place as part of a deliberate, systematic or widespread pattern. Under these circumstances, these human rights violations acquire the status of *crimes against humanity*, and they are thus committed primarily by governments but also by insurgent or other groups exercising a high degree of de facto authority in their regions. When committed in the course of war, these actions (and an array of similarly condemnable acts) are *war crimes* or grave breaches of the laws of war. It is worth noting that an isolated war crime gives rise to an obligation to prosecute and punish, whereas a single act of torture in a non-conflict situation is insufficient to trigger this obligation. When either war crimes or crimes against humanity are committed with the intent to destroy, in whole or in part, an ethnic, religious or national community, they constitute *genocide*. Genocide, war crimes and crimes against humanity give rise to an obligation on the part of the primary state, as well as on the part of the international community. The latter obligation may be satisfied by creating an international criminal court but also by allowing the courts of other nations to exercise the principle of *universal jurisdiction*.

These affirmative obligations include first and foremost an obligation to investigate, prosecute and punish. This obligation on the part of the state is a *right to justice* when viewed from the perspective of the victims and their families. Secondly, there is an obligation to disclose to the victims and to society all that can reliably be known about the circumstances of the crime, including the identity of the perpetrators and instigators. We call this a *right to truth*. Thirdly, the state is obliged to offer to the victims or their kin some measure of reparation that should not be limited to monetary compensation. Finally, whether or not perpetrators are punished, the state has a duty to reform state institutions and to eliminate from the ranks of the security forces those agents who are known to have participated in such crimes. All four obligations are independent from each other, and all must be executed in good faith. It follows that if one of them is rendered impossible to execute (say, by a defective amnesty law), the state must still strive to comply with the other three to the best of its ability.

In each of the Latin American countries, a combination of actions to fulfill these four obligations took place, though not so much by design as in response to societal pressure. Chronologically, Argentina was the first country to include policies of this sort in its transition to democracy. Elections in 1983 were held against a backdrop of a not-too-orderly retreat of the military dictatorship, hastened by its defeat the previous year in the Falklands-Malvinas war with the United Kingdom. Raúl Alfonsín won unexpectedly, in no small part because his campaign embraced the idea of settling accounts with torturers and murderers. Among his first acts of office, he created a National Commission on Disappearance of Persons, which was headed by the writer Ernesto Sabato and included other personalities who were also regarded as persons of integrity. The Commission worked for a ten-month period, receiving testimony from survivors, families of the victims and some defectors, and conducting field investigations throughout the country. It produced a damning report that identified almost 300 secret detention centres and named some 9,000 people who had been made to 'disappear' after arrest by security forces. Most importantly, its findings left no doubt as to the official, deliberate and carefully planned nature of the campaign of disappearances led by the military dictatorship. This report set the stage for the other main feature of the Alfonsín government, the prosecution of those responsible.

In 1985, after historical oral hearings before the Federal Court of Appeal for Buenos Aires, several members of the three juntas were convicted and sentenced—General Videla and Admiral Massera to life and other generals to long prison terms—for planning and supervising the killing of dozens of victims. Although several other cases against lower-ranking officers were before the courts, unrest in the armed forces led Alfonsín to promulgate two laws that put an end to most prosecutions. The cycle of impunity was later closed by his successor Carlos Menem, who in 1989 and 1990 granted pardons to the few high-ranking officers still facing prosecution at the time, as well as to the members of the juntas who were serving sentences. However, pushed by human rights organisations and by decisions of the Inter-American Commission of Human Rights, the Menem administration carried out an extensive programme of reparations for victims and their relatives. There has been no 'purge' of the armed and security forces, but each time a well-known perpetrator is proposed for promotion to higher ranks, public outcry forces the government and the armed forces to backtrack and send the person in question into retirement. Significantly, the Argentine Army, now under commanders who did not participate in the atrocities, is a very different body today. In 1995, General Martín Balza offered an apology to the nation on account of the 'dirty war' tactics of his comrades-in-arms.

With respect to the truth, the Sabato Report was a seminal event, marking the standard for many similar reports in other countries. It did not, however, establish the individual truth in relation to each victim, since that was left to be dealt with through the criminal investigations and prosecutions that should have followed.

In Chile, the Pinochet regime was able to 'manage' the transition more effectively than in Argentina, and the democratic forces that took over the government in 1989 were left with far fewer options. To his credit, President Patricio Aylwin resisted all pressures to expand the scope of impunity. In essence, a broad consensus among democratic parties held that the self-amnesty law passed by Pinochet in 1978 could not be repealed, which effectively precluded most criminal investigations. As a result, the emphasis was placed on truth-telling, also via a Commission of well regarded persons, which was headed by Jorge Rettig. In some aspects, the Rettig Commission improved upon the Sabato precedent by holding hearings and by writing a detailed report on each of the cases brought to its attention. A major contribution of the Chilean Truth and Reconciliation Commission is precisely this insight: that the state owes each victim not only a general truth about the patterns and practices of repression but also an individualised truth about what happened to each and every victim.

Prosecutions in Chile moved very slowly, and even then, only in those cases that were explicitly exempted from Pinochet's system of self-amnesty. Nevertheless, the *Letelier* case (about the murder of a major dissident in the streets of Washington, DC) yielded the conviction of General Manuel Contreras, Pinochet's chief of intelligence and his second-in-command. For years to come, several cases remained only nominally open, but the courts— still dominated by judges from the Pinochet era—repeatedly impeded serious investigations or applied the self-amnesty law. The arrest of General Pinochet in England, however, has altered this picture decisively. In a major breakthrough in 1999, a judge in Santiago ordered the prosecution of some of the highest-ranking officers of the Pinochet years, for a particularly gruesome episode known as the Caravan of Death. After his return to Chile in early 2000, Pinochet himself was stripped of his parliamentary immunity as an appointed 'senator for life' and faced criminal charges for ordering very serious human rights violations. The 'self-amnesty' law of 1978 is still on the books, but for years now the courts have refused to apply it.

Reparations in Chile have taken the form of life pensions to the victims' families, offered by a State Corporation set up to complete the work of the Rettig Commission. The Corporation wrapped up its work in 1997 but continued investigations into the fate and whereabouts of hundreds of other victims of disappearances and extra-judicial execution on which the Rettig Commission had not had time to complete its inquiries. A second truth commission investigated torture that had not resulted in death and established its pervasive, brutal application by the Pinochet regime. The Chilean armed forces had remained loyal to Pinochet and thus had been shielded from any civilian authority, so there has been no serious attempt to cleanse them of known perpetrators of human rights violations.

After Argentina and Chile, the next Latin American exercises in truth-telling and doing justice to human rights violations came in the context of interventions by the international community to put an end to armed conflicts in Central America and to restore democracy in Haiti. Nicaragua was the first country to put an end to its civil war with international support. The Sandinista regime never thought it would lose the elections of 1989 and never prepared for the contingency of having to leave office. Between the election and the inauguration of Violeta Chamorro, the Sandinistas passed a blanket amnesty for themselves and for their enemies, the *contras*. Complete impunity has been the rule ever since, despite some futile attempts by human rights organisations to investigate clandestine burials from time to time.

In El Salvador, however, the international community had a better sense of what needed to be done to obtain a more lasting peace. The United Nations (UN) brokered an agreement that called for, among other things, a Truth Commission formed by three prominent foreigners, one jurist and two political leaders. Though it had only a few months and limited resources to conduct investigations in the field, it produced a highly credible and damning report. Unfortunately, the right-wing Salvadoran government immediately passed a blanket amnesty law to preclude any serious prosecutions. The members of the Farabundo Martí National Liberation Front (FMLN), eager to rejoin public life, did not object. Human rights organisations have continued to insist on some forms of accountability, however. An interesting project of this sort includes an attempt at reuniting families with children who were lost to Army campaigns in the countryside and given away in irregular adoption. El Salvador fared a lot better in regards to purification of the armed forces. An ad hoc Commission—this time formed by Salvadoran citizens—created as part of the peace process reviewed the records of scores of officers and recommended discharge of more than 100 of them. Despite threats and pressure from the Army, their recommendations were complied with.

In Haiti, the United Nations and the Organization of American States (OAS) were called upon to obtain the return to power of Jean-Bertrand Aristide, a democratically elected President who had been ousted by a military coup. During the protracted negotiations, the military and their allies in goon squads committed many atrocities against Aristide supporters. With UN and OAS help, the Aristide government organised a Truth Commission after regaining power. This one, however, was a failed exercise. After months of investigation, the Truth Commission did not produce any serious new information over what was already known, even as it concentrated its efforts on the well-known cases of prominent Aristide supporters killed during the previous regime. It also kept its full report secret for a long time, initially releasing only a summary; after the report was fully released, there was no serious effort to disseminate it. An opportunity to allow Haitians to come to terms with this recent past was totally squandered.

Guatemala has been the latest Latin American country to go through a UN-sponsored peace process. Of all the many separate agreements that it includes, the one calling for a Commission on Historical Clarification (CEH for its initials in Spanish) was the least promising, because the parties to the conflict insisted that it should not name names or attribute individual responsibilities. It was also charged with establishing only a *historical* interpretation of the long years of conflict rather than individualised truths as in Chile. As it happened, however, the Commission, led by the German jurist Christian Tomuschat and seconded by two prominent Guatemalans, conducted a very credible investigation, with strong UN support in human and material resources. Its report is perhaps the strongest of its kind, as it does not hesitate to use the word 'genocide' to categorise the Army's campaigns against the indigenous peoples of the Guatemalan highlands. And, to its credit, it does so only after an exhaustive analysis of the terrible facts it has found. Undoubtedly, a good measure of the success of the CEH is owed to the wholehearted support of Guatemalan nongovernmental organisations (NGOs), something that did not take place in El Salvador or Haiti, for different reasons. In fact, before the CEH, the Guatemalan Catholic Church had already produced its own report on human rights violations during the armed conflict, after a long and thorough investigation in key areas of the countryside. This project, called Recovery of Historical Memory (REHMI) almost certainly resulted in the murder of its chief architect, Mons Juan Gerardi, 48 hours after the public release of the report. On the other hand, Gerardi's vision and the painstaking effort of his colleagues undoubtedly prepared the way for an exemplary collaboration between Guatemalan civil society and the CEH.

This is necessarily only a very sketchy overview of the efforts undertaken by Latin Americans in the past two decades to overcome the burden of the human rights violations of the recent past. It would be a mistake, however, to list only state actions of this sort. In some cases, important contributions were made solely by civil organisations, especially in those countries where the democratic governments steadfastly refused to recognise any obligation in this regard. In Brazil, a remarkable research project was initiated by the Archdiocese of Sao Paulo for obtaining and reviewing secret files from the military courts that prosecuted civilians in the 1960s and 1970s. The files are full of evidence about the savage torture used systematically by inter-rogators to extract confessions and intelligence, and of the tolerance toward this practice by those courts. The study is the more important since it was clandestinely conducted while still under the military dictatorship. The result was a book called *Tortura Nunca Mais*, which became Brazil's all-time bestseller in non-fiction and contributed enormously to shaping the debate during the *abertura*, as Brazilians called the period immediately preceding the transition to democracy (Dassin 1986; see also Weschler 1990). In 2007, federal prosecutors have initiated actions in courts to declare the amnesties of the military period null and void and thus reopen prosecutions.

In Uruguay, the democratically elected leaders who succeeded the military dictatorship of the 1970s and 1980s have not only refused to allow prosecu-tions or truth-telling but also intervened decisively to make them impossible. A pseudo-amnesty law (see below), called by the untranslatable name of *Ley de Caducidad de la Pretension Punitiva del Estado*, was passed early in the democratic period. Human rights organisations then campaigned for its repeal via plebiscite, for which a very high number of signatures is needed (25 per cent of registered voters). The authorities tried to thwart the effort by forcing many of those who signed to ratify their signatures, which involved considerable inconvenience and the risk of revealing their identi-ties. Nevertheless, an outstanding organising effort overcame this obstacle, and the plebiscite had to be called. President Julio M Sanguinetti then cam-paigned very forcefully against repeal of the law, in effect asking Uruguayans to choose between justice and democracy. The law was retained by a narrow margin, but the months-long episode shaped the debate about the future of democracy and further delegitimised the military elite, not only because of the crimes committed but also because of their shameless blackmail. More recently, Uruguayan human rights organisations have continued to press for exhumations of clandestine graves, an apology from the Generals similar to that of their Argentine colleagues, and a presidential truth commission (Michelini 1996; see also Weschler 1990). In recent years, Uruguayan courts have found exceptions to the *Ley de Caducidad* and some spectacular cases and proceedings, including the prosecution of figure-head president Bordaberry, who presided over the Uruguayan 'dirty war'.

In Paraguay, Martin Almada, a former political prisoner and torture victim of the Stroessner regime, filed court actions to obtain documentation on his case and, with the help of committed young judges, stumbled upon a trea-sure trove of documents on repression by intelligence forces. The judges then organised a study of these files, known in Paraguay as the Archives of Terror, allowing scholars and human rights activists access to them. After Pinochet's arrest, these files have proved invaluable in establishing evidence of one of the major charges against him: a secret plan of illegal cooperation between security forces in the Southern Cone, known as 'Operation Condor'.

III. ISSUES ARISING IN THE COURSE OF THESE EXPERIENCES

A. *De Facto* and *De Jure* Impunity

The dramatic experiences described in the previous section represent an effort by civil society to overcome a pervasive Latin American phenomenon: impunity. We refer to impunity for the most egregious human rights crimes, such as extra-judicial execution, torture and disappearances, when committed in a systematic or widespread scale. Of course, many other crimes also go unpunished for one reason or another. In addition, many Latin Americans rightly decry the pervasiveness of impunity for other illegal actions committed by high officials, particularly acts of corruption. We note that our views apply to only impunity for the most serious human rights crimes because, in their regard, emerging principles of international law require their effective prosecution and punishment, disclosure of the facts, reparations to the victims and an effort to cleanse the security forces of the perpetrators in their lifetime (Mendez 1997a).

Impunity for such crimes can be de facto or de jure. The former occurs when crimes are not investigated thoroughly or not prosecuted, simply because of lack of will to do so on the part of officials in charge of institutions with specific duties in that regard. It can also result from multiple interferences, overt and covert, into the discharge of those duties by others with more power or influence. In contrast, de jure impunity applies when states resort to manipulations of the domestic legal order to establish rules that effectively preclude investigation and punishment or stand as obstacles to discovery and disclosure of the facts surrounding those crimes. We refer here to amnesty and pseudo-amnesty laws, to presidential pardons and other forms of clemency. We note, however, that we do not mean to imply that *all* amnesties or pardons violate an international law obligation. In fact, some forms of amnesties are required by international law.[2] Blanket amnesties, however—the effect of which is to prohibit any serious inquiry into the facts or punishment of those responsible—are a breach of international law if they cover the most severe human rights violations, those that

---

[2] Art 6.5 Protocol II Additional to the Geneva Conventions of 1949 (1977) with regard to conflicts not of an international character.

can be characterised as war crimes or crimes against humanity. It follows that amnesties and pardons are valid if they do not result in a general and all-embracing atmosphere of impunity.

Some mechanisms of impunity straddle the line between de facto and de jure impunity. The application of military court jurisdiction to these kinds of crimes is often an example. In principle, military jurisdiction is a legitimate forum to hear offenses of a specifically military nature, such as disobedience to orders, cowardice and so on. Military tribunals are, however, inherently not independent or impartial, since they act wholly within a sphere of administrative law; for that reason, their use for criminal cases may violate a cardinal provision of human rights law, namely the due process clause requiring an independent and impartial adjudicator. In fact, however, and turning to the actual Latin American experience, military court jurisdiction is used very expansively, covering every possible matter in which a member of the armed forces may be involved. And worse, military court jurisdiction is often put into practice only for the purpose of preventing investigation and action by other courts or prosecutors. In that sense, military courts are the 'black hole' where all serious inquiries are lost, and they have thus become a major mechanism of impunity of both a de facto and a de jure nature.

Amnesty laws are in any event the preferred form of de jure impunity. Military dictatorships have almost always enacted by decree a self-amnesty law by which they try to prevent any future inquiry. Though there is little disagreement in international law that such laws are unacceptable, by and large succeeding democratic governments have allowed them to stand, as in the cases of Pinochet's Decree 2191 of 1978 and the Guatemalan amnesties of 1982 and 1986. Brazil negotiated an amnesty law in 1979, years before the military government started the carefully controlled *abertura* process towards democracy. The Guatemalan example is particularly egregious. The military government decreed the 1986 law only a few days before handing over power to an elected President and Congress. There was an attempt in Congress to declare it null and void, but President Vinicio Cerezo effectively blocked the effort. In Argentina, military rulers attempted to do the same in 1983, only a few days before the elections that marked the return to democracy. The military, however, were then too weak after the Falklands-Malvinas defeat to impose too many conditions on the transition. As a result, judges refused to apply the decree-law, and the newly elected Congress declared it null and void.

Unfortunately, newly democratic regimes in South America have been too inclined to yield to military pressure and enact further amnesties with the intervention of freely elected representatives of the people. Guatemala passed a new amnesty law in 1987. In El Salvador there was an amnesty law in the same year and a subsequent one in 1993, days after the Truth Commission issued its report. There were also blanket, comprehensive amnesty laws in Nicaragua in 1990 and in Honduras in 1981, 1987 and 1991. More recently, the Fujimori regime in Peru enacted an amnesty law in 1995 (Decree Law 26.479, 14 June 1995), just in time to release members of an army death squad from prison and prevent their conviction. Those laws were declared null and void in 2001, after the Inter-American Court of Human Rights decided they violated Peru's obligations under the American Convention on Human Rights. Because of that, in 2009 former head of state Alberto Fujimori was convicted of serious crimes and sentenced to 25 years in prison. His case is on appeal as at the time of writing.

'Pseudo-amnesty' laws have the same effect as amnesty laws but merely avoid using the word. Examples are the Uruguayan law of 1986 (Ley de Caducidad de la Pretensión Punitiva del Estado) and two Argentine laws, *Punto Final* (Full Stop) in 1986 and *Obediencia Debida* (Due Obedience) in 1987, enacted during Raúl Alfonsín's government under pressure from rebellious army officers.[3]

The struggle against impunity did finally yield some results, however. The most recent amnesty law was enacted in Guatemala in December 1996, in order to facilitate the return of guerrilla leaders from exile and to sign a comprehensive peace agreement brokered by the UN. It is the first amnesty law in Latin America that specifically exempts the most egregious crimes from its coverage. Its terms are in line with the emerging principles mentioned earlier. Of course, the law did not end impunity in Guatemala, but it is encouraging that the principle of accountability for human rights crimes has been preserved.

The struggle to overcome impunity had to confront the legality and widely accepted morality of amnesty laws, first using each country's legislative process, then through challenging impunity in courts, and eventually through litigation before international bodies and by international procedures. In the Western Hemisphere, these legal battles have offered a wealth of arguments and ideas and yielded precedents that have been applied in many other circumstances around the world. Victims of egregious abuse and of state-sponsored impunity have been granted both a right to justice and a right to truth in landmark decisions that were the final result of these struggles.

The *Velásquez Rodríguez* decision by the Inter-American Court of Human Rights (IACtHR) was the first case in which an international body confronted the phenomenon of forced disappearances.[4] Angel Manfredo Velásquez was a Honduran student leader who was apprehended by a unit of the Honduran Army and subsequently disappeared. The case was the first fully tried 'contentious case' brought before the IACtHR. Though the matter of amnesty was not directly at issue, the Court declared that forced disappearance of persons

---

[3] For details of amnesty and pseudo-amnesty laws in Latin America, see Norris 1992.
[4] *Velásquez Rodríguez*, IACtHR, Judgement on the Merits, 29 July 1988.

was a crime against humanity, citing—among other documents—declarations to that effect by the most representative political bodies of the international community.[5] The Court also clarified the legal effects of such a categorisation:[6] the state has an obligation to conduct serious investigations into alleged human rights violations and to identify those responsible.[7]

> Even in the hypothetical case that those individually responsible for crimes of this type cannot be legally punished under certain circumstances, the State is obligated to use the means at its disposal to inform the relatives of the fate of the victims and as may be the case, the location of their remains.[8]

At about the same time, the Inter-American Commission on Human Rights (the region's other human rights protection body) received complaints about the impact of amnesty and pseudo-amnesty laws on the rights of victims to pursue criminal action before the courts of their own countries. The Commission had already had occasion to condemn self-amnesty laws passed by military dictatorships in previous years.[9] In fact, by the mid-1980s the matter was considered by the Commission to be of great institutional gravity, meriting an important place in that body's annual reports to the General Assembly of the OAS.[10] In Argentina and in Uruguay, relatives of victims who had pursued criminal actions in domestic courts had seen their cases dismissed by application of the pseudo-amnesty laws passed in those countries by recently established democratic governments (see above). After lengthy deliberations and hearings involving the complainants and diplomatic representatives of those states, the Commission issued Reports 28/92 and 29/92 on Uruguay and Argentina respectively.[11] Citing, among other authorities, the IACtHR's decision in *Velásquez*, the Commission declared that the Ley de Caducidad in Uruguay and the Argentine laws of Punto Final and Obediencia Debida, plus Menem's pardons, were all incompatible with the obligations imposed on the state by the American Convention.

The argument against the validity of such blanket amnesties lies in the nature of the offenses themselves, ie their seriousness, which is comparable to that of crimes against humanity. It is also based on the fact that murder, torture and disappearance are violations of rights so fundamental that the Conventions specifically made them non-derogable, meaning that they

---

[5] Declarations of the General Assembly of the United Nations and of the Organization of American States, cited at para 151, 152 and 153.

[6] See *Velásquez Rodríguez* (1988) para 158 et seq.

[7] *Ibid*, para 174.

[8] *Ibid*, para 181.

[9] See General Secretariat of the Organization of American States. 1997. Report 36/96, p 162 of the Spanish version.

[10] General Secretariat of the Organization of American States. 1985–86. Annual Report, p 205 of the Spanish version.

[11] General Secretariat of the Organization of American States. 1985–86. Annual Report of the Inter-American Commission on Human Rights, pp 42 and 162 of the Spanish version.

cannot be suspended even during states of emergency. It follows that amnesties that cover such violations are ex post facto derogation that is equally impermissible. The obligation (of the state) to investigate, prosecute and punish is also a right of the victim and his or her families, based on the Convention's clause instituting a 'right to a remedy' (Articles 8 and 25). When it comes to this kind of crime, the remedy cannot consist simply of payment of money but must include reparations also of a non-monetary nature. Among the latter, the victims have a right to see justice done. They are not entitled to a specific form of penalty, but they are definitely entitled to a process that restores justice by criminally prosecuting those who may be responsible (Van Boven 1993; see also Joinet 1997).

Since the Inter-American Court and Commission issued these landmark judgments, other international bodies have followed the same path. The UN Human Rights Committee (HRC), which is the organ for the authoritative interpretation of the International Covenant on Civil and Political Rights (ICCPR), has consistently taken a strong position on the accountability for grave human rights violations. It has done so in the context of applying its case complaint mechanism, as well as when issuing comments on some countries' periodic reviews of implementation of the ICCPR.[12] The HRC objects to amnesties that create an 'atmosphere of impunity', meaning that an amnesty law may be valid under some circumstances but not if the net result is a legal impossibility to investigate and prosecute these kind of crime. The HRC has also based its objection to blanket amnesties and pardons on the fact that when applied, they prevent victims from exercising their right to a remedy.[13] In August 2004, Secretary-General Kofi Annan adopted this doctrine in a document called 'Rule of Law and Transitional Justice in Conflict and Post-Conflict Situations'.

The European Court of Human Rights (ECtHR) has also recently dealt with the question of what is an appropriate response by the state to a human rights violation of this seriousness. In a decision against Turkey, it stated in no uncertain terms that violations of the right to life and to physical and moral integrity of the person cannot be satisfied merely by the payment of monetary damages. Victims and their families have a right to serious investigation, prosecution and punishment of those found to be responsible for such crimes.[14]

---

[12] *Elena Quinteros Almeida v Uruguay.* UNHCR Case 107/1981. See also Report of the Committee on Human Rights, Volume I. General Assembly Official Documents, Fiftieth Session, Supplement No 40 (A/50/40): Argentina, para 153; Paraguay, para 200; Haiti, para 230. See also Report of the Committee on Human Rights, Volume I. General Assembly, Official Documents, Fifty-first Session, Supplement No 40 (A/51/40): Peru, para 347.

[13] CCPR/C/79/Add.46, adopted at Meeting No 1411, Fifty-third Session, 5 April 1995, Item 10.

[14] *Aksoy v Turkey.* ECtHR. Judgment of 18 December 1996.

Theo Van Boven and Louis Joinet, Special Rapporteurs appointed by the UN to deal with these questions, have persuasively established this right to justice. In their authoritative reports on Reparations and Impunity respectively, they cite and compile the Courts and their judgments as well as the Commissions mentioned above. Both conclude that victims have a right to demand prosecution for crimes against humanity (Velásquez Rodríguez 1988, para 158).

Most recently, the Inter-American Commission on Human Rights had the occasion to plead the right to truth explicitly before the IACtHR, in a case involving the disappearance of a Peruvian student and Peru's non-investigation of the matter. The Court stated that the right to truth 'does not exist in the American Convention, although it may correspond to a concept that is still in doctrinal and jurisprudential development'.[15] Although the Court here evidently ducked the opportunity to contribute to that doctrinal and jurisprudential development, it did add that the matter was covered in any event by its own finding that Peru was under a duty to investigate the facts that produced violations of the American Convention.[16] In more recent decisions, the court has firmly established the right to truth as emanating from the American Convention on Human Rights.[17]

B. Truth and Justice

The common denominator of all truth commissions is their mission: *to tell the truth*. Although this may seem obvious, it is not if we consider the context in which they have to perform their work and the provisos to which *the truth* is subjected. These commissions have to work in societies that operate under almost impenetrable mechanisms of denial and that are accustomed to hearing a single, reassuring and definitive version of the facts—societies that in general are not very open to changing their way of thinking about past events. Furthermore, commissions operate in times of extreme institutional and political complexity and major social instability, which makes it very difficult to discover and, above all, tell the truth. Their task is not easy: they are responsible for overcoming barriers to the discovery of the facts and for redeeming society from the reign of lies and oblivion. In spite of these difficulties, commissions, together with judicial proceedings, are effective instruments for establishing an indisputable factual basis, above and beyond differing interpretations.

---

[15] *Castillo Paez v Peru*. IACtHR. Decision on Merits, 3 November 1997, para 86.
[16] *Ibid.*
[17] *Almonacid Arellano v Chile; Goiburu v Paraguay.*

On many occasions the arguments against the commissions' work were based either on an application of Max Weber's ethics of responsibility or else on the (wrong) assumption that criminal justice proceedings and ensuing punishment are inspired by the desire for revenge. Influential Latin and North American intellectuals have maintained that in order to ensure governance during the transition to democracy, those responsible for massive human rights violations should not be submitted to judicial proceedings. As a consequence, they have declared their preference for action exclusively by truth commissions. The statement that truth promotes reconciliation, while judicial proceedings are vindictive, is conceptually and historically incorrect. In our view, it also cannot be proved empirically. Criminal procedures expressly emerged in order to take the conflict out of the hands of the parties involved (*'expropiación del conflicto'*) so as to avoid revenge. Its institutionalisation and institutions are the result of the long road that humanity has traveled in order to process social conflicts rationally. Consequently, justice is not private revenge; and criminal justice excludes revenge (Maier 1996, 259; Osiel 1995). We believe that the process whereby victims and their families are invited to be heard before a truth commission is fundamental to healing their wounds and to changing the relationship that they previously had with the state and society (Mendez 1997b, 529). However, state responsibility does not end there. Although knowledge and recognition of the truth are fundamental steps, they are insufficient. When revealed responsibly and impartially, the truth is an important step towards justice, provided it forms part of a global, comprehensive policy to overcome impunity and is not merely an attempt to replace the right to justice with a report on what happened.

C. Naming Names

A truth commission whose findings could have judicial effects of a criminal nature over a person would violate the principle of *juge naturel* (the right of every defendant to be tried only by courts having jurisdiction over the case at the time the crime was committed). As to identifying individuals and including them in a report, an important controversy has arisen over whether truth commissions should explicitly identify perpetrators or rather refrain from naming names. The legitimacy of one or the other solution depends on the specific case. If there are limits to establishing the truth eventually in judicial proceedings, it is evident that keeping secret the names of those found to be responsible does not contribute to either clarification or reconciliation. Arguably, it diminishes the credibility of a report that, while claiming to tell the truth, hides significant facts and information. On the other hand, if there is a significant possibility of prosecution, it would appear prudent not to reveal names until criminal proceedings, with all due guarantees, can determine the guilt or innocence of each individual. In either case, it must be recognised that 'naming names' entails severe stigma for those identified. Consequently, if there is no possibility of court action, commissions should study the information they receive very closely and envisage mechanisms that would allow a minimum right of defense for those who may be implicated.

D. Truth as a Justiciable Right

The Inter-American Commission has said that the truth should be discovered and revealed by

> creating investigative commissions, whose integration and competence shall be determined in accordance with the corresponding domestic law of each country, or by granting the necessary means so that the Judiciary itself can undertake the necessary investigations (General Secretariat of the OAS 1985–86, 205).

However, more than ten years passed before the judiciaries of the States of the Americas assumed their obligations with regard to the right to truth. While the actions of the courts have still not been completely satisfactory, today the right to truth is one of the most important issues in Latin America, and significant steps have been taken , including for instance, the discovery of the files of Stroessner's secret police in Paraguay, and in Uruguay, the denunciation presented by Senator Rafael Michellini regarding the alleged clandestine burial of those who disappeared following execution.[18]

Argentina began to follow this route as of March 1995. Just when discussion of what happened during the *años de plomo* finally seemed to have been buried under the laws of impunity and the presidential pardon, the revelations of Captain Adolfo Scilingo of the Argentine Navy, who explained how people were thrown alive into the sea from planes, gave new momentum to the discussion (Verbitsky 1996). The former soldier's confession rekindled the climate of the early years of the return to democracy. Once again, there was open discussion and social indignation, and the mass media offered extensive coverage. However, following the revelations, time went by, and there was no official or institutional response.[19] Consequently, human rights organisations and victims almost reflexively looked to the judiciary as the only place within the state structure able to provide answers. This

---

[18] This was based on the Inter-American Convention on Forced Disappearance of Persons, together with Uruguayan domestic law that prohibits invoking exceptional circumstances to violate commitments assumed under the Convention.

[19] It was not only judicial officials who remained silent. It was extremely noticeable that the political class, with few exceptions, preferred silence. Considerable time passed before, in April of that year, the head of the Argentine Army, General Martín Balza, gave his famous speech in which, on behalf of the Army, he asked the nation's forgiveness for the atrocities committed during the illegal repression.

also happened because historically, the fight for human rights and against state terrorism in Argentina has been closely linked to the behaviour of the judiciary. Before it fell into apathy and ceased questioning the 'political' decisions of the legislative and executive branches, the judiciary had been a protagonist in the prosecution and conviction of those who had violated human rights during the Argentine military dictatorship.

The relatives of victims appeared before criminal courts on many occasions, invoking the right to truth of the families and of society, as well as the right to mourn.[20] After a very ambivalent initial reaction by lower courts, the issue of the right to truth reached the Supreme Court in August 1998.[21] This tribunal, in a decision of two paragraphs—by a majority of five votes to four—rejected a mother's claim to seek information about her disappeared daughter through regular criminal proceedings.[22] As a consequence of this poorly argued and erroneous decision, the Tribunal was harshly criticised by almost all sectors of society. Two months later in a new decision, the Supreme Court recognised the existence of a right to individualised truth that is enforceable by the courts. Such right arises from the Constitution and from the international human rights conventions that are part of it.[23] Through this decision, the State has accepted that it owes information on what happened in the past to the general population and to victims, and that the courts have the chief responsibility for uncovering and telling the truth. It is significant that in reaching this landmark ruling, both the Supreme Court and lower appellate tribunals have repeatedly cited precedents from the Inter-American Commission and the IACtHR. From now on, when it comes to serious human rights crimes, the State must respond to five basic questions: who, where, when, how and why. 'Truth trials' then proceeded at several courts throughout the country. Their revelations brought about the Supreme Court decision, in 2005, to declare the *Punto Final* and Due Obedience laws null and void as contrary to Argentina's treaty obligations.[24] In time, all cases of human rights violations during the 'dirty war' were reopened and several officials of various ranks were convicted.

---

[20] For further details of these presentations, see Abregú 1996.

[21] Perhaps one of the most obvious examples of what is argued here are the majority votes of the Federal Criminal and Correctional Court of Appeals for Buenos Aires in both the *Mignone* and *Lapacó* cases. *Lapaco case*. Supreme Court of Argentina. Judgment of 13 August 1998. Due to its importance, Human Rights Watch (Americas) and the Center for Justice and International Law (CEJIL) appeared in the proceedings as *amici curiae*. See Case 761, *Hechos ocurridos en el ámbito de la Escuela de Mecánica de la Armada* (ESMA), known as the *Esma case* or *Mignone case*. Following contradictory arguments, these decisions established '*prosigan los autos según su estado*' (the process should continue according to its status), an unprecedented and meaningless legal formula (for details of the cases see Abregú 1996, 34).

[22] *Lapaco case*. Supreme Court of Argentina. Judgment of 13 August 1998. see also FN 20.

[23] *Urteaga case*. Supreme Court of Argentina. Judgment of 15 October 1998.

[24] *Simón* case … (oka *Poblete-Hlacik* case).

Finally, a more recent development has spurred a new wave of political and social activity in Latin America and is related to the recovery of memories of human rights violations of the recent past. In some European countries prosecutions have been brought against military leaders and other perpetrators of those violations, under the theory of universal jurisdiction. It is on the basis of one of these cases that General Augusto Pinochet was arrested in the UK in October 1998 and held in custody, pending extradition proceedings requested by judge Baltazar Garzón of Spain, until March 2000. In fact, Judge Garzón and at least one other Spanish judge (García Castellón) had been gathering evidence of atrocities in Argentina and Chile for several years, originally confining their search to events in which Spanish subjects were the victims, but later broadening it to include Argentine and Chilean victims as well. Simultaneously, similar cases were brought before Italian and German courts. Until Pinochet's arrest, these matters raised interest only in the relatively small community of human rights activists on both sides of the Atlantic, though they also elicited, from time to time, intemperate reactions from the South American governments.

The actions of Judge Garzón and other European magistrates have been made possible by the cooperation of South American human rights organisations and a strong and active community of exiles living in Europe, as well as European human rights and solidarity groups. In turn, however, the attention raised in Latin America by these actions—even before Pinochet's arrest—has brought the outstanding issues of memory and justice to the front and centre of national debates. In Chile especially this debate has had the very beneficial effect of bursting the bubble of complacency in which many sectors of democratic society were living, as if one could 'declare' the country reconciled and expect the families of victims to accept a *status quo* characterised by silence and impunity. After Pinochet's arrest, as noted above, at least one other major human rights case progressed to the level of actual prosecution. Upon his return, the Supreme Court of Chile stripped Pinochet of immunity so that there was then a clear possibility of prosecution for human rights crimes. In addition, the military had to abandon its arrogant stance towards this matter, and in an effort to bring their cause home, it offered to start conversations with the families of victims to see what could be disclosed of those tragic events. Several human rights organisations, though not all, have boycotted these talks on grounds that they see them as no more than face-saving on the part of the Army.

Of course, other Latin American governments joined in a form of 'democratic solidarity' with Chile and denounced both the Spanish judges and the British government for engaging in extraterritorial criminal jurisdiction and violating Latin American sovereignty. Explaining why this position is legally and ethically wrong, and even politically unsustainable, exceeds the scope of this essay. But it is worth noting that there is a huge gap between the official position of governments and the prevailing mood in Latin American public opinion that is mainly supportive of ending impunity. Concerning the law, it is also worth noting that Chile's most convincing argument against Pinochet's arrest had to rely on the premise that Chile could and was willing to prosecute him for the same crimes. If Chile prosecuted in good faith, its claim to do so should prevail over any other, and the *raison d'etre* of universal jurisdiction would not apply. It was obviously very difficult to make such a claim in good faith when so many years had passed without any effort in Chile to hold Pinochet accountable. As the Chilean government was making this claim, there was neither any warrant of arrest against Pinochet produced in that country, nor any effort to dismantle the array of legalistic shields that he had constructed for himself before leaving power. But sceptics (including this author) have been proved wrong, and Pinochet's prosecution in Chile has in itself been a great victory for the human rights movement.

IV. CONCLUSION

As with many other issues in social sciences, a comparative analysis between Latin American experiences and those of other regions in the world is burdened with complications. There are many reasons why the situation in Latin American countries and elsewhere are not only different but even not comparable. However, such comparisons have nonetheless been made, fruitfully in my mind, for the last several years (Rosenberg 1991 and 1995; Kritz 1995).[25] Latin American 'lessons' in this regard may be difficult to apply to the forms and instruments that other newly democratic states devise to come to terms with past violations. Since the most important purpose of truth and justice efforts is a *national* catharsis that prevents repetition of the tragedy, it stands to reason that each democracy must find its own way to deal with the past according to its culture and its mores.

On the other hand, this country-specific approach applies to methodology, not to whether some effort in that direction is necessary. Given a tragic recent past of egregious violations of human dignity, silence and oblivion is simply not an option. The right of victims and families to be recognised and respected in their plight cuts across culture and is truly universal. And even when it comes to the methods for doing so, vastly different societies have reached out and borrowed pages of law and rules from each other. In that sense, the South African TRC is not only the most prominent example of an approach that has been validated across cultures; it is also an important improvement over its Latin American precedents. It may be that there is

---

[25] See also publications from the Institute for Democracy in South Africa (IDASA) on their website http://www.idasa.org/.

still a lot of impunity for the crimes of apartheid in South Africa; but the thoroughness of the TRC and the novelty of granting conditional amnesty ('indemnity' from prosecution in South African legal terminology) to perpetrators who come forward and tell their stories truthfully and completely, are indeed major steps in the right direction.

With regard to Eastern Europe the differences may be more marked. Most Latin Americans would find fault with Eastern European efforts at accounting for the crimes of communism, including lustration laws and some of the controversial attempts at prosecution that have taken place, especially in Germany, for crimes that were either too far back in the past or for actions that were not crimes under the laws of the land when they were committed. In the end, using criminal trials to assert some interpretation of the historical record is a disservice both to history and to the administration of justice (Osiel 1995, 463, 680). It should be obvious that we do not object to prosecutions but only to prosecutions (and administrative sanctions like *lustration*) that violate cardinal principles of due process. We certainly object to prosecutions that attempt too much or that sweep over important norms such as *juge naturel*, the principle of legality or *non bis in idem* (the rule against double jeopardy) (Mendez 1997c). The nature, scope and length in time of the abuses committed by the communist regimes in Europe are very different from the repressive tragedies of Latin American in the 1970s and 1980s. In particular, the communist regimes were characterised by a pervasive intrusion into everyone's privacy and by a web of complicity with spying and informing. This means that once you start pulling the yarn, a lot of people share in the guilt of how the lives of others were ruined. In Latin America, however, large sectors of society supported and cheered on when the military elites took over, and most of them chose to look the other way when confronted with the evidence of atrocities. But truth commissions and prosecutions are not meant to deal with political and moral accomplices; they are directed strictly at the killers, the torturers and those who gave the orders—and these are comparatively few.

Still, Latin American experiences do apply to the principles that are being developed internationally in law and policy about what societies owe to themselves and to the victims of massive human rights violations. In the first place, blanket amnesties are now clearly outlawed, even though only a few years ago we took their enactment for granted. Second, truth-telling is an integral part of any regime of reparations that is not meant to insult the dignity of victims. Third, accountability for the crimes of the past must be achieved as early as possible, but it is not only a problem for the transition to democracy. Decent societies must continue to conduct every possible effort to investigate the events, to disclose to the victims and their relatives what can be established and to make those facts public, including the identities of perpetrators, unless to do so would interfere with ongoing criminal prosecutions.

The most significant feature of Latin American experiences with accountability is perhaps this recent insight into the nature of the problem: that efforts at truth and justice have outlived the narrow limits of the transition and take on new forms in the now relatively stable democratic period. In conformity with the dicta of the IACtHR in the *Velasquez* decision, these obligations on the part of the state live on for as long as there is any uncertainty as to the fate and whereabouts of any disappeared person. Of course, the fact that there still is uncertainty is not something to be proud of. The good news, however, is that the victims and their families have not abandoned their quest and that they are succeeding in making their demands an integral part of each country's democratic agenda for the coming decade.

REFERENCES

Abregú, Martín. 1996. La tutela judicial del derecho a la verdad en la Argentina. *Revista IIDH* 24(1): 11–49.

van Boven, Theo. 1993. *Study Concerning the Right to Restitution, Compensation and Rehabilitation for Victims of Gross Violations of Human Rights and Fundamental Freedoms: Final Report.* UN Doc E/CN.4/Sub.2/1993/8. New York: UN Commission on Human Rights, Sub-Commission on Prevention of Discrimation and Protection of Minorities.

Dassin, Joan (ed). 1986. *Torture in Brazil.* [Brasil: Nunca Mais.] Translated by Jaime Wright. Austin: Institute of Latin American Studies, University of Texas.

General Secretariat of the Organization of American States (ed). 1985–86. Annual Report of the Inter-American Commission on Human Rights. Washington DC.

——. 1997. Annual Report of the Inter-American Commission on Human Rights. Washington DC.

Joinet, Louis. 1997. *Revised Final Report on the Impunity of Perpetrators of Human Rights Violations (Civil and Political Rights) Prepared under Sub-Commission Resolution 1996/119.* E/CN.4/Sub.2/1997/20/Rev.1 of 2/10/97. New York: UN Commission on Human Rights, Sub-Commission on Prevention of Discrimation and Protection of Minorities.

Kritz, Neil J (ed). 1995. *Transnational Justice: How Emerging Democracies Reckon with Former Regimes.* Washington DC: US Institute of Peace.

Maier, Julio. 1996. *Derecho Procesal Penal. Tomo I: Fundamentos.* Buenos Aires: Ed Del Puerto.

Méndez, Juan E. 1997a. Accountability for Past Human Rights Violations. *Human Rights Quaterly* 19(2): 255–82.

——. 1997b. Derecho a la verdad frente a las graves violaciones a los derechos humanos. In *La aplicación de los tratados sobre derechos humanos por los tribunales locales*, edited by M Abregú and C Courtis. Buenos Aires: Ed Del Puerto-CELS.

——. 1997c. In Defense of Transitional Justice. In *Transitional Justice and the Rule of Law in New Democracies*, edited by AJ MacAdams. Notre Dame: Notre Dame Press.

Michelini, Felipe. 1996. El largo camino de la verdad. *Revista IIDH* 24: 157–72.

Norris, Robert E. 1992. Leyes de impunidad y los derechos humanos en las Américas: Una repuesta legal. *Revista IIDH* 15: 47–121.

Orentlicher, Diane. 1991. Settling Accounts: The Duty to Prosecute Human Rights Violations of a Prior Regime. *Yale Law Journal* 13: 2537–615.

———. 1994. Adressing Gross Human Rights Abuses: Punishment and Victim Compensation. In *Human Rights: An Agenda for the Next Century*, edited by L Henkin and J Hargrove. Washington: Asil.

Osiel, Mark J. 1995. Ever Again: Legal Remembrance of Administrative Massacre. *University of Pennsylvania Law Review* 144(2): 463–704.

Roht-Arrazia, Naomi. 1995. *Impunity and Human Rights in International Law and Practice*. New York: Oxford University Press.

Rosenberg, Tina. 1991. *Children of Cain: Violence and the Violent in Latin America*. New York: Morrow.

———. 1995. *The Haunted Land: Facing Europe's Ghosts after Communism*. New York: Random House.

UNCHR. 1997. *Report of the Committee on Human Rights, Volume I*. General Assembly Official Documents, Fifty-first Session, Supplement 40 (A/51/40). New York: United Nations.

———. 1999. *Report of the Committee on Human Rights, Volume I*. General Assembly Official Documents, Fiftieth Session, Supplement 40 (A/50/40). New York: United Nations.

Verbitsky, Horacio. 1996. *The Flight: Confessions of an Argentine Dirty Warrior*. New York: New Press.

Weschler, Lawrence. 1990. *A Miracle, a Universe: Settling Accounts with Torturers*. New York: Pantheon.

II

Divided Memories, Contested Truths, Silenced Voices

3

Reflections on Law and Memory

EMILIOS CHRISTODOULIDIS AND SCOTT VEITCH

LIKE ALL WAYS of knowing and acting, legal concepts and actions constitute and conceal at the same time. Concepts such as right and duty, citizen and sovereign, provide ways of acting and being in the world that simultaneously close off other ways of being and acting in the world. In so doing, they form some of the elementary social tools for the ways in which remembering and forgetting take place.

What is remembered and what forgotten intrigues, necessarily, with the temporal. Legal concepts apportion time, start it off, cut it up, extend it, terminate it: the will is written, the duty owed, the deed done or the contract executed. Memory here may be tapped or trapped, released or abandoned. Legal concepts work, they labour, to make ways of being and, acting through the subjection of normative ordering, to make sense of ways of being over time.

In no sense is law unique at closing down possibilities of thinking about the past. But law, like any template that makes meaning possible, must accommodate and institute memory in its own specific way, allow it to find expression in its pathways, in a representational space that may disclose and reveal it. Any accounting of the past cannot but be selective. In this selection process, aspects of the past will be actualised and repressed—and those actualised will in a crucial sense depend on what is repressed.

What does this mean? It means that the *referent* of memory is not the reality of things past: it is instead, at its most abstract, the *stake of a question*, of several questions that we may ask about the past. As famously expounded by Rudolf Bultmann in *Glauben and Verstehen*,

> All understanding, like all interpretation, is continually oriented by the manner of posing the question and by what it aims at [by its *Woraufhin*]. Consequently it is never without presuppositions; it is always directed by a prior understanding of the thing about which it interrogates the text (quoted in Ricoeur 1967, 351).

Memory is the stake of a question, selecting out and thus reducing the infinite complexity of potential renderings of the past, and crucially here, doing it by means of 'sequencing', releasing established sequences and reconfiguring others. In all this there is suppression and actualisation operating simultaneously: the recalling of events is both a constitution—the past made present—and a concealment—what is called forth as past *is present* at the expense of how it might *have otherwise been.*

More needs to be said on memory's workings, and in this chapter we will focus on law's mode of interrogating the past, what questions it asks of it, and how in the process it is set up as appropriate to the demands of the future, the ordering of society. The examples we choose are taken from situations of political transition in South Africa because the focus on transitional justice there has fruitfully brought to the fore crucial questions, as limit situations force law to manifest what under normal conditions might have remained latent. Rather than attempting a complete survey of the issues involved, we offer in this chapter reflections in a fragmentary form that allow us to tap selectively only a few aspects of the fashioning of memory in law.

I. MEMORY AND EMANCIPATION

Karl Marx wrote:

> Men make their own history, but they do not make it just as they please; they do not make it under circumstances chosen by themselves, but under circumstances directly encountered, given, and transmitted from the past. The tradition of all the dead generations weighs like a nightmare on the living (2000, 329).

Herbert Marcuse qualified this with an optimistic reliance on the liberating effect of politicising memory:

> The rediscovered past yields critical standards that are tabooed in the present. ... The weight of these discoveries must eventually shatter the framework in which they were made and confined. The liberation of the past does not end in its reconciliation with the present. Against the self-imposed restraint of the discoverer, the orientation to the past tends towards an orientation on the future. The *recherche du temps perdu* becomes the vehicle of future liberation (1966, 33).

Of course what Marcuse did first was argue against one of memory's most disarming features, its complicity with the past and thus also its inertia:

> [T]he flux of time is society's most natural ally in maintaining law and order ... The flux of time helps men forget what was and what can be: it makes them oblivious to the better past and to the better future (Marcuse 1966, 33).

Likewise, Adorno acknowledged that '[e]nlightenment about what happened in the past must work, above all, against a forgetfulness that too easily goes along with and justifies what is forgotten (1986, 125). He warned against the regressive pull of the past which passes as wisdom. This 'wisdom' threatens because of its complicity with a history that is over-determined by loss, failure and mutability, comfortably withdrawn behind a past that instills the present with inertia. This instilling of inertia characterises even the recall of past revolutionary moments, as Marx reminds us in his exhilarating *Eighteenth Brumaire of Louis Bonaparte*. Just at the moment when people seem most capable of 'revolutionising themselves and things' they fall back on these past traditions and express themselves through them. In past revolutions 'the awakening of the dead [...] served the purpose of glorifying the new struggles' (2000, 330). But the revolutions of the nineteenth century could not afford the risk of this relapsing into the past, of allowing the past to defeat revolution and praxis:

> An entire people which had imagined that by means of a revolution it had imparted to itself an accelerated power of motion suddenly finds itself set back in a defunct epoch .... [But] the social revolution of the nineteenth century cannot draw its poetry from the past, but only from the future .... [L]et the dead bury their dead (Marx 2000, 330–331).

In short: Marcuse's endeavour to marshal memory in the service of praxis relies on countering its complicity and inertia, and on tapping memory's *disruptive* potential—its ability to preserve promises and potentialities. He wrote:

> [Memory's] recovered past is not reconciled with the present but challenges it ... Truth loses its power when remembrance redeems the past ... Without release of the repressed content of memory, without release of its liberating power, non-repressive sublimation is unimaginable (Marcuse 1966, 163).

And thus:

> Liberation is the most realistic, the most concrete of all historical possibilities and at the same time the most rationally and effectively repressed—the most abstract and remote possibility (Marcuse 1966, xv).

Marcuse's conclusion is significant. It concerns the question of ideology, and as we proceed to look at the law in more detail, the limits of law's representations. Can the repression of memory, its complicity with and redemption of the past, be redressed, and can it be redressed in law? Can memory allow the past to be released from ideology's hold of it? And here we mean ideology in the broader (but still Marxist) sense of the term—that is, as a system of meaning (symbols) that perpetuates oppression by simultaneously keeping it latent ('glorifying the past') and undercutting the potential for resistance at the point of recovery of meaning. Ideology here works through linking up with a past and establishing a continuity that is over-determined by what is already in place. The past is made commensurate with terms that allow social reproduction in a way that—to use Nietzsche's words—establishes continuity 'with a past from which we seem to have derived rather than one from which we may spring' (Nietzsche

1983, 45): 'To spring' as revolutionary subjects (as in Marx and Marcuse) or more generally as subjects capable of a beginning that is neither a denial of history on the one hand, nor a hostage to a past of iniquity and exploitation on the other.

II. MEMORY AND COMPLICITY

If the question that calls us as political actors to responsibility is whether the repression of memory, its complicity with and redemption of the past, can be redressed, a key concern must be the extent to which contemporary institutional attempts to 'deal with the past' confront underlying structural conditions or whether they merely serve to perpetuate hegemonic memories. Might they subvert memories, or do they in fact slot into an ongoing narrative by selecting only part of the past to be dealt with? It is in the latter context that the question of complicity arises most acutely.

The work of the Truth and Reconciliation Commission (TRC) in South Africa has brought to the fore important questions of how a nation deals with its past. It has been subjected increasingly to criticism that its *modus operandi* meant that, despite its good intentions, it not only privileged certain ways of remembering the past, but failed to engage with the structural conditions within which apartheid operated, and therefore that it became complicit with a particular form of the reproduction of unjust social relations.

One can look at this with regard to the role of the judiciary under apartheid. If apartheid was a crime against humanity, we are forced to engage with the question raised by Hannah Arendt (1963) in her coverage of the Eichmann trial and elsewhere: What happens when crime is legal, when criminals can enthusiastically enforce the law? As Mahmood Mamdani pertinently put it, 'Perhaps the greatest moral compromise the TRC made was to embrace the legal fetishism of apartheid' (2000, 60). The question of complicity arose centrally here not in terms simply of direct physical violence but in terms of structures of power *and* legality.

This is the point that David Dyzenhaus made in his defence of an alternative, Fullerian account of legality, an account which makes procedural fairness and justice constitutive. And it is indeed the judges who appeared at the forefront of Dyzenhaus's investigation into complicity. For judges, as Dyzenhaus noted, are both ordinary and special citizens. In the context of playing their part in upholding the apartheid state, they had a doubly privileged position:

> They could carry out their duty without fear of serious personal repercussions and their duty was not one which required following orders; it required careful consideration of argument and careful attention to the particulars of cases (Dyzenhaus 1999, 89–90).

Judges, unlike apartheid's security forces footsoldiers, were not simply following orders. Despite often holding to a 'plain fact' view of law—the view that judges ought to apply the law as the legislators in fact intended it, regardless of questions of 'substantive justice'—judges had choices. Their education and professional experience gave them the necessary legal skills for argument and debate in interpreting and applying the law. It introduced them to an awareness and history of law that would be caricatured by the notion that it was merely a series of orders, as if lawyers and judges were simply nothing more than privates in an army (something their status and self-image alone would belie). Moreover, and despite their material privileges, they, perhaps of all ruling citizens, were most able to witness that special place of conflict in which their society's battles often took place: the courtrooms. Given the oppression they were involved in—the crime against humanity that, despite attempts to separate violence from the judicial word, was knowingly taking place—given this, and more, it is *their* complicity that needed to be understood. As Dyzenhaus put it in the context of the TRC hearings which considered the role of the legal profession:

> South Africans were therefore entitled to know how and why the majority of judges failed so miserably in keeping to their oath of office. They needed to know how men in so privileged a position, with such an important role, and with so much space to do other than they did, made the wrong moral choice... (Dyzenhaus 1999, 90).

Dyzenhaus's argument is that the vast majority of apartheid judges were in dereliction of their duty to uphold and apply the rule of law. The decision to attempt a 'plain-fact' view of law was not a neutral one politically or morally, but involved partaking in a specific view of the legal order. That view, he says, was not only morally wrong but unfaithful to the notion of legality as such. Hence their failure:

> [T]he injustice was of a kind which subverted a particular ideal of the rule of law. That ideal holds that individuals subject themselves to the law—accept the authority which the law claims for itself—only on condition that they are treated equally, fairly, reasonably and so on. A law which subverts equality, or which results in gross unfairness, or can only be implemented unreasonably, is suspect from a moral perspective which is also a perspective inherent in the law. In other words, when a statute is suspect in this way, not only its morality but its legality is in doubt. If a judge is complicit in sustaining this kind of injustice, then he will find himself complicit in undermining the role to which he has sworn fidelity (Dyzenhaus 1999, 176).

Dyzenhaus's position here provides a defence of values *inherent* to law, such that when they are wilfully damaged, we must question whether we are still dealing with the rule of law at all.

What was most striking about the TRC hearings into the South African legal system was that, whilst a handful of judges responded in writing to a series of questions posed by the Commission, not one judge appeared in person. This showed, says Dyzenhaus, a serious contempt for the whole process. In the main, a 'no use in raking over the past now' argument was combined—paradoxically—with an argument for judicial independence (if we want to respect judicial independence now we must respect it in the past, too). Added to this was a range of other excuses: denial of the knowledge and extent of human rights violations under the old regime; the need for collegiality on the bench during the transitional period; and, most revealing in its contempt for the black majority as well as for any sense of political and legal history, the claim (repeated also by some legal academics) that '95 per cent of our [lawyers'] work had nothing to do with apartheid' (Dyzenhaus 1999, 137).

So the judges stayed away, and their failure to account for their role, it can be argued, extends their complicity, though that did not separate them from countless others in the former ruling elite who during the TRC proceedings also managed to whitewash their role. The process of self-absolution was thus carried through by default and with ease. And whilst legal philosophers such as Ronald Dworkin have often been chastised, and rightly so, for over-focusing their analyses of law on judges and the courts to the exclusion of other types of regulation, there is no doubt that the judges' prominent position in implementing apartheid demanded a response and an availability for cross-examination at least, in order to begin to acknowledge the wrongs of the past and come to terms with these wrongs.

The TRC's inability to address these issues, despite its best efforts to do so, also betrays deeper problems. That is, whether or not the judges appeared, they, and the judicial apparatus which they headed, could neither be defined as criminals who enforced the law, nor was crime perfectly legal—both questions that had so perplexed Arendt. Their involvement in the legal apparatus of apartheid could not be redeemed as 'crime' and especially 'crime against humanity' so long as the cloak of legality which the TRC maintained, covered this as a possible understanding of their actions. This difficulty was in fact aired in a discussion of the judicial role more generally. Edwin Cameron, a serving judge, wrote in his insightful submissions to the TRC:

> [M]y role in the enforcement of a system that contains injustices necessarily makes me complicit in them … [In the context of contemporary, democratic South Africa] judges still participate in a system which, in many diverse and complex respects, perpetuates injustice (quoted in Dyzenhaus 1999, 174).

This exceptional acknowledgement notwithstanding, the judiciary's complicity in the crime against humanity that was apartheid, was built into the reconciliation process—not simply as silence, but merely as an inadequate answer to a question.

It was precisely this sort of complicity then that the TRC had difficulty in addressing, and it was indicative of a more general problem it faced. As Colin Bundy has stated,

> [The TRC] could not come to terms with the underlying structures and processes that have determined our identities and patterned our society. Because of its mandate, we may run the risk of defining a new order as one in which police may no longer enjoy immunity to torture opponents of the government, but fail to specify that ordinary citizens should not be poor and illiterate and powerless, or be pushed around by state officials and employers (Bundy 2000, 20).

The institutions set up for dealing with the past have in fact allowed complicity to be covered over. This has happened most obviously in the way that the TRC allowed the apparatchiks of the system to walk away with pardons or exemptions or silence in the name of reconciliation (Dyzenhaus 1999); or it happened in a more subtle way, in the failure to disaggregate victim and beneficiary, which, as Mamdani has described, meant that a 'diminished truth was created that wrote the vast majority of apartheid's victims out of its version of history' (2000, 61).

And it is precisely this problem that led François du Bois to question whether there is really a viable third way between victor's justice and impunity, concluding emphatically that there is not:

> [A] choice *has* to be made between past and future, between impunity and punishment. In a transition to democracy where an oppressed populace has emerged victorious the only viable and legitimate option is to pursue victors' justice (Du Bois 2001, 114).

In order to understand why this might be so, we must address some of the phenomenal underpinnings of the conceptions of truth and reconciliation at play.

III. MEMORY 'COLLECTED' AND 'COLLECTIVE'

> The pursuit of national unity, the well-being of all South African citizens and peace require reconciliation between the people of South Africa and the reconstruction of society.
>
> The adoption of this constitution lays the sure foundation for the people of South Africa to transcend the divisions and strife of the past ...
>
> These can now be addressed on the basis that there is a need for understanding but not for vengeance, a need for reparation but not for retaliation, a need for *ubuntu* but not for victimisation ...
>
> With this Constitution and these commitments *we*, the people of South Africa, open a new chapter in the history of our country.
>
> Postamble to the Interim Constitution of South Africa (Act no 200 of 1993)

> [The report fails to reflect] the truth that the struggle *we* waged helped *our* country to avoid the death of millions of civilians and radically reduced the hostility of [...] our people to those who belonged to the 'oppressor nation'.

> Submission of the African National Congress to the Truth and Reconciliation Commission in Reply to the Section 30 (2) of Act 34 of 1996 on the TRC "Findings on the African National Congress" (October 1998)

> *Our people* [...] have been robbed.

> The ANC Freedom Charter (1955)

Is the 'we' of the ANC's 'country' the 'we' of the Constitution? Does the 'we' include the 'oppressor nation'? Does it include it *a posteriori*? Who has robbed 'us'? Have 'we' done the robbing? The critical risk that reconciliation runs in this context is that conflict can work in two ways: in bringing people together in their overcoming of the conflict that a community assumes to be internal (and here reconciliation and restorative justice is possible) or in maintaining it (in which case reconciliation never gets off the ground). It is a mistake to assume that either form of conflict is detrimental to community. Both enhance community but set its constituency differently. And it is a mistake to elide that distinction: the risk that there will be no reconciliation cannot be avoided even if we decide *a priori* to ignore it.

Let us see in more detail why. The 'phenomenal' connection between conflict and collective social identity is that between the struggle and who 'we'—who are engaged in the struggle—assume to be. In conflict are identities formed and consolidated, through conflict is entry into public space effected in a way that attracts commitment and allows solidarity in consolidating oppositions. In this context, Georg Simmel wrote:

> Conflict may serve to remove dissociating elements in a relationship and re-establish unity. Insofar as conflict is the resolution of tension between antagonists it has stabilising functions and becomes an integrating component in the relationship. However not all conflicts are positively functional for the relationship, but only those which concern goals, values or interests that do not contradict basic assumptions upon which the relationship is founded (1955, 20).

This difference allows Simmel to draw a distinction between 'communal and non-communal conflicts':

> Non-communal conflict results when there is no community of ends between the parties to the conflict ... Non-communal conflict is seen as disruptive and dissociating. Communal conflict, that is based on a common acceptance of basic ends, is, on the contrary, integrative. When men settle their differences on the basis of unity, communal conflict will ensue (Simmel 1955, 75).

Talk of reconciliation all too often elides the distinction that matters by disposing of the dangerous non-communal type of conflict and assuming that conflict is always already of the communal type. Then, of course, by definition, people's engaging in conflict will bring them closer together because there isn't a basic cleavage in the first place that could have driven them further apart. Having presupposed that the conflict was of the communal type anyway, having therefore begged the question, the argument about the restoration of community can be made without reference to the risk that conflict may in fact drive communities further apart.

This conflation of conflicts is at the heart of the impossible task the TRC set itself. Its use of the language of law allowed it to elide the distinction and ignore the risk—the risk that non-communal will not become communal conflict, just because the TRC has provided a forum for accounting for it. But the problem goes deeper and undercuts law's claim to be a means of establishing community. In terms of the past, surely we cannot but assume that during the apartheid years, quite explicitly in the policy of separate development, there was no community, just a stark confrontation of narratives, of two positions that only generated community within and not between them. The one was a narrative of oppression and of the promise of emancipation through struggle, while the other, insofar as it was not split into further, even more partial, patterns, was one of privilege and achievement, of a sense of ownership of the land, of guardianship, of heroic conquest in the narrative of the Boers who undertook 'the Trek' North to conquer territories that later came to be known as Natal, the Orange Free State and the Transvaal, but also a narrative of insecurity and fear. If communities draw from oppositional and mutually exclusive narratives, surely they have very little, if anything, to recollect in common as memory.

So much for sharing any kind of fund of narrative and normative commitments and memories. But further: to the extent that the transition to the 'new' South Africa was successful, does it follow that this led to integration into communal identity? Why ever would it? Why would superimposing the status of equal citizenship in the new nation upon a genuine diversity of identities, needs and expectations fulfil the quest for community? In fact could not the converse be argued: that the success of the movement rather than creating a community, actually divided one; that a substantial minority of white segregationists found themselves pushed out of a community of new sensibilities? Theirs would be a story of the birth of a new narrative that explains past common history of the white community in a new way. Probably this new narrative would explain away the unity of the original white community. How can this possibility be dispensed with, since the danger is, as Adam Czarnota identifies, that 'legal institutions will, by their very nature, support hegemonic collective memories to the suppression of others' (2001, 238)? Why should one assume that the end result of our accounting of the past will move us any closer to a shared community rather than a breakdown of community? What makes the danger impossible and the risk invisible?

In the first case memories collected from master and slave constitute in the law's eyes the inventory of communal experience, those proto-understandings that are shared in some *a priori* sense. They will be shared again, having undergone the transition from pre-interpretative to interpretative and in the process allowed a collective memory to crystallise around them. Yet however convenient a demarcation the new South African nation might be, the question of constituency cannot be elided in this way without either belying collected memories or over-determining them; in either case the purported transition from collected to collective memory is unwarranted. And the history that the Constitution invokes—that it legislates from and for—is that of a collective memory that *could never have been* yet seemingly *must be*.

This links to a second legal *a priori*: that collected memories will survive their transition to collective memory in the first place. That there will be consensus over the explanation of the struggle is an unwarranted assumption, warranted merely by the fact that law is driven by a decisionist imperative and must 'resolve' disagreement over the 'truth of contested memories' and has devised a body of rules and criteria about what truly constitutes what, the terms of contestation, as well as *what* can be remembered, *what* forgotten. Most importantly this requires a special orientation to selection, to its balancing of institutional memory and forgetting.

Of course, as Niklas Luhmann has written,

> [What] is specific to history is that it enables optional access to the meaning of past [and thus also] of future events, and thus leaps within the sequence. History originates in the release from sequence (1995, 79–80).

The argument about law's selectivity working against genuine reconciliation turns on the attempt to police the access and set the contours of institutional memory in a way that installs it as communal. In all this the institutional moment highjacks the discursive by inserting at the social's most crucial junction the *a priori* of the existence of community. The TRC, the forum of collected memories, becomes the institution that marshals collective memory; the assumption that *collected* can become *collective* usurps and over-determines; it is an *a priori* assumption that when read into reconciliation cancels it out by doing violence to the understandings that might have established it.

IV. INSTITUTIONALISED RECONCILIATION AND MEMORY'S TRUTHS

Of all places where this logic of reconciliation was deployed, the most visible in the TRC process was that part which was most explicitly legal in its operations. The Amnesty Committee, despite its quasi-legal staffing, nonetheless followed the detailed criteria and procedures set out in the 1995 Promotion of National Unity and Reconciliation Act; it wielded powers which had direct legal effect; and it survived the close scrutiny of challenge in the Constitutional Court.

The rationale behind the amnesty process, which was enshrined in the Epilogue to the 1993 Interim Constitution, was pragmatic, a means of achieving political progress during the negotiations. Amnesty—immunity from civil and criminal liability—was to be granted in return for truth, the main grounds for the granting of amnesty being the full disclosure of all relevant facts and that the acts in question were acts associated with a political objective. Such a conditional amnesty was seen not simply to be a matter of compromise, but to have a normative component that blanket amnesties used in other transitional scenarios largely lacked, a *quid pro quo*, backed by the threat of future liability for wrongs which remained undisclosed.

It is undoubtedly the case that many truths were uncovered in amnesty hearings that had not been aired publicly before.[1] In particular, victims too had the chance to have their views put on record. Yet the use of the legal method here had interesting implications. Consider the following statement by the Amnesty Committee on an application for amnesty by a former apartheid state police officer:

> Almost all policemen giving evidence before the Amnesty Committee referred to their background and at the end of their testimony expressed regret for what they had done. This may be very relevant in an ordinary criminal hearing when extenuating factors are considered, but these factors or any other factors relating to morality that may lend colour to an offence do not in terms of Act 34 of 1995 render one offence more justified than another. They are not requirements or relevant factors to be considered in the granting of amnesty or refusal thereof. They may however be factors that could contribute to reconciliation and a better understanding of the conflicts of the past and for this reason the Committee allowed the evidence to be led.[2]

The impetus behind this seems to be the desire for an even-handed approach to the conflicts of the past. It was not for the judges to engage with the morality of the acts under review but merely to test their conformity with the legal provisions: full disclosure and association with a political objective. In this, regret, as a personal or individual matter, was not to be taken into account; it was extra-legal, as would be any sense of reconciliation that flowed from the claimed regret.

Yet the institutional dimension could not contain or run with such open-ended risk, the risk that reconciliation may or may not take place. For this

---

[1] Whether or not criminal trials would have been more desirable is a matter of some debate. See eg, du Bois 2001.

[2] Amnesty Decision: Cronje, JH (2773/96).

would be inadequate to ground the required legal *a prioris*. Indeed, the whole process depended upon the risk, or promise of reconciliation. As this is a forward-looking dimension of community as always 'not-yet', the process needed to rest upon a reinforced political consensus, one that all legal operations implicitly rest upon.

This can be glimpsed by considering the ways in which truth and memory are used in the amnesty process. The granting of amnesty was premised on 'full disclosure' in line with the TRC's modus operandi that the revelation of 'truth' is a prerequisite for getting on the 'road to reconciliation'. Full disclosure appears to involve an act of memory, of bringing back to mind and then to the attention of the panel the details of events that took place in the past. But this memory is not itself simply an object, since it is inseparable from the performative process that recalls it as event and therefore which constitutes the very object of legal scrutiny. The question that is implicitly not engaged with is: what is the standard by which 'full disclosure' is deemed to have occurred? Especially given the often secretive nature of the offences committed, as well as the lapse of time since the commitment of the offences, how did the panel know whether full disclosure was achieved?

What is exposed here is the very essence of the problem: that is, the referent of memory is not the event but the truth as constructed by memory. In other words, that which is to be accounted for in law demands not the truth of the event but rather the truth of its accounting—not 'What really happened?' but rather 'Is this believable?', not 'Are these facts verifiable?' but rather 'Were these acts as remembered acts associated with a political objective?', 'Full disclosure' signifies answers to the latter questions, not a revelation of the truth of the event; the latter remains, from the point of view of legal adjudication, unnecessary.

It is not therefore the 'object' of memory, the event itself, which allows for amnesty to be granted: the process is somehow already bound up with its own possible outcomes, which require not truth but the fulfilment of an expectation of a legal memory that could have no original correspondence to legal truth. This is because of the *political* condition of the recall, which is dependent on the political reconciliation at one level having *already taken place* in order to decide whether the plea constitutes an act committed in relation to a political objective. And there is no correspondent 'truth' that could have pre-existed that reconciliation. The need to recognise the events of the past—this realignment of the *mens rea* within a different set of legal coordinates—shows that no matter how risky the connection between truth and personal reconciliation, the amnesty process formally depends on a conceptual connection between reconciliation having taken place in order to ascertain what will count as both truth and political objective. And it is that connection—on which so much depends, not least the possibility of legal adjudication—that is no longer a matter for politics.

This detail signals, however faintly, the way in which—to return to Simmel's terminology—non-communal conflict is hidden from view in the amnesty process. Such a risk is not simply too risky to endorse, but in the way in which legal technique and justification are deployed, made structurally impossible to register. Once endorsed by the Constitutional Court, the amnesty process proceeded without danger of reopening the question 'Whether reconciliation?' except insofar as it is made safe by being an adjunct (a 'merely personal' question which has no institutional impact) to the main task—namely, of deciding yes or no to a particular amnesty application, a political question made answerable in these terms only by the use of legal decision. That the overall raison d'etre of the process was the revelation of truth does not disturb this structural ordering of memory and outcomes that help fashion and legitimate the transition.

This is not to say that things did not come out publicly that had not hitherto done so. Rather it is to point out that the jump from collected to collective memory was, from the TRC's point of view, one in which the risk of non-communal conflict was highly reduced and, in the case of the Amnesty Committee's legal decisions, rendered invisible. This was not simply structural in its operation but, as already noted, pragmatic in genesis. And as Michael Ignatieff has pointed out, such pragmatism matters:

> In such a context, where truth seems a less divisive object than justice, Tutu's commission, even as it forces the disclosure of painful truth, may well reinforce the political consensus that created his commission (1998, 174).

In this sense the process of reconciliation institutionalised through the TRC was underwritten not by the risk of the new political community as unknown project—whatever that might turn out to be—but instead by the needs of the new political community, which had to be promoted explicity as *national* unity; it was underwritten by the risk of non-communal conflict defined as the return to violence.

This was a serious, pragmatic and real concern. But that is not to say that the theoretical understanding offered here is not to the point. Quite the opposite. If anything, the ways in which the language and resources of the idea of reconciliation and, more importantly, the ways in which these were given institutional force, are important in offering one way to understand the emerging sense of irrelevance of the TRC to large sections of the South African public. To the extent to which the project of promoting national unity depended upon great concessions being given to the beneficiaries of apartheid, whether by conscious design or not, the institutionalised process for reconciliation played a major legitimating role. In particular, the manner in which the fostering of a collective memory was propounded as a way of coming to terms with the past, of healing the divided psyche of a nation, worked to the exclusion of conflicts of class, race and ethnicity—the impact of which remains profound, devastating and, most significantly, ongoing.

And it is this which forces us to consider the extent to which memory's disruptive potential has in this instance been actualised or whether instead, in terms we noted earlier, it has been used to link up with a past and establish a continuity that is over-determined by what is already in place. In other words, has the deployment of memory instilled the present with inertia rather than preserve the promise of reconciliation as precisely that—a promise whose obligation persists as obligation and whose debt is not dischargeable?

V. CONCLUSION

In this chapter we have attempted to show that while the giveness of the past is in always so many ways in question, structural features and specifically the demands of legal action, provide necessary limits on the use and role of memory. We argue that the questions that we ask of the past are constitutive of how we fashion it and that the processes of recalling the past operate on the basis of a selectivity that suppresses even as it actualises memory. We conclude, however, by suggesting that treating memory as a force of liberation from what appears as given, confining and inevitable, requires a quite extraordinary effort to counter the many ways in which 'hegemonic' memories become entrenched and to retrieve memory's many truths. Furthermore, in periods of political transition we must guard against both the severing of a 'new community' from its past and its over-determination as community in the first place.

What did Nietzsche mean by the disjunction between 'a past from which we may spring rather than that from which we seem to have derived'? It is at this (dis-)junction that we would like to locate these short reflections on memory. It reminds us that entry into public space is not predetermined by fixed origins of past mythologised battles, as nationalism and patriotism so devastatingly demonstrate; entry into public space must instead be treated as opportunity for praxis that is renewal, not repetition—not the drawing of a collective memory as 'a picture that holds us captive' but instead one that urges us always to 'let the dead bury their dead.'

REFERENCES

Adorno, Theodor. 1986. What Does Coming to Terms with the Past Mean? In *Bitburg in Moral and Political Perspective*, edited by Geoffrey Hartman. Bloomington: Indiana University Press.

ANC (African National Congress). 1998. Submission of the African National Congress to the Truth and Reconciliation Commission in Reply to the Section 30 (2) of Act 34 of 1996 on the TRC "Findings on the African National Congress" (October 1998); http://www.anc.org.za/show.php?doc=/ancdocs/misc/trcreply.htm.

ANC (Congress of the People). 1955. *The Freedom Charter*. Adopted at the Congress of the People, Kliptown, on 26 June 1955; http://www.anc.org.za/ancdocs/history/charter.html.

Arendt, Hannah. 1963. *Eichmann in Jerusalem*. Harmondsworth: Penguin.

Bundy, Colin. 2000. The Beast of the Past: History and the TRC. In *After the TRC: Reflections on Truth and Reconciliation in South Africa*, edited by W James and L van de Vijver. Johannesburg: David Philip.

Czarnota, Adam. 2001. Law as Mnemosyne and as Lethe. In *Lethe's Law: Justice, Law and Ethics in Reconciliation*, edited by E Christodoulidis and S Veitch. Oxford: Hart.

Du Bois, Francois 2001. Nothing But the Truth: The South African Alternative to Corrective Justice. In *Lethe's Law: Justice, Law and Ethics in Reconciliation*, edited by E Christodoulidis and S Veitch. Oxford: Hart.

Dyzenhaus, David. 1999. *Judging the Judges, Judging Ourselves*. Oxford: Hart.

Ignatieff, Michael. 1998. *The Warrior's Honor*. London: Chatto and Windus.

Interim Constitution. 1993. http://www.info.gov.za/documents/constitution/index.htm

Luhmann, Niklas. 1995. *Social Systems*. Stanford: Stanford University Press.

Mamdani, Mahmood. 2000. A Diminished Truth. In *After the TRC: Reflections on Truth and Reconciliation in South Africa*, edited by W James and L van de Vijver. Johannesburg: David Philip.

Marcuse, Herbert. 1966. *Eros and Civilisation*. Boston: Beacon Press.

Marx, Karl. 2000. The Eighteenth Brumaire of Napoleon Bonaparte. In *Karl Marx: Selected Writings*, edited by D McLellan. Oxford: Oxford University Press.

Nietzsche, Friedrich. 1983. *Untimely Mediations*. Cambridge: Cambridge University Press.

Ricoeur, Paul. 1967. *The Symbolism of Evil*. Boston: Beacon Press.

Simmel, Georg. 1955. *Conflict*. New York: Free Press.

Truth and Reconciliation Commission (TRC) (South Africa). 1998. *Findings and Conclusions: TRC Report, vol 5*. Cape Town: CTP Book Printers Ltd.

4

Divided Memories: How Emerging Democracies Deal with the Crimes of Previous Regimes

HERIBERT ADAM[1]

I. THE POLITICS OF MEMORY

HUMAN MEMORY IS never an objective fact, a kind of fixed, stored data that can be downloaded or accumulated for later use. What is being remembered and how events are being recalled depends very much on social conditions. Interests shape individual as well as collective memory. Memory, therefore, amounts to a contingent social construction.

Ian Buruma has rightly pointed out that 'Memory is not the same as history and memorializing is different from writing history' (1999, 9). If the two are lumped together, the distinction between fiction and fact, falsehood and truth, is lost. A history concerned with establishing factual events is to be distinguished from their interpretation. About this interpretative and moral truth, opinions can legitimately differ, particularly in divided societies. Since individual morals, feelings and interests vary widely in a heterogeneous collectivity, it is problematic to assume a collective psyche.

[1] This analysis is based on involvement in the early conceptualisation of the South African Truth and Reconciliation Commission (TRC) during several international conferences and frequent discussions with TRC Deputy Chair Alex Boraine and other commissioners' participant observation of the Commission's work. An earlier shorter version of this chapter was the opening address at a symposium on the Walser–Bubis dispute at the Max Weber College at the University of Erfurt and was subsequently published in the *Frankfurter Allgemeine Zeitung*, 24 June 1999. A different version of this chapter with an emphasis on the South African TRC was published in 2000 in *Telos* (118: 87–108) under the title 'Divided Societies: Confronting the Crimes of Previous Regimes'. An English version was presented at the workshop 'Legal Institutions and Collective Memories' at the Oñati International Institute for the Sociology of Law, 22–4 September 1999, and at the Summer School, University of Cape Town, 28 January 2000. All translations of German quotes are by the author. I am grateful for critical comments from previous audiences as well as from Kogila Moodley, Pierre van den Berghe and Ian Angus.

Without a collective persona, there can hardly be a collective memory. Only in a loose, metaphorical sense can we speak of a collective identity, a national character or a collective memory.

Collective memory constitutes the informal, widely accepted perceptions of past events in which the collective identity of a people is mirrored. This identity is strongly influenced by the official definitions, rituals and laws of the state. The memorials that a state erects, the national holidays selected, the museums subsidised, the speeches of politicians that celebrate or mourn the past and define a state's self-perception in laws and public institutions—these are all contributions to collective memory, which changes over time. Divided memories exist when sizable groups within the same state simultaneously attribute different meanings to the same history, just as individual witnesses to crimes or car accidents testify to the same event in surprisingly contradictory terms.

II. WAYS OF REMEMBERING AND FORGETTING

It is difficult to generalise for all situations and all times. Perhaps the most useful generalisation distinguishes between two kinds of remembering: a progressive and a retrogressive one. *Progressive memory* inquires into the causes of past suffering with a view to preventing a future recurrence of past misery. It amounts to political education in the best sense. Progressive memory results in politically literate citizens whose current and future choices are guided by a historical awareness of their society, its misguided paths, wrong turns and missed opportunities. *Retrogressive memory*, on the other hand, locks people into vicious circles of past conflicts. History becomes a set of mental shackles from which people cannot free themselves. They remember ancient battles, particularly lost ones, in order to re-enact revenge. The quest for revenge blinds its adherents to alternative options. When individual and collective identity is tied to wounds, never to be forgotten, its adherents become prisoners of their past.

In short, the valid exhortation not to forget should always be accompanied by two questions: *what* is remembered, and particularly remembered *for* what? Progressive remembering uses hindsight to draw lessons. It guards against repeating the mistakes of the past. Retrogressive remembering on the other hand, aims at continuing a battle in the hope of achieving a triumphant outcome this time. Nationalist mobilisers dwell on this hope. They manipulate with the mirage of victory, rescue from remembered humiliation and wipe out past degradation by following the rallying cry of the unified collective. Theirs is the false language of sacrifice in order to be free from the shame of the past in an imagined glorious future, even if the Utopia causes renewed pain to adversaries and followers alike.

A test for progressive or retrogressive remembering lies in the collective attitude towards the political crimes of the past. Again, there can be no universally valid rules as to how an emerging democracy should deal with the crimes of a previous regime. It seems useful to explore empirically how different democracies have coped with the problem of state-sponsored crimes, how victims are recognised or compensated, how the new order attempts reconciliation between warring factions and how the repetition of an unsavoury past is prevented.

Six forms of grappling with the past can be distinguished and compared in their historical contexts: amnesia (post-war Germany, Japan, Spain, Russia); trials and justice (the Nuremberg trials, the International Criminal Court (ICC)); lustration, ie, the disqualification of former collaborators from public office (the German Democratic Republic (GDR), Eastern Europe); negotiated restitution (Germany's reparations to Israel and compensations for forced labour, Canada's and Australia's negotiations about land rights of indigenous minorities); political re-education (post-war Germany); and finally, truth commissions (Latin America and South Africa).

Several of these strategies are frequently employed simultaneously or with different emphases over time. Of all cases, two countries are of particular significance: Germany, because of its unique past with Auschwitz as the universal paradigm of barbarism; and South Africa. The South African Truth and Reconciliation Commission (TRC) deserves critical scrutiny for three reasons: it is a novel experiment of restorative justice and nation-building through reconciliation; the TRC is often recommended as an international model for similar conflicts elsewhere, from Cambodia to ex-Yugoslavia; and achievements of the TRC are widely overrated outside South Africa, while largely dismissed inside. Among its flaws and problematic assumptions is the fallacy that 'revealing is healing'. Legislated reconciliation negates the deeply personal nature of reconciliation, that only victims can forgive. The skewed composition of the TRC and its theological perspectives have both affected its credibility. The quest for an official truth and common memory denies pluralist interpretations of history. Above all, the focus on gross human rights violations frees the many beneficiaries of apartheid from responsibility and obliterates the structural violence of racial laws for millions of victims not recognised by the TRC process.

A. Amnesia

In Germany the post-war period up to the mid-1960s represents a typical example of official amnesia and private denial. Chancellor Konrad Adenauer, who himself was an anti-Nazi politician nevertheless defended his heavily implicated aide, Hans Globke, with the demand in Parliament 'to stop the sniffing for Nazis!' Instead of honestly dealing with the shame of the past, it was not to be remembered. The future and the rebuilding of the nation should be focused upon. Wallowing in a terrible past could not reverse it anyway. The past was considered a catastrophe, like a natural disaster, rather than the result of political decisions. The Nazi period was portrayed as an accident of German history.

'In the middle of the 1950s', writes the historian Norbert Frei, 'a collective consciousness had emerged that attributed solely to Hitler and his inner circle all responsibilities for the atrocities of the Third Reich' (1996, 405). Germans as a whole were ascribed the role of a politically seduced people whom the war and its consequences had made into victims themselves. To this day, the 8th of May is designated as 'the day of liberation' by Allied forces, implying that Germans were mainly victims of Nazi rule. Daniel Goldhagen's 'willing executioners' (1996) had shrunk to a small minority. The active complicity and passive collusion of a silent majority was out of sight and memory. The phrase of the 'hour zero' (Stunde Null) dismissed historical continuity, insisting instead on a newborn society that had no relationship with the previous period.

In the communist GDR, official anti-fascism also denied all links with the Nazi past. Since that dark period had—in the lexicon of economistic Marxist dogmatism—resulted from a capitalist crisis, the heroic rise of socialism in the anti-fascist struggle had also taken care of all fascist remnants and preconditions.

In the West, the theory of totalitarianism reigned supreme in the ensuing cold war. The free West proudly distinguished itself from both the brown and red totalitarianism. The sociologist Helmut Dubiel writes that 'the true scandal of German memorializing was not that the Nazi past was simply ignored, but immersed in the ideological competition between East and West' (1999, 276). Both states accused each other of failing to draw the necessary conclusions from history. Each side blamed the other for perpetuating conditions in which freedom was denied.

There are two main explanations for the post-war amnesia. The most widely accepted version holds that the economic and bureaucratic reconstruction required the inclusion of Nazi collaborators, given the scarce skills available. German rearmament in the 1950s, for example, would have been impossible without falling back on the expertise of previous officers. Large sectors of the colluding population needed to be integrated into the new democracy rather than marginalised.

A second explanation, psychologically based, focuses on the subconscious reaction to collective trauma. A fragile collective identity—psychoanalytically speaking, a weak ego—had to protect itself against an unbearable truth by repressing and rationalising it. Theodor Adorno pointed to the paradox that the factual collapse of the National Socialist world had not been reflected in the psychic disposition of the population. With reference to Sigmund Freud,

Adorno draws the questionable conclusion that this proves the survival of Nazi mentalities:

> What is missing when collective identities unravel, according to the theory of 'Mass Psychology and Ego Analysis', is the phenomenon of panic. Unless one wants to dismiss the insights of the great psychologist, this allows for only one conclusion: that the old identifications and collective narcissism were not destroyed but continue secretly dormant in the unconscious and therefore particularly powerful (cited in Perels 1998, 58).

However, one could speculate equally persuasively that perhaps the Nazi identifications were not as deeply internalised and the consciousness of injustice was more widespread than the suspicions of Adorno allow. Otherwise the Allied democratic re-education would not have run so successfully and smoothly. As critical studies in the tradition of 'the Authoritarian Personality' have proven, this character type is more shaped by conformity pressure than by internalised ideological convictions. With the change of powerholders, the dominant attitudes of ego-weak characters also change. They replace easily one ideological doctrine with an opposite equally authoritarian master narrative. Therefore it is helpful to criminalise hate speech. While attitudes cannot be legislated, discriminatory behaviour at least can be constrained by being outlawed.

It was not until the late 1960s that the children of the war generation revived questions about the past, spurred on by the student revolt against authoritarian traditions and by general politicisation. Debates about the statute of limitation of prosecutions after widely publicised trials of concentration camp guards under German jurisdiction together with moving personalised films about the Holocaust also evoked new interests. Yet another generation later, the meaning of the past has never been more intensely debated—starting with the 1986 dispute among academic historians about the comparability and relationship between Stalinist and fascist terror (see Wehler 1988) and continuing with the Goldhagen controversy in 1996[2] (see Wippermann 1997), the Walser–Bubis argument in 1998[3] (Wiegel and Klotz 1999; Rohloff 1999) and the simultaneous controversial exhibition about the collusion of the German army in the war atrocities

---

[2] In his book *'Hitler's Willing Executioners'* Goldhagen had argued that a deep-rooted anti-Semitism in the German population and culture was the ultimate cause of the Holocaust. The ensuing controversy mainly focused on the question whether and to which extent German culture was intrinsically anti-Semitic.

[3] On the occasion of receiving the prestigious 'Friedenspreis des Deutschen Buchhandels', the novelist Martin Walser criticised the continuous omnipresence of the Holocaust in the media, in schools and in politics, declaring that 'the instrumentalisation of Auschwitz for ulterior purposes' should stop. The President of the German Jewish Council, Ignaz Bubis, immediately started a public debate, refuting Walser's arguments as unacceptable.

against the civilian population (see Thiele 1997; Hamburger Institut für Sozialforschung 1999).

There is probably no other country that currently scrutinises and redefines its collective memory so thoroughly. Eleven years of debate about a central Berlin memorial for the victims of Nazism (see Reichel 1999; Cullen 1999; Jeisman 1999) culminated in a sophisticated parliamentary debate in June 1999 with the decision that a) the memorial should be built as proposed by architect Eisenmann; b) it will be dedicated exclusively to European Jews; and c) it should also have an information and learning centre attached to it. Earnest arguments split all parties, and the overwhelming supporting vote surprised everyone, including the head of the German Jewish Council, the late Ignaz Bubis. He had predicted that the memorial would never be built (*Konkret* 2/1999). The support of the political class for the immense and challenging Eisenmann monument also revealed a substantial discrepancy in public opinion surveys. These had indicated a split population: 46 per cent for and 44 per cent against the memorial, with 93 per cent of supporters in favour of its dedication to all Nazi victims. Parliament's decision to dedicate it exclusively to European Jews indicated that concern about negative foreign reactions outweighed local opinion.

Behind the German debate about whether the nation should define itself as a 'normal' polity stands the question whether the unified state should also shed the constraints on its 'moral sovereignty'. Full political sovereignty was restored with re-socialisation into Western democratic habits. Later in 1989, the unification of Germany with the framework of Europe and its rules and values was the final crowning achievement. A growing number on the political right and centre now wishes to shed the moral inhibitions resulting from the Nazi legacy. Until the involvement of the German army in Bosnia and Kosovo, the country had shirked its responsibility for international human rights enforcement with reference to its unique history sixty years ago.

How should one evaluate this process of profoundly redefining collective memory? Is the decision for the Holocaust Memorial the progressive acknowledgment of collective moral and political responsibility, although 'Germans collectively do not bear criminal and moral guilt' (Neier 1998, 228)? Is it an official rejection of the earlier Walser warning about the 'banality of the good', the instrumentalisation of Auschwitz for ulterior purposes?[4] Or is the victory of the seemingly progressive remembrance of shame merely the monstrous tombstone in the final burial of an embarrassing past, just as Walser advocated to the applause of the establishment in the Paulskirche?

---

[4] See *ibid.*

It would seem that the Berlin memorial, above all, fulfills the function of visibly exculpating the new 'Berlin Republic' from the suspicion of past nationalist ambitions. With narcissistic self-congratulation, the debate lays to rest the Nazi legacy by demonstrating that the self-confident unified state has successfully come to terms with its shame—just as the victims wished. 'The more unique the German crimes, the greater the own achievement of collective cleansing', comments the historian Gerd Koenen sarcastically (1999, 98). Hermann Lübbe (1989) speaks of 'Sündenstolz', the German pride in their sins. Just as minorities the world over clamour for the 'vicarious virtue' of victimisation, as Ian Buruma (1999) has argued in an intriguing article entitled 'The Joys and Perils of Victimhood', so the German political elite of all parties is now keen to demonstrate the opposite: that it has mastered the much more intricate task of coming to terms with being the worst collective perpetrator in history. This negative uniqueness, the ritual acknowledgment of the Nazi break with civilisation ('Zivilisationsbruch'), is now almost paraded as interesting a feature of a new national identity as the positive achievements of an economic miracle after total destruction in 1945. However, a shameful past as nationalist exhibitionism would be merely the other side of the dubious coin of denial and amnesia.

Helmut Dubiel in his study of parliamentary debates diagnoses a correlation between 'the inability of Germans to accept collective responsibility for their history and their underdevelopment of democratic virtues' (1999, 288). However, neither was the post-war German amnesia a specific German characteristic, nor does historical denial of collective infamy stand in a necessary relationship with the development of democratic culture. Britain, France and Holland had buried their colonial crimes until very recently but are considered model democracies nonetheless. The United States still lacks a single national memorial to slavery or to the near genocide of the aboriginal people. Nations memorialise their own suffering but not what they inflict on others. The Washington memorial of the Vietnam War lists all the names of Americans who lost their life but not a single Vietnamese name. In Japan, history textbooks do not mention the atrocities of the imperial army in Korea and China. *The Rape of Nanking*, Iris Chang's English bestseller (1997) about the murder of 300,000 inhabitants, has not been published in a Japanese translation, bogged down in controversy regarding its accuracy. The Tokyo government refuses to issue a clear apology even to Chinese or Korean state visitors, despite worldwide feminist concern with thousands of so-called 'comfort women'.[5] Recently the official designation 'capitulation' was renamed as the more neutral 'end of war'. National guilt is widely considered to be absolved by the first atomic bomb dropped on Hiroshima and Nagasaki.

---

[5] See Young-Hee Shim in this volume.

After political transformation, many nations rationalise their guilt with new myths. In Austria, collective memory redefined the former popular enthusiasm for Hitler into 'forced unification' (Zwangsanschluss), thereby portraying collusion as victimhood. In France, only the recent trials against collaborators of the Vichy regime have undermined the popular myth that half of the French population had joined the underground resistance against the German occupiers. Spain has totally avoided coming to terms with its 40 years of Franco dictatorship because it would reopen the wounds of the Civil War. Paradoxically, Germany has apologised for Guernica and paid compensation but not the Madrid Parliament. Turkey still cherishes its taboo belief that the Armenian genocide never happened and is an invention of foreign propaganda.

The 80 to 100 million victims of Stalinism still wait to be rehabilitated and even properly recognised. When Stephane Courtois edited *Livre noir du communisme* (*The Black Book of Communism*, 1997) on the 80th anniversary of the October Revolution, it met with a hostile reception on the Left, similar to the earlier exposure of communist crimes by Arthur Koestler, Alexandre Solshenytzin, Robert Conquest and Francois Furet (see Möller 1999). Recognising that Marxist-Leninism had a rational, humanitarian goal while Hitler's biological master narrative was by definition irrational should not preclude comparisons with the racial genocide here and class genocide there. Nor are the fascist crimes relativised or trivialised by comparing them with the terror of Stalinism. Comparing does not mean equating.

The sketch of varied collective responses to past state crimes allows some general conclusions. Grappling with the past is not a necessary precondition for a functioning democracy. As Michael Ignatieff has written:

> All nations depend on forgetting: on forging myths of unity and identity that allow a society to forget its founding crimes, its hidden injuries and divisions, its unhealed wounds. It must be true, for nations as it is for individuals, that we can stand only so much truth. But if too much truth is divisive, the question becomes, how much is enough? (1998, 170)

It is commonly assumed that public interest in a shameful past fades away among later generations. They carry no personal guilt, unlike their parents who engaged in denial because they were psychologically incapable of admitting the enormity of their own collusion with state atrocities. Paradoxically, public interest in and recognition of national crimes seems to increase over time. Subsequent generations feel free to accept collective responsibility for the sins of their ancestors, although motivations differ in each context and divided memories prevail.

In their eagerness to prevent the gruesome past from haunting the future, well-meaning social engineers are intent on creating 'a common history' between hostile groups. In their most extreme form, they repress the airing of past hostilities, as Tito did with the enforced slogan 'Brotherhood and Unity'. Such totalitarian designs are the surest recipe for renewed conflict: 'By repressing the real history of the interethnic carnage between 1941 and 1945, the Titoist regime guaranteed that such carnage would return' (Ignatieff 1998, 185). Only a pluralist interpretation of history may achieve a shared truth at best or reinforce divided memories at worst. History as an ongoing argument is still preferable to the myth-making of official collective memory.

B. Trials and Justice

Prosecution of perpetrators of gross human rights violations requires clear victors and vanquished. Where there is a stalemate—as in South Africa or in Chile between democrats and the military—historical compromises and amnesties are negotiated (see also Mendez in this volume). Prosecutions would most likely provoke new violence and even endanger the survival of the emerging democracy. Apart from the morality of pursuing justice for its own sake, there are good pragmatic reasons for trials of political criminals. Aryeh Neier, one of the most ardent advocates of punishment, has expressed the most convincing reason: 'When the community of nations shies away from responsibility for bringing to justice the authors of crimes against humanity, it subverts the rule of law' (1998, 213). If the victimised see no one held accountable, they may seek revenge on their own and continue the cycle of violence. Prosecution of individual perpetrators also counteracts the misleading notion of collective guilt. Individualising guilt does not smear the name of an entire group. Finally, indictments by the proposed ICC cannot be accused of 'victor's justice'.

However, there are also clear pitfalls to be avoided. If a sovereign state can head off ICC prosecution by bringing alleged war criminals before its own courts, a fair trial depends very much on the independence and quality of its judiciary. This spectrum can range from biased judges of the old order (as alleged in South Africa) to an internal 'victor's justice' whereby the judiciary has been purged and replaced with partisans of the new regime.

The ICC would be emasculated if prosecutions could be launched only with the consent of the states involved where the crime occurred or the alleged criminals live. A similar paralysis would ensue if vetoes by United Nations (UN) Security Council members could indefinitely block prosecution. The unilateral military intervention by the North Atlantic Treaty Organization (NATO) in Kosovo without UN approval already responded to this predicament. NATO's 'military humanitarianism' postulated that gross violations of universal rights within a sovereign state necessitates outside intervention in the same way as an aggression against a foreign territory would justify war in self-defence. The NATO action, the

Geman philosopher Jürgen Habermas (1999) argued, anticipated a world citizenship that unfortunately does not yet exist as an enforceable order.

If the ICC were to be the first practical indicator of a more effective world order for universal human rights, it would be even more imperative to prevent 'core' crimes rather than merely punish violators afterwards. It is doubtful whether the threat of indictment is sufficient to restrain future Pinochets or Milosevics. In fact, the opposite might happen. Faced with the prosect of being imprisoned in The Hague, future dictators may cling to power strenuously, resulting in more victims, rather than abdicate or remove themselves into unsafe exile.

A great step towards prevention of crimes against humanity could be the establishment of a similar international tribunal (or the inclusion of the task into ICC duties) to which aggrieved minorities could appeal for redress. The world lacks an impartial forum to which oppressed groups can formally turn for action against their government. With the realistic prospect of justiciable relief by an international body, armed resistance and civil war would be effectively discouraged. Should a sovereign state refuse to heed the verdict of the tribunal on the treatment of minorities, a variety of sanctions against the outcast could be meted out. The state's chief representatives could even be indicted themselves for contempt of court. While the European Court in Strassbourg already hears complaints against unjust treatment by European governments and the International Court of Justice pronounces on interstate disputes, aggrieved national minorities need to be offered a similar legal alternative to taking up arms.

C. Lustration

The term lustration is frequently meant to describe all actions against former regime affiliates, from violent or lawless purges to formalised procedures or even mere 'ceremonial cleansing' of the new order (see Karstedt 1998, 15–56). In this analysis, lustration is used in a narrower sense to define the regulated screening of former collaborators for disqualification from public office. Victors establish categories of guilt and responsibility to which varying sanctions correspond. Typical examples would be denazification procedures in post-war Germany and 'destasification' after reunification.

Attitudes of the general public show remarkable similarities between the two cases, which are 55 years apart. Susanne Karstedt (1998), in a perceptive comparative analysis of polling data, notes an initial strong approval of punishment of the top decision makers and beneficiaries but a readiness to exempt ordinary party members and recipients of orders in the lower echelons. This reaction reflects and reinforces the notion of a 'betrayed people'. A small clique can be blamed while the collusion or silence of ordinary people is transformed into their being victims as well. With time, the call for indictment of the leadership fades, and a general atmosphere of closure on the past takes hold.

Lustration is possible only in situations in which extensive files of the previous regime reliably document collaborators. Disqualification for public office also presupposes the availability of sufficient skilled substitutes. This was the case with the reunification of East and West Germany; the Eastern part was taken under the economic and bureaucratic tutelage of the West. In South Africa, the continued employment of apartheid administrators in the civil service for a while was not only part of the negotiated settlement but also a necessity in the absence of sufficiently trained personnel within the new order.

D. Restitution and Compensation

Even established democracies pay reparations to victims mainly under political pressure but rarely out of moral commitment or guilty conscience. Only more than 35 years after the establishment of internment camps for Japanese Canadians during WWII did the Canadian government finally pay a meagre average amount of CAD$20,000 to the survivors. Reparations amounted to only a symbolic restitution of their expropriated property.

The Chinese Canadian National Council has been lobbying the Canadian government in vain since 1984 for redress of the Chinese 'head tax'. This racist legislation, enacted 1 July 1923, imposed a special tax on Chinese immigrants only. It was aimed at deterring further Asian immigration, considered to be the 'yellow danger' at the time. However, since wealthy Asian immigrants are now courted by the Canadian government and only a few hundred head-tax payers survive, the government can ignore calls for compensation of the CAD$23 million extracted by the head-tax. The diverse Canadian Chinese community itself does not like to be reminded of its unwelcome past in the country that many now consider a home of unlimited opportunities, where they no longer need their 'grandparents' money'.

Another dynamic is at work with regard to the long-standing grievances of native people. Canadian courts have found the main churches and the federal government 'jointly liable' for horrific sexual abuses of thousands of aboriginal children. They were sent to religious boarding schools as part of a government effort to assimilate native youth. Hundreds of former students have filed individual and class-action lawsuits, seeking damages for their suffering, inflicted mostly by Roman Catholic and Anglican Church officials. In the case of land claims and hunting and fishing rights by aboriginal groups in both Australia and Canada powerful moral pressure is exerted. The three per cent scattered Canadian native population possesses neither the voting strength, physical power nor the economic clout to force the national government to recognize its historical grievances. Yet despite strong opposition from influential oil, mining and forest companies, Canadian courts have recognized aboriginal land claims and forced governments to enter into good faith negotiations about the transfer of large tracts of crown land to native jurisdiction. Preferential fishing and hunting rights have long been granted, despite strong local voters' opposition and concern for conservation measures. Australia has even instituted a symbolic national 'Sorry Day' to create a collective memory of the country's illegitimate conquest by foreign settlers.

At work here is the moral politics of embarrassment. A state is forced by relatively powerless groups into a clear choice: either to forfeit its claims of a model democracy, based on the rule of law, or to live up to broken treaties and admit historical injustice. Since Canada proudly markets itself as an anti-colonial, multicultural model, it can hardly allow itself to be exposed as practicing open internal colonialism. With the help of legal assistance by sympathetic lawyers, even powerless minorities can exercise power over indifferent governments. The Canadian state even bears the costs of the court challenges against itself and finances research into further claims in the name of historical injustice.

The political interest of reintegration into the international community motivated substantial German reparation to Israel and individual Jewish victims at the beginning of the 1950's, despite disapproval of the majority of the electorate. Foreign policy considerations also play a major role in Germany's compensation for an estimated one million out of eight to ten million survivors of forced labour in Nazi Germany. Paradoxically, it was globalization with the fusion of German and foreign conglomerates that made the German side vulnerable to boycotts abroad and adverse court judgments in the US. Like the Swiss banks and insurance companies who had to account for Nazi gold transfers, German industry is faced with huge claims by US lawyers of the influential Claims' Conference. The negotiations, coordinated by the Chancellors office, not only concerned the amount of reparation to be paid into a Foundation Fund but above all, the legal exclusion of future claims, whether individual restitution should be paid to the needy only, whether national wage levels and differential living costs should be taken into account, and whether the compensation should be based on underpaid wages or the suffering of Nazi slave laborers.

Although the German government promised to treat all claimants equally, the strength of their lobby and the status of their government played a decisive role. Sinti and Roma, unorganized gays or Jehovah's Witnesses will surely be shortchanged in the end. Claims of US citizens will be given greater weight than those originating from Eastern Europe. Constantin Goschler (1998, 49) points out that only the end of the Cold War made these demands possible:

> Individual Nazi victims play a minor role in the calculation of East European states in light of their own interests in German support and therefore receive less

endorsement from their own government than comparable claims originating from the US.

Even in a state with a government of liberation, the liberated victims cannot be sure to receive material reparations. The South African government agonized over the recommendations of the Truth and Reconciliation Commission (TRC) to pay 20,000 recognized victims a modest amount of Rand 20,000 for six years. At the same time the TRC process illustrates the danger of establishing a hierarchy of victimhood.

Advocates of the TRC praise the involvement of broad sectors of society in providing information. The communal experience of public hearings, of being listened to and officially recognized as victims, is said to be as important for the healing of trauma as the testimony itself. Unfortunately, this broad involvement also raises false expectations. In South Africa, one hears disappointment in many communities that no follow-up took place, and particularly that the expected compensation for suffering has not materialized. 'We have stimulated hopes and then abandoned the people', explains one commissioner self-critically (personal conversation, February 7, 1999). However, the SA TRC, with limited resources and a limited life span, had not been empowered to fulfill the expectations it raised. It could only make recommendations to government which was free to accept and, more likely, to 'fudge' even the modest TRC suggestions. ANC leaders now argue that liberation should not be reduced to material benefits.

Speculations that 'the palpable insufficiency of reparations could stoke fires of revenge or further victimize the victimized as trivializing their harms or suggesting a payoff for silence' (Minnow 1998, 132) do not apply in South Africa. Since a government of victims is responsible for non-payment it would be a rejection of their own representatives. Nor is anyone co-opted into silence. Those 20,000 recognized by the TRC as theoretically eligible for compensation are envied by the millions of ordinary victims of apartheid laws who did not fall under the legal category of 'gross violations'. Their suffering caused by the expropriation of the Group Areas Act, low wages under the discriminatory labor policy, and arrests under the Pass Laws, is comparatively trivialized by not being worthy of restitution under the TRC legislation. In short, by focusing solely on the illegal transgressions of illegitimate laws, the TRC legislation ignores the structural, legal violence of a racist system. The TRC concerned itself mainly with a select group of victims, Mahmood Mamdani (1998) argues, instead of beneficiaries.

E. Re-education

Memory politics frequently includes conscious measures for re-education, from re-writing of history books to exchange programs and the official re-definition of collective identity. At the height of the Kosovo war, Daniel Goldhagen recommended, as the only lasting solution, the occupation of Serbia and the resocialisation of the population, as had happened successfully after the war in Germany and Japan. Others emphasize the importance of focusing on the suffering of the adversary rather than on own group pain in order to achieve empathy and tolerance through a shared history.

Education for multicultural understanding always deserves support but must not be overrated in its impact. Another educational method promises greater success: strengthening the self-confidence of adolescents, to develop their critical consciousness and rules of negotiated conflict resolution.

The lessons of Auschwitz do not lie in repeating empty rituals of remembrance or in indoctrinating collective guilt. Political education in the next century must go beyond Auschwitz by keeping alive an awareness of and sensibility to future injustice. By exposing the all-pervasive dispositions for racism and discrimination the lessons of Auschwitz are best preserved.

The ashes and corpses of previous victims are best honored by providing the living with insights about the causes of their fate. In Germany that should include all victims of Nazism, not only Jews. To be sure, Jews were the most numerous victims, and in the paranoia of the Nazis their most dangerous enemy. Only for Jews a 'final solution' was designed. Yet it would seem wrong to dedicate the Berlin memorial exclusively to Jews, as the German parliament decided. Promises of similar memorials for the other victim groups elsewhere, leads to rivalry and establishes a hierarchy of suffering. Germany again makes selections among victims. Above all, the false impression is created that the motivation for the murder of Jews was based on their particular behavior. Yet Jews as scapegoats were interchangeable.

Memorialisation in form of an official monument always suggests the Nazi past has been laid to rest once and for all. Some consider such finality an advantage. A truth commission, writes Minnow (1998, 127) 'fails to create potential closure afforded by criminal trials that end in punishment'. However, continuing soul-searching should be welcomed rather than regretted. Political education is advanced by disputes over interpretations of past events that are easily relegated to oblivion with the closure of an authoritative judgment. The more controversial a memorial in the center of Berlin, the better for raising consciousness. It ought to hurt as a thorn in national self-satisfaction rather than please. The central German memorial cannot be, as the glib suggestion of former Chancellor Schröder implied, 'a place which one likes to visit'.

The central memorial need not even be confined to Nazi victims. Fascist mentalities survive among an alienated minority in the form of xenophobia and violence against foreigners, particularly in former East Germany where hardly any foreigners lived before. To highlight this continuity, the memorial could open itself to the future and engrave the names of all foreigners murdered for racist reasons in the post-fascist state.

To be sure, this everyday racism amounts to individual deviance and not the state-criminality of the Nazis. It is important to stress this difference, because racism is frequently viewed as always originating from fascist social conditions. East German skinheads, who harass 'others', know that they will not be tolerated by the state. They embody a syndrome similar to hate crimes in London, Paris or Toronto.

How and under what conditions such universal individual predispositions emerge and are successfully mobilized in a mass movement for genocide, could be illuminated with the unique Nazi crimes. In this way the 'normal society' of the 'Berlin Republic', because of its abnormal past, could prove to itself and the world that it has effectively learned to mourn all victims of discrimination.

F. Truth Commissions

Truth Commissions were first established after the successors of the military dictatorships in various Latin American countries came under pressure to reveal the fate of thousands of alleged dissidents who had disappeared. The celebrated South African Truth and Reconciliation Commission (TRC) differed from its Latin American counterparts by being established as an act of Parliament rather than by presidential decree, holding open hearings instead of in camera investigations and making an amnesty dependent on full disclosure of perpetrators. The SA TRC sees itself in the tradition of 'restorative justice', foregoing punishment in favor of reconciliation. Assuming that 'revealing is healing', encounters between forgiving victims and remorseful perpetrators were meant to achieve the ambitious goal as the only alternative to continued strife.

Due to the international stature of the TRC's chair, Desmond Tutu, his hopes and predictions have even entered the academic literature as empirical facts. In this vein Gesine Schwan (1997, 245) in her celebrated 'Politik und Schuld' falsely credits the TRC with 'having engendered pity, empathy and remorse on the part of perpetrators by being confronted with the unspeakable suffering of victims'. That was the intention of the TRC hearings but in reality only occurred in rare cases. Interestingly, two of the worst killers, Eugene de Kock, dubbed 'prime evil' by the SA media as commander of the special Vlakplaas police unit, and his predecessor Dirk Coetzee, fall into this category of remorseful converts (de Kock 1998). However, in most other cases, judging from participant observation and recorded confessions, apartheid's assassins tried to save their skin by applying for amnesty or turning state witness without recognition of the moral terpitude of their actions (Pauw 1997). The public shaming of confessing perpetrators presupposes a moral reference group that shares the shame. This is doubtful when exposed killers retreat into ethnic enclaves for whom they committed their crimes and whose dominant attitudes range from understanding to open sympathy.

Typically, perpetrators acknowledged suffering caused or even expressed coded regret but rationalized their deeds in terms of the political climate at the time or their assigned role in the apartheid machinery. Like their political leaders in the National Party, genuine acknowledgment of guilt or acceptance of responsibility was not forthcoming. None offered private compensation within their means.

Indifference towards the plight of victims was also displayed by black perpetrators on the other side, most prominently Winnie Madikizele-Mandela. Despite an embarrassing beckoning for a sign of remorse by the TRC chair, she finally complied only half-heartedly and reluctantly. The ANC leadership as a whole has yet to remove from office cadres within its ranks for admitted human rights abuses. The ANC only took collective responsibility for 'excesses' in the heat of the struggle. In fact, Mbeki criticized the TRC for its 'erroneous determination' that indiscriminate bombings or the taking of civilian hostages constitute human rights violations. The TRC findings were seen by the ANC as an attempt to criminalize a significant part of the struggle of their people for liberation. The TRC was accused of elevating the ANC's unfortunate 'collateral damage' in pursuit of a just cause to the moral equivalent of the defense of an unjust one. To its lasting credit, the TRC has always insisted that no such moral leveling was intended or indeed possible, but even in the fight for a just cause, Geneva Convention rules of justice have to be upheld.

The SA debate has confirmed Michael Ignatieff's (1998, 176) insight from the Yugoslav conflict that it is relatively easy for both sides to acknowledge each other's pain:

> Much more difficult—indeed usually impossible—is shared acknowledgment about who bears the lion's share of responsibility. For if aggressors have their own defense against truth, so do victims. People who believe themselves to be victims of aggression have an understandable incapacity to believe that they too have committed atrocities.

While Truth Commissions can confirm the factual truth of an atrocity, they usually fail to establish a common interpretative truth. This moral truth of who is responsible and why it happened, is always heavily contested. Divided memories prevail because truth is tied to institutional and collective identity. Apportioning blame in a moral narrative, affects the standing of a political party or the self-respect of a people. Even if something is an obvious truth to any 'objective' outsider, it is far from acceptable to an insider. For a member of the in-group the myth about the others or the goodness of their own is not just a tissue of lies that can be unmasked. This identity is a daily reality to be lived by, a lense through which the world is interpreted and a tool to make sense and give meaning to life. As Ignatieff (1998, 173) has rightly stressed:

> It is unreasonable to expect those who believed they were putting down a terrorist or insurgent threat to disown the idea simply because a truth commission exposes the threat as having been without foundation. People, especially people in uniform, do not easily or readily surrender the premises upon which their lives are based.

Particularly if truth is imposed from outside, it is rejected. Foreigners therefore should refrain from interpreting history for indoctrinated locals, no matter how high their academic standing outside and how good their intentions. It is also wise to guard against internal exiles, people of the same ethnicity but little ideological credibility among their own group: human rights activists or cosmopolitan minds who are viewed as sympathetic to the enemy. If collective identity is to be successfully redefined, it must be communicated by credible ideologues of the inside. If a few respected opinion leaders can be won over to the painful truth, their standing alone assures susceptibility, or at least stimulates some initial doubts about dearly held positions. The South African TRC neglected to enlist such figures from the Afrikaner intellectual or religious establishment. Unlike the Chilean Commission with four members of the old and four of the new regime, none of the seventeen members of the SA TRC belonged to the formerly ruling National Party (the two Afrikaners on the Commission were members of rival parties and were isolated among the rest of the ANC-oriented staff). This skewed composition of the TRC, comprised of otherwise well-intentioned people with predominantly legal qualifications or theological training, nevertheless compromised the reception of its findings. It almost promises better results to appoint reasonable hardliners from both sides to argue about a shared historical truth in the calm of a committee room than to select presumable non-partisan, 'objective', politically low-profile representatives of various stakeholders, as the SA legislation stipulated. Should ethnic fundamentalists achieve some minimal consensus, they can communicate their controversial compromise more effectively than even Nobel-prize winning personalities. In fact, the more the outside world courts leaders or heaps praise on interlocutors, in order to strengthen their difficult reconciliation, the more suspect they become among their followers. Bestowing honor should wait until results have been achieved.

The South African historic compromise initially benefited from having a range of credible leaders on both sides. With little internal democracy and authoritarian traditions in both the ANC and NP, followers trusted their leaders blindly. Mandela could sell a controversial negotiated settlement to a skeptical constituency on the basis of his hallowed record of suffering and militancy. The conservative, cautious de Klerk was given an overwhelming mandate to negotiate because nobody suspected his team would surrender all political power in exchange for preserving economic privileges.

However, more than sanctions and rising costs of minority rule, it was the very nature of racial domination that distinguished South Africa from Yugoslavia. Mobilized ethnic identity in the Balkans prevented reconciliation, while discredited racial identity in SA facilitated compromise. Long before negotiations about the abolition of apartheid started, the system had been delegitimized from the outside as well as from the inside. Most Afrikaner intellectuals had defected from the ruling group and championed 'reform'.

Furthermore, the economic interdependence limited ruthlessness in apartheid South Africa. Terror was not applied indiscriminately against all members of an outgroup, as under fascism or the ethnonationalist strife of Yugoslavia, but mainly against political activists. The vast majority of 'non-whites', though heavily discriminated against, could escape direct attacks on their life by being apolitical and complying with 'the law'. Apartheid ruled through a supposedly equal legal system rather than placing its victims outside the law as rightless persons, as fascism did.

Racial discrimination in such a context does not lend itself to the same group cohesion and collective trauma as ethnic mobilization does. Unlike Nazi ideology, based on imagined national blood bonds of common ancestry, apartheid needed to racialize culturally different whites in order to unify a weak demographic base but ethnicize blacks in order to divide and rule. This artificial and imposed social engineering had to fail because it lacked the freely embraced legitimacy of ethnonationalism elsewhere. When the cold war ended, Eastern European leaders turned successfully to previously suppressed nationalism to fill the ideological vacuum. In South Africa, costly segregation could finally be abandoned because the elites of both sides benefited from reluctant co-operation. In short, the discredited racism lacked the appeal of a just cause because even apartheid advocates had come to see blacks as victims while the humiliated colonized eschewed vengeance in the name of nonracialism and reconciliation.

A once powerful Afrikaner nationalism had become a victim of its own economic success through state patronage. Once a mild African nationalism merely claimed political power and civil service positions without threatening the accumulated wealth and relative cultural autonomy of its historic adversary, Afrikaner nationalism unravelled into heterogeneous interest groups and different identity definitions without a common enemy. Graves of ancestors, territory acquired in ethnic cleansing or conflicts over holy sites, as in other nationalist conflicts, would be the last issues on the minds of black or white South Africans. Instead, a thoroughly Americanized society worries about access to the latest consumer goods and capitalist frills and diversions. The white 'haves' are silently thankful that black 'would-be-haves' now keep a huge mass of black 'have-nots' reasonably pacified and, if necessary, under authoritarian control. It is this constellation, not a Christian ethic or democratic consensus that enabled a Truth Commission to go through the ritual of grappling with the past in order to proclaim in vain a reconciled memory for the future.

III. CONCLUSIONS

Collective memory of human rights violations could be separated into two broad categories of cases to which appropriate responses differ: (1) historical injustice and (2) contemporary abuses.

(1) Historical injustice comprises cases where blameless groups have been the victim of state aggression a long time ago. Few direct survivors exist and the claims of their descendants relate to the appropriate recognition rather than to the restoration of the situation before the event. Victims of Nazi atrocities, Japanese imperial expansionism, Stalinism and colonial conquest and slavery fall into this category. Punishment of guilty perpetrators is no longer possible. Repossession of expropriated property or forced resettlement of people after civil wars or ethnic cleansing would create new strife and injustices or is not feasible because of interim economic development. In these cases collective responsibility consists more of symbolic restitution than material compensation. Keeping the memory of the injustice alive and mourning the victims through political education about the historical crime best does justice to the collective legacy.

(2) Contemporary abuses call for both justice through legal recourse as well as developing new institutions that facilitate reconciliation or, perhaps more realistically, peaceful coexistence. Particularly where sizable historical antagonists share the same state (South Africa, Northern Ireland, Rwanda, Latin America), truth commissions together with trials of guilty perpetrators can affirm victims, contribute towards common norms, or even create constitutional patriotism. Where ethnonationalist groups do not support common nation-building (Balkans, Israel/Palestine) and where mutual atrocities engendered divided memories, separation in independent or semi-autonomous polities would seem the only feasible solution. Here, international trials for state criminals of recent abuses could also act as a deterrent. An international forum to which aggrieved groups can turn for redress would constitute an alternative to renewed violence.

Remembering cannot be the same for perpetrators and victims. Both can fall into the trap of false memory. For the perpetrators this usually encompasses rationalizations of past misdeeds ('following orders', 'blinded by the atmosphere of the time', 'no choice'). Denial can be expected, the greater the atrocity. The moral identity of a perpetrator is challenged by full acknowledgement, not to mention the material and legal consequences of full confessions. Even the guaranteed amnesties in return for full disclosure did not entice many South African perpetrators before the Truth Commission to admit their involvement in gross human rights abuses. A much more vexed case is the memory of bystanders, or more specifically the beneficiaries of conquest or the descendants of aggression a long time ago. Theirs is no personal guilt, but in Karl Jaspers' (1996/1946) famous distinction, they still bear responsibility. In the broadest sense responsibility can be defined as progressive remembering, the knowledge of the causes of privilege, the awareness of infamy committed in the name of the group they belong to through no fault of their own. Even guilt by association does not apply to them, because they had no choice. Therefore a historically conscious, ie, a politically literate beneficiary of past injustice must, above all, develop an awareness of historical privilege. Responsibility means political consciousness. It is a precondition for restitutive measures.

No general rules can be discerned, how much and how long a collective of conquest should compensate its surviving vanquished. Nor can it be left solely to the victims and their descendants to determine how much repentence is enough, whether material or symbolic remorse is appropriate. Survivors too are tempted by greed. Exploiting past crimes or instrumentalizing the guilty conscience of beneficiaries for selfish enrichment would be an all too understandable strategy. In any case it is impossible to put an exact price tag on past suffering. Past injustice is also trivialized if victims can be bought off. Patient negotiations in good faith about a mutually acceptable compromise would seem the only feasible route to follow in the absence of an international court on ethical behaviour by governments and business. In the end, threats of boycott, harmful publicity for the image of a multi-national company or state and general shaming may suffice to reach a reasonable compromise. Moral education in ethical awareness always facilitates appropriate choices in genuine predicaments.

In the long run conquered and conquerors both benefit from leveling their playing field, from social justice that equalizes or at least reduces the vast historically caused material gaps in education, income and quality of life. However, social justice policies or even preferential treatment in affirmative action strategies may be insufficient to satisfy historically disadvantaged groups. For many of their members, liberal equity policies smack of co-optation. They will not be placated with the upward mobility of their elite which robs the majority of historical victims of their leaders and leaves ordinary members further impoverished. Policies of pacification usually fail if they only benefit the few. Even the pampered leadership often demands more than material rewards, namely symbolic recognition, an official acknowledgement and apology for historical wrongs, or even secession in the case of Palestinians, Quebecois or Sri Lankan Tamils. It may be worth specifying mutually acceptable conditions under which secession of people with divided memories may proceed, as the Canadian government has attempted.

If perpetrators and victims have to live together in the same state, the victims too have to adjust their attitude. It is counterproductive to cultivate self-pity. Memory that wallows in victimhood may well be disempowering. History cannot be reduced to victimology because the powerless are never entirely without power. By remembering defeat as well as resistance, suffering as well as survival against all odds, victims empower themselves as human agents. Self-pity is replaced with enabling for appropriate action for change. The most useful memorial for past injustice is keeping the debate about it alive rather than freezing it in a monument. Past victims are best honoured by sensitizing a new generation for future injustice.

REFERENCES

Buruma, Ian. 1999. The Joys and Perils of Victimhood. *New York Review*. 8 April, 4–9.

Chang, Iris. 1997. *The Rape of Nanking: The Forgotten Holocaust of World War II*. New York: Basic Books.

Courtois, Stephane. 1997. *Livre noir du communisme: crime, terreurs et repression*. Paris: R Laffont.

Cullen, Michael S (ed). 1999. *Das Holocaust-Mahnmal: Dokumentation einer Debatte*. Zürich: Penta.

Dubiel, Helmut. 1999. *Niemand ist frei von der Geschichte*. München: Hanser.

Frei, Norbert. 1996. *Vergangenheitspolitik. Die Anfänge der Bundesrepublik und die NS-Vergangenheit*. München: Beck.

Goldhagen, Daniel Jonah. 1996. *Hitler's Willing Executioners*. New York: Alfred A Knopf.

Goschler, Constantin. 1998. Offene Fragen der Wiedergutmachung. *Leviathan* 18: 38–52.

Habermas, Jürgen. 1999. Bestialität und Humanität: Ein Krieg an der Grenze zwischen Recht und Moral. *Die Zeit* 18: 7.

Hamburger Institut für Sozialforschung (ed). 1999. *Eine Ausstellung und ihre Folgen*. Hamburg: IfS.

Ignatieff, Michael. 1998. *The Warrior's Honour. Ethnic War and the Modern Conscience*. Toronto: Penguin Books.

Jaspers, Karl. 1996/1946. Reprint. *Die Schuldfrage. Von der politischen Haftung Deutschlands*. München: Piper. Original edition, 1946.

Jeismann, Michael (ed). 1999. *Mahnmal Mitte*. Köln: Du Mont.

Karstedt, Susanne. 1998. Coming to Terms with the Past in Germany after 1945 and 1989: Public Judgements on Procedures and Justice. *Law and Policy* 20: 15–56.

de Kock, Eugene. 1998. *A Long Night's Damage: Working for the Apartheid State*. Saxonwold: Contra Press.

Koenen, Gerd. 1999. Der verstörende Unterschied. Warum Stalinismus und Nazismus doch nicht über einen Kamm zu scheren sind. In *Der rote Holocaust und die Deutschen. Die Debatte um das, Schwarzbuch des Kommunismus'*, edited by H Möller. München: Piper.

Konkret. 1999. Die Haare sind mehr geworden. 02/1999: 12–15.

Lübbe, Hermann. 1989. Verdrängung? Über eine Kategorie zur Kritik des deutschen Vergangenheitsverhältnisses. In *Die Gegenwart der Vergangenheit: Historikerstreit und Erinnerungsarbeit. Zeitkritische Beiträge der Evangelischen Akademie*, edited by H-H Wiebe. Bad Segeberg: Nodelbien.

Mamdani, Mahmood. 1998. *When Does Reconciliation Turn into a Denial of Justice?* Pretoria: HRSC Publishers.

Minnow, Martha. 1998. *Between Vengeance and Forgiveness.* Boston: Beacon Press.

Möller, Horst (ed). 1999. *Der rote Holocaust und die Deutschen. Die Debatte um das 'Schwarzbuch des Kommunismus'.* München: Piper.

Neier, Aryeh. 1998. *War Crimes: Brutality, Genocide, Terror, and the Struggle for Justice.* New York: Random House.

Pauw, Jacques. 1997. *Into the Heat of Darkness: Confessions of Apartheid's Assassins.* Johannesburg: Jonathan Ball.

Perels, Joachim. 1998. Die Zerstörung von Erinnerung als Herrschaftstechnik. Adornos Analysen zur Blockierung der Aufarbeitung der NS-Vergangenheit. *Leviathan Sonderheft* 18: 53–8.

Reichel, Peter. 1999. *Politik mit der Erinnerung. Gedächtnisorte im Streit um die national-sozialistische Vergangenheit.* Frankfurt: Fischer.

Rohloff, Joachim. 1999. *Ich bin das Volk. Martin Walser, Auschwitz und die Berliner Republik.* Hamburg: Konkret Literatur Verlag.

Schwan, Gesine. 1997. *Politik und Schuld.* Frankfurt: Fischer.

Thiele, Hans-Günther (ed). 1997. *Die Wehrmachtsausstellung. Dokumentation einer Kontroverse.* Bremen: Temmen.

Wehler, Hans-Ulrich. 1988. *Entsorgung der deutschen Vergangenheit.* München: Beck.

Wiegel, Gert and Klotz, Johannes (eds). 1999. *Geistige Brandstiftung? Die Walser-Bubis Debatte.* Köln: PapyRossa.

Wippermann, Wolfgang. 1997. *Wessen Schuld? Vom Historikerstreit zur Goldhagen-Kontroverse.* Berlin: Elefanten Press.

5

Common Past, Divided Truth: The Truth and Reconciliation Commission in South African Public Opinion[*]

GUNNAR THEISSEN

L EGAL INSTITUTIONS HAVE played a central part in dealing with past atrocities in newly established democracies. Besides criminal trials, truth commissions have become a frequently used tool to investigate past human rights abuses (Hayner 1994). This chapter explores the ways in which the South African Truth and Reconciliation Commission (TRC) has contributed to a shared understanding of the apartheid past in South Africa. The TRC is worth studying as it can be distinguished from earlier truth commissions in Latin America and Africa by two important features. It was the first truth commission that collected information on past human rights violations largely in public and not behind closed doors, enabling the national and international media to report extensively on the Commission. The other innovation was the amnesty process. Unlike other truth commissions, the South African TRC could grant amnesty to perpetrators of past political crimes if they made a full disclosure about their acts.

The TRC was based on the idea that criminal punishment is less important than truth, official acknowledgement and reparation. The amnesty provisions of the TRC were a reflection of a political compromise between the African National Congress (ANC) and the National Party (NP). They followed the assumption that in the aftermath of large-scale atrocities, the need for public reckoning with past horrific events is more important to democratisation than the criminal law's more traditional objectives of deterrence and retribution. With an organised process of public storytelling the architects of the

---

[*] This chapter reflects empirical research and public opinion polls published up until November 1998. Only minimal changes have been made to reflect more recent developments. For a more recent empirical study on the public perception of the TRC process see Gibson (2004).

South African TRC hoped to put an end to official denial of past atrocities and thereby promote national unity and reconciliation. In a similar vein, Mark Osiel (1997) has stressed that legal procedures dealing with past human rights violations should be conducted with an educational purpose in mind. They should stimulate public discourse about past atrocities and foster the liberal values of tolerance, moderation and civil respect. However, little empirical research is available that has investigated whether legal institutions have been able to achieve these goals. Public opinion surveys are therefore an important source to analyse the potentials and limits of legal institutions in shaping collective memory, social solidarity and respect for human rights.

First, I would like to point out why a democratic country like South Africa needs a certain degree of agreement about its atrocious past. Thereafter, I will analyse the strengths and weaknesses of the South African TRC process for building an inclusive and shared understanding of this past. Finally, I will turn to the question of how the South African TRC was accepted by the general public and try to explain why remembrance remained strongly determined by past allegiances.

I. THE NEED FOR A COMMON UNDERSTANDING OF THE PAST

A critical reader may ask if Maurice Halbwachs' (1985) notion of a collective memory makes sense in a society as sharply divided as South Africa. Was apartheid not all about entrenching difference and constructing separate racial identities? Indeed, the term 'collective memory' may be a misnomer for societies that are based on racial segregation and experience prolonged and deeply rooted social conflict. In such societies there is rather a lack of a common understanding of the past. Halbwachs' main argument, however, that individual memory is largely shaped by those social groups we belong to, is even more accurate for divided societies. Conflict-ridden countries often lack a common understanding of the past on a national level but are frequently characterised by antagonistic social groups that have built their own collective memories reflecting their selective perspectives of past political conflict.

Although South Africans experienced the apartheid past very differently, there cannot be disagreement about the fact that citizens were given unequal rights and privileges based on their colour or constructed ethnicity. Nor is there any doubt that many thousand South Africans were imprisoned, tortured or killed during the apartheid era. Although 'the past' is always a cognitive representation—a selective process of remembrance that can be changed to fit the present self-concept or current policies—one should avoid the trap of postmodern indifference. Whether somebody was killed or not can be proven, and not all interpretations of the past can be justified as acceptable. The uncritical glorification of the so-called benefits of separate development on the one hand and images of a 'clean' and always heroic liberation struggle on the other hand both need to be challenged.

Nonetheless, arguing for a need to build a common understanding of the past does not deny a pluralism of historical perceptions. Democratic societies should not be characterised by a single or imposed account of national history that is beyond rational argument. To the contrary, an active and ongoing discourse about the past and its moral implications is an indicator of a vibrant democracy. National unity and reconciliation cannot, however, be built on the basis of completely incompatible stories of the apartheid past. First, justifications of the apartheid system and past human rights abuses question the basic commitment to the new democracy and its fundamental values, which are entrenched in South Africa's new Constitution. Secondly, it is impossible to build interpersonal trust between victims and beneficiaries of the apartheid system, when past injustices are ignored, justified or denied. A certain degree of common understanding is therefore essential to transcend past racial and political divisions.

II. THE SOUTH AFRICAN TRUTH AND RECONCILIATION COMMISSION

The capability of legal institutions to produce a detailed and at the same time inclusive, picture of past injustices is often limited by the constraints of the judicial process. Criminal procedures focusing on past human rights violations are often in danger of being selective, losing perspective in minutiae, becoming lost in judicial detail or distorting systematic torture as grievous bodily harm (Osiel 1997). Truth commissions face these risks, too. There is, however, more flexibility to draft the mandate of a truth commission in such a way that it enables the public to get a fuller picture of the extent, context and gravity of past human rights violations. Furthermore, the way in which a truth commission works has a strong impact on whether it will be able to promote public discourse about past human rights violations or whether it will fail to do so.

Criminal proceedings are usually limited to cases in which substantial evidence against the alleged perpetrators exists. The South African TRC, however, was asked to establish as complete a picture as possible about gross human rights violations committed from March 1960, the month of the Sharpeville massacre, which subsequently led to the beginning of the armed liberation struggle, until 10 May 1994, the date of Nelson Mandela's inauguration as State President.[1] This enabled the Commission to document and investigate human rights abuses that would never have

---

[1] The cut-off date was originally 5 December 1993, the day before the Interim Constitution of 1993 came into force (see s 3(1)a and s 20(2) in conjunction with s 1(1)vii of the TRC Act (1995)). It was extended to 10 May 1994 in order to be able to grant amnesty for bombings and other human rights violations by members of the right wing before and during the first democratic election in April 1994.

been brought to trial because of lack of evidence, death of the accused or because the identity of the perpetrator remained unknown. Criminal trials would also have been severely hampered by the fact that nearly all security police records were systematically destroyed before 1996 (TRC 1998, vol 1, 201–36). Furthermore, many victims did not trust the inherited criminal justice system, which had completely failed during the apartheid era to bring perpetrators of past human rights violations to book (Bizos 1998). Even if victims would have charged, the South African criminal justice system, already overloaded with an extraordinarily high crime rate (Stack 1997), would have been ill-equipped to investigate the atrocities of the previous 30 years.

The mandate of the TRC was also broad enough to circumvent problems that would have been related to the territorial applicability of South African criminal law. Gross human rights violations could be investigated irrespective of whether they were committed inside or outside the Republic, or whether they were committed by the government's security forces or by the liberation movements. A gross violation of human rights was defined by the TRC Act (1995)[2] as 'the killing, abduction, torture or the severe ill-treatment of a person' (s 1(1)ix). This limited the scope of inquiry, privileging certain forms of human rights abuse in comparison to others. As a consequence certain legalised injustices widely accepted as gross human rights violations, like forced removals or prolonged arbitrary detention, were excluded from the investigations of the TRC. Thus the Commission focused on the excesses of the apartheid system, while the human rights abuses inherent to the apartheid legal order remained largely untouched. Apartheid as a crime against humanity (Slye 1999) was not a central topic in the TRC proceedings, though the Commission reiterated the view that apartheid was an 'illegal, oppressive and inhuman system' and a 'crime against humanity' (TRC 1998, vol 1, 68–9).

The Human Rights Violations Committee of the TRC held public hearings in more than eighty towns. About 1,200 victims and survivors reported on their experiences or the fate of their loved ones.[3] They could tell their stories without inhibition or being subjected to a debasing or degrading procedure of cross-examination by their alleged perpetrators. The human rights violation hearings of the TRC focused not only on the criminal act, but also on the psychological, physical and social consequences that victims and survivors had to endure. This allowed victims to put their perspectives in a more complete and dignified manner to the public than criminal proceedings

---

[2] TRC Act (Promotion of National Unity and Reconciliation Act). Act No 34 of 1995.
[3] A compassionate account of the TRC hearings has been written by the poet Antjie Krog (1998), who followed the hearings as a radio journalist. The transcripts of the Human Rights Violation Hearings and Amnesty Hearings are available on the TRC website: http://www. doj.gov.za/trc/.

would have allowed for. At least at the beginning of the TRC's work, the media attention and empathy went to the victims, their mothers and wives, fathers and husbands, daughters and sons. The stage was not set, like so often in criminal proceedings, for the perpetrators and their perspectives. In total an impressive 21,296 statements relating to more than 36,000 gross human rights violations were collected (TRC 1998, vol 3, 3).

Another obvious advantage of the TRC was that it could enquire into the 'causes, nature and extent of gross human rights violations ... including the antecedents, circumstances, factors and context of such violations' (TRC Act 1995, s 3(1)a). Therefore various forms of collaboration, conformity and public support for the apartheid regime could be examined—manifestations of culpability that are usually beyond the scope of criminal law. For this purpose a series of institutional hearings were held, during which various influential sectors of society were called to account: the media, business, the legal system, the health sector and the religious communities (TRC 1998, vol 4; Chapman and Rubenstein 1998; Cochrane, De Gruchy and Martin 1999; Dyzenhaus 1998; Nattrass 1999). All these sectors had over the years come under attack for their complicity in human rights violations and the apartheid system.

The shocking accounts of victims and perpetrators were extensively reported in the media. The TRC featured constantly in radio and national television news. From April 1996 to March 1998, the South African Broadcasting Corporation (SABC) aired every Sunday a magazine pro-gramme summarising the TRC proceedings of the week. The 'Special Report on the TRC' often found its way into the 'Top Ten' favourite TV programmes of the week and was extremely popular among Africans. An average of one million adults watched the 'Special Report' every Sunday, representing about 8.7 per cent of all adults who had a television at their home.[4] Public inter-est in the TRC proceedings was significantly lower among white television viewers (4.1 per cent) compared to African viewers (13.7 per cent). This demonstrates how the TRC proceedings generated high but split levels of public interest for a prolonged period. Other truth commissions that have worked behind closed doors have rarely achieved similar media attention. Although some truth commission reports have become bestsellers, the radio and television broadcasts of the TRC proceedings reached nearly everyone in South Africa. In the context of a multilingual country in which many people are illiterate, a lengthy printed academic report alone would not have achieved a similar impact. Probably, criminal trials would never have achieved such a level of public attention, since broadcasting from the court room is usually prohibited, and many legalistic aspects of the judicial process are too

---

[4] The South African Broadcasting Corporation (SABC) regularly collected average ratings of the Special Report on the TRC, from 1996 to 1998; data were provided by the SABC Research Department to the author.

boring for the general public. Criminal trials focus media attention more exclusively on high-profile cases. The human rights violations hearings of the TRC heard well-known matters together with previously unknown cases, and victims from all groups and political backgrounds testified. This ensured that media reporting reflected a comprehensive account of the multiple forms of victimisation experienced under apartheid, instead of reproducing stereotypical conceptions of good and bad guys.

The South African TRC was also unique as it combined a truth-finding process with amnesty proceedings. Perpetrators of past political crimes could be granted amnesty if they came forward and made a full disclosure (TRC Act 1995, s 20(1)c). Suspects who failed to apply for amnesty before 30 September 1997 or who were refused amnesty might face criminal prosecution.[5] The Amnesty Committee of the TRC had the difficult task of deciding whether each applicant had made a full disclosure and whether an act was politically motivated or not. Politically motivated crime is defined in the TRC Act (s 20(2)a–g) as a crime committed on behalf of or in support of the state, a liberation movement or any other publicly known political organisation. In order to ascertain whether the crime was associated with a political motive the Amnesty Committee was guided by various criteria, including the proportionality of the act in relation to its objective, the motive, gravity and context of the crime (s 20(3)). The Amnesty Committee received in total 7,116 applications. In total 5,142 applications were administratively refused, because they were outside of the jurisdiction of the Amnesty Committee (Coetzee 2003, 193). Most of these applications came from sentenced prisoners who portrayed their crimes as politically motivated in an attempt to secure for them an early release from prison. Only about 1,800 amnesty applications related to 2,341 gross human rights violations (Coetzee 2003, 193). These applications had to be heard in public. The Amnesty Committee was rather generous to perpetrators who were invited to a public hearing: 84 percent of all amnesty applications concerning politically motivated gross human rights violations were granted (Du Bois-Pedain 2007, 80).

Members of the liberation movements were more willing to apply for amnesty: 1,094 applications came from ANC members and 201 from members of the left-wing Pan-Africanist Congress. Only 289 members of the State security forces and 85 members of the Inkatha Freedom Party (IFP) applied for amnesty (Du Bois-Pedain 2007, 68–69). This stood in strong contrast to the victim testimony attributing the overwhelming portion of torture and killings to the State security forces and the IFP (TRC 1998, vol 3, 9–11).

---

[5] The cut-off date was originally 14 December 1996 (see s 18(2) of the TRC Act). It was extended twice by regulation according to § 40 (1)i of the TRC Act.

While perpetrators are usually better off if they deny as much as possible in criminal trials to increase their chances of acquittal, the amnesty procedures of the TRC encouraged confession. The more details an amnesty applicant provided, the more likely it was that the criteria of full disclosure were met, which increased the chance of being granted amnesty. Although amnesty applicants frequently played down the brutality with which their victims had been tortured or murdered, their accounts were detailed and shocking enough to convince the South African public that these atrocities must indeed have taken place. Human rights violations could not be denied any more as unfounded allegations. The amnesty process furthermore reduced the likelihood of the public showing solidarity with former perpetrators. A soldier or police officer confessing to heinous crimes and pleading for amnesty is hardly likely to become a martyr of victor's justice.

Instead of reinforcing opposing worldviews held by the former parties in the conflict, as is often the result of human rights trials (Malamud-Goti 1996), the South African TRC process had more potential to produce a mutual recognition of past atrocities. Victims were allowed to challenge the perpetrators during the public amnesty proceedings, and amnesty applicants were often forced to give their story coherence to remain credible and to succeed with their application. Although stories told by victims and perpetrators often remained different, they had at least one essential fact in common, namely that a person had killed, abducted, tortured or ill-treated another one. The South African amnesty process was therefore more likely to build some shared understanding of past human rights violations than criminal trials would have done.

The advantage of punishment compared to amnesty is that it sends a stronger message that a specific violation is a blameworthy criminal act and not to be excused. But criminal trials also have the potential to support revisionist perceptions of past injustices. High-profile suspects may be acquitted because of the court's failure to call on important witnesses, a lack of evidence or procedural flaws. Such acquittals may send the unintended message to the public that individuals who are widely suspected of having been the masterminds of state repression are either innocent or get away with it, as the court case against the former South African Defence Minister Magnus Malan has demonstrated (Varney and Sarkin 1997).

Another advantage of truth commissions is that they provide the public with a comprehensive report about their findings. Judgements in criminal proceedings tend to be made for individual cases, often remain unpublished and are not primarily written for the purpose of public education. The detailed five-volume report of the TRC was handed over to President Mandela on 29 October 1998. At this time the Report had not been finalised, as amnesty hearings were still ongoing. In 2003 two additional volumes covering the amnesty process and short summaries of all identified human rights violations and their victims were published.

The TRC did not equalise the struggle of liberation with the human rights violations of the apartheid regime in its Report. Apartheid was defined as a crime against humanity, and the armed resistance against apartheid was recognised as a 'just war'. The Commission maintained, however, that 'the fact that the apartheid system was a crime against humanity does not mean that all acts carried out in order to destroy apartheid were legal, moral and acceptable' (TRC 1998, vol 1, 68–9). The Report states that the 'predominant proportion of gross violations of human rights was committed by the former state through its security and law-enforcement agencies' and gives a detailed account how 'elimination' of political activists became increasingly frequent after the mid-1980s (TRC 1998, vol 5, 212–18). The Report reveals findings about high-ranking perpetrators. Prominent politicians who had not applied for amnesty, like President PW Botha, IFP leader Gatsha Mangosuthu Buthelezi and Winnie Madizikela-Mandela, are found to be responsible for gross human rights violations (TRC 1998, vol 5, 223–43). After a successful last-minute court appeal, the findings on former President FW de Klerk were eliminated from the report and made subject to a later legal hearing. A similar court appeal by the ANC to suppress the publication of negative findings about the organisation failed. The report recommends that 'where amnesty has not been sought or has been denied, prosecution should be considered' and that the 'granting of a general amnesty in whatever guise should be resisted' (TRC 1998, vol 5, 309). About 500 cases were handed over to the national director of prosecutions, Bulelani Ngcuka, who stated that some prosecutions might be dropped in the name of national reconciliation.[6]

Before praising the South African TRC process as a better tool for building a shared memory than an approach based on criminal prosecutions, the fact has to be acknowledged that the South African amnesty process could not be successfully carried through without the threat of criminal prosecutions. Most perpetrators not yet prosecuted were motivated to confess to their crimes only because they realised that the office of the state prosecutor was already at their heels.[7] Furthermore, it should be pointed out that the South African amnesty process considerably restricted the rights of victims to sue, since successful applicants were granted amnesty in respect to criminal as well as civil liability (TRC Act 1995, s 20(7)a). Thus victims and survivors were not allowed to lay any civil charges for their suffering against perpetrators, against political organisations they had been members of or against the state. These amnesty provisions were challenged by relatives of Steve Biko and other famous slain anti-apartheid activists before the South African Constitutional Court. In July 1996 in

---

[6] See the *Sowetan*, 2 November 1998.
[7] I owe this point to my colleague Volker Nerlich, who researched the impact of imminent prosecutions against members of the South African Police on convincing them to apply for amnesty.

AZAPO v President of the RSA, the Court upheld the constitutionality of the legislation.[8] However, whether the South African amnesty provisions are compatible with current international law remains questionable (Dugard 1997; Motala 1996; Theissen 1998).

As far as victims are concerned, the TRC could not meet the high expectations it raised when it claimed to put 'victims first'. The Reparation and Rehabilitation Committee of the TRC was mandated only to recommend a future policy of reparation to the State President and Parliament (TRC Act 1995, s 4(f) and s 25(1)b) and could not provide any substantial reparation to victims. This was regarded as a shortcoming of the TRC legislation by former Commissioners and its Chair Desmond Tutu (Orr 2000; Tutu 1999, 61–3), and provisions for reparations have been debated ever since.

The Commission proposed a system of individual- and community-based reparation measures (TRC 1998, vol 5, 170–95). The latter include, amongst others, symbolic reparations (eg, erecting headstones, building memorials, renaming public facilities, establishing a day of remembrance, etc), legal and administrative interventions (eg, expunging criminal records, (re)issuing certificates of death, etc), exhumations, reburials and ceremonies. The first payments of urgent interim reparation—a lump sum of about 3,300 Rand (USD$500) per victim—were only made in July 1998, two and a half years after the Commission had been established (TRC 1998, vol 5, 181–2). By 30 January 2000, only 6,252 of these grants had been paid out (CSVR 2000a). Besides urgent interim reparations the TRC has recommended individual reparation grants for victims or their next of kin. The proposal includes annual grants of 17,029–23,023 Rand (about USD$2,800–3,800) for a period of six years to some 18,000 victims. To minimise administrative costs, the proposed calculation system does not take the degree of physical, psychological or financial harm into account (TRC 1998, 184–7). Furthermore only those victims of gross human rights violations who have made a statement to the TRC before December 1997 or who were identified as victims of gross human rights violations during an amnesty process will be eligible for reparation (TRC Act 1995, s 26(1); TRC 1998, vol 1, 86). In April 2003 State President Thabo Mbeki announced that all victims identified by the TRC would receive a once-off reparation grant of 30,000 Rand. This is less than 25 percent of the amount proposed by the TRC. As of 31 March 2007 reparation grants had been paid out to 15,610 victims (Department of Justice and Constitutional Development 2007, 4).

TRC staff and academics were often too fast in hailing the TRC process as a superior process of genuine restorative justice. Of course the TRC had many positive restorative features: the Commission helped to restore the dignity of the victims, facilitated strong community participation in its

---

[8] 1996 (8) BCLR 1015 (CC).

hearings and assisted in reintegrating perpetrators (Llewellyn and Howse 1999). It should, however, not be overlooked that the TRC legislation excluded all restorative obligations on the side of indemnified perpetrators and their organisations. As far as reparations are concerned, the Chilean Truth and Reconciliation Commission achieved more. A National Corporation for Reparation and Reconciliation was established shortly after the publication of the Chilean Truth Commission's report, providing some 4.600 survivors with lifelong pensions and many of their children with educational scholarships (Kritz 1995, vol 3, 502–9; CNRR 1996, 102–17). With the South African amnesty process dragging on, public interest decreased dramatically and media attention shifted to the amnesty hearings of perpetrators. At the same time the political pressure to secure Parliamentary approval of the recommended reparation policy was low.

The TRC was extraordinarily successful in documenting past human rights abuses. But one should not forget that for many victims the promise of truth has not been fulfilled. Time pressure made it necessary to concentrate investigations on those cases for which an amnesty application was received. Most victim statements presented to the TRC were only corroborated—checked for internal consistency and for external consistency with official records like death certificates or medical reports—in order to classify them as victims. In probably 90 per cent of all cases the TRC was unable to present victims with any new evidence. What remains is an acknowledgement of their suffering. From the victims' perspective the TRC experience can be summarised as: some acknowledgement, some truth, and little reparation.

Notwithstanding these limitations, the TRC provided a more detailed and inclusive picture of past human rights violations, produced less divergent stories about past atrocities by perpetrators and victims, and confronted the South African public more intensively with the apartheid past than a process based on criminal trials would ever have achieved.

III. PUBLIC OPINION ABOUT THE TRC

There can be no doubt that the TRC was a suitable approach to foster public debate about the apartheid past. The capacities of legal institutions to reshape collective memory are, however, often overestimated. Divergent historical perceptions are rooted in people's biographies and their social milieus. They are usually resistant to any fast changes. Although the following data cannot assess the long-term impact of the TRC on the political culture of South Africa, a review of various public opinion surveys may provide us with some preliminary indicators about the TRC's limits and potentials to nurture a common understanding of the apartheid past.

A. The Surveys

The surveys discussed in this chapter are based on national area-stratified probability samples of more than 2,000 respondents from metropolitan, urban and rural areas, including people living in formal and informal settlements (Table 1). Interviews were conducted face-to-face and in the language of the respondent. Usually people from all racial backgrounds were interviewed. The two Research Surveys Polls (1996, 1998) included only African and white respondents, and both surveys of Market Research Africa (MRA 1996, 1998) excluded rural inhabitants of former home-lands. The poll of the Centre for the Study of Violence and Reconciliation (CSVR 1996; Theissen and Hamber 1998) focused exclusively on white public opinions. Due to financial constraints the CSVR survey was con-ducted by telephone and limited to a small national probability sample of 124 white South Africans. With the exception of the latter kind of exploratory survey the statistical standard error of the samples can be estimated at about three per cent. Survey research on the TRC was largely conducted in an ad hoc and unsystematic manner. Questions asked on similar topics were worded differently by various polling institutions. This poses some difficulties in conducting reliable analysis of trends in the public's view of the TRC.

B. Findings

Before the TRC started operating, public opinion was already split along historical cleavages. While most African respondents wanted justice to be done by the new government, most white South Africans resisted the idea of bringing white perpetrators to trial. In 1992, 74 per cent of all African respondents demanded that 'whites who harmed blacks during apartheid be charged in court', but 83 per cent of white respondents opposed this idea, most of them strongly (HSRC 1992; Schlemmer 1992). A first survey conducted by the Institute for Democracy in South Africa on the proposed truth commission showed that 60 per cent of all South Africans were in favour of 'a Commission to investigate crimes that occurred under the pre-vious government' as the question was phrased (IDASA 1994). Again, sup-port varied strongly between the different groups of the population. While 65 per cent of all Africans were in favour of a truth commission, only 39 per cent of white South Africans endorsed such a proposal. In May 1995, 63 per cent of white students doubted whether the TRC would be able to find out what really happened with regard to human rights violations. In contrast, 72 per cent of the African respondents were confident that the TRC would accomplish this task (Figure 1).

Table 1: Surveys

Survey	HSRC 1992	Idasa 1994	HSRC 1995	CSVR 1996	MRA 1996	Research Surveys 1996	Mark Data 1997	Gibson & Gouws 1999	MRA 1998	CASE 1998	Research Surveys 1998	HSRC 1998
Fieldwork in	October 1992	August 1994	May 1995	May 1996	May 1996	October 1996	July 1997	Nov–Dec 1997	March 1998	April 1998	Nov 1998	Nov 1998
Number of Respondents (= N)	1998	2517	2229	124	2507	2700	2240	1518	2503	1200	2000	2200
Surveyed Population Groups	All	All	All	Whites Only	All	Africans and Whites Only	All	All	All	All	Africans and Whites Only	All
Type of Survey	Area stratified random sampling	Area stratified random sampling	Area stratified random sampling	Telephone survey random sampling	Area stratified random sampling	Area stratified random sampling	Area stratified random sampling	Second wave of panel study	Area stratified random sampling	Area stratified random sampling	Area stratified random sampling	Area stratified random sampling
Remarks				High statistical standard error (+/-9%)	Excluded former homelands				Excluded former homelands		Conducted only in metropolitan areas	

Survey Question: Do you think the TRC will be able to find out what really happened with human rights violations?

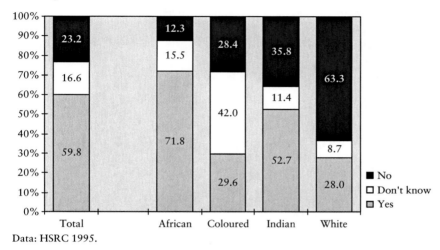

Data: HSRC 1995.

Figure 1: Public Perception of the TRC's Truth-finding Capability (May 1995)

A comparison of three surveys—one conducted before the establishment of the TRC in May 1995, one at the beginning of the TRC's proceedings in May 1996 and one after the publication of the TRC Report in November 1998—indicates that the TRC increasingly gained public approval. Although the questions of the consecutive surveys were not phrased in the same way, they elicited the respondents' general attitudes towards the TRC process. Figure 2 shows the development of public support. In November 1998, after publication of its Report, 57 per cent of all South Africans felt that the TRC had been a good or very good thing for the country; only 27 per cent held the opposite view.

Generally speaking the South African public was overwhelmingly pleased with the TRC—despite the many hurting memories it evoked. Thus claims that the TRC has only made few friends in South Africa (Gibson and Gouws 1999, 514) are not confirmed by these empirical data. Such an argument is valid only with respect to the white minority in South Africa. As the following results will show most whites disliked the TRC from the beginning, and their attitudes towards the Commission hardened further during the process. In November 1998, 72 per cent of them claimed that the TRC had been a bad or very bad thing for the country. Only a few whites disagreed with this perception (see Figure 2). The opposite trend can be found for African respondents: the TRC seems to have lived up to their high expectations. In November 1998, 72 per cent claimed the TRC was a good or very good thing. In sum, the actual work

May 1995:   Are you for or against the establishment of a truth commission? (Answers include only respondents
               who had heard about such a commission.)
June 1996:   Should the Commission be allowed to continue for as long as necessary and not have to end in
               18 months' time, as planned?
November 1998: Do you think the Truth and Reconciliation Commission (TRC) has been a good or a bad thing
               for the country?

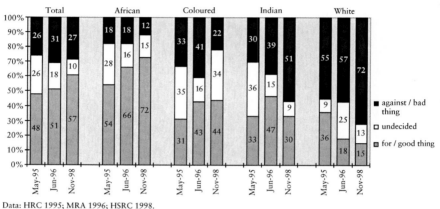

Data: HRC 1995; MRA 1996; HSRC 1998.

Figure 2: Public Perception of the TRC (May 1995–November 1998)

of the TRC has reinforced rather than changed preconceived opinions about the TRC.

There was no strong divergence of opinion between Africans speaking different languages but a significant difference between English-speaking whites (mean rating: –1.06) and Afrikaans-speaking whites (mean rating: –2.73) (see Table 2). Although positive evaluations prevailed in the coloured community (mean rating: +0.59), many were undecided (34 per cent). Indian respondents had mixed views about the TRC process but tended to be more negative than positive about it (mean rating: –0.30). Interestingly, people from urban informal settlements, hostels and former black townships—areas that had been strongly affected by political violence in the past—were very positive about the TRC process, while respondents living in the former homelands were less enthusiastic. Residents of small towns and former 'white' farming areas were usually very negative about the TRC. These areas have largely remained strongholds of white conservatism in the new South Africa as Table 2 demonstrates.

There is a distinct pattern that divided younger and older generations. Young white South Africans under the age of 25 (mean rating: –1.00) were less negative about the TRC than their parents' generation (mean rating: –2.28). These results point to an emerging generation of white South Africans who have fewer problems accepting the legacies of apartheid. In total, however, negative evaluations prevail throughout all

Table 2: Perceptions of the TRC among Different Social and Ethnic Groups (November 1998)

Survey Question: Do you think the TRC has been a good or bad thing for the country?

	very good thing (+4)	good thing (+2)	neither/ don't know (0)	bad thing (−2)	very bad thing (−4)	mean
All	37%	20%	10%	10%	17%	+1.03
African	51%	21%	15%	6%	6%	+2.08
Coloured	17%	27%	34%	12%	10%	+0.59
Indian	18%	22%	9%	28%	23%	−0.30
White	3%	12%	13%	17%	55%	−2.18
Home Language						
White/Afrikaans	2%	6%	13%	13%	66%	−2.73
White/English	6%	26%	13%	19%	36%	−1.06
African/Zulu	46%	23%	17%	10%	4%	+1.95
African/Sotho-Languages	54%	19%	13%	5%	8%	+2.12
African/Xhosa	51%	24%	16%	6%	4%	+2.23
Other African Languages	48%	25%	22%	4%	1%	+2.30
Place of Dwelling						
Urban Informal	69%	20%	6%	3%	2%	+3.05
African Townships	59%	24%	7%	6%	4%	+2.60
Hostel Dwellers	55%	18%	9%	17%	1%	+2.19
Rural, former Homelands	44%	18%	23%	6%	9%	+1.61
Coloured Townships	16%	26%	34%	11%	12%	+0.48
Indian Townships	22%	17%	4%	34%	23%	−0.36
Metropolitan City-Areas	12%	23%	15%	13%	38%	−0.83
Rural 'white' Farmland	4%	15%	12%	20%	49%	−1.93
Non-metro Towns & Cities	1%	13%	16%	11%	59%	−2.28
Whites/Metro	3%	17%	15%	15%	51%	−1.87
Whites/Non-Metropolitan	1%	8%	12%	19%	60%	−2.57
Generations						
Africans under 25 years	46%	23%	14%	10%	8%	+1.81
Africans over 25 years	52%	20%	16%	6%	6%	+2.15
Whites under 25 years	20%	17%	4%	11%	48%	−1.00
Whites over 25 years	2%	12%	14%	17%	56%	−2.28
Education						
Non-Whites > Std. 10	50%	25%	12%	8%	4%	+2.17
Non-Whites Std. 10 or less	44%	21%	18%	9%	8%	+1.70

(continued)

Table 2   Continued

	very good thing (+4)	good thing (+2)	neither/ don't know (0)	bad thing (−2)	very bad thing (−4)	mean
Whites > Std. 10	1%	15%	18%	16%	50%	−1.94
Whites Std. 10 and less	4%	10%	10%	17%	59%	−2.34
Political Orientation						
ANC	55%	21%	12%	5%	7%	+2.24
PAC	46%	9%	22%	17%	6%	+1.44
UDM	50%	5%	27%	4%	14%	+1.46
IFP	25%	24%	17%	25%	8%	+0.66
NP	16%	18%	17%	17%	31%	−0.58
DP	7%	24%	15%	22%	33%	−1.00
FF	0%	3%	4%	9%	84%	−3.48
Non-Voters	17%	17%	31%	11%	24%	−0.16

Data: HSRC 1998.

white age groups. A contrasting but only marginally significant trend can be observed among African respondents. The TRC seems to have been more important to Africans who experienced the old days of apartheid as adults (mean rating: +2.15) than to the young African generation under 25 years of age (mean rating: +1.81). If race classification is controlled for, the TRC was more often endorsed by subjects with higher educational qualification than by those with less than 10 years of schooling (Table 2).

Political orientation also had a strong impact on the respondents' evaluation of the TRC (Table 2). Supporters of political parties that grew out of the liberation movements, like the ANC and Pan Africanist Congress (PAC), were overwhelmingly positive about the TRC. This is also true for the followers of the United Democratic Movement of the former 'homeland' ruler Bantu Holomisa and of Roelf Meyer, a former prominent NP politician. Although the leadership of the IFP vehemently opposed the TRC, it is an interesting fact that their supporters were more inclined to claim that the TRC had been good rather than bad for the country. Negative evaluations prevailed among voters of the former ruling NP and the Democratic Party (DP), which both have their constituencies in the white population. Dissatisfaction with the TRC was strongest among adherents to the right-wing Afrikaner Freedom Front (FF).

In sum, past allegiances and their respective distance from the apartheid regime were the best predictors of attitudes towards the TRC. The Commission was most rejected by conservative or right-wing Afrikaans-speaking whites who grew up under the old apartheid order, had less education and lived in rural areas or small towns. On the other hand, those South Africans who supported progressive liberation movements and lived in areas that were strongly affected by state repression were on average very satisfied with the TRC process. Although support for the TRC was lower among IFP-supporters, the Commission was welcomed by most African respondents throughout the political spectrum as a positive contribution. This analysis suggests that the TRC was more successful in resolving the many conflicts that divided black communities during apartheid, than bridging the divisions between the black and white communities.

In comparison to other government institutions the TRC rated very favourably. It even garnered more sympathy than the ANC-led national government. Public opinion was strongly polarised along racial lines, but still, in comparison to other legal institutions like the police and the courts, the TRC got rather positive evaluations (see Figure 3). White attitudes towards public institutions of the new South Africa were a reverse image

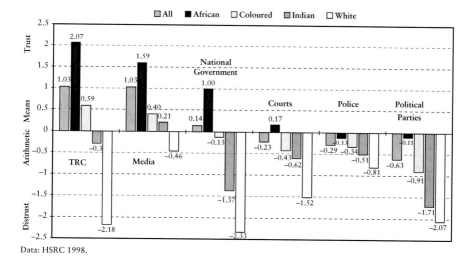

Data: HSRC 1998.

Figure 3: Public Trust in Institutions (November 1998)[9]

[9] Unfortunately the HSRC 1998 survey did not include the TRC in the sequence measuring confidence in public institutions. The response to the TRC was measured by the question 'Do you think that the Truth and Reconciliation Commission (TRC) has been a good thing or a bad thing for the country?' while trust in all other institutions was measured by 'How much trust or distrust do you have in the following institutions in South Africa at present?' Although the question in respect to the TRC is more output-orientated, it is included here, on the assumption that those who claim that an institution has done a good job must also have some confidence in it, and those who claim that the TRC was bad for the country are very unlikely to trust the institution.

of the high levels of support these institutions had formerly enjoyed during apartheid (Booysen and Kotzé 1985; Gagiano 1986; Rhoodie, De Kock and Couper 1985; Booysen 1989). Given the general mistrust of white South Africans towards all public institutions of the new state, the negative evaluation of the TRC by white respondents seems less of an exception. Since South Africans from all racial backgrounds had only little trust in the traditional criminal justice system, it is highly doubtful whether the police and courts would have been capable of gaining enough cooperation and support from the public should they have been entrusted with the investigation of past human rights abuses.

Public views on the impartiality of the TRC corresponded strongly with the general evaluation of the TRC. While most African respondents regarded the TRC as impartial, white South Africans denied this, and this increased during the hearings. The perception of white respondents that the TRC was fair to both sides dropped from 35 per cent in May 1996 to a mere 13 per cent in November 1998 (see Figure 4).

The reasons why respondents regarded the TRC as biased varied. Two out of three white Afrikaans speakers claimed that the TRC was biased towards the ANC. This feeling was shared by every second white English-speaking respondent (48 per cent), but only 13 per cent of all African respondents held this view (Mark Data 1997). African respondents frequently mentioned that the TRC was unfair because perpetrators are not punished according to their crimes (25 per cent)—an opinion hardly expressed by white respondents (0.8 per cent; Research Surveys 1996).

Notwithstanding these reservations and divisions, most South Africans believed that the TRC was successful in uncovering past atrocities. In November 1998, 60 per cent of all African respondents maintained that the TRC had been successful in finding the truth about past human rights violations; only five per cent disagreed (see Table 3). Zulu-speaking South Africans were slightly less sure whether the TRC had succeeded in this. This is explained by the refusal of the IFP to participate in the TRC process, which inhibited the investigation of many human rights violations committed in Kwa Zulu Natal. Again, this evaluation was not shared by the white minority, who were undecided (46 per cent) or denied that the TRC had found the truth (39 per cent). Among white respondents the view prevailed that the TRC had not revealed the whole truth, had given a one-sided account of the past or had misrepresented past human rights violations, an opinion held especially by Afrikaans-speaking respondents (Table 3).

South Africans have mixed opinions about the TRC's contribution to reconciliation. 67 per cent of the respondents agreed with the basic principle underlying the TRC process that 'there can be no reconciliation in South Africa unless people—both black and white—have confessed to their apartheid crimes' (Gibson and Gouws 1999). But more and more South Africans believed that 'hearing what went on in the past will make people even more

Affirmative answers to the statement 'The Truth Commission will be/is fair to all sides':

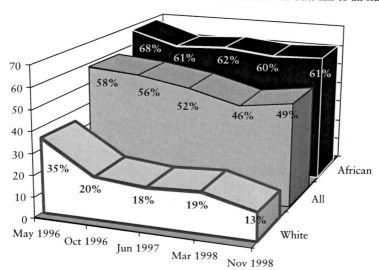

May 1996:   Here are some comments that people have made about what the
               Commission is doing. Please tell me how much you agree or disagree
               with each one. . . 'The Commission will be fair to all sides and to all
               races.' (MRA 1996)

October 1996: Do you think the Truth Commission is fair or do you think it is biased?
               (Research Surveys 1996)

June 1997:   Do you feel that the Truth and Reconciliation Commission is fair and
               unbiased towards all political parties, or does it favour certain political
               parties and is hostile to others? (MarkData 1997)

March 1998:   Here are some comments that people have made about what the
               Commission. Please tell me how much you agree or disagree with each
               one. . . 'The Commission was fair to all sides and to all races.'
               (MRA 1998)

November 1998: Do you think the process of the Truth Commission was fair or do you
               think it was biased? (Research Surveys 1998, conducted only in
               metropolitan areas)

**Figure 4: Public Perceptions of the Impartiality of the TRC
(May 1996–November 1998)**

angry and result in worse feelings between the different races' (MRA 1996:
60 per cent; MRA 1998: 65 per cent). While African respondents overwhelmingly (56 per cent) believed that the TRC has contributed to peace
and reconciliation, most white respondents (54 per cent) maintained that
the TRC has failed to promote either (Research Surveys 1998).

Whether this perception failure might be attributed to the TRC alone is
highly questionable. Instead of examining their own failures to overcome
past divisions, most South Africans tended to blame the Commission.

Table 3: Trust in the Findings of the TRC

	How successful do you think [the Truth Commission] has been as far as uncovering past atrocities is concerned?					
	very successful (+4)	successful (+2)	neither/ don't know (0)	unsuccessful (−2)	very unsuccessful (−4)	mean
African	27%	33%	33%	4%	1%	+1.61
White	3%	12%	46%	18%	21%	−0.83
White/Afrikaans	2%	8%	43%	20%	27%	−1.13
White/English	4%	16%	49%	16%	16%	−0.48
African/Zulu	19%	32%	41%	6%	2%	+1.18
African/Other Languages	35%	33%	28%	3%	1%	+1.96

Data: Research Surveys 1998.

Empirical research by the Human Science Research Council (HSRC 1998) has shown that all groups of the population show significant pride in their own group, while attitudes towards their fellow citizens from other cultural backgrounds are often indifferent, less accepting or outright negative. In the HSRC survey many white South Africans openly admitted disliking Africans (43 per cent) and Indians (38 per cent). Although two out of three African respondents (63 per cent) claimed to like English-speaking whites, negative feelings prevailed towards Afrikaners: 61 per cent of all African respondents said they disliked Afrikaans-speaking whites (HSRC 1998). It seems that many black South Africans still identify Afrikaans-speaking whites as former oppressors. The rejection of the TRC process by Afrikaans-speaking whites has probably further fostered feelings in the black communities that their suffering during apartheid remains unacknowledged by many Afrikaners. It comes as no surprise that mistrust still prevails in post-apartheid South Africa. In April 1998, 61 per cent of all South Africans claimed that 'black and white South Africans will never trust each other'; only 17 per cent disagreed (CASE 1998).

The TRC legislation did not differentiate between past political crimes committed by the liberation movements and those committed by the apartheid regime. The Commission was therefore often criticised for furthering moral indifference, as crimes committed by the illegitimate apartheid government were treated in a similar way as those committed by the liberation movement. In May 1996 most white South Africans in fact claimed that there was no moral difference between acts committed by the liberation movements and those of the security forces during apartheid. When white respondents in our telephone survey were asked whether there is 'a moral difference between somebody who committed an act as a freedom fighter and somebody who committed a crime in order to defend the former political system', 81 per cent responded with 'no'. 11 per cent felt that crimes committed in order to defend the apartheid system were more justified, and 8 per cent said that if those acts were committed during the freedom struggle they were more justified on moral grounds (Theissen 1997, 66). Although these figures provide only rough estimates because of the small sample size of the CSVR study, they nevertheless show that the vast majority of white South Africans did not accept the legitimacy of the armed liberation struggle against apartheid.

These findings are supported by research conducted by James Gibson and Amanda Gouws (1999). The second wave of a representative national panel study included an experimental design. Each respondent was presented with a vignette story about a man named Phillip, who had killed people during the past political conflict in South Africa, but with different, systematic variations of the circumstances in order to find out under which conditions the respondent would blame Phillip. The fictional Phillip was presented either as a member of the armed wing of the ANC, Umkonto we Sizwe (MK), or as member of the security branch of the police. His victims who had been killed were presented either as having been actively involved in the struggle about apartheid or not at all. A further systematic variation of the situation presented 'Phillip' either as following orders or as being in command himself; and his actions were either motivated by hatred against his opponents or as not motivated in this way. This resulted in 16 different versions of the story, which were randomly assigned to African, Coloured, Indian and white South African respondents. Version 1 read as follows:

> Phillip was a member of the Security Branch of the South African police. He was a senior official in the organisation; he gave orders that others had to follow. As a result of his actions, people who were not directly involved in the struggle over apartheid were killed. Phillip says that his actions were motivated by hatred towards those he killed.

Version 16 read:

> Phillip was a member of MK, the ANC's military wing. He was not a senior official in the organisation and therefore had to take orders from others higher up in the organisation. As a result of his actions, people who were directly involved in the struggle over apartheid were killed. Phillip says that his actions were motivated by the belief that what he was doing was necessary and justified by the struggle.

Respondents were asked whether they 'blamed Phillip personally for what happened in this story', and the responses were measured on a ten-point scale. Extreme responses (1 and 10) were categorised respectively as completely blameless and completely blameworthy, while the remainders (2–5 and 6–9) were classified respectively as 'blameless' and 'blameworthy'.

The results of the experiment are shown in Table 4. There are no large differences between African, coloured, Indian and white South Africans in overall response to all 16 versions of the story. On average, all groups of the population tended to attribute the same blame to Phillip. Coloured respondents are only slightly less inclined to blame Phillip (mean: 5.80) compared to African (mean: 6.18), white (mean: 6.29) and Indian (mean: 6.37) respondents. This, however, changes dramatically for variations of the different factors.

In the bottom half of Table 4, the responses to Phillip's membership (in either the MK or the government Security Branch) are analysed. The South African population generally differentiated between acts committed during the armed liberation struggle and those committed by apartheid security

Table 4: Human Rights Violations and Attribution of Blame

Phillip is …	Completely Blameless (1)	Blameless (2–5)	To be blamed (6–9)	Completely to be blamed (10)	Mean	N
All Vignette Versions						
All South Africans	15.4%	28.4%	27.2%	29.0%	6.18	1237
African	17.1%	27.0%	24.3%	31.6%	6.18	1005
White	5.9%	37.8%	43.6%	12.8%	6.29	188
Coloured	17.1%	27.4%	29.1%	26.5%	5.80	117
Asian Origin	6.5%	37.0%	33.8%	22.7%	6.37	157
Phillip as member of MK (ANC)						
All South Africans	21.5%	34.4%	22.8%	21.3%	5.30	636
African	25.6%	36.0%	18.3%	20.0%	4.92	519
White	1.1%	27.3%	53.4%	18.2%	7.16	88
Coloured	14.5%	29.0%	24.2%	32.3%	5.92	62
Asian Origin	7.1%	33.3%	32.1%	27.4%	6.54	84
Phillip as member of Security Branch						
All South Africans	8.9%	22.1%	31.8%	37.1%	7.11	601
African	8.0%	17.3%	30.7%	44.0%	7.52	486
White	10.0%	47.0%	35.0%	8.0%	5.52	100
Coloured	20.0%	25.5%	34.5%	20.0%	5.66	55
Asian Origin	5.7%	41.4%	35.7%	17.1%	6.17	70

Data: Gibson & Gouws 1999.

forces. Members of the MK were blamed less (mean: 5.30) than Security Branch officers (mean: 7.11) by all respondents. The perpetrator was also blamed more strongly when he was portrayed as a senior officer who gave orders. The other two variations, being motivated by hatred and the involvement of victims in the struggle had no significant impact on blame attribution (Gibson and Gouws 1999, 503).

Significant differences in reactions were found for the different racial groups of respondents. While 62 per cent of all African respondents found Phillip as an MK member not really blameworthy for his actions (mean: 4.92), only 28 per cent of white respondents shared this view (mean: 7.16) (see Figure 5). The opposite pattern emerges when Phillip is portrayed as a member of the Security Branch: 75 per cent of all African respondents felt that Phillip should be blamed for his actions (mean: 7.52), but only 43 per cent of white respondents felt the same (mean: 5.52). The population was decisively polarised in the attribution of blame for past human rights violations. While African respondents were less inclined to blame MK members, most white South Africans are more inclined to condone the human rights violations of the Security Branch than those of the armed liberation forces.

In addition, the subjects were asked whether they would forgive Phillip, grant him amnesty, punish him or allow his victims to sue him in court. As might be expected, Gibson and Gouws (1999, 512) found that those who ascribed blame were less likely to forgive (r = −0.66), were much more

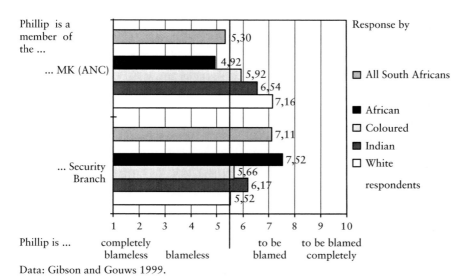

Data: Gibson and Gouws 1999.

Figure 5: Attribution of Blame for Different Allegiances across South African Society (Means)

likely to opt for punishment (r = 0.75) and were less likely to grant amnesty (r = −0.66). But while 71 per cent of all African respondents would have granted amnesty to a member of MK, only 40 per cent were willing to do so for a Security Branch police officer. White respondents shared the opposite view: only 41 per cent agreed to exonerate the MK Phillip, but 79 per cent supported an amnesty for the member of the Security Police (Gibson and Gouws 1999, 513). Thus white and black South Africans strongly disagreed about amnesties granted to perpetrators belonging to the former 'enemy'.

Despite these differences it should be noted that a quite significant minority of all respondents accepted that amnesties should be granted to those who belonged to the other side during the past political conflict. This finding is confirmed by other survey data: although respondents from all groups of the population had reservations about the amnesty process, every second (48 per cent) South African agreed that amnesty should be granted if people come forward and confess to their crimes (Research Surveys 1996). Thus, the principle of amnesty for truth is accepted by a near-majority of South Africans. According to public opinion, the amnesty process should, however, be restricted to a limited number of people (52 per cent support; Mark Data 1997), and those who failed to apply for amnesty should be prosecuted (50 per cent support; Research Surveys 1998). African respondents were slightly more inclined to support amnesty than Coloured, Indian and white South African respondents (MRA 1996; Research Surveys 1996). One aspect of the South African amnesty provisions has obviously violated predominant conceptions of justice. Contrary to the TRC Act, 69 per cent of all respondents felt that victims should be allowed to sue perpetrators in court (Gibson and Gouws 1999, 507). The majority opinion seems to be that justice is not sacrificed if perpetrators are not punished, but justice is not done if victims are not allowed to lay civil claims against their perpetrators.

A common understanding of the apartheid past has still to emerge. Although most South Africans disapproved of apartheid—only 9 per cent of all white respondents claimed in May 1996 they would prefer the return of apartheid—many white respondents (44 per cent) claimed that 'apartheid was merely a good idea badly carried out' (Theissen 1997). At the same time only few white South Africans admitted to having profited from apartheid (19 per cent) (Gibson and Gouws 1997). The predominant view among white South Africans was that life under apartheid was better (45 per cent; 14 per cent thought it was worse) (Gibson and Gouws 1997). In contrast to all other groups, they did not see the liberation of South Africa from authoritarian rule as such a significant contribution to a better life that it might neutralise negative perceptions about the new democratic order. For most whites the new political and social order in South Africa is associated with increased crime, government corruption and economic decline. Given the extremely high crime rate, negative feelings about the new South Africa are understandable, but their strength can only be explained by traditional stereotypes about black majority rule, which were nurtured during the apartheid era. Instead of acknowledging their share of responsibility for past injustices, many beneficiaries of the apartheid system have rather redefined themselves as victims of the new order, an opinion shared by every second white South African (51 per cent; CSVR 1996).

South Africans have highly divergent views not only about who should be blamed for the repression of black communities but also about the consequences of such blame. White respondents were more inclined to attribute responsibility for the repression of black communities to anti-apartheid activists and black 'troublemakers' (57 per cent) than to the government or security forces (46 per cent each) (CSVR 1996). Only a small number of white respondents said that those who supported the NP in the past share some of the responsibility for past repression (14 per cent agreement; 75 per cent disagreement) (CSVR 1996). Even though the majority of white South Africans conceded to feeling ashamed about past human rights violations, only a minority of white respondents supported compensations for the victims of human rights violations and their families (32 per cent, according to HSRC 1995; 39 per cent according to CSVR 1996). Instead, the view prevailed that 'too much is being done for blacks at the expense of white people nowadays' (54 per cent endorsement of this statement) (CSVR 1996).

These data should be interpreted with caution given the small sample, but results from other surveys conducted after 1996 indicate that the TRC process seems not to have substantially changed these trends. The research by Gibson and Gouws (1999) clearly confirms a tendency to blame former enemies. And a poll conducted by the Independent Newspaper Group (1999) indicated that only eight per cent of all white respondents are in favour of compensation policies for disenfranchised communities, such as the return of land—compared to 55 per cent of Indian, 70 per cent of coloured and 73 per cent of African respondents.

Negative attitudes of white South Africans towards the TRC are furthermore strongly correlated with uncritical perceptions about the apartheid past and negative views about black citizens and the new democratic order. White South Africans who were against the TRC tended to glorify the apartheid past ($r = 0.48$; $p<0.001$), were rather unhappy with the new democratic order ($r = -0.42$; $p<0.001$) and were more likely to express racial prejudices ($r = 0.52$; $p<0.001$) (Theissen 1997). They were less supportive of human rights statements ($r = -0.45$; $p<0.001$) and were also less likely to support policies to undo past socioeconomic injustices, including affirmative action, land reform and equal opportunities in education ($r = -0.38$; $p<0.001$) (Theissen 1997). The disapproval of such policies again correlated strongly with the denial of responsibility for past human rights violations ($r = 0.45$; $p<0.001$) (Theissen 1997). Thus, attitudes towards the

TRC and the apartheid past have strong implications for the acceptance of the new democracy, the approval of redistribution to undo past injustices; and they furthermore correlate strongly with attitudes towards African citizens.

C. Discussion

Despite the TRC's efforts to highlight past atrocities, public opinion about the apartheid past has remained largely determined by past political and racial allegiances. Preconceived opinions about the TRC were reinforced rather than changed during its operation. Although many state institutions that have been built after 1994 represent the new emphasis on human rights in South African politics, these institutions are not necessarily embedded in a supportive political culture. Like other transitional societies, South Africa is characterised by a 'cultural lag' (Welch 1993). Public opinion does not yet reflect the spirit of the new official South Africa. The TRC has produced a new account of the apartheid past and instigated public debate, but a collective memory of the apartheid past that is shared across former political and racial divisions has still to emerge.

The hardening of white attitudes towards the TRC and the increasing support by African respondents can be explained by Muzafer Sherif and Carl Hovland's assimilation-contrast hypothesis of attitude change (1961). According to their model, confrontation with information that contradicts positions that are very important to the recipient can lead to a shift of opinion in the non-intended direction. They assume that people change their attitudes only if they are confronted with messages that fall into the realm of non-commitment. If a message falls into the realm of rejection, people are instead motivated to increase the contrast by moving into the direction of further rejection. The assimilation-contrast hypothesis predicts that the TRC will be increasingly supported by those who find their own views and experiences reflected in the work of the Commission. This prediction is confirmed by the empirical evidence, as Africans supported the TRC increasingly during its operation.

For many white South Africans the TRC produced information contradicting their previously held views about apartheid and its system. According to Leon Festinger's theory of dissonance (1957), discrepancies in an individual's cognitive system are a source of psychological distress. People will therefore act to reduce dissonance by actively seeking information that stabilises their belief structure and disregarding information threatening established beliefs. This may explain why most white South Africans were less interested in following the TRC proceedings on television and why some people engaged in strategies of neutralisation by denying the evidence, doubting the accuracy of the information or wrongly attributing responsibility for past atrocities (Cohen 1995, 32–7). Cognitive dissonance can also be reduced by discrediting the source of information, for example, by claiming that the TRC is biased.

The empirical evidence shows that attitudes about the apartheid past are strongly correlated with a set of congruent attitudes. Thus, changing perceptions about the past involves more than accepting mere historical facts. White South Africans also have to break with past justifications of apartheid and acknowledge the harm caused by it. Acknowledging responsibility means as well that demands for reparation or redistribution cannot be ignored. It is therefore easier to engage in strategies of counterclaims or denial, than to accept hurtful truths about the past political system that demand substantial attitudinal and behavioural change. Many white South Africans are locked up in what I have called a 'post-apartheid syndrome' (Theissen 1997), a set of opinions and beliefs that makes adoption of the new political order difficult. In a similar vein Anthony Greenwald (1980) has compared the human mind with a totalitarian state. Like non-democratic totalitarian states resist social and governmental changes, individuals resist cognitive changes. Totalitarian governments distort events and rewrite history to make them fit the 'party line'. Similarly, human minds select and interpret information to fit established beliefs and attitudes. Individuals will only 'rewrite' their memories if there is benefit in making past actions and thoughts cohere with new interests and prevailing social norms. The TRC put the history of past atrocities on the national agenda, but the Commission was hardly able to shift dominant social norms and opinions in conservative white milieus. In a society as divided as South Africa, divergent group values and norms will continue to stabilise conflicting historical perceptions for a long while.

Attitudes that are central to individuals' self-definition are furthermore very resistant to change (Zimbardo and Leippe 1991, 35). To ask former apartheid supporters to change their attitudes about the past quite literally means to ask them to change who they are. Having supported a government that resorted to brutal suppression of opponents threatens the self-concept of having been a good and decent citizen. As people want to keep a positive self-concept about themselves they tend to attribute their mistakes and socially disapproved behaviour to external circumstances and other actors (Ross 1977). According to social identity theory (Tajfel and Turner 1979; Tajfel 1982), individuals will not want the groups that they belong to to be cast in a negative way, and their self-esteem will be enhanced or diminished by the past or present behaviour of the groups they identify with.

The empirical findings discussed in this chapter are largely consistent with these theoretical considerations. As a consequence, legal institutions do not necessarily reach all those they want to teach. The fact that many white South Africans did not like the truth should not lead to the conclusion that the TRC was a fruitless as an endeavour of public education.

Short-term influences on white public opinion should not be confused with long-term prospects for attitudinal change. Furthermore we should not overlook that the process was strongly supported by the black majority and responded to the strongly felt need for official recognition of past injustices. It would also be wrong to reduce the political conflicts during the apartheid era to a simple black-and-white issue. Many human rights violations were committed as part of the informal repression of the apartheid regime by and among black South Africans who were aligned to different political organisations, homeland structures and local authorities. Even if the TRC was able only to reduce these divisions and produce a shared understanding about what had happened inside the black communities, it was a worthwhile exercise.

Finally, there are good reasons to assume that the TRC will contribute in the long run to changing the dominant perceptions of the apartheid past among the white community. According to Karl Mannheim's concept of political generations (1952), dramatic political upheavals, such as wars or the collapse of the past political order, have a particularly strong impact on adolescents. Major political events prompt discussion and re-evaluation of the ideals and values of the political order, and young adults, whose political orientations are not yet fully established, are more willing to participate in these reflections. Particular experiences can mark an entire age-cohort, leading to long-term reorientation of their political beliefs.

Mannheim's generation hypothesis can be sustained by the theoretical considerations and empirical evidence presented above. Young white South Africans, for example, do not have to ward off negative self-perceptions arising out of their own past conduct, like feelings of guilt or immorality, when acknowledging that apartheid has caused harm to others. Although their rapid reorientation is restricted by the social environment in which they grow up, the empirical evidence shows already divergent perceptions of the TRC process by young white South Africans compared to older generations. Prevailing historical perceptions in the white community will therefore shift, partially under the influence of young generations replacing older generations, who experienced the apartheid system. Similar long-term changes of the collective memory of a 'perpetrator society' are well documented for Germany after 1945 (Bergmann and Erb 1997; Institut für Demoskopie 1993). In the South African context, Booysen and Fleetwood (1994) have found considerable reorientation of political attitudes among white students between 1989 and 1991.

Although attitudes of whites towards the TRC may have temporarily hardened to absorb the distressing information that was revealed during the TRC process, it is rather unlikely that most white South Africans will sustain uncritical perceptions about the apartheid past. The dominant political culture of the new South Africa reflects the historical perspectives presented by the TRC process, and even though revisionist perspectives may still exist and be shared by certain minorities, they will become increasingly disapproved of. The fate of former NP leader de Klerk is a typical example. Increasingly losing credibility because of his inability to explain past human rights violations during his rule as President, he decided to resign. Another indicator is the erosion of white political milieus that still represent to a certain degree the old apartheid order. In the second general election of 1999 white political support shifted to the liberal DP, which exploited successfully the general dissatisfaction of many white South Africans. Both, the right-wing Afrikaner Freedom Party and the New National Party, still struggling to get rid of its image as the former party of apartheid, lost considerable ground. The final dissolution of the New National Party (NNP) in April 2005 reflects a symbolic shift in the political culture of South Africa. The party disintegrated. Its leader, Marthinus van Schalkwyk, and other NNP politicians who had not defected to other opposition parties, decided to take up ANC membership. For crossing the floor Schalkwyk was offered the post of Minister of Environmental Affairs and Tourism in the cabinet of Thabo Mbeki. Thus, eleven years after the first democratic elections in South Africa the remains of the former apartheid party ended in a strange marriage with its previous opponent.

IV. CONCLUSION

The South African TRC was a very successful tool for stimulating public debate about the apartheid past in South Africa. The public hearings of the TRC were extensively reported by the media and captured the attention of most South Africans. Only few societies have been able to achieve such an intensive public debate about their recent past during the immediate post-authoritarian era. Compared to criminal trials, the TRC provided the South African public with a more comprehensive and victim-orientated account of past human rights violations. The TRC also enquired into injustices that are usually beyond the narrow scope of criminal law. Instead of reinforcing denials and polarised views of former adversaries, the amnesty process of the TRC forced perpetrators to admit to their crimes, thus increasing the mutual recognition of past political crimes. Thus the TRC is more likely to produce a shared understanding of the past than criminal trials or a general amnesty would have. This should not distract attention from some shortcomings of the TRC process: its mandate was too narrow to investigate the 'legalised injustices' of the apartheid system. Although many victims could tell their stories, all their expectations could not be met. The promise of truth could often be fulfilled only if perpetrators were forthcoming. It remains also to be seen whether the TRC was indeed such a genuine process of restorative justice as is often proclaimed. After the TRC submitted a detailed reparation policy to the public, the South African government has failed to provide victims and survivors with what these regarded as substantial reparations.

The review of various public opinion surveys shows that the TRC gained authority, especially among those who suffered during apartheid, but was distrusted by former apartheid supporters. It was capable of presenting a 'new' history of the apartheid past but not of fundamentally changing the prevailing views of those who had backed racial discrimination and repression. The armed struggle against apartheid and the repression by the forces of apartheid are still largely judged differently by white and black South Africans. While the principle of refraining from criminal punishment if a perpetrator makes a full disclosure was accepted by many South Africans, most felt that justice is sacrificed when victims are prohibited from laying claims for compensation against perpetrators.

But are truth commissions fruitless endeavours of public education if their findings are not accepted by particular minorities? I do not think so. The short-term reactions of white South Africans towards the TRC process are not a reliable yardstick for future changes of public opinion. The empirical evidence shows that young white South Africans are more likely to subscribe to the historical record of the TRC than their parents' generation. Legal institutions should not primarily strive for public consent. If they do not stir controversy or disapproval in certain quarters of society, they have failed. If there had been no discontent, deeply rooted justifications of past abuses must not have been challenged. Undemocratic and authoritarian tendencies would have been imported secretly into the new democratic institution without being subjected to public discourse. Although new revelations are often met with denial and legal institutions dealing with past atrocities may be distrusted by some social groups, these denials cannot be sustained forever. Truth commissions therefore have an important function in establishing a new normative foundation for society. They do offer a new version of history. If their narratives become dominant, denial will be considered as political incorrect and be socially disapproved of. Even former supporters of the past regime will try to rewrite their memories and adapt step by step to the new dominant narrative.

REFERENCES

Bergmann, Werner and Erb, Rainer. 1997. *Anti-Semitism in Germany: The Post-Nazi Epoch since 1945.* New Brunswick: Transaction Publishing.

Bizos, George. 1998. *No One to Blame? In Pursuit of Justice in South Africa.* Cape Town: David Philip.

Booysen, Susan. 1989. The Legacy of Ideological Control: The Afrikaner's Youth's Manipulated Political Consciousness. *Politikon* 16(1): 7–25.

Booysen, Susan and Fleetwood, J. 1994. Political Events as Agent of Political Socialisation: A Case of Change in Racial Attitudes in South Africa. *South African Journal of Sociology* 25(3): 95–103.

Booysen, Susan and Kotzé, Hennie. 1985. The Political Socialisation of Isolation: A Case Study of the Afrikaner Student Youth. *Politikon* 12(2): 23–46.

Centre for the Study of Violence and Reconciliation (CSVR). 1996. *Attitudes of White South Africans towards the Truth and Reconciliation Commission and the Apartheid Past, May 1996*. Principal Investigators: Gunnar Theissen and Brandon Hamber. Johannesburg: CSVR/South African Data Archive (SADA 0080).

——. 2000a. *Reparations Update*. Johannesburg: CSVR, February 2000. Available at http://www.reconciliation.org.za.

Chapman, Audrey R and Rubenstein, Leonard S (eds). 1998. *Human Rights and Health: The Legacy of Apartheid*. Washington, DC: American Association for the Advancement of Science.

Cochrane, James, De Gruchy, John W and Martin, Stephen (eds). 1999. *Facing the Truth: South African Faith Communities and the Truth & Reconciliation Commission*. Cape Town: David Philip.

Coetzee, Martin. 2003. An Overview of the TRC Amnesty Process. In *The Provocations of Amnesty. Memory, Justice and Impunity*, edited by C Villa-Vicencio and Erik Doxtader. Cape Town: David Philip.

Cohen, Stanley. 1995. *Denial and Acknowledgement: The Impact of Information about Human Rights Violations*. Jerusalem: Centre for Human Rights, Hebrew University.

Community Agency for Social Enquiry (CASE). 1998. *Monitoring Socio-economic Rights in South Africa: Public Perceptions, June 1998*. Principal Investigators: Piers Pigou, Ran Greenstein, and Nahla Valji. Johannesburg: CASE.

Corporación Nacional de Reparación y Reconciliación (CNRR). 1996. *Informe Final de la Corporación Nacional de Reparación y Reconciliación, Diciembre 1996*. Santiago: CNRR.

Department of Justice and Constitutional Development. 2007. *President's Fund, Annual Report 2006/07*. Pretoria.

Du Bois-Pedain, Antje. 2007. *Transitional Amnesty in South Africa*. Cambridge: University Press.

Dugard, John. 1997. Is the Truth and Reconciliation Process Compatible with International Law? An Unanswered Question. *South African Journal on Human Rights* 13: 258–68.

Dyzenhaus, David. 1998. *Truth, Reconciliation and the Apartheid Legal Order*. Cape Town: Juta.

Festinger, Leon. 1957. *A Theory of Cognitive Dissonance*. Stanford: Stanford University Press.

Gagiano, Jannie. 1986. Meanwhile on the 'Boereplaas': Student Attitudes to Political Protest and Political Systems' Legitimacy at Stellenbosch University. *Politikon* 13(2): 3–23.

Gibson, James L. 2004. *Overcoming Apartheid: Can Truth Reconcile a Nation?* New York: Russell Sage Foundation.

Gibson, James L and Gouws, Amanda. 1997. Support for the Rule of Law in the Emerging South African Democracy. *International Social Science Journal* 152: 173–91.

——. 1999. Truth and Reconciliation in South Africa: Attributions for Blame and the Struggle over Apartheid. *American Political Science Review* 93(3): 501–17.

Greenwald, Anthony. 1980. The Totalitarian Ego: Fabrication and Revision of Personal History. *American Psychologist* 35: 603–18.

Halbwachs, Maurice. 1985. *Das Gedächtnis und seine sozialen Bedingungen.* Translated by H Lhoest-Offermann. Frankurt: Fischer.

Hayner, Priscilla B. 1994. 15 Truth Commissions, 1974 to 1994: A Comparative Study. *Human Rights Quarterly* 16(4): 597–655.

Human Science Research Council (HSRC). 1992. *October 1992 Multibus.* Data collecting agency: Mark Data. Pretoria: HSRC.

——. 1995. *Omnibus, May 1995.* Data collecting agency: Mark Data. Pretoria: HSRC.

——. 1998. *Perceptions, November 1998.* Data collecting agency: Market Research Africa/AC Nielsen. Pretoria: HSRC (E.1698).

Idasa. 1994. *Idasa National Elections Survey, August 1994.* Cape Town: Institute for Democracy in South Africa/South African Data Archive (SADA 0109).

Independent Newspapers. 1999. *Reality Check.* CASE and Strategy & Tactics. Survey published in the *Cape Times, The Star, The Mercury, Diamond Fields Advertiser* and *Pretoria News*, 19–23 April 1999 and 28 April 1999.

Institut für Demoskopie. 1993. *Jahrbuch für öffentliche Meinung, 1986–1992.* Wien: Saur.

Kritz, Neil J (ed). 1995. *Transitional Justice: How Emerging Democracies Reckon with Former Regimes*, 3 vols. Washington, DC: United States Institute for Peace Press.

Krog, Antjie. 1998. *Country of My Skull.* New York: Random House.

Llewellyn, Jennifer J and Howse, Robert. 1999. Institutions for Restorative Justice: The South African Truth and Reconciliation Commission. *University of Toronto Law Journal* 49(3): 355–88.

Malamud-Goti, Jaime. 1996. *Game without End: State Terrorism and the Politics of Justice.* Norman: University of Oklahoma Press.

Mannheim, Karl. 1952. The Problem of Generations. In *Essays on the Sociology of Knowledge*, edited by Karl Mannheim. London: Routledge & Kegan Paul.

Mark Data. 1997. *Reactions to the Truth and Reconciliation Commission among Members of the General Public, July 1997.* Press Release. Principal Investigator: Lawrence Schlemmer. Pretoria: Mark Data.

Market Research Africa. 1996. *Truth Commission Conducted for Business Day, May 1996 Multibus.* Johannesburg: Market Research Africa/AC Nielsen (E0624).

——. 1998. *Truth Commission Evaluation Conducted for Business Day, March 1998 Multibus.* Johannesburg: Research Africa/AC Nielsen (E1422).

Motala, Ziyad. 1996. The Constitutional Court's Approach to International Law and its Method of Interpretation in the 'Amnesty Decision': Intellectual Honesty or Political Expediency? *South African Yearbook of International Law* 21: 29–59.

Nattrass, Nicoli. 1999. The Truth and Reconciliation Commission on Business and Apartheid: A Critical Evaluation. *African Affairs* 98: 373–91.

Orr, Wendy. 2000. Reparation Delayed is Healing Retarded. In *Looking Back, Reaching Forward: Reflections on the Truth and Reconciliation Commission in South Africa*, edited by C Villa-Vicencio and W Verwoerd. Cape Town: University of Cape Town Press.

Osiel, Mark. 1997. *Mass Atrocity, Collective Memory and the Law.* New Brunswick, NJ: Transaction Publishers.

Research Surveys. 1996. *Truth Commission, October 1996.* Cape Town: Research Surveys.

——. 1998. *Truth Commission, November 1998.* Cape Town: Research Surveys.

Rhoodie, Nic J, De Kock, Chris and Couper, Mick P. 1985. White Perceptions of Socio-political Change in South Africa. In *South Africa: A Plural Society in Transition,* edited by DJ Van Vuuren. Durban: Butterworths.

Ross, Lee. 1977. The Intuitive Psychologist and His Shortcomings: Distortion in the Attribution Process. *Advances in Experimental Social Psychology* 10: 174–221.

Schlemmer, Lawrence. 1992. Public Attitudes and South Africa's Future Democracy. *Information Update (Pretoria)* 2(4): 4–6.

Sherif, Muzafer and Hovland, Carl I. 1961. *Social Judgement: Assimilation and Contrast Effects in Communication and Attitude Change.* New Haven: Yale University Press.

Slye, Ronald C. 1999. Apartheid as a Crime Against Humanity: A Submission to the South African Truth and Reconciliation Commission. *Michigan Journal of International Law* 20(2): 267–300.

Stack, Louise. 1997. Courting Disaster? Justice and South Africa's New Democracy. Research Report No 55, September 1997. Johannesburg: Centre for Policy Studies.

Tajfel, Henri and Turner, John C. 1979. An Integrative Theory of Social Conflict. In *The Psychology of Intergroup Relations,* edited by W Austin and S Worchel. Monterey, CA: Brooks/Cole.

Tajfel, Henri (ed). 1982. *Social Identity and Intergroup Relations.* Cambridge: Cambridge University Press.

Theissen, Gunnar. 1997. *Between Acknowledgement and Ignorance: How White South Africans Have Dealt with the Apartheid Past.* Johannesburg: Centre for the Study of Violence and Reconciliation.

——. 1998. Amnesty for Apartheid Crimes? The South African Truth and Reconciliation Commission and International Law. Unpublished LL M Thesis, University of the Western Cape.

Theissen, Gunnar and Hamber, Brandon. 1998. A State of Denial: White South Africans' Attitudes to the Truth and Reconciliation Commission. *Indicator South Africa (Durban)* 15(1): 8–12.

Truth and Reconciliation Commission (TRC). 1998. *Truth and Reconciliation Commission of South Africa Report,* vols 1–5. Cape Town: Juta.

Tutu, Desmond. 1999. *No Future without Forgiveness.* New York: Doubleday.

Varney, Howard and Sarkin, Jeremy. 1997. Failing to Pierce the Hit-squad Veil: An Analysis of the Malan Trial. *South African Journal of Criminal Justice* 10: 141–61.

Welch, Stephan. 1993. *The Concept of Political Culture.* New York: St Martins Press.

Zimbardo, Phillip G and Leippe, Michael R. 1991. *The Psychology of Attitude Change and Social Influence.* Philadelphia: Temple University Press.

6

From Silence to Testimony: The Role of Legal Institutions in the Restoration of the Collective Memories of Korean 'Comfort Women'

YOUNG-HEE SHIM

I. FIFTY YEARS OF SILENCE

THE ISSUE OF the so-called Korean 'military comfort women' is not only an unprecedented case of systematic violence against women and infringement of human rights and women's rights, but also an unprecedented and shocking case of a systematic violation by a state power: the Japanese government and military. More shocking is that the Japanese government kept on denying its involvement until it finally had to concede its involvement recently. The plight of the comfort women—the name given to women who were forced to become sexual slaves for Japanese troops during World War II—remained hidden for about fifty years and surfaced as a public issue only in 1991. Why was there such a long silence?

In Japan, neither the government nor the Japanese people wanted to face the issue, because they were the offenders and were to blame. Furthermore, when the Japanese Government General in Korea retreated from Korea in 1945, they destroyed most of the files related to war atrocities and forcible draft, so there is very little data left. Even today in Japan, social pressures not to challenge the status quo are overwhelming. War atrocities are a particular taboo. After the war, Japan focused on having been the victim of the bombing of Hiroshima and Nakasaki, abandoning the more painful path of reflecting on their own conduct. Even some Japanese recognise this. Yoshimi, a Japanese historian, has stated, 'I have lived here all my life, and I know that Japan only talks about half of its history, the half where Japan is victimized' (*New York Times*, 28 January 1992).

The silence on this issue has been similar in Korea, but for different reasons. Korea, left with no supporting data, was not in a position to bring the issue up. Furthermore, in Korea, a patriarchal society with a strong tradition of women's chastity, it would have been embarrassing and shameful to talk about the issue. This is demonstrated by the fact that many of the survivors were shunned by their families when they returned. Until recently South Korea's school textbooks, like Japan's, have scarcely mentioned the women's plight. Even the victims themselves were too humiliated to talk about it.

However, with media organisations focusing on the 50th anniversary of Pearl Harbor and with the formation of the Korean Council for the Women Drafted for Sexual Service by Japan (KCWD), some of the surviving Korean comfort women decided that this was the moment to press for their case. Three went to Tokyo in December 1991 to claim damages against the Japanese government. However, the government's chief spokesman, Koichi Kato, reiterated that Japan considered all of its war reparations to South Korea paid and denied that the army had organised or run brothels. During the visit of Japanese Prime Minister Kiichi Miyazawa to Seoul in January 1992, the issue that has seared the consciousness of Koreans unleashed an outpouring of shocked responses. A telephone line was installed for comfort women to report their cases, and victims finally began to talk. Only recently, a research team was organised in Korea and tried to demand reparation from Japan.

The Korean comfort women had remained silent for fifty years before they came forward to testify on the war atrocities they had suffered. Hwang Kum Joo, a survivor who was 69 years old in 1992, said that she still finds it difficult to talk about her experiences: 'There's still a feeling of humiliation in talking about it' (*New York Times*, 23 February 1992). Why did she and many others remain silent so long? Why did it take so long before they could talk? What kind of trauma did they suffer all their lives after their return? What made them come forward in the end and speak out? What has been the role of legal institutions in this process? And more generally, what is their part in restoring collective memories these days?

This chapter attempts to answer these questions by analysing the lives of Korean comfort women after their return to Korea with a focus on the concept of collective memory. It consists of two parts, the first focusing on losing collective memories and the second on their recovery. In this chapter, I use the term 'collective memories' in contrast to personal memories: collective memories are situated between personal memories and history. It is important for the establishment of collective memories that a group or society not only shares its memories—the act of speaking is decisive (Kim 1998, 157–211; Yoon 1992).

The famous saying 'out of sight, out of mind' hints at the relationship between 'seeing' and memory. A similar relationship seems to hold between talking and memory. Remembering a certain event or forgetting about it is closely related to whether one talks about it or keeps silent on it. This suggests not only that we can talk about a certain event based on our memory, but also that we can bring the fading or 'dead' memory to life again by talking, such as during an interview. Thus memory/forgetting on the one hand and talk/silence on the other are two important dimensions for analysing memories.

Memory/forgetting and talk/silence are decisive not just for personal memories but also in the collective or social realm. The process of forgetting affects both individuals and collectivities, and for the latter it leads to the loss of collective memories. If memories are kept alive on the individual as well as collective level, it leads to the social production of collective memories, such as the commemoration of events. Analogous processes are related to the dimension talk/silence. If memories are silenced on both individual and collective levels, social amnesia is the result. But when individuals start talking, this influences others and often induces others to talk, thus leading to a restoration of collective memories. In a longstanding situation of silenced memories, like the comfort women in Korea, various intellectual and political factors, such as social movement organisations, public discourse and government, are often necessary to prompt the beginning of talking.

The importance of simply talking cannot be emphasised enough when we consider in which way personal memories produce collective memories, Based on the relationship between these two dimensions of memory/forgetting and talk/silence, the following typology can be developed (Table 1).

This typology simultaneously can be read as stages of change (Figure 1). In this context the process of losing and recovering the collective memories of the Korean comfort women can be interpreted as a process that goes through different stages from personal memory to collective forgetting and to the recovery of memory, which is then reflected in the simultaneous process from silence to talk and then to testimony.

Table 1: The Relationship between Memory/Forgetting and Silence/Talking

	Silence	Talking
Memory	Memory but Silence (Stage I)	Memory through Talk (Stage IV)
Forgetting	Silence and Forgetting (Stage II)	Talk but Forgetting (Stage III)

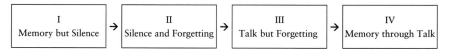

I Memory but Silence	→	II Silence and Forgetting	→	III Talk but Forgetting	→	IV Memory through Talk

Figure 1: Stages of Memory and Forgetting/Silence and Talk

I will approach the problem basically within this framework. More specifically, with regard to the loss of the collective memories, I will focus on the following four questions: (1) How was the situation immediately after the comfort women returned? (2) Why did these women remain silent for almost 50 years, and why was it so difficult to talk? (3) What were/are the effects of this silence? (4) How did they try to cope with the pain caused by being silenced? With regard to the *recovery* of collective memories, this chapter will focus on the following three questions: (1) How did the comfort women come forward to testify—more specifically, did legal institutions play any major role in this process? And if so, how? (2) What effects has testifying had on their lives? (3) What contributions did they make to the recovery of collective memories in Korea, and in Japan?

The total number of Korean comfort women who finally came forward and broke the silence on their plight is 199 (including those who acquired citizenship after they had returned to Korea and those who are now deceased). Amongst these, forty-eight (including those whose testimonies are published in the three volumes of collected testimonies and not including those who have testified but live in China) were contacted by the researcher. I conducted in-depth interviews with six of the women from March to August 1999. The characteristics of the interviewees are shown in Table 2. I will also refer to the cases published in three volumes of collected testimonies (KCWD 1997a, b, c; see also KCWD 1993; KCWD 1998).

Who are these women interviewees, and how do they differ from other comfort women? This can be answered by examining some of the important moments in their lives such as their return to Korea, reporting, giving testimony, etc. First, unlike many other victims, these women were fortunate

Table 2: The Interviewees

Case	Age (Year of Birth)	Method of Recruitment	Location and Duration of Sex Slavery
1	79 (1922)	Draft (1941)	Jilin, China, four years
2	74 (1925)	False pretence of employment	Manchu, China, duration unknown
3	73 (1926)	False pretence of employment	1 and a half years, location unknown
4	73 (1926)	False pretence of employment	Burma, duration unknown
5	73 (1926)	Sold	Hunchun, China, 3 years
6	76 (1923)	False pretence of employment	Kainando Island, China, 5 years

enough to get back to Korea after their sexual slavery. Notwithstanding the hardships of their return given their economic situation, physical pain and mental conflicts, compared with those who died or could not come back, they can be considered as lucky ones. Second, among those who returned these are the women who reported themselves as comfort women victims. Though the reasons for reporting might have been diverse, it cannot have been easy to reveal themselves as comfort women. Of course there are some women who lived in silence and died without reporting, and others who are still alive but have not reported for various reasons; their numbers are not known. Third, these women all testified and thus went one step further than those who only reported. There are some women who reported but died without making testimonies and others who may yet testify.

The interviewees indeed can be considered as 'survivors' of various moments of extreme difficulty in their lives. Considering the mental anguish they probably suffered during the course of returning to Korea and reporting, it is rather a miracle that they still decided to testify and make their stories public. Maybe history like this can only be written by 'survivors' like these women.

In order to put these women's lives in their historical and social context, I want briefly to describe their situation during and immediately after the war.[1]

II. KOREAN COMFORT WOMEN DURING AND AFTER THE WAR

Japan started building 'comfort stations' in the mid-1930s, and from 1937 (the beginning of the Sino-Japanese War) to 1945 (the end of World War II) 100,000 to 200,000 women were eventually lured or forcibly taken to Japanese battlefronts across Asia, including China, Southeast Asia and the Pacific Islands (McDougall 1998). Eighty per cent of these women were from Korea, and most of them teenagers (*New York Times*, 27 January 1992). Confined to small rooms under surveillance, the women were forced to have sex with 20–30 soldiers a day, the men being 'processed' through the 'comfort stations' day and night often at 15-minute intervals. Venereal disease was rampant, and thousands of the women died, including many who were apparently killed by soldiers (*New York Times*, 27 January 1992).

'It was like being raped everyday. It was not a life of a human being. The Japanese treated their dogs better than they treated us', Hwang Kum Joo, one of the victims told the *New York Times*. She recalled how she and other teenage girls from their village in the southern Korean Peninsula were put on trains and told they would be given manufacturing jobs like hundreds of thousands of men drafted into forced labour (*New York*

---

[1] For a more detailed description, see Shim 1994 and Chung 1997.

Times, 23 February 1992). Instead, the women—as young as 12 years old—were kept like animals in filthy barracks, where Hwang reported they had to serve up to 50 men a day. Women who contracted venereal disease were shot or simply left to die. Anyone resisting the advances of the men was beaten, she has said. 'Young women in their 30s come and ask me, "Why did you go?" How could anyone ask me that? How could anyone be willing to go into such indescribable conditions?" (*New York Times*, 23 February 1992).

A Japanese woman, who was 71 in 1992 and had been a sixth-grade teacher in Korea during the war, recalled how she was ordered by the principal to choose 'physically well-developed' girls for war service. She chose eight girls, believing, she said, that they would be put to work in a factory for aircraft parts. Back in Korea a few years ago, she visited some other former students and learned the truth. She said, 'I could not meet the women. They were still too hurt, physically and mentally. I am so very sorry' (*New York Times*, 27 January 1992).

In the early 1990s, some Japanese soldiers born between 1910 and 1925 and then in their seventies and eighties also began to talk about their experiences during the invasions by the Japanese army. They might have broken their silence because of a traditional Buddhist belief that one should confess to one's sins and crimes before death. For example, Yoshida Kiyoji, former head of the mobilisation department at the Simonoseki Branch of the Japanese Army, published a book entitled *I Dragged Korean People This Way*. Furthermore, in Tokyo a telephone line set up in January 1992 by groups supporting the comfort women got 230 calls during one week, the vast majority from men in their late sixties and seventies, who confirmed that the military had established and run brothels and moreover confessed to having used them (*New York Times*, 27 January 1992).

As can be imagined, the living conditions of the comfort women were terrible. They were forced to work from noon to midnight, serving soldiers during the day and officers during the night. They were confined to shabby tents or rooms made of boards and divided by curtains, where they were provided with one or two blankets only and no sheets (KCWD 1991a and 1992). They lived under constant surveillance, were prohibited from leaving the fenced area and were severely beaten when they refused to serve. Furthermore, the Japanese prevented their escape by sending them to China or other foreign regions where they could not speak the language and did not know the place.

The physical and health conditions of these women were horrific. Even though there were regular medical inspections, venereal disease was rampant, they took quinine most of the time and many died. As much as from illness, they suffered from the humiliation and torment of being sexually abused. The Japanese soldiers openly expressed their contempt for them and treated them as disposable objects or as common property (KCWD 1991a and 1991b). They were frequently transported to other places to serve more soldiers and sometimes mobilised to move ammunitions and other military materials and even to fight in the war (KCWD 1991a and 1991b).

After their defeat in 1945, the Japanese troops did not tell the comfort women that the war was over. When the military finally retreated, the Korean comfort women were deserted and left to starvation and terminal illness, or were forced to suffer 'deaths of honour' together with the troops. Others were gathered in tunnels and killed by bombs or were handed over to the Allied Forces and again forced to serve. In this way, military comfort women were treated as 'expendable goods' (KCWD 1991b and 1992). Some of those who were lucky enough to survive returned to Korea. Upon seeing their homeland from aboard the returning ships, some of these women committed suicide by throwing themselves into the sea rather than face their families with their torn bodies and hurt minds.

III. THE LIVES OF KOREAN COMFORT WOMEN AFTER THEIR RETURN

The returned comfort women had difficult lives. Most of them showed serious symptoms of physical and mental illness for the rest of their lives. Most suffered from venereal disease, some died early and others could never have children. Psychological trauma led some of them to shun other people and avoid any sort of social interaction; some had even forgotten their mother tongue. Many could not go back to their families, and most of them could not get married. They lived in poor economic circumstances and mostly held only menial jobs like peddling or working as poorly paid housemaids (KCWD 1991a, 1991b and 1992). Many of those who did return to their hometowns were shunned or simply did not tell the truth about what they had lived through.

In order to return to Korea, these women had to overcome huge difficulties. However, return to the home country did not mean that problems were resolved; on the contrary, more difficulties were waiting for them. Post-war Korean society was still agricultural and very traditional. Families and hometowns were the basis of life, and it was difficult even to imagine that a young woman could live alone in a city that was not her hometown. Nonetheless, many comfort women decided not to return to their hometowns: their lives were uprooted and their family ties dissolved. In other words, they could not live normal lives as women in post-war Korea. Table 3 gives an overview of the family situation, work and income, and personal relationships of the six interviewed women.

Table 3: The Lives of the Interviewees after Returning to Korea

Case	Return, Hometown and Family Ties	Work and Income	Personal Relationships
1	• Returned to Seoul • Hometown was Buyo but had lived in North Korea • No parents	• Worked as a waitress • Peddled matches, cigarettes, etc	• Not married • Brought up 5 orphaned children during the Korean War • None of the children lives in a household with her
2	• Returned to hometown in Kyongsang Province • Had a family, but drifted around	• Worked as a waitress	• Not married • Brought up her sister's grandson and now lives with him
3	• Returned to Pusan • Hometown was Pyongyang, North Korea • Had no close family in the South	• Worked as waitress in bars • Peddled vegetables, bread, etc	• Married at age 34 to a 60-year-old widower with 4 daughters • Has a daughter of her own
4	• Returned to Inchon • Hometown was Kwangju, Cholla Province • No parents, but had lived with her uncle • Had cousins in Kwangju	• Worked in a restaurant for 10 years • Worked as a housemaid for 25 years	• Lived with a man who later was found to have a wife • Has two daughters
5	• Returned to Cholwon, Kangwondo Province • Hometown was Pyongchang, Kangwondo • Parents had died • Two sisters, one deceased, the other is deaf	• Worked as a waitress in bars • Peddled US military goods • Worked as a housemaid • Joined a temple in a monkish life	• Not married • Had a lover who was forced to marry another woman and subsequently committed suicide • Had a daughter, who died at the age of 7 months
6	• Returned to hometown, Taegu • Had parents and 8 siblings	• Husband traded scrap iron • Gathered and sold herbs and medical plants	• Married to a widower who already had 5 children • No children of her own

Among the six women interviewed, four did not go back, and only two returned to their hometowns. What kept them from going back to where they had come from? First, some did not want to go back because their close family members no longer lived there. Second, those whose hometown was in North Korea could not go back even if they wanted to, because most of them arrived in Pusan, at the southern end of Korea. Most importantly though, many did not want to go back because they were afraid of encountering someone who might know about their war-time past.

Even those two among the interviewees who went back to their home-towns did not stay there but drifted around. One interviewee gave as a reason that she could not stand her family's pressure to get married to someone who did not know about her past (case 2). Another was afraid that she might encounter those men whom she had met at the 'comfort sta-tions' (case 6). Thus, all these women became uprooted—sooner or later, voluntarily or unvoluntarily—and were cut off from their familial and social networks.

For those who were cut off from their families or who could not talk about their experiences even after returning to their hometowns, their families could hardly provide any support. Nonetheless, the returned comfort women missed family life and familial emotional bonds dearly. One woman (case 1) brought up abandoned children during the Korean War, when it was difficult for even adults to survive on their own. Another one (case 2) took in a niece's son when he was three years old, eventually relying on him as her own child. One could assume that they did such things because they were scared to live alone. However, con-sidering how difficult it is to bring up children and how much care and love they need, and considering that one of them brought up five aban-doned children, a much better explanation seems to be that they wanted to establish families of their own and did so in the only ways that were open to them.

In the post-war period in Korea it was still considered natural that most women should get married, have children and look after their families and households (and women's socio-economic participation in larger society was accordingly highly restricted). However, most of the comfort women victims did not or could not marry and/or did not or could not have children, as was expected from 'normal women'. Three of the six interviewees did not get married. Of the other three, one married an unusually old man (case 3), one lived with a man who it was discovered already had a wife (case 4) and one married a widower who had a large number of children to take care of (case 6). Only two of them had children of their own (cases 3 and 4).

Thus, to these women it was their greatest *han* (pain) and torment not to have lives like other 'normal women' as one of the interviewees said (case 2). The issue regarding whether marriage is a good thing in a patriarchal society might be relevant for a small number of women even today, but it was totally irrelevant for the former comfort women during the post-war period. As a result, their intimate relationships, marriages and family life could not be considered as 'normal'.

After World War II, Korea was in a bad economic condition, and the population found survival difficult, due to long exploitation by Japanese colonial rule. The comfort women victims suffered from particularly appalling conditions. Those who could not go back to their hometowns were especially bad off because their families could not provide support in times of economic distress. They had to earn a living, but there was very little from which they could choose, since women's participation in the labour market was extremely restricted at that time. The Korean War, which broke out in 1950 and continued until 1953, exacerbated their situation. They barely survived, mostly by working in sex-service industries, as personal servants and/or as peddlers. The comfort women I interviewed worked as waitresses in restaurants (cases 1, 2 and 4) and taverns (cases 2, 3 and 5), peddled matches, cigarettes, clothes, US military goods like clothes and food (cases 1, 3 and 5), worked as housemaids (cases 4 and 5), gathered and sold herbs and medical plants (case 6) and joined a in a monkish life (case 5).

IV. THE TRAUMA AND THE AFTERMATH: THE IMPACT OF SILENCE

For the women who were forced to become comfort women, their trauma had a massive impact on the whole of their lives after they returned, and their whole lives can be considered as nothing but the aftermath—physical, mental and social—of these experiences. In this section I will focus on the consequences for the physical and mental health of the comfort women victims and in particular on the traumatic consequences of being barred from 'normal' intimacy and normal marital relations. Reports on the women's health were taken during the interviews and are shown in Table 4 along with relevant details about their personal relationships.

Probably the women victims themselves were not aware of it, but during interviews, they all expressed in one way or the other that upon returning to Korea they had been frightened by coming back to 'real life'. Their lives on Japanese army bases in foreign countries had been a sort of 'moratorium' from their normal lives, far away from social relations and expectations in Korea, not to mention a deviation from the expected course of their development and lives. Furthermore, they had been living in a context in which normal social ethics and values had been suspended. When they realised that they were going back to their previous lives and relationships, they probably felt fear and anxiety. Even though the life in the comfort stations

Table 4: Traumatic Consequences for the Physical Health, Mental Health and Social/Personal Lives of Six Comfort Women

Case	Physical Health	Mental Health	Social/Personal Life
1	• Had serious gynaecological surgery from which seven other comfort women did not survive	• Disgust of men (horrified at the mere thought of them)	• Did not get married and did not have children of her own • The children she brought up left her when they were grown up
2	• Had her side seared with a hot iron	• Nightmares • Ran away from home and drifted around to avoid marriage	• Did not get married and did not have children
3	• Her shoulder was twisted and permanently deformed due to soldiers' kicking • Has a bent back • Has a hearing problem due to being beaten	• Disgust of men	• Was married to a man of 60 years when she was only 34 • Was deceived about the marriage
4	• Has bladder problems • Has arthritis	• None mentioned	• Lived with a man who was found out to be already married • Had two daughters
5	• Has multiple health problems • Has had seven operations • Has a hearing problem because her eardrum was destroyed due to being beaten	• Six attempts at suicide • Preoccupation with her difficult life and unfortunate fate	• Avoids contact with others and with the outer world • Joined a temple
6	• Was hit by a sword • Had an operation to remove gallstones	• Drifted around • Feels that her life was 'destroyed' due to her experience as a comfort woman	• Married a widower • Could not have a child of her own because she had to take care of five children from her husband's previous relationship.

was painful and humiliating, there were no family members, friends or neighbours to witness their situation or judge them morally. However, on coming back they became conscious of the moral judgment of their families and communities, and this certainly was an enormous burden.

The fact that many women victims did not return, gave up on returning or committed suicide before returning, demonstrates that they were aware of what was awaiting them at home. Those who did return nearly never told the truth about their experiences to anybody. All this demonstrates the intensity of the pain they went through during the return, in the first months after their return and during the long years afterwards. The social pressure they felt prompted many women not to tell their stories, not even to their families, but rather to keep complete silence. In fact, none of the six women we interviewed had told anybody about their experiences until they went public or reported to the victims' organisation nearly 50 years later. According to the relationship between memory and silence that we outlined above (see Table 1) and the corresponding stages of development (see Figure 1), upon their return to Korea the comfort women entered stage I: having personal memories but keeping silent.

As time passed by with memories repressed and silence kept, these women probably felt the burden of both, and the layers of *han* kept piling up. Although they had decided to keep silent in order to soothe or relieve their mental pains and conflicts, they could hardly forget them given their altered living conditions and bare survival. However, as their silence lasted longer, it is very likely that their memories became blurred or that they repressed the traumatic experiences. Eventually, they entered stage II of the process outlined in Figure 1: silence and forgetting. Since the issue of the comfort women was not recognised by Korean society, it never entered collective memory and also started to fade away from personal memories. The women's long silence also came with various psychological and behavioural consequences (see Table 4): nightmares and sleepwalking (case 2), disgust at the thought of men (cases 1 and 3), general distrust of others (case 3), shunning other people and the outer world in general (case 5), drifting around (cases 2 and 6) and attempted suicide (case 5). These psychological and behavioural problems clearly speak to the burden of trauma and silence.

How did these women endure all this physical and psychological pain and distress? Where did they look for relief from the torment of being silenced? Some took to smoking and (ab)using alcohol (cases 3 and 6); others tried to build up new social networks by getting acquainted with neighbours and new friends (cases 4 and 6) or compensating for the lack of family by bringing up orphans or children of kin (cases 1 and 2). Some committed themselves to prayer (case 4), to religion (case 5) or to work (see Table 5). Many of the women also found that the acts of reporting and testifying about their experiences helped them to cope with their pain.

Table 5: Coping with Stress, Pain and Trauma

Ways of Coping	Individualistic/Negative	Social/Positive
Personal	Smoking, drinking, crying	Relating to neighbors and friends
Religious	Individual praying	Devoting oneself to a religion
Social/Public/ Political	Testifying	Taking part in KCWD movement and/or in demonstrations

Taking part in the KCWD movement or in regular public demonstrations also seemed to be helpful in this regard.

Table 5 classifies these ways of coping. First we find personal, religious and finally social, public and political ways of dealing with their trauma. I have further differentiated between individualistic and negative in contrast to social and positive ways of coping. Thus, personal coping strategies like drinking and smoking are seen as individualistic and negative, whilst establishing new networks is deemed social and positive.

V. SILENCE: WHY WAS IT SO DIFFICULT TO TALK?

These women victims remained silent for fifty years despite their initial suffering at the hands of the Japanese army and their subsequent torment due to the silence about their plight. What were the factors that made and kept them silent? Three factors seem to have been particularly decisive in establishing and maintaining their silence: their living conditions, cultural factors and issues of language and identity.

It must be pointed out that the comfort women had no choice but to remain silent, because there was no opportunity to talk. Most of these women had nobody to talk to, since they could not or did not go back to their hometowns and were thus cut off from their families, friends and most of their former relationships (cases 1 and 3). Others went back to their hometown but could not talk of what had happened to them, not even to their own families, because of the widespread ideology of women's chastity (cases 2 and 6). Others said that the relatives who were told about their experiences then pressured them not to speak further about them, even with regard to reporting and registering as comfort women victims with the government (case 4).

In addition to internal torment, daily life for the returned comfort women was also a heavy burden. Korea had only just emancipated itself from Japanese colonial rule and was not even a proper nation-state yet. The Korean War, which lasted from 1950 to 1953, then all but destroyed what little was left. As a result, institutional support such as financial help, counseling, etc was unthinkable at that time, and there were no other relief systems in place.

For some of the interviewees, the Korean War, which brought about a new wave of destruction for the whole population helped that their memories faded. Past pains have a tendency to fade away from memory when the present puts new layers of pain on it.

The ideology of chastity prevailing in Korean society was a decisive factor in preventing the comfort women from talking to even their families. The stigma of having been comfort women became a defining aspect of their lives in the still highly patriarchal society of Korea. One of the interviewees said that even after she reported her experiences, people 'looked at me as if they were looking at a leper' (case 6). Others feared that speaking out might alienate them from families and friends.

Another cultural factor to consider is the widespread and overt anti-Japanese sentiment that emerged not long after Japanese colonial rule ended in Korea. The women feared that even though they had been victims of the Japanese military, if they told their stories, they might be accused of cooperation with the Japanese military and collaboration with the enemy.

In addition to the ideology of chastity and anti-Japanese sentiments, language and factors related to identity also made it extremely difficult for returned comfort women to convey their experiences. Even after they had reported they seemed incapable of defining and expressing their experiences in the interviews. The women interviewed knew that they had been seriously harmed and mistreated, but they had difficulties in defining this as victimisation. They were not sure themselves whether it had been rape or prostitution or something different, and they were at loss to find words to describe their experiences. Of course, before the (legal) terms 'sexual harassment' or 'wife battering' were coined, women were victims of both, but most could not define their victimisation in such terms, much less take action against it. In this case, the comfort women's unarticulated sense of victimhood was compounded by the social atmosphere in Korea, which likewise did not treat the women as 'victims' but rather sought to cover up this humiliating episode of Korean history.

The absence of verbal expression on the part of the returned comfort women is strongly related to this confusion about their identity as victims. At first, they probably thought that they had been raped, but later they might have defined themselves as no different from prostitutes. At some point they might have thought that they were Korean victims who had been forcibly drafted under colonial rule, but after Japanese indoctrination some of them might have considered themselves as Japanese patriots serving in the 'Japanese Imperial Army' and identified with the Japanese military. Due to this confusion of identity they probably had even more difficulty in defining their victimisation and were even more likely to conceal their pasts and keep silent. Table 6 links the development of their identity and consciousness to the dominant discourses in society that prevailed in the two periods from their return until they reported, and after they had reported. The fact

Table 6: Changes in the Identity and Consciousness of Comfort Women

	From the time of their return to Korea until they reported	After reporting
Status of the women's identity	• Confusion of identity • Concealment of identity	• Consciousness raising
Dominant discourse	• Patriarchy and women's chastity • Anti-Japanese sentiments	• Feminist discourse • Nationalist discourse • Post-colonial discourse

Source: Hwang 1998

that they concealed their victimization and their identity is attributed to the traditional discourses around patriarchy and women's sexuality.

There are two types of situations in which individuals find themselves incapable of speaking: (1) they find themselves impeded by others, even though they know what and how to express; (2) though they want to express themselves, they do not have the right concepts or terms at hand. The comfort women had to struggle with both situations: they were pressured by the ideology of women's chastity and widespread anti-Japanese sentiments not to talk about their experiences; at the same time, they did not and could not find words to describe their experiences and had no concepts at hand to articulate their victimisation even if they had wanted to. Thus, when the KCWD, or the academies in women's studies, and feminists advocated their position, their words began to pour out like a flood (Shim 1998).

VI. FROM SILENCE TO TESTIMONY: STARTING TO SPEAK?

How did the comfort women get over their long silence and finally come forward to report and testify? Reporting can be classified roughly into two categories according to who reports: voluntary reporting by the victims themselves and other people's reporting on their behalf. The comfort women who finally reported voluntarily had different reasons for doing so.

Three of the interviewees reported voluntarily (cases 1, 2 and 4). One (case 1) reported as soon as she watched Kim Hak-Soon, the comfort woman who first reported and testified on Korean television in 1990. Another interviewee (case 2) reported after she heard about the events through her adopted grandson, who had seen an advertisement in the street. One interviewee (case 4) had seen a newspaper report about Yoshida Seiji, the author of *I Dragged Korean People This Way*, was overwhelmed by tears and decided to report.

For some of those who reported voluntarily, their poor living conditions played an important role. One woman (case 6) said that she had decided to report because it was 'too hard for her to live'. She hoped that reporting might result in some compensation and/or a monthly stipend.

The other interviewees did not report themselves; others did so on their behalf. The daughter of one of the women (case 3) opposed her reporting, but her landlady, who lived in the same house, reported on her behalf. The landlady had heard the victim's story from her personally, though the woman herself did not remember the fact that she had told her. Another women (case 5), who lived alone in the mountains, was visited by county welfare officials for other reasons. They found it strange for a woman to live alone in the mountains and in the course of their inquiries found out about her past and reported on her behalf.

I want to reconstruct the comfort women's process of reporting and testifying according to the relationship between memory/forgetting and talk/silence laid out in Table 1 and the corresponding stages laid out in Figure 1. Figure 2 shows the different stages of individual change and adaptation to the suppression of memory and imposed silence, but also the possibilities of retrieving memory and speaking out.

The first stage—discontent—is characterised by trying to keep silent though the victim has a clear memory of the past events: she may remember her life at the comfort stations and feel anger against Japan, her parents, her country and patriarchal society, but there is no way to break the silence and tell the story. Even if there were opportunity to speak, her past as a comfort woman would be revealed. Consequently, she keeps on concealing it. The second stage—adaptation—centres on trying to forget while having to remain silent. She may try to conceal her past identity as a comfort woman and hope for a life as a 'normal' woman—getting married and having children. However, she finds her hopes and expectations shattered by the reality of her life of exclusion. At the third stage, resignation prevails: she gives up and resigns herself to her burden. During this stage her memory gradually fades. A case in point for this process is the woman mentioned above (case 3), who had confided to her landlady about her past but then completely forgot about it. The fourth and last stage—resistance—entails speaking out, which results in the restoration of

Figure 2: Stages of Individual Change and Adaptation

Table 7: Different Emotional States in the Process from Silence to Testimony

	Silence	Talking
Memory	Discontent (Stage I: Memory but Silence)	Resistance (Stage IV: Memory through Talk)
Forgetting	Adaptation (Stage II: Silence and Forgetting)	Resignation (Stage III: Talk but Forgetting)

memory. Table 7 represents these links between these processes of change and the concomitant imposition of silence and opening up possibilities of talking respectively, as described above: adaptation e.g. is the typical result of silence and ensuing forgetting.

VII. THE ROLE OF SOCIAL MOVEMENTS AND LEGAL INSTITUTIONS IN THE RESTORATION OF COLLECTIVE MEMORIES

With the emergence of the Korean Council for Women Drafted for Sexual Service by Japan (KCWD), and feminist and nationalist discourses, the comfort women were encouraged to report and testify, and to restore their memory, now in the public sphere. By April 2000, 199 women had reported to government agencies and the KCWD. The Korean Government had an important role in helping the comfort women to come forward, report and testify. A law was enacted that provided for victims' reports, their registration and support procedures. However, the government did not move voluntarily, and only after ten years' efforts on the part of the KCWD was this change of policies finally achieved.

The KCWD was founded in 1990 as a network organisation of the Korean women's movement. It advocates the cause and rights of comfort women victims, targeting the Japanese government and people as well as the Korean government. Their activities include, first, making comfort women issues social issues and raising awareness of their plight in Korean society, and second, advocating their cause against the Japanese Government. Their activities include legal advocacy and raising public support, demands for revealing the truth and seeking restitution of damages. The KCWD has also established international networks with other Asian nongovernmental organisations (NGOs) and reached out to international humanitarian organisations.

In 1992, the KCWD submitted seven demands to the Japanese government: (1) to reveal the truth regarding comfort women; (2) to concede the facts; (3) a formal apology; (4) legal restitution and compensation for the victims; (5) criminal prosecution and punishment of those responsible;

(6) a rewriting of history textbooks and schoolbooks; and (7) a monument for the victims and an archive for relevant documents. I will focus here on some legal aspects of the KCWD measures and the establishment of discourses and a social movement.

The cause of the comfort women received wide publicity in the international press and emerged as an important international issue when three former comfort women, including Kim Hak-Soon, filed a lawsuit for restitution of damages at the Tokyo District Court in 1991. This lawsuit was advocated and supported by the KCWD. Their work with the media in extensively covering the issue was also decisive in putting it on the national and international agenda. Thus, legal advocacy as a core task of this social movement helped to make comfort women a social issue and establish a public discourse about the fate of the women.

The Jungshindae Studies Association was founded in order to accumulate relevant data, collect comfort women's testimonies and conduct and publish research about their issues. The Association has published collected testimonies of the victims, which have been vital to revealing the war atrocities committed by Japan and to rewriting history. The Association first focused on revealing the truth with the aim of punishing those responsible and ensuring restitution for the victims. Their work was grounded in historical research and a more nationalist discourse. However, since then they have engaged in post-colonial discourses and shifted the focus of their research in this direction. The development of women's studies in Korea and the emergence of feminist discourses helped the comfort women finally to find words to express themselves and to recover their self-esteem and dignity.

The lawsuits, the women's movement, the press, feminist discourses and the media all put pressure on the Korean Government. Finally, the so-called Special Act to Support Comfort Women Victims passed through the Korean Parliament in 1992, providing for a support system at the government level. The Department of Health and Welfare received the reports of the comfort women victims, and after screening and examination procedures had been established, official registration was started and a financial support system established for the victims. In 1993 the Ministry of Health and Welfare began to pay one-time subsidies as well as monthly pensions to the women.

A decisive factor in helping the comfort women victims to break their silence was the change in their identity and consciousness (Hwang 1998). This change has been mainly influenced by two factors: the spread of nationalist and feminist discourses as a result of the activities of KCWD; and the establishment of the government support system as a result of the Special Act to Support Comfort Women Victims. Without doubt, the government support system has provided financial incentive for reporting and thus has played a large part in overcoming the inhibitions of the comfort women and the moral attitudes of the public. Figure 3 gives an overview of

Silence	→	Reporting
Ideology of women's chastity Anti-Japanese sentiments	→	Feminist discourse Nationalist discourse Post-colonial discourse
Living conditions of bare survival	→	Improved living conditions
Lack of support systems	→	Government support system
Marginality and exclusion in national society	→	International solidarity

Figure 3: Changes Prompting the Korean Comfort Women Survivors to Forgo Silence

the changes that have contributed to the comfort women finally breaking their silence and speaking out.

VIII. THE IMPACT OF SPEAKING OUT: NEW LIVES AND NEW TRAUMATA

After the enactment of the Support Act, the number of former comfort women who revealed their identities and reported increased steadily, reaching 155 in January 1998 and 199 in April 2000. In this section I will focus on three aspects of these women's lives that have been affected by speaking out about their experiences: their material and economic situation, their mental well-being and their social relations.

The first change most comfort women experienced after reporting was an improvement in living conditions. The government subsidy programme for each woman includes a lump sum of five million Won (about US$4,800 in 1993), a monthly stipend of 500,000 Won (US$480) and 110,000 Won (US$106) for those who needed care, in addition to free health check-ups. Since most former comfort women had suffered from poverty after their return to Korea, many of them reported considerably improved living conditions.

In addition to the financial support from the government they were offered substantial payments from the Asian Women's Fund of Japan, a civil fund for the comfort women victims. The KCWD campaigned against accepting the money, since this would imply an indirect denial of the involvement of the Japanese government and consequently exempt the Japanese government from its responsibilities for war crimes and the restitution of damages. Furthermore, acceptance of the payments might weaken or even void all further demands for an apology from the Japanese Government and for the criminal prosecution of those who were responsible. This mood was shared by the overwhelming majority of the Korean Parliament. 90 per cent of its members opposed the Japanese Women's Fund, they asked for restitution by the Japanese state and sent a letter to the Japanese Government.

Although many of the comfort women had promised that they would not accept the money from this fund, many payments have actually been applied for and accepted, presumably due to the women's life-long economic hardship and the sense that even such sums are meagre compensation for their shattered lives. As shown in Figure 1 above, the fourth stage of coping with the trauma of being a comfort woman involves the recovery of memories through talking. However, among the victims who have broken their silence to report, there has been a wide spectrum of immediate effects. Some have said that they 'felt better and relieved, having poured out everything', as if 'nothing bad has remained' (case 5). In contrast, others stated that making public testimonies made them feel 'uneasy, suffering from pains in the heart or having a headache' (case 4). One victim who had suffered from nightmares while keeping silent (case 2) said that the nightmares returned in force after reporting and testifying. This clearly shows how vividly memory can be recovered after speaking out.

After breaking their silence and articulating their identity as comfort women victims, they differ considerably in their interpretations of and adaptation to the process. Some show regret for wishes unfulfilled, others show signs of giving up, resignation and retreatism, while others have sublimated what they once desired for themselves. One interviewee (case 2) said that she still wanted to 'get married and give birth to a child' even though she was far beyond the age when those things are likely. Another interviewee (case 5) said that she does 'not want to be born again', thus giving a kind of religious interpretation to the fact that she does not want to go through the experience of life again, and 'just wants to pass away without much fuss'. For another woman (case 6), after reporting 'no dreams or hopes' were left, and she wanted to 'die without causing any shame'.

However, a few former comfort women go beyond resignation once they have reported and spoken out about their experiences. One of the interviewees (case 5) said that she 'wanted to help the poor boys and girls who do not have parents so that they would not get into the same difficulties she went through'. In fact, she donated the 50 million Won (US$48,000) she received from the government to a newly established foundation named The People's Solidarity for Participatory Democracy, which supports orphans (Munhwa, 30 August 2000).

In any case, it is clear that most of the comfort women victims still suffer from their past trauma, and for many the painful experiences of the last 50 years are not a problem of the past but continue to be of the present. Nonetheless, the psychological impact of speaking out seems not only to make them 'feel better and relieved' but more importantly to open up opportunities for a new life by acquiring a new sense of dignity and worth and giving them a new identity.

With regard to the comfort women's social relations, there have been both positive and negative effects of speaking out and reporting. As for the positive effects, the process of speaking out and reporting provides opportunities for new relationships and networks. In particular, the KCWD provides a forum for comfort women victims to get acquainted with and forge new bonds with other women who have had similar experiences. On the other hand, foremost among the negative effects of speaking out are problems and conflicts with family members who are unhappy about or do not support the reporting and testifying process. Further conflicts have emerged between individual victims after they learn of each other's stories and compare experiences. These conflicts arose from contesting memories and stories, including the question whether they had been forcibly drafted or not, or had suffered from particular torments. Also, failing memories contributed to such conflicts and accusations of exaggerating their stories. With an increasing number of public testimonies, repetition has become an issue, and the content of the women's testimonies has changed significantly. Of course, this may be caused by the distortion of passing time or the natural blurring of memories. However, occasional intentional distortions and exaggerations have also been revealed when victims try to speak in specific ways that are thought to be appealing to the public or to give 'the right answers' to authorities and journalists. Such changes in testimonies also reflect adaptation to changes in the mood of the public and its support for the KWCD or its resentment against the Japanese.

The acts of reporting and testifying seem to be turning points in the lives of many comfort women victims; many have spoken of beginning a new life and forming a new identity. Some have even decided to dedicate themselves to the restoration of the collective memories of the victimisation of the comfort women. They have become actively involved in this process and enthusiastic about this work. One of the interviewees (case 1) made explicit reference to her own preoccupation and obsession with testifying and with the testimony process.

Moreover, despite their old age and poor health, many women have participated in the 'Wednesday Demonstrations', which started in 1992 and took place weekly in front of the Japanese Embassy in Seoul, in an effort to increase public awareness and to demand legal and historical justice from the Japanese government. Until 2000, more than 400 of these protest demonstrations took place, however they have stopped soon afterwards to be conducted on a regular basis. They were organised by the KCWD and other social movement organisations.

IX. CONCLUSION

This chapter has dealt with the issues surrounding the lives of the comfort women victims after their return to Korea. In particular, it focused on the following questions. Which torments did fifty years of silence impose on them? Why did they keep silent so long? How did they manage to break the silence and report their stories? And finally, what was the impact of speaking out? In sum, their whole life after they returned can be considered as a continuously ongoing aftermath of their comfort women experiences. The testimonies of the comfort women victims have a strong impact on the restoration of collective memories and on rewriting history. The fact that they had to keep silent for fifty years makes their voices particularly powerful now. The process seems to be driven by the power of truth, which neither political power nor military force can suppress. This became very obvious in their testimonies.

The fifty years' silence was finally broken by ten years of effort on the part of the KCWD to persuade the government to implement policies for the support of comfort women survivors. Legal institutions and measures are important in restoring collective memories, but civil movements, especially the women's movement, have been essential in achieving legal and policy changes with regard to the comfort women.

In order to start the new millenium in a new spirit, East Asian NGOs established a Women's International War Crimes Tribunal on Japan's Military Sexual Slavery in 2000. It was the task of the tribunal not to punish those who were responsible or to demand restitution but to reveal the truth, to make the war atrocities of Japan public and to influence international public opinion regarding the establishment of preventive measures. Although it was a symbolic court and trial, it demonstrates the discursive power of legal institutions. Such symbolic measures can have a vital role in restoring collective memories alongside more concrete measures such as financial restitution and health and social support networks.

Public discourse on the issue of comfort women is still ongoing in Korea, and has been nourished by a higher international awareness of the plight of women in armed conflicts. Presently, the feminist discourse in Korea focuses on the universality of war atrocities against women and therefore endorses international coalitions and solidarity. Nationalist discourses focus on the specific situation of Korean comfort women in the context of colonialism. In addition, a post-colonial discourse has emerged around the issue. It is thus clear that the issues surrounding comfort women not only relate to the past but are embedded in the present.

REFERENCES

Chung, Chin Sung. 1997. The Origin and Development of the Military Sexual Slavery Problem in Imperial Japan. *Positions: East Asia and Cultures Critique* 5(1): 219–53.

Hwang, Eun-Jin. 1998. A Study on the Process of Consciousness Change of the Korean Comfort Women Victims. MA Thesis, Hanyang University, Interdisciplinary Program of Women's Studies.

Kim, Young-Bum. 1998. Socio-historical Horizon and Dynamics of Collective Memories. In *Studies in Social History: Theory and Practice*, edited by the Academy of Korean Studies. Seoul.

Korean Council for the Women Drafted for Sexual Service by Japan (KCDW). 1991a. *Proceedings on Jungshindae Problems*, vol 1. Seoul.

——. 1991b. *Korean Women Drafted for Sexual Service by Japanese Imperial Army: Petition Against the Japanese Government by the KCWD.* Seoul.

——. 1992. *Proceedings on Jungshindae Problems*, vol 2. International Agreement on Human Rights and the Comfort Women Issues: A Seminar with Theo van Boven, 11 December 1992. Seoul.

——. 1993. *Proceedings on Jungshindae Problems*, vol 4. The Comfort Women and the Legal Responsibility of Japan. Seoul.

——. 1997a. *Proceedings on Jungshindae Problems*, vol 6. North Korea's Positions and Activities on the Comfort Women Issues, Seoul.

——. 1997b. *Proceedings on Jungshindae Problems*, vol 7. Let's Forbid the Entering of Japanese War Criminals into Our Country. Seoul.

——. 1997c. *Proceedings on Jungshindae Problems*, vol 8. Asian Solidarity Conference on the Comfort Women Issues. Seoul.

——. 1998. *Proceedings on Jungshindae Problems*, vol 10. An Analysis of the Simonoseki Trial, Together with the Jungshindae Studies Association. Seoul.

McDougall, Gay J. 1998. *Systematic Rape, Sexual Slavery and Slavery-like Practices during Armed Conflict.* E/CN.4/Sub.2/1998/13. Geneva: UN Commission on Human Rights, Sub-commission on Prevention of Discrimination and Protection of Minorities.

Seiji, Yoshida. 1990. *I Dragged Korean People This Way.* Seoul: Chongye.

Shim, Young-Hee. 1994. Women as Sexual Slaves: The Case of Korean Military Comfort Women. *Journal of Social Sciences* 13: 78–101.

——. 1998. Human Rights of Women. In *Human Rights in Contemporary Society*, edited by Sang-Jin Han. Seoul: Nanam.

Yoon, Taek-Rim. 1992. From Memory to History: A Study on the Theoretical and Methodological Issues of Oral History. *Korean Journal of Cultural Anthropology* 25: 43–68.

Yoshimi, Y. 1992. Japan Battles Its Memories. *New York Times*, 11 March.

III

Law, Memory and the Politics of Culture and Identity

7

Negotiating the Past: Culture Industry and the Law

HEINZ STEINERT

I. THE POLITICS OF TRUTH

ISN'T IT A surprising idea that the *trial*—a dramatic adversarial mise-en-scène with a high risk of loss of moral status, money, freedom or even life for at least one participant and the remarkable 'face' involvement for all parties—should in the end produce something like 'truth'? Taking into account that the 'courtroom drama' is a very successful genre of entertainment and that there is probably no other state action short of war that is as heavily covered by the media as at least some trials are (Do we need to argue this after OJ Simpson?)—what chance is there for a vulnerable product of thorough checking and patient reflexivity like 'truth'? Moreover, theorists speak of 'procedural truth', a particular form of reconstruction that is restricted by legal protection against the state's power to gain and collect information.[1] Most judges will tell us that we are not at all entitled to anything like 'Truth' or 'Justice'; all we are entitled to is a (hopefully fair) trial. And any decent defence attorney is aware that the client need not be innocent to deserve the competent use of all his/her tricks of the trade, some of which are aimed at confusing rather than sorting out aspects of what might in the end constitute 'truth'. The best 'courtroom dramas' focus precisely on the many aspects of what may have happened for the different persons in it and the impossibility to decide between them—think of Akira Kurosawa's famous film *Rashomon*.[2]

---

[1] Such restrictions are the right of the defendant to refuse to give evidence, the right of witnesses to withhold evidence that might implicate them, the right of relatives and certain professions to refuse giving witness evidence and the inadmissibility of evidence that is gained by unlawful means. Strict adherence to such rules is the main legitimisation of the trial, its main virtue, exactly because it restricts the state's reach into what might be 'truth' (see Hassemer 1990, esp 268ff).

[2] On the movie genre of 'courtroom drama', see Laster (with Breckweg and King) 2000.

The argument I intend to put up here, then, is a simple one. Law's reconstructions of the past—particularly in political trials—are not about truth. Or to be more exact, the claim to 'truth' has a function of its own in the context of culture industry—which is where a public trial takes place. 'Truth' does not necessarily translate into 'this is how it really happened' but rather means 'this reconstruction is best suited for our present purposes and understandings'.[3] (By this criterion law has always been a postmodern institution.) We should ask why and how the social belief is upheld (in spite of all that we, in our less state-submissive moments, know and assume about the criminal law) that trials are about historical truth. Or better still: we should find out what conception of 'truth' is compatible with such an improbable belief.

'The past' is not only constructed for different purposes and under sometimes heavy conflicts; it is also constructed systematically by what can be called a 'memory and heritage industry', a special sector of culture industry characterised by the material interest the (national) state takes in it.[4] 'Culture industry',[5] the cultural form of capitalism and the capitalist form of culture, is mainly characterised by the *commodity form* which it imposes

---

[3] I say this to imply that there are other possibilities and other forms of 'truth': it all depends on what those 'present purposes and understandings' are. In the case of law they are domination and its convincing public display. In other institutions—science, for instance—they mostly are technical mastery but can also be understanding and empathy. Fashionable postmodern relativism has—in the interest of competition-management in the intellectual marketplace—over-generalised the easy denunciation of knowledge as power and failed to analyse the different forms and degrees of power in knowledge. See Evans 1997.

[4] It is a little bit absurd that there is high reflexivity about and increasing—sad and helpless—criticism of what some call 'Shoah business' yet comparatively little about the *nationalist* productions of different states. 'National identity' seems to have become an uncontested (and uncontestable) 'right'. The same is true for 'group identities' that nobody dares to question as long as they are claimed to be authentic and to be (or to have been) suppressed. Populist 'identity politics' have made 'victimism' an accepted political strategy—as if it were not a politics of resentment, weak in effect and quite costly for those who have to 'identify' as 'victims'. It seems to have been forgotten that 'identity' used to be something imposed on people, that the demand to 'identify' ourselves usually comes from the police and has often been the first step to being imprisoned, tortured and even killed. Think of being 'identified' as 'Tutsi' in Rwanda—see the impressive story of one woman told by Gourevitch (1998, 41–5). On 'victimism', see Sykes 1992; Hughes 1993; and the chapter 'Populismus und Viktimismus im Wissen über Kriminalität' in Cremer-Schäfer und Steinert 1998. 'Victimism' is very well adapted to media demands for emotional, gruesome and thus sensational stories and pictures, but it can in its inflationary and competitive use produce what has been termed 'compassion fatigue'. See Zelizer 1998; Moeller 1999. The German writer Anders described this political necessity and human inability to love one's 'most distant' ('Fernstenliebe') in contrast to one's neighbour ('Nächstenliebe') in his book *Die Antiquiertheit des Menschen* as early as 1956.

[5] The seminal text and still the most useful formulation of this concept is the chapter 'Culture Industry' in Adorno and Horkheimer's *Dialectic of Enlightenment* (1944/1947)—notwithstanding recent developments in which the concept has been cleansed of its critical implications. 'Culture industry' has since the 1940s come to be taken for granted. This makes it all the more necessary to at least occasionally remember the enormity of influence this industry has on intellectual life. For a contemporary reconstruction of the concept and its critical function, see Steinert 1992; 1998.

upon intellectual products—from art to popular entertainment, from scientific theory to journalism, in short, upon all forms of self-presentation and self-reflection of society. Such forms of knowing about society include, of course, reconstructions of the past.

Generally the commodity form of the past (as well as the contracts it implies) is guaranteed by the state and its mass administration—which in turn have an active interest in defining the (national) past as part of their legitimacy. Such appeals to a national whole are a defining characteristic of populist politics.[6] Culture is the praxis of living and its reproduction—with its material manifestations and resources—and as such an integral aspect of a mode of production. In capitalism, culture is organised as 'culture indus-try' and according to the needs of commodity-form production and distri-bution, mass administration and populist politics. To secure and organise suitable pasts, to produce memories—and to produce forgetting—is one of the activities of the culture industry. Documentations of different kinds as well as fictional renditions of the past are among its products.[7]

In this chapter, I approach the question of law and memory in two ways. I will first describe some of the mechanisms of the 'memory and heritage industry' by outlining a few distinctions between ways of remembering, ie, reconstructing a past out of private, commercial and state-organised memo-ries. This should help us see the role and space that state-organised memo-ries and particularly criminal law and trials have in the broader context of creating and negotiating different possible pasts. Then I will—the other way round—try to determine the consequences (and functions) of negotiating the past in terms of (criminal) law.

II. CHANGING THE PAST

A. From Private into Public Memories—and Vice Versa

The question is not 'Does the past change?' It does. It is redefined again and again—as are other products of culture (literature, artistic artefacts, memorial sites, styles, knowledge, understandings of what a person is, what

---

[6] For an analysis of populism as culture-industry politics, see Steinert 1999. On state-organised memories, see for example the chapters in Gillis 1994; Winter and Sivan 1999; and Huyssen 1999.

[7] In the theory of 'cultural memory' developed by Assmann 1999, a line is drawn from per-sonal remembering (including its social organisation) to the media of memory and to forms of storage. In this most comprehensive treatment presently available we find numerous examples of relevant phenomena but no systematic analysis of 'culture industry' as a determinant of socially organised renditions of possible and dominant pasts. By concentrating on this complex of functions I also suggest here conceptualising 'cultural memory' not so much as a model of storage and of an inventory selectively used (which corresponds to work aesthetic in art theory) but rather as a model of continuous *processes* of (re)construction and (re)definition in which the organisation of the duration of memory is a special (and unlikely) case.

he or she is entitled to, whether the person is 'he', 'she' or something more abstract): cultural meanings change and are changed.

Seen from the perspective of the individual, *private* memories are embedded into a rich surrounding of *commercial* memories, the stories of fictional and historical persons, families, communities, tribes, peoples and even 'humanity'.[8] Such stories are presented in different media from the bard reciting heroic tales to theatre, novels, movies and television series. And there are *state* memories, which are owned, implanted and administered by state agencies and have their own media—memorial days, monuments, school curricula and, as a special form, laws and legal decisions. Religious tales have always been an essential (and early) part of the structure of domination and can therefore be seen as 'state memories'. The state media named above are often religious at the same time or are modelled after religious inventions; in particular, the state rituals in which domination and submission are celebrated are usually secularised versions of religious rituals. Religious media proper, for instance scripts like the Holy Bible and similar genealogical tales or the legends of saints and kings—also in different pictorial forms—have also been widely used in commercial memory productions.

Our private memories have to find some relation to commercial and state memories and thus are influenced by them. If they pertain to the same historical event there may be validation as well as tension in contents, in what is personally remembered of a complex event like a battle, or a war, of a place like a death camp or a whole genocidal campaign.[9] But more generally, in forming an idea of person, family, country, up to whole historical periods etc, we have to use or refuse the formal models publicly presented and at times propagated: is it career, progress, liberation from some dark past, possible attainment of some end-state, progressive deterioration, perpetual struggle with ups and downs, deadly competition or possible cooperation, revolution, evolution—or, in Macbeth's words, 'a tale told by an idiot, full of sound and fury, signifying nothing'? Even the most private memories are socially (and, we might add, politically) framed and ordered.

Memories, then, are produced and obliterated. How is this done?

---

[8] In Western tradition 'humanity' has often been reduced to 'civilised peoples'. There is, of course, local variation as to who belongs to this category.

[9] This tension between private trauma, mourning, testimony, and public, culture-industry politics has best been analysed and reflected in analyses of what has been called 'Shoah Business'. Cf e.g. Young 1988; Schneider 1997; van Alphen 1997; LaCapra 1998; Zuckermann 1999; Cole 1999. While it is obvious that the Shoah has had changing political functions in the post-war history particularly of Israel, but also of the U.S. the recent attack by Finkelstein (2000) has widely been criticised for reducing a highly complex political field to greed and money-making (which at the same time feeds an anti-semitic stereotype). Cf. on Israel, Segev 1991 (English edition 1993); on the U.S. Novick 1999; on Germany Herf 1997; Fulbrook 1999.

B. Anticipatory Memory Production

Let me start with two examples of memory construction:

1. I have recently been in Naples and found it very odd to see bridal couples at several locations: they were followed by groups of people, including photographers, video operators and other people responsible for lighting, etc; they went from one romantic spot to the next to have their picture and video taken—brides triumphant, grooms awkward. They spent part of their marriage day on staging a memory.

2. The Romanian dictator Nicolae Ceaucescu left behind a monster of a palace that dominates Bucharest from every perspective and is much too enormous to ever be removed by anything short of an earthquake or carpet bombing (and it was designed to survive even those).

In these two examples we find an *anticipatory* construction of memories—organised attempts to give duration to a moment and thus determine memories for the future. Enormous monuments of domination have been an established means of such anticipatory memories since the Egyptian pyramids, but Ceaucescu has made his domination inescapable for a whole city. There are, of course, similar attempts by banking and insurance companies, who build skyscrapers, or the 'Family Towers' in Renaissance Italian cities like Bologna. The difference is that they have competition and are not allowed the kind of monstrosity boasted by Ceaucescu.[10]

Our private attempts to do similar things for ourselves and our grand-children through photography are harmless and helpless in comparison because they lack power. Even though the bridal couples in Naples display the same urge for permanence, something quite different is achieved: the marriage contract is complemented by a documentation of how desirable they once were to each other.[11] There is no continuum between private and

---

[10] Today's monstrosities of anticipatory memory construction are bureaucratic. Governments produce archives on an absurd scale. The US National Archives is 'currently the custodian of four billion pieces of paper; 9.4 million photographs; 338,029 films and videos; 2,648,918 maps and charts; nearly three million architectural and engineering plans; and more than nine million aerial photographs. Storage consumes nearly half of the agency's budget, so, ironically, the more information it keeps the less money it has to spend on making this information accessible to the public.' This problem of access consists in cataloguing and documenting the new material delivered for storage in the first place: 'A study done in 1996 by the Archives concluded that at current staff levels it would take approximately a hundred and twenty years to transfer the backlog of nontextual material (photographs, videos, film, audiotape, and microfilm) onto a more stable format' (Stille 1999, 38f).

[11] Marriage photographs seem to have markedly changed: older ones typically show a proud husband displaying his newly acquired property of a wife; then there are triumphant brides who have got hold of husbands; lately these pictures have become sexy and show the couple kissing and in even more suggestive positions. Desirability seems to be defined as looking as much like one of the models in the bridal magazines as possible.

state-organised memories—and there is no continuum between nostalgia and the permanence of domination.

Lawmaking has this latter dimension, too: casting some rules as law is intended to give them permanence and thus make them memorable. It is the prolongation of a piece of domination into the future. And we, living according to or against laws of venerable age, appropriate that past and accept the domination of the past over the present. It is not certain though that knowledge about the origin of a particular law is available and accurate. The original intention is not necessarily relevant: the law can be reinterpreted and used in new ways and for changed purposes.

C. From Anticipation to Pre-history

Memory production, thus, comes in several types, distinguished by the time that elapses between the event and its memory. We can define the following possibilities:

Memory is produced

— ... *right at the moment an event takes place.* There are special cases in which an event is actually—and maybe exclusively—staged for the purpose of being documented; the other limiting case is when an event is kept secret and its traces erased immediately.

— ... *by those who are part of the event after they have lived through the experience.* This includes private memories (usually of some extraordinary event) and testimony, as well as adventure stories. Historical memory is elusive and problematic and cannot be (and has never been) left to private remembering only. Individual memories of historical events are unreliable and give one perspective only, they need being compared and reaffirmed in the company of other participants.

— ... *when the event passes from a living memory to 'pre-history'.* Historical memories fade and lose their power after one generation unless they are passed on and revived in an organised effort. They need to be turned into 'testimony' and socially validated by being accepted and even celebrated by a community. At this stage, when they become 'second hand', participants' memories need to be complemented by documents and traces of the event of a more 'objective' and usually 'official' nature. Private memories turn into tradition and become part of a canon of knowledge—or they are lost.

— ... *when changed historical conditions make it desirable to redefine 'pre-historically' past events.* Traditions can be redefined. They will attract efforts of reinterpretation when new powers need legitimacy and challenge old powers by attacking their tradition. This will often result in the discovery of new historical facts, but a shift in perspective, a re-evaluation of well-known facts may also be sufficient.

Memories, with this understanding, are (even in their private forms) *social* events: narratives for a smaller or larger audience; narratives distinguished from pure fiction by claiming to refer to something that 'has actually happened', by claiming to be 'documentation' rather than 'fantasy', thus inviting others to confirm or contest these narratives; 'invention' or 'falsification', more or less elaborate by using 'traces', which hint at something that is not readily to be seen, and of which only a representation is available like administrative documents or ruins of buildings, thus building on collective memories of past events; 'reminders', which are opportunities for well-known stories to be (re)told about the original events (monuments and memorial days are obvious examples); and full-blown presentations of 'stories' in which an event is reconstructed in all detail, eg, descriptions in history books, but also historical novels or movies, which interpolate a reality as it might have been.

III. DOMINATION OVER THE PAST

Let me add two other examples at this point:

3. Europe and the USA (and the rest of the world as a result of their influence) are full of Capitols and White Houses, Greek temples that house parliaments and other seats of state power. The bourgeois republic has right at its origins in the American and the French revolutions constructed a Greco-Roman 'tradition' that is still around. The combination of rationalist order, engineering achievement and classicist decor is nowhere brought together more strikingly than in Washington, DC, the 'mother of all Capitols', its artificial grid of streets and diagonal layout forged over formerly swampy ground.[12]
4. The German convention of dubbing movies made it possible for *Casablanca* to be released in 1952 as an adventure story, twenty minutes shorter than what we see today and without a single Nazi in it. Similarly, Alfred Hitchcock's *Foreign Correspondent* (German version 1961) was purged of all Nazis, while *Notorious* (German version 1951) became a story about drug dealers. The German-speaking public got to know the original renditions of these films only in 1968, 1975 and 1986 respectively (Fuld 1999, 47f, 109).[13]

---

[12] The classicist heritage is invoked in a more narrative way in historicist paintings like those of the French painter Jacques-Louis David (1748–1825).

[13] It is hard to imagine *Casablanca* without key scenes: the Marseillaise being sung as counterpoint to the Deutschlandlied, without Laszlo being a resistance leader and without Rick shooting the Nazi officer at the end of the film. It must have been pretty unintelligible. The reinterpretation of *Notorious* as a drug dealer story, on the other hand, is easier to imagine—particularly

History has always been a matter of domination. Establishing a 'narrative of origin' is (the 'traditional') part of investing legitimacy in institutions.[14] In European history, this became particularly problematic when nationalism was the foundation of states. In contrast to aristocratic domination, which always had a genealogical claim to rule, bourgeois domination has a particular challenge: it needs to criticise and do away with aristocracy but is itself not content with purely functional legitimacy. There is, of course, no easy consensus on such myths, neither inside national states, nor between them. There are struggles over the self-representation of the state, and quite often there are clearly distinct candidates for this function pushed and supported by different classes and class-subdivisions. War and war-propaganda tend to be great unifiers in this respect.

In the example of Greco-Roman antiquity as the model for the Western bourgeois republic, the problem of such constructions becomes obvious. How do we connect that faraway 'original' with the present? The Paris revolutionaries did it mostly through role-playing and masquerades—and, of course, with a political theory that relied on the authority that the Renaissance and Enlightenment had given to Greek and Roman thought, art and politics. The easiest way to effect such a connection, to demonstrate the relevance of the historical original for the present, is through the flexible medium of 'high culture'. High culture still refers to the 'classical' original, revived during the Renaissance and Enlightenment, that was brought to its peak in Germany with the politically reactionary 'classical' Weimar of poets Goethe and Schiller. It is a narrative of (uneven) progress from youthful rebellion followed by a wise return to tradition after excesses of the youthful age and rebellion had been repented and thus the connection between high culture and classics could be re-established.

There may be other such narratives than that of original and re-make that forge links between the past and the present. One is 'progress'; another is an account that still needs to be settled, some injustice that still has to be rectified; often it is a parable of (more or less tragic) heroism, a model held up for emulation or a heritage that we have to honour. In general, 'truth' is not the focus of these narratives. The event at the very origin of its memory can clearly be mythical, even pure fairytale. If it does have some factual basis, it does not matter if only very little is known about it. It is rather used as a morality tale and told precisely because of this moral quality. This *moral* connection is the most simple reason for giving relevance to the past in the

---

since the viewing public has been desensitised by TV-serials and action movies that neglect narrative coherence. The reinterpreted German version is still available.

[14] The other parts of the process of legitimacy are a (charismatic) 'statement of purpose' and a (bureaucratic) 'instruction for use'. Max Weber's (1968) categories are not exclusive—usually institutions try to have all forms of legitimisation—and they are to be translated into operational descriptions of social practices, ie types of discourse.

present. Present moral fibre is thus strengthened by the moral example of the past, be it by imitation or by the warnings it presents. Truth may not be morally uplifting: it may even be inimical to the moral purpose of historical narratives.[15]

In the example of the purified German renditions of Hitchcock's movies we see how history—film history and real history—can be rendered harmless by *not* remembering. The German distributors must have feared that an unfriendly—or any—depiction of Nazis would still (in the 1950s, even early 1960s) diminish the attraction and financial returns of these movies. There is no need to assume that those who made the cuts had a political tendency of their own; it is probable that they were merely anticipating the attitudes of the public and thus prospective profit.

IV. SITUATIONS OF MEMORY

What is socially and politically important is not historical truth but rather keeping a narrative at all alive and relevant. This does not need truth, but rather organised effort. There need to be: occasions for retelling the story; media (including people) that can and will tell the story 'correctly'; and measures ensuring that the 'correct' morality lesson is received by the audience. I will base my description of different 'situations of memory' on this simple list. There are three exemplary situations that in combination make up the spectrum of culture-industry memory constructions: private memories, commercial renditions of the past and state-organised memories. Law and the courts are a special case of state-organised memories and will be analysed in this context.

A. Private Memories

Social occasions for private memories occur when individuals who have participated in the same memorable event gather together to 'exchange memories' or when one or more of these original participants narrates the event to a group of listeners, passing along the details as 'news'. Such exchanges can include questions being asked, doubts being voiced and allayed, and confirmations being given. More complicated exchanges produce other, parallel or counter-narratives of the same, similar or contrasting events.

---

[15] In the Kosovo war both sides were following through with their historical narratives: for the Serbs, a tragic history of persecution and heroic defence against annihilation as a 'nation', starting with their resistance to oriental domination in the battle on the Amselfeld (now in Kosovo); for the Germans (a decisive part of the NATO air attacks), the Nazi past provided the lesson, which made intervening in a case of genocide a national imperative. See Höpken 1998.

A special case of such exchanges involves telling the story to members of the next generation in order to found a tradition.

There are no *media* involved on these occasions; the telling of memories is direct and face-to-face. However, this does not mean that there are no structures and rules. The memories in question must form a story, ideally with exposition, development and resolution—a proper ending. There are genres, as in the more mediated forms: there is the 'sad story' and the 'happy story', and the most advantageous genre seems to be the story of a near-catastrophe, of a challenge just surmounted with luck and prowess. In this situation the correct narrative of morality is ensured through the comparison of different participants and their stories of the same event and the eventual understanding reached between all those present. In other words, it is subject to negotiation and (re)consideration.

The function of the narrative is interpersonal understanding and/or recognition. Sometimes an event was traumatic and has to be retold in order for participants to come to grips with it. There is nothing wrong with intense emotions in such storytelling. Another special case may be the collective denial of shock and ill treatment experienced, which gets turned into an adventure—as is often the case with stories of war. On the other hand, collective denial of a wrong done by the narrator will most probably involve that stories are not told and people keep silent about these events or tell consensually agreed cover stories, ie, stories about other events or different aspects of the same event.

B. Memory for Sale: Entertainment and Education as Commercial Renditions of the Past

The main distinction between commercial renditions of memory and private memory is that we get narrated and/or pictorial reproductions of the event in the public media, nowadays primarily in the form of documentaries and fictional movies. Such forms bring a new quality in vividness, (seeming) objectivity and authority, reproducibility and, not least, *memorableness*. Social occasions for private memories occur when individuals who have participated in the same memorable event gather together to 'exchange memories' or when one or more of these original participants narrates the event to a group of listeners, passing along the details as 'news'.

Before modern-day films, the next-best equivalent were pictures accompanied by narration. Quite early examples include the 'comic strip' legends of saints, as for instance the Benedict Cycles (the most remarkable being Signorelli's version in Monte Oliveto Maggiore near Siena). All these presentations have to obey rules of the genre and conventions of the medium; they must follow dramaturgical demands and be entertaining, exciting, sensational, perhaps expensive—a good show that can be sold to a mass public.

Culture as commodity easily fits into and makes use of the structure set by memorial days fixed by the state and religion. It complements them with memorials of its own—most of the culture industry's agenda is defined by such a timetable of occasions (which just shows there is not much more to it than a (co)incidental relevance to the agenda of public topics). Culture industry in its own right, however, has a 'mechanism of 'fashion' with which to draw up its different agendas—short-lived crazes for the latest novelties, which quickly become boring and are replaced by new ones that bear no traces of their predecessors. (It is imperative for culture industry that we do *not* remember yesterday's news but are kept hungry for tomorrow's.) Stability and a framework of recurring cycles (daily, weekly, monthly and yearly) are established by state and religion (and to some degree by the seasons) and readily used by culture industry.

Culture industry takes over from the state in controlling content. The 'correct morality' lesson to be learned is secured by state censorship in crude cases only but more thoroughly by market forces. Acceptable is what sells, ie, what commands attention and appeals to great numbers; acceptable is what relates to common sense—which in turn is what media products tell us all the time. The *function* is entertainment and education. The fact that states censure and implement state censorship shows that such entertainment is critically observed by all kinds of interests (mainly state, but also religious) and instrumentalised for their purposes. The genre of the Western is an archetypal contemporary example of historical stories edited for entertainment.

C. State-organised Memories

Occasions and locations for telling the narrative of state-organised memories are structured by memorial sites, memorial days and monuments. The state also can take advantage of such occasions to institute compulsory education of the young. Quite often states cooperate with religious organisations in the construction of a past and use the occasions they provide (and vice versa).

Typically, the retelling of state-organised memories are elaborate media spectacles, such as official speeches, parades and rallies. Today states also make use of new electronic media, but the paradigmatic medium for state-organised memories remains stone structures—government and historical buildings, memorial sites, and statues designed to last through the centuries. State-organised memories aim at eternity or at least a thousand years (and they seem to have a tendency to also go back very far), and they do so by structuring land and cityscapes (for Germany, see Koshar 1998; Reichel 1995).

State-organised memories often entail staging the same spectacle in many places. Thus, instructions are issued to sub-organisers through a chain of bureaucratic command. Schools are important for these simultaneous staging, as are churches. They often have their own media and they imitate each other—although again it is religion that has set the standard for solemn celebrations (and provided much of the infrastructure). A preaching tone is still what is proper on such occasions. Music, especially singing choirs, is another element originally developed in religious ritual and transferred to more secular ones.

The 'correct morality' story is ensured by carefully selecting those who are allowed to speak and by making the audience assume a pre-set role, which they have to rehearse like in the proper order of marches and rallies. The production aims at overwhelming all participants and thus producing among them feelings of 'we' and of unity (which is most easily done by whipping up shared hatred of those who are made *not* to belong). Speeches and other elements of the production excite and emotionalise. The educational element, the teaching, can be quite explicit—as it is, of course, in the context of school. Texts and other educational technology are provided. The function of these spectacles is obvious: celebration of and identification with authority—an authority that is elevated and beyond reach (and criticism) and thus has to be endorsed.

V. CRIMINAL LAW: A SPECIAL TYPE OF STATE-ORGANISED MEMORY PRODUCTION

A. A Most Theatrical Mis-en-scene

States have instituted a dramatic and elaborate performance in the form of 'the trial'—which is an occasion for the reconstruction of past events and, under special circumstances, events of historical importance. This occasion is offered to and used by a harmed party to ask for state intervention into a conflict. (This party can be the state itself, represented by an official.) The historical cases are primarily those in which a new government or state (after a revolution, after a military victory, etc) denounces the old one. Often in such cases, extra efforts are made to ensure that the trial verdicts are desirable to those (now) in power. Tribunals and forced confessions are the most obvious examples.

In a trial, the inquisitorial or the antagonistic dimension may be variously more or less emphasised , but on the whole it is a theatrical performance in which juxtaposed forces try to win over an audience—which includes the jury and the judge, as well as a larger public, who may or may not be physically present. This is done through improvisation (which does not mean that the actors are not well prepared, but it is not rehearsed as a whole), which has to conform to particularly strict rules.[16] The judge acts as a referee to guarantee that the rules are adhered to. He/she also acts as the representative of the state proper—impartial, wise, serious and solemn, the ultimate power whose decisions are binding. His/her decisions encompass declarations of guilt and innocence as well as acts of punishment and exoneration. It is a powerful image that is part of many religions—God as the last and superior judge and the end of the world as an enormous mass trial and final judgment (with no appeal possible). The close connection between state and religion is not often as evident as in the criminal trial.

The medium of this theatrical performance has special features derived from the power involved. Participants can be forced to play their part, to produce evidence and, in the end, to suffer the verdict (which may be death). However, the antagonistic dimension of the trial confers a sense of fairness to the procedures: defendants are able to fight according to rules that provide an equal chance for all. Consequently, any unfavourable result will be partially of their own making.

Finally, a trial is a bureaucratic procedure with strict protocols for everything (so that acts and utterances can be held against defendants later), with rules of what is admissible and relevant. In short, it is a frame of artificial relevance that differs from everyday life, but can be forced upon the narratives and everyday life conflicts that are the staple of criminal courts. The performance is a show of detailed domination that entangles participants so that they become an intricate part of the structure of domination—and through this fine-tuned medium they become part of the larger structure of domination of which the trial, the law and the state itself are only parts. It makes them participate in their own verdict, which is simultaneously the enforced allocation of social position and moral status, and their identification as (inferior) social beings. It makes the actors who are involved 'belong' to a state and a society in the different roles and entitlements of judge and defendant/condemned. They can be forced to 'belong'—even if for the defendant this means a subjugated position.

The 'correct morality' is ensured by the whole procedure, the aim of which is, ideally, confession, if possible after a dramatic breakdown of defences—coming clean after a struggle of conscience, Alternatively, a repentant confession before execution—which has a literary genre of its own—is also welcome. We are still dissatisfied by trials without confessions, even though we have become aware that there are false confessions and self-accusations that have motives we cannot accept. The confession must be convincing, particularly after a history of staged trials and forced confessions. The pathos of authority and overwhelming domination alone is not sufficient anymore; we need it complemented by the pathos of having

---

[16] The structure is somewhat analogous to that of attractive spectator sports such as soccer.

found the truth. This is why torture has become dysfunctional for the trial: it disclaims the truth of the confession. The function of the criminal trial as a way to recreate a past event is to affirm a version that is validated by the highest authority: the state (and beyond that God).

B. Criminal Law and Culture Industry

The very theatricality of the trial finds an obvious affinity in the culture industry . It is no coincidence that there is a well established genre of 'court-room drama' with a fixed dramaturgical structure of gradual revelation and last-minute reversal. But it is also obvious that the trial itself is good entertainment. There are people who visit courts for entertainment; there are TV stations that specialise in reporting about trials ('The Law Channel'). Part of the appeal is the drama and its tensions, but there is more to it. The drama of justice is about morality, ie, about the right way to live and honour basic social institutions: property, family, the state monopoly on force. In particular, the sections of the criminal law on property offenses deal with the income–consumption nexus (or more precisely, the wage–labour–money nexus); the sections on violent crime raise the necessity of abstaining from physical force, particularly in politics; and the sections on 'sexual' crimes in the penal code symbolise the desirability of paying due respect to 'normal' family (including sexual) relations. What makes the criminal trial even more convincing is that it ultimately conveys the right way to live by giving (deterrent) examples of what appears as undisciplined, but highly attractive, and consequently needs to be punished.

Before I go on I want to add three more examples on the production of memories to the four given above.

5. In one of the follow-up trials in Nuremberg in 1946/47 twenty-three medical doctors were accused of crimes against humanity, which in these cases included systematic torture, murder and sterilisation (as a result of medical experiments conducted on inmates in concentration camps) and euthanasia (mostly of mentally ill patients in psychiatric hospitals). Most of the accused were found guilty, and seven death sentences were handed down. A young doctor, Alexander Mitscherlich, was allowed to attend and observe the trials as a representative for a medical professional association and published his report with the title 'Wissenschaft ohne Menschlichkeit' ('Inhumane Science'). A first, provisional publication had been met with protests from some high-ranking members of the medical profession, who, on the whole, did not deny the crimes but wanted them to be attributed to the criminal and pathological behaviour of individual doctors. Their aim was to separate such medical torture and murder from the general scientific

orientation of medical practice, whereas Mitscherlich had implied that the latter was responsible for the former. The second, more comprehensive report was probably hidden from the public by the Association of Physicians (Ärztekammer), who had commissioned it in the first instance, but nonetheless continued to use it as evidence of their democratic goodwill in order to return to the general standards and ethics of the world's community of physicians. (Mitscherlich and Mielke 1969; Mitscherlich 1978; Lohmann 1987).

6. In the first Nuremberg trial of Nazi legal professionals, the Allies encountered no insurmountable difficulty in obtaining guilty verdicts. Ten were found guilty, and of these, three were given life sentences; four were acquitted. However, in later trials by German courts, it became less and less likely for officials within the Nazi legal system to be found guilty. The Allies saw Nazi Germany as a criminal state that had come to an end in 1945. Law had become 'Maßnahmen-Recht' ('instrumental law') in the Nazi state, instrumentalised for political aims, subject to 'Führer-Befehl' (command by the Führer) and thus a de facto arm of the executive. Therefore, according to the Allied prosecutors, officials in the Nazi legal system had acted in a criminal way by serving the Nazi state in designing and applying its 'law'.[17] Later, however, continuity between the Nazi and West German state was assumed, and Nazi law was seen as the law legally in force during the Nazi era. Civil servants who 'did their duty' under and according to such law could therefore not be held responsible for any unusual or cruel results. In 1978, Hans Filbinger, then Prime Minister of one of the German states was accused in public by the playwright Rolf Hochhuth of having, in his capacity as presiding judge in a military court, sentenced a young deserter in Norway to death by execution even after the end of the war in 1945. In justifying himself, he relied on the now firmly entrenched view regarding the legality of Nazi law, (in)famously declaring "What had been legal then cannot be illegal now'. (Much to his surprise, he found himself confronted with a public outcry and had to step down from office.) As a result of this widespread understanding of 'continuity', the legal profession was 'de-Nazified' only very reluctantly, and even then not on the grounds of the Nazi laws it had made or the sentences that had been passed down. It was also based on this understanding that the widow of Roland Freisler, the President of the Nazi 'Volksgerichtshof' ('Court of the People'), an instrument of Nazi terror by show-trial, was entitled to a considerable state pension in West Germany (Perels 1998; Gosewinkel 2000; Rückerl 1984; Rüthers 1988).

---

[17] See also see also Emilios Christodoulidis and Scott Veitch in this volume.

7. Erich Mielke, head of the Stasi, the internal and external secret security force of the German Democratic Republic (GDR), was after 1989 never tried for any of the cases involving murder, torture, illegal incarceration, abuse of his power, telephone tapping, breach of confidence, property seizure, smuggling, fraud and forgery, which were systematically perpetrated by his organisation over decades. Instead, in 1993, he was tried and found guilty (on quite shaky evidence) of murders committed in 1931 when he was very young and involved in civil strife and revolutionary action. In the same year he received a criminal conviction, the courts dismissed a civil lawsuit for damages against Mielke that had been filed by a man who had been incarcerated on what even the Stasi themselves saw as 'illegal grounds'. Although a note written by Mielke was found in the Stasi files to the effect that 'suspects' should be incarcerated regardless of legality, it was not deemed to be sufficient evidence of Mielke's personal responsibility. The court ruled that civil servants cannot be held personally responsible for state crimes (Broder 1996).

The first two of these examples (5 and 6) give an account of the unwillingness on the part of West Germany to find high-status practitioners of highly regarded professions guilty of criminal professional activities. This unwillingness is even more pronounced in the case of Mielke because there was a strong general intention to bring him to trial. In the case of the legal professionals, the suspicion that professional solidarity may have had some influence is not too farfetched. The ruling of the civil law court in the Mielke case suggests that this solidarity may even extend to civil servants and state officials in general. Officials of the state have a common interest in the stability and reliability of the state.

Bourgeois law is a class law in its very construction: Criminal law is directed against actions of the lower classes and is not designed to prosecute actions of the ruling classes in the state and the economy. This is probably due to a common understanding of the need to rule and regulate 'subjects' who are to be guided and led and who must, if necessary, be sacrificed for the common good. There is, however, a common interest in stability shared by the classes in the state.

In a nation state and its national society it seems difficult to condemn even in historical writing and accounts what the ruling class of one's 'own' country has done. It is nearly impossible to do so by using the criminal laws of that country, unless there is a clear break from the past, a definite new beginning—something that even revolutions do not easily achieve. The German example shows that it can be done from outside, by what is then denounced as 'Siegerjustiz' ('victors' justice')—and this term illustrates that the results will very likely not be accepted by the nation, at least for a very long time. The German example also shows that part of the former ruling class can be 'externalised' from the state and society, as happened to Hitler and the highest Nazi elite who were brought to trial in Nuremberg.

The case of Mielke, and perhaps the example of the whole GDR, shows that communists were not deemed to be proper members of the international ruling class and definitely not after they had lost power.[18] The ruling class of the communist states does not resemble Western capitalist elites, and in consequence they are not accepted as such.[19] Accordingly, it seems to be easier to prosecute them and when on trial, find them guilty. Neither were the Nazi leaders accepted by the established ruling classes of the Weimar Republic; they were seen as upstarts and unpolished, uneducated people. Apart from ideologically motivated political opposition (by communists, socialists and some Catholics), the only active German resistance against the Nazis came from the aristocracy, who socially despised them. It is easy to find men and women guilty who conform to the law's image of 'the criminal'—individuals who are selfish and brutal in their personal ways. It is not easy at all to find individuals guilty who conform to the image that the legitimate elite have of themselves—working for the common good and not for their self-interest.

C. Truth and Instrumentality

Where criminal law trials are organised according to the 'inquisitorial' model (which aims to find truth independent of accusation and defence), as in continental Europe, criminal law, it seems, has always been 'outcome-oriented'. The public and even judges have a precise idea of what a just and satisfactory judgment should look like. It is craft of the legal profession to find a legally safe way to reach and justify this result. Presently, the law is openly moving away from truth-finding towards the attainment of results.[20]

---

[18] They were eventually reluctantly accepted as members of the ruling class, first by politicians who have a lot of respect for power (eg, the influential conservative German politician Franz-Josef Strauß). Once the communists had lost their power, the German public was willing to accept educated and witty, even though highly suspect individuals like Markus Wolf (former head of the foreign intelligence branch of the Stasi) and Gregor Gysi (leader of the Party of Democratic Socialism (PDS), the successor party of the former communist SED), but not proletarian functionary types like Mielke or former head of state Erich Honecker.

[19] Exceptions just prove this point: see the enormous Western sympathy for the educated Mikhail Gorbachev and particularly for his elegant philosopher wife Raisa. Boris Yeltsin, self-enriching, scheming, heavy-drinking and womanizing—even though he was seen in the West as a hero in the beginning—had no chance in comparison.

[20] That political trials at least secure evidence of human rights violations is one of the 'minimalist' claims made for them. In a recent study on how such violations by the former GDR have been handled by the criminal courts of unified Germany, the authors, who on the whole take a cautious and sceptical stance, come to the following conclusion: 'The actual information secured in criminal trials is of greatest use for social memory and historical research. The high standards set for proof in the trial give special weight to facts stated in judgments. Criminal

As a case in point, conflict resolution is now used to reach an agreement between the parties on what happened; establishing the 'truth' about the event is not necessarily the goal. 'Politically necessary' verdicts are another consequence of this development. Hence Mielke was convicted of a murder he committed while fighting against the Weimar Republic and the Nazis, but was not tried for his actions in a position of power in the former GDR. It was obvious that the former head of the Stasi had to be convicted, but it was equally obvious that it did not matter for what, as long as he went to jail: not truth but punishment. This avoided setting a precedent for punishing innumerable civil servants: not truth but containment.

Why then is criminal law attractive as a mechanism to secure historical truth at all? Most probably 'truth' is just a euphemism for the need to see individuals being punished and to make visible the 'truth' about what they quite clearly did and is consequently known by all.[21] The attraction, I assume, is the possibility of *forcing* the truth to be revealed about what was done: to use the measures provided by criminal law to force people to reveal documents and to make confessions; to stage all this within the performative space provided by the trial; to see the spectacle of formerly powerful people crumbling in the face of evidence; to see the revelation of the 'truth' that we have known all along in a way that cannot be disregarded. It is more than truth—it is *truth victorious, truth triumphant*.

Even notwithstanding the difficulty in achieving verdicts of guilt beyond the operative (as it were: blue-collar) level of historical 'crime', there are a number of unfortunate consequences of attempting to uncover historical truth by criminal law.

— Historical misdeeds are reduced to what can be defined as individual 'criminal acts'; there is no clear tendency to see these acts as part of 'executive' actions, political decisions or institutional structures. Rather, the opposite is often true, as has been shown above by the example of the legal profession under the Nazi regime. In order to avoid this, the entire structure must be declared 'criminal' before attempting to adjudicate individual guilt.
— Historical misdeeds are reduced to actions by individuals—which they actually are and what we want to be taken account of in trials

judgments, therefore, are important measures against repression, denial and glorification of historical facts' (Marxen and Werle 1999, 260, translation mine).

[21] The truth established in a form of procedure—whether criminal or not—is often deemed to be a prerequisite for 'reconciliation' and for living peacefully again after war, occupation, atrocities and traumas. It is more than doubtful that the criminal trial fulfils this function, and there are many other ways of obtaining the goal more directly. For a historical study of such attempts at peace-making, cf Barkan 2000. The amazing capacity of individuals to forget in order to get on with everyday life and to leave behind the role of victim is shown in Hartman 1996.

of the past. We want individuals to be personally responsible, too. But this is only a part of the story, and it does not help in orientating ourselves toward setting up new types of organisations and administration, or finding safeguards against a repetition of what has been done. In order to achieve this, changes of organisational structures are needed, and an analysis of what has gone wrong in the old ones. Criminal trials are incapable of doing this.

— 'Legal purges' have a tendency towards a certain kind of evidence, the most obvious being lists of membership. Those who took part in political organisations (for whatever reason) are the easiest target. The more complex dimensions of what has been done (eg, in the case of Nazi Germany, racism, anti-Semitism, nationalism, militarism, belief in the master race, instrumentalism, etc) do not directly show up and can get lost behind the 'membership' category.[22]

— All three consequences mentioned so far combine to make insignificant the small acts of everyday opportunism, shabbiness, greed, refusal to help and simple willingness to look the other side.[23] By concentrating on 'great crimes' and on 'official' politics the many forms of cooperation that fall short of 'criminality' in the narrow and technical sense of the legal term, but without which no system of repression can work, are made insignificant. This coincides with the myth of a 'resistance' that was extremely 'heroic' on the one hand, and while resistance was made nearly impossible at all on the other hand.

— Casting the problem in terms of guilt means that the opposite must also be acknowledged: innocence. Those who are not found guilty can demand to be treated as innocent. The German example is again illustrative: people began to think or felt confirmed in thinking that they themselves were 'innocent'. Many even took on public office again, and increasingly at highest levels, demanding entitlements for their faithful services rendered to the (Nazi) state.

These consequences are summed up in the assumption and the image of what happened in the period of history about which we are to learn by

[22] This is what my grandmother learned from repeated personal experience in Austria in 1918/19, 1934, 1938 and 1945: 'Never join a political party', she told me, 'Afterwards it will have been the wrong one again.'

[23] The 'disappearance' of Jews in Nazi Germany, for example, resulted in innumerable small advantages of a material kind for most of the rest of the population: less competition, new opportunities for employment, cheap second-hand clothes and carpets, housing and economic enterprises. Denunciations and 'Arisierungen' (take-over of former Jewish businesses) must have been everyone's everyday experience of Nazi politics. Nobody could have not known about it (like they could say with more credibility about the atrocities at Auschwitz), and most took part, though often on a very small scale.

legal 'Aufarbeitung' ('legal reappraisal') and which are best known from the case of Germany—the image of a foreign horde that took hold of a decent population and did atrocious things that none knew about. When we have got rid of that barbarian horde—by strictly legal means, of course—we can return to our decent normality unchanged. Neither authoritarianism nor 'Herrenmenschentum' ('master race ideology') are the problem, but individuals. We all know how few of those perpetrators we can actually make responsible by strictly legal means, but these few force us to treat all others as 'innocent'. By focusing on individuals we avoid having to deal with structures, organisations and principles of living together; what we actually get is living with murderers by turning a blind eye.[24]

Law—even though it appears a promising candidate for getting at historical 'truth'—is not at all a proper means to this end. Instead, it produces a model of what happened that is thoroughly and systematically distorted, as well as politically conservative (to put it cautiously). There is, however, not much besides law that looks capable of managing the immediate aftermath of dictatorship and military action. The other possibilities are simple revenge (of which plenty and at the same time surprisingly little occurs after such upheavals), suicide, flight, or exile. Trials have the function of re-establishing state domination—but we cannot assume that we get to any historical truth this way. Rather, 'truth', as Aulus Gellius wrote, 'is the daughter of time'.

We will approach truth only when the conditions for reflexive analysis have been developed, when the (legitimate and illegitimate) interests of survivors and perpetrators can be acknowledged and when the cultural (ie, culture industry) models of understanding what happened in the past are thoroughly scrutinised.

VI. HISTORICAL TRUTH AT THE POINT OF PASSAGE INTO PRE-HISTORY: SHOAH MEMORY REFLEXIVITY

I want to finish with an example of how the possibilities of finding historical truth have changed in Germany recently through forces beyond criminal law. This is the passage of the Shoah from living memory to pre-history. Troubled by its unscalable past, Germany has an ample supply of differing historical accounts and of conflicts about them, yet even so, the present surge of writing on 'memory' is remarkable. It seems that the memory industry as part of culture industry has entered a stage of reflexivity in

---

[24] It is estimated that there were about 6,000 guards on duty in Auschwitz alone (Decker 1990). In the important Frankfurt Auschwitz Trial of 1963–65 information was collected on about 800, a mere few dozen of them finally stood trial. See the resigned conclusion reached by Decker 1990.

which we no longer reconstruct pasts and try to make one of them universally accepted, but rather question the process of memory itself. Is there enough of it? Of the right kind? What role is the state to have? What role is the culture industry to have? Do we really want to establish our national identity on the Holocaust?

In Germany (as in Israel, New York and Hollywood), a new generation, mainly the grandchildren of survivors and perpetrators increasingly treats the Nazi past as 'historical'. This involves a profound change to the meaning of those past events. When the past shifts from personal memory to (pre-)history, the meta-narrative about 'memory' tends to come to the fore. This seems to make it easier to agree on a broad outline of historical events. Documentation is much better today and readily available. The Shoah is not some dark secret any more that has to be kept from children; it is part of school curricula and a frequent background for if not the outright topic of popular novels, movies and TV productions. The contents of memory are less contested as its form changes. These changes imply several things.

First, there is an increased chance that 'small' misdeeds will be considered—eg, the 'perfectly legal' appropriations of Jewish property ('Arisierungen'), the denunciations and non-criminal acts of mere neglect and denial, the whole culture of anti-Semitism that pervaded even groups of (eg, communist) resistance, the part played by organisations that have so far managed to maintain that they stood outside the cycle of 'Auschwitz' (such as, unbelievably, the Wehrmacht). The old model of a Germany that was on the whole decent yet overrun by (a small number of) barbarian Nazi hordes who did terrible things that nobody knew about seems to be giving way at last. It is being replaced by a richer and more nuanced picture of widespread anti-Semitism and a willingness to exclude groups singled out by the state, of opportunism and everyday meanness and indifference. As a corollary, the heroic understanding of resistance is giving way to one in which resistance is an everyday affair of not participating, of speaking up when possible and of subversive disobedience when participation is demanded by the state. There is now a chance of understanding that what is needed to guard against a recurrence of Nazism is not heroic actions in the realm of institutional politics (although clever and courageous ones are necessary) nor even armed combat (which drove a small faction of the German student movement into terrorism) but rather a theory and practice of antiauthoritarianism based on human solidarity and civil disobedience. At least that is what I think in my more optimistic moments.

Second, forms of 'restitution' can now reach beyond personal 'guilt' and make visible the shameful role of the successor states after 1945. The governments and economies of West Germany, Austria and Switzerland profited from property 'without owners', which they had appropriated by not engaging actively in its restitution to those exiled and to potential heirs of those who had been killed, over the course of nearly four decades. This was done by not issuing invitations to return and restoring their property, but it also included more or less overt extortion, as in the case of artwork that was declared part of Austria's 'national heritage' and thus prohibited from being removed. Further, settlements regarding compensation to slave workers have finally been agreed upon now that US lawyers have taken on the issue.

Third, on the flip side for parts of the population, these changes mean that 'self-defilement' can end so that being 'German' can be something to be proud of again, or at least something that is as 'normal' as belonging to other nations. It is increasingly argued that the enormity of German crimes against humanity can be balanced against the Russian Gulag, the rapes of German women by the Red Army, the Allied bombings of Dresden and Hiroshima, as well as the post-war ethnic cleansing of Germans from Poland, the Czech Republic and other Eastern European countries. The dominant mood in this part of the population seems to tend toward 'closing of the account' ('Schlussstrich').

Fourth, for culture industry renditions of the Holocaust, 'documentation' is no longer the main topic. There is no more need to 'prove' the truth of it: it can be taken for granted. Steven Spielberg, in his quasi-documentary movies, which include *Schindler's List* (1993) and (regarding a different topic) *Saving Private Ryan* (1998), has not only become old-fashioned but even (objectively) cynical by making us sit back and look at mass murder as what Imre Kertész has rightly called pseudo-documentary 'kitsch' (1998, 55f).[25] 'Laughing at Hitler'—as in George Tabori's *Mutters Courage* (*My Mother's Courage*, 1995), Roberto Benigni's *La vita è bella* (*Life is Beautiful*, 1997) and the French/Romanian movie *Train de vie* (*Train of Life*, 1998)—is acceptable again as it was in Chaplin's masterpiece *The Great Dictator*—and is more up to how the problems are perceived at present (Laster and Steinert 1999).

Finally, since the reunification of the two German states in 1990, it has become very obvious that there is no way of getting around questions of 'national identity' in the historical memories cultivated by nation states. Now that most of the population of Germany (as well as of Austria and other European countries) can rightly claim that the events of the Shoah have nothing to do with them personally, it can finally be seen as the historical disaster it was for all of humanity. Only now, with this perspective in mind does it become apparent that the Shoah has in fact become part

---

[25] It remains to be seen how much this verdict will hold for Spielberg's other initiatives that aim at 'truth', including the testimonies collected by his Survivors Foundation and the documentaries that will come out of it. (The first was *The Last Days* in 1999) There has been criticism that others have done such collecting before and done it more professionally, ie, with more regard for what retelling does to the survivors themselves. Spielberg's naive realism is untainted by any consideration of the culture industry framework in which he—a master of children's movies—produces tear- and fear-jerkers.

of nationalist discourse in these countries and is even used as a catalyst for nationalism. The Shoah is seen as part of 'our' (German) heritage, and its very enormity gives 'us' a national distinction. On the extreme right this distinction involves the great struggle/battle of the 'Herrenmenschen' ('master race'), who happened to be defeated but to whose values some remain faithful. Far more interesting is the widespread pacifism, internationalism and European orientation in Germany (to some extent in Austria too) that is derived from the Nazi past. On the extreme left this inclination is linked to strong anti-nationalism, but only a little further to the middle of the political spectrum lies the nationalist theory of 'German exceptionalism'. This attitude is most frequently seen and promoted in the German weekly *Der Spiegel* by public figures like novelist Martin Walser and ex-leftists like Green foreign minister Joschka Fischer, who argue for a special German obligation to wage war (which is prohibited by Law) on behalf of human rights.

In any case, the passage of the Shoah from living memory to pre-history and the concomitant reflexivity allow us to see how the 'memory and heritage' industry works and to analyse it in the framework of the culture industry in general. It is obvious from the example of Germany that the cultural commodities produced are of utmost importance to the (nation) state, and we find here, as in other cases of culture, a strong connection between industry and populist politics.

REFERENCES

Adorno, Theodor W and Horkheimer, Max. 1944/1947. *Dialektik der Aufklärung. Philosophische Fragemente*. New York: Social Studies Association Inc/Amsterdam: Querido Verlag.

van Alphen, Ernst. 1997. *Caught by History: Holocaust Effects in Contemporary Art, Literature, and Theory*. Stanford: Stanford University Press.

Anders, Günther. 1956. *Die Antiquiertheit des Menschen*. München: Beck.

Assmann, Aleida. 1999. *Erinnerungsräume: Formen und Wandlungen des kulturellen Gedächtnisses*. München: Beck.

Barkan, Elazar. 2000. *The Guilt of Nations: Restitution and Negotiating Historical Injustices*. New York: Norton.

Broder, Henryk M. 1996. Die Hand auf der Schulter. *Der Spiegel* 25: 62–9.

Cole, Tim. 1999. *Images of the Holocaust: The Myth of the 'Shoah Business'*. London: Duckworth.

Cremer-Schäfer, Helga and Steinert, Heinz. 1998. *Straflust und Repression: Zur Kritik der populistischen Kriminologie*. Münster: Verlag Westfälisches Dampfboot.

Decker, Friedrich. 1990. Vergangenheitsbewältigung durch Strafrecht? *Kritische Viertel jahresschrift für Gesetzgebung und Rechtswissenschaft* 73: 299–312.

Evans, Richard J. 1997. *In Defence of History*. London: Granta.

Finkelstein, Norman. 2000. *The Holocaust Industry: Reflections on the Exploitation of Jewish Suffering*. New York: Verso.

Fulbrook, Mary. 1999. *German National Identity after the Holocaust*. Cambridge: Polity.

Fuld, Werner. 1999. *Das Lexikon der Fälschungen*. Frankfurt: Eichborn.

Gillis, John R (ed). 1994. *Commemorations: The Politics of National Identity*. Princeton: Princeton University Press.

Gosewinkel, Dieter. 2000. Politische Ahndung an den Grenzen des Justizstaats. In *Geschichte vor Gericht: Historiker, Richter und die Suche nach Gerechtigkeit*, edited by N Frei. München: Beck.

Gourevitch, Philip. 1998. The Unimagined. *The New Yorker*, 7 September, 41–5.

Hartman, Geoffrey. 1996. *The Longest Shadow: In the Aftermath of the Holocaust*. Bloomington: Indiana University Press.

Hassemer, Winfried. 1990. Grundlinien eines rechtsstaatlichen Strafverfahrens. *Kritische Vierteljahresschrift für Gesetzgebung und Rechtswissenschaft* 73: 260–78.

Herf, Jeffrey. 1997. *Divided Memory: The Nazi Past in the Two Germanys*. Cambridge, MA: Harvard University Press.

Höpken, Wolfgang. 1998. Kriegserinnerung und nationale Identität(en): Vergangenheits politik in Jugoslawien und in den Nachfolgestaaten. *Transit: Europäische Revue Heft* 15: 83–99.

Hughes, Robert. 1993. *Culture of Complaint: The Fraying of America*. New York: Oxford University Press.

Huyssen, Andreas. 1999. Monumental Seduction. In *Acts of Memory: Cultural Recall in the Present*, edited by M Bal, J Crewe and L Spitzer. Hanover: University Press of New England.

Kertész, Imre. 1998. Wem gehört Auschwitz? *Die Zeit* 48, 19 November, 55f.

Koshar, Rudy. 1998. *Germany's Transient Pasts: Preservation and National Memory in the Twentieth Century*. Chapel Hill: University of North Carolina Press.

LaCapra, Dominick. 1998. *History and Memory after Auschwitz*. Ithaca: Cornell University Press.

Laster, Kathy (with Krista Breckweg and John King). 2000. *The Drama of the Courtroom*. Sydney: Federation Press.

Laster, Kathy and Steinert, Heinz. 1999. La vita è bella: Absurdismus und Realismus in der Darstellung der Shoah. *Mittelweg 36*, 8(4): 76–89.

Lohmann, Hans-Martin. 1987. *Alexander Mitscherlich*. Reinbek: Rowohlt.

Marxen, Klaus and Werle, Gerhard. 1999. *Die strafrechtliche Aufarbeitung von DDR-Unrecht: Eine Bilanz*. Berlin: de Gruyter.

Mitscherlich, Alexander. 1978. Der Patient—nur ein Werkstück? *Der Spiegel* 38: 238–9.

Mitscherlich, Alexander and Mielke, Fred (eds). 1969. *Medizin ohne Menschlichkeit: Dokumente des Nürnberger Ärzteprozesses*. Frankfurt: Fischer.

Moeller, Susan D. 1999. *Compassion Fatigue: How the Media Sell Disease, Famine, War and Death*. New York: Routledge.

Novick, Peter. 1999. *The Holocaust and Collective Memory: The American Experience*. London: Bloomsbury.

Perels, Joachim. 1998. Der Nürnberger Juristenprozeß im Kontext der Nachkriegsgeschichte. *Kritische Justiz* 31(1): 84–98.

Reichel, Peter. 1995. *Politik mit der Erinnerung: Gedächtnisorte im Streit um die nationalsozialistische Vergangenheit*. München: Hanser.

Rückerl, Adalbert. 1984. *NS-Verbrechen vor Gericht: Versuch einer Vergangenheitsbe-wältigung.* Heidelberg: CF Müller.

Rüthers, Bernd. 1988. *Entartetes Recht: Rechtslehren und Kronjuristen im Dritten Reich.* München: Beck.

Schneider, Richard Chaim. 1997. *Fetisch Holocaust: Die Judenvernichtung— verdrängt und vermarktet.* München: Kindler.

Segev, Tom. 1991. *The Seventh Million: The Israelis and the Holocaust.* New York: Hill & Wang (English edition 1993).

Steinert, Heinz. 1992. *Die Entdeckung der Kulturindustrie oder: Warum Professor Adorno Jazz-Musik nicht ausstehen konnte.* Wien: Verlag für Gesellschaftskritik.

——. 1998. *Kulturindustrie.* Münster: Verlag Westfälisches Dampfboot.

——. 1999. Kulturindustrielle Politik mit dem Großen & Ganzen: Populismus, Politik-Darsteller, ihr Publikum und seine Mobilisierung. *Internationale Gesellschaft und Politik* 4: 402–13.

Stille, Alexander. 1999. Overload. *The New Yorker*, 8 March, 38–44.

Sykes, Charles J. 1992. *A Nation of Victims: The Decay of the American Character.* New York: St Martin's Press.

Weber, Max. 1968. On Charisma and Institution Building. Selected Papers. Chicago: Chicago University Press.

Winter, Jay and Sivan, Emmanuel (eds). 1999. *War and Remembrance in the Twentieth Century.* Cambridge: Cambridge University Press.

Young, James. 1988. *Writing and Rewriting the Holocaust: Narrative and the Consequences of Interpretation.* Bloomington: Indiana University Press.

Zelizer, Barbie. 1998. *Remembering to Forget: Holocaust Memory through the Camera's Eye.* Chicago: University of Chicago Press.

Zuckermann, Moshe. 1999. *Gedenken und Kulturindustrie.* Berlin: Philo.

8

Australia's Sorry Judges: Nationalism and Collective Memory

KATHY LASTER[*]

ALL OVER THE world governments are confronting the legacy of oppression against sections, even the whole, of their society. At first sight, it seems odd to find Australia in such company. Australia, after all, is a 'good' society, free of the turmoil that besets many political systems across the globe.[1] However, Australia's appalling treatment of its indigenous Aboriginal population, past and present, has begun in the past decade to undermine its international standing.[2] The guilty secret is out: aboriginal people in Australia have been massacred, forced off their land and discriminated against in all aspects of life. Even now, they are arrested and imprisoned in disproportionately higher numbers than white Australians, their life expectancy is far lower and their general level of health and education is scandalous for a prosperous, post-industrial society.[3]

[*] I am grateful to Stan Cohen, Susanne Karstedt and Heinz Steinert for helpful comments on an earlier draft of this chapter.

[1] This perspective is, for example, consistently held by successive waves of immigrants and refugees who come to Australia as a safe haven. See Laster 1995a.

[2] In 1999, the monitoring body of the Convention on the Elimination of All Forms of Racial Discrimination (CERD) found that Australia was in serious breach of its obligations (AAP, August 18 1999). CERD condemned the Australian government's approach to indigenous land rights as they were reflected in amendments made to the 1993 Native Title Act in 1998. These amendments created legal certainty for Governments and third parties at the expense of indigenous entitlements (Federal Capital Press 1999). The CERD Committee recognized that, within the broad range of discriminatory practices that had long been directed against Australia's Aboriginal and Torres Strait Islander peoples, the effects of Australia's racially discriminatory land practices had endured as an acute impairment of the rights of Australia's indigenous communities.

[3] The life expectancy of Aboriginal and Torres Strait Islanders for the period 1991–1996 was 57 years for males and 66 for females, which is approximately 15–17 years lower than the life expectancy for the general Australian population (Australian Bureau of Statistics 1996). Aboriginal deaths from common infectious diseases are up to 300 times higher than the average for the general population and among the highest in the world (Pilger 1992, 45). The income of indigenous households is more than AUD$200 lower than that of the average Australian household (Australian Bureau of Statistics 1996). The inequalities are highlighted in indigenous people's experiences of incarceration. The 1989 Royal Commission into Aboriginal

Methods of bringing past abuses into the open vary from country to country, from violent insurrection to quasi-legal procedures, which are used to identify (but only sometimes formally punish) those deemed responsible (see Cohen 1995; 2001). Extraordinary measures are necessary to restore public confidence in the rule of law and trust in new governments. Australia, however, is relatively unique in allowing these weighty matters to be dealt with as part of its routine court-based system of adjudication.[4] Here, confronting the wrongs of the past has largely been undertaken in the civil jurisdiction, and standard legal methods, grounded in a conservative jurisprudence, have been employed.

The landmark decision of the High Court of Australia in *Mabo v Queensland (No 2)*[5] (hereafter *Mabo*) was the formal beginning of Australia's engagement with its racist past. The case overturned legal doctrine that considered Australia to be '*terra nullius*' ('land of none') at the time of white settlement. The privileged position of white settlers with regard to Australian land was suddenly called into question. This dramatic legal about-face paved the way for recognition of aboriginal peoples' claims to an interest in land and provided a material basis for black–white reconciliation in Australia.

At first blush, the *Mabo* decision provides an optimistic case study of how judicial law-making has been employed in 'coming to terms with the past'. However, in this chapter, I argue that this too quick liberal assessment ignores some less pleasant aspects of collective memory jurisprudence. Specifically, I suggest that the Australian experience demonstrates that law's engagement with collective memory is inexorably tied to national identity politics. The link between collective memory and nationalism, even in the relatively benign form it has assumed in Australia, is probably toxic to the real spirit of 'coming to terms with the past'. Worthy intentions do not necessarily lead to good outcomes. I argue that *Mabo* perpetuates an artificial 'Guilty White/Victim Black' divide. The outcome, in the longer term, is counterproductive for the achievement of reconciliation and social change. Law, I contend, works best when the needs and interests of socially marginalised groups are embedded in cultural values

---

Deaths in Custody examined more than 105 deaths that occurred in the mid to late 1980s, by which time the rate of deaths in custody was thirteen times higher than that in South Africa (Australian Archives 1996; Pilger 1992, 54).

[4] Australia has maintained a stable political system throughout its short history, and its institutions of governance have consistently enjoyed high levels of public support (see Bean 1995). Neal (1991) recounts that the first civil case in Australian courts was brought by a convict couple—the Cables, who sued the ship's captain for return of property belonging to them. Neal's thesis is that confidence and trust in the rule of law were transported from Britain by the convicts as part of their cultural baggage. Surprisingly, convicts who had suffered on account of the legal system nevertheless relied upon it to forge a new political and social order in Botany Bay.

[5] (1992) CLR 175 1.

other than victim status. In Australia, 'coming to terms with the past' has led to stereotyped conceptions of national identity that have occluded more sophisticated and fruitful understandings of social and political pluralism.

In the first part of the chapter, I set out the relationship between history and nationalism, with special regard to Australia. I show how the traditional understanding of Australia's past as essentially 'good' is now being challenged by a radical, post-colonialist republican political agenda. Through an analysis of the Australian High Court's *Mabo* judgment, I show how even the well-meaning legal activism of the High Court is part of a misconceived public debate over national identity. I go on to argue that the main beneficiary of the *Mabo* decision was the High Court and the common law system itself. I then consider the limitations of law in meeting the longer term interests of Australia's indigenous people, and use concepts like victimism, and identity politics that are based on an apparently shared experience of harm or marginalisation, as my main political paradigm. In the final section of the chapter, I consider how aboriginal peoples' interest would be better placed within the broader framework of Australia's successful experience with cultural pluralism and multicultural ideology.

I. PAST AS PRESENT

Australia's engagement with collective memory admits the 'awfulness' of 'our' past behaviour toward indigenous people. Since the past is always the captive of the present, the current mea culpa rationale for radical reform requires closer analysis. How and why has Australian history suddenly come to be seen as 'wrong'? Specifically, how do we account for the collective memory impulse?

There is a general pattern in all societies' interpretations of their past. Conservative regimes, for example, tend to regard the past as 'the good old days', a nostalgic representation of all that has been lost in the excesses/degeneration/secularism/rush/individualism of 'modern' life. This argument is often made in the context of 'Orientalism'—the idealisation of less advanced cultures as representations of a dominant society's vision of its own past (Said 1978). The 'Other' is romanticised because it appears to exhibit elements of the dominant society's revered lost history. This past may or may not be able to be resurrected for a brighter future. By contrast, revolutionary societies of both the Right and Left locate their 'golden age' in the immediate or distant future, built upon the radical foundation of the present. For these societies, the past is the 'dark age', the point of departure that makes the present both justifiable and inevitable.[6] These competing worldviews (and all shades in between) coexist, vying for dominance. A sudden shift in a society's attitude toward its past therefore is usually a marker of a significant change in power relations.

History is inevitably part of a national narrative: to tell 'us' about who 'we' are 'today' by examining 'our' past.[7] The history of the vast island-continent of Australia, for instance, has mainly been understood from the perspective of the artificial construct we dub the 'nation' (White 1997, 19).[8] The Federation of the Colonies into States of the Commonwealth in 1901, for example, occurred under the slogan 'A Nation for a Continent'. A constant succession of significant historical anniversaries (such as the bicentenary of White Settlement in 1988 and the centenary of Federation in 2001), as well as national events (such as the 2000 Sydney Olympics), feed the nationalist enterprise.[9]

Until recently, the dominant vision of Australian history, and therefore national character, has been overwhelmingly positive and positivist. Rejecting a circumspect approach to the celebration of the Australian Bicentenary in 1988, for example, Geoffrey Blainey, the most well-known and influential Australian historian, argued, 'By the standards of almost any utopia they care to name, Australian history in the last 200 years, for all its failings, has been

[6] I have here amplified some of Geoffrey Blainey's views, most notably those expressed in *The Great See-Saw* (1988), an examination of the cyclical trends in attitudes to progress in Western history. It is odd, given Blainey's insights on attitudes to history, that he is quite unreflexive about his own role in the public debate about 'collective memory' in Australia.

[7] The instrumental use of history for diverse nationalist agendas is most evident in official histories of the nation state (or, conversely, the fall of kings) and its institutions. But it permeates even more modest endeavours purporting to record the contributions made by a select group (trade union, school, 'pioneer women') or select individuals (social reformers, military leaders and intellectuals) and thereby (either positively or negatively, depending on your leaning) influenced the course of that society's future development. Even micro studies of individuals and groups (including those informed by postmodernist, anti-master narrative theories) are easily co-opted as (qualifying) footnotes illuminating a national(ist) mosaic.

[8] Big-name Australian historians, such as the conservative Geoffrey Blainey and his radical teacher, the late Manning Clarke, are influential precisely because they deliver a clear vision of the (imagined) nation of Australia and are forthright in their views about Australian national character and identity. Significantly, Clarke and Blainey were both identified as Great Australian Thinkers of the Twentieth Century in a special issue of *The Australian* newspaper, 'This Living Century', 28–29 August 1999. Henry Reynolds, another nationalist historian but of the 'Black Armband' school, was the third nominee on this exclusive list.

[9] Increasingly, there is dissent from this characterisation. Commentators point to these celebrations of Australian nation-building as illustrating Australia's rapid transition from colonialist self-denigration to nationalist self-admiration (eg, Lowenthal 1990, 137). At the time of the bicentenary, which commemorated two hundred years of white settlement, prominent novelist David Malouf bemoaned that the event 'is too blackened with sorrow for some of us ... and with shame for the rest: too loaded with despair and courage ... for its re-enactment to be any more than a farce' (Lowenthal 1990, 152). Yet, as I argue below, there is also some smugness in the concessions made by settler society to aboriginal sensibilities.

a fortunate history.' Australians, he maintains, can be justly proud that this country established one of the first democracies in modern history, enjoys a high standard of living and has contributed to 'the world's stock of valuable skills and ideas' in art, science and technology (Blainey 1991, 49–50).

Blainey's expansive declaration was a defensive response to recent revisionist accounts of Australian history. A younger band of Australian historians have sought to debunk naive Whig accounts of Australia's past. The influential historian, Henry Reynolds, for example, has made it his mission to expose the long denied violence, subversion and genocide punctuating Australian history (Reynolds 1987; 1999).[10] Blainey dubbed this alternative perspective 'the Black Armband' view, implying that Australians were now parading around in obvious formal mourning for their past when they should instead be proud of all they had achieved as a nation.[11] His pithy phrase came to encapsulate the rejection of both the collective memory of and collective guilt for the wrongs committed by white settlers against Aboriginal people. The imagery also pokes fun at those bleak prophets casting aspersions on the bona fides of their ancestors.

Though ostensibly competing with each other, the perspectives of the 'Three Cheers' Whig account of Australian history and the 'Black Armband' approach share a common nationalist preoccupation—'Were Australians "good" or "bad" in the past?' The answer to this historical question lies at the heart of contemporary Australian domestic politics. If, on balance, Australia's past was 'worthy' there is no need to break with it and the institutions that have served it well. If, on the other hand, 'our' history is 'bad', there is good reason to sever the imperial umbilical cord and its legacy.

II. NATIONALIST POLITICS IN AUSTRALIA

For a significant section of Australia's elite, 'a republic is our destiny'.[12] However, in November 1999, when a referendum on whether Australia should cut ties with the British Crown through the election of an Australian Head of State was put to the Australian people, the people overwhelmingly

---

[10] Blainey maintains that it is 'vocal minorities' who now seek to present Australian history as 'the story of violence, exploitation, repression, racism, sexism, capitalism, colonialism, and a few other "isms"' (Blainey 1991, 49).

[11] This was the title given by Blainey in his influential article in the July/August 1993 edition of *Quadrant*, the main Australian conservative intellectual monthly. The term was immediately taken up by John Howard and other conservatives. Historians were quick to point out that historical narratives are informed by the ideologies of the storytellers (Walter 1990), and they accused them of 'naive triumphalism', based not on primary research but on nostalgia for a past that never was. (See, for example, Fitzgerald 1990; Burgmann and Lee 1988.)

[12] Peter Costello, 'A Republic Is Our Destiny' (Wright 1999b).

voted 'no' to constitutional change.[13] There was, it seems, no justification for breaking with 'our' British heritage.[14]

The republican movement had implicitly based its campaign on a 'Black Armband' perspective. In a now famous speech launching the International Year for the World's Indigenous People in 1992, then Labor Prime Minister Paul Keating, the main instigator of the republican agenda, maintained that 'there is nothing to fear or to lose in the recognition of historical truth'. He boldly declared:

> We took the traditional lands and smashed the traditional way of life.
> We brought the disease. The alcohol.
> We committed the murders.
> We took the children from their mothers.
> We practised discrimination and exclusion.
> It was our ignorance and our prejudice.[15]

Aboriginal people in Australia have actively sought a public acknowledgment and admission of responsibility for their suffering. They have also demanded reparation for their losses as individuals and as a community.[16] Keating's remarks signalled a major shift in the government's responsiveness to these claims. The concession, though, is marred by its flagrant nationalism. Built into that powerful possessive pronoun 'we' is a fictional invocation of a homogeneous white Australian entity conveniently united in a formal expression of responsibility, if not guilt.

The republican movement in Australia though is far from loaded down with guilt. Rather, a robust, nationalist self-confidence motivates much of

[13] The referendum asked whether voters wished to alter the Constitution 'to establish the Commonwealth of Australia as a republic with the Queen and Governor-General being replaced by a President appointed by a 2/3 majority of Parliament'. In order to succeed, the referendum required a majority 'yes' vote throughout Australia in addition to a majority 'yes' vote in at least four of Australia's six states. Neither of the two requirements was fulfilled. Not one state achieved a 'yes' vote due to the very strong 'no' sentiment in rural areas (The Sunday Age 1999; Wright 1999c). Many republicans voted 'no', preferring a directly-elected President model (Gorden 1999). The 'yes' campaigners blamed Prime Minister John Howard for the result, accusing him of confusing the issue by not allowing a referendum on the simple choice of a republic over a monarchy (Gorden 1999).

[14] This view was expressed by Prime Minister Howard in his announcement that his principal reason for voting 'no' was his support for the present system. He could not support change to a constitutional system that had 'worked so well' and had 'brought stability to the nation' (Wright 1999a). The view that the monarchy protects Australia from instability underscores the monarchist position (Slezak 1999).

[15] Paul Keating, at Redfern Park in Sydney on 10 December 1992.

[16] An official apology for brutal policies inflicted upon indigenous communities is integral to the reconciliation process according to the Aboriginal and Torres Strait Islander Commission (*The Australian*, 21 May 1997). Former Head of the Commission, Ms Lois O'Donoghue, argues for reparation in the form of state funds for the education of aboriginal children as an illustration of the Australian governments' commitment to righting past wrongs (*The Australian*, 21 May1997).

its rhetoric and political activism.[17] There is a kind of double-think underlying the republican reconstruction of Australian history and identity: 'our' Australian past was 'bad', but since that was an 'English' past, and 'we' are not really 'English'—indeed, 'we' consider ourselves to have been overborne by the English—'we' do not wholly own that identity, even if 'we' must accept formal responsibility for 'their' actions.

It is easier to disown a past you are intent on shedding. Yet it would be wrong to dismiss the republicans' use of Australia's treatment of aboriginal people as mere political opportunism. For mixed reasons, there is genuine empathy for the plight of indigenous people oppressed by a stronger 'foreign' power. For some, there is empathy with the socially marginalised. For others, a post-colonialist framework provides a more abstract way of denouncing the vices of imperial domination. Nevertheless, the image of Australia as an ancient country with a strong aboriginal heritage has proved to be a commercial boon. 'Australiana' sells well. Aboriginal artefacts, artworks and sacred sites are internationally acclaimed and appropriated by Australian companies and governments alike. In the opening ceremony of the 2000 Olympics in Sydney, for example, the mystical exoticism of Australia's original inhabitants was seamlessly blended with the 'can-do' pioneering spirit of white settlers. According to restitution theorist Elazar Barkan, however, 'in the moral economy of restitution, Australia seems to pay little for the privilege of acquiring this long indigenous history' (Barkan 2000, 237).

The business opportunities afforded by reconciliation, however, have not been sufficient to persuade the current Liberal (conservative) Prime Minister, John Howard, to embrace a new black/white national identity. Despite extreme pressure, the Prime Minister stubbornly refuses to turn 'collective memory' into 'collective guilt'.[18] He has stated unequivocally,

---

[17] For example, Henry Reynolds explains that 'much critical, revisionist history springs from a belief that Australia should do better and is capable of doing so. It is written in hope and expectation of reform, crafted in the confidence that carefully marshalled, clearly-expressed argument can persuade significant numbers of Australians to change their minds and redirect their sympathies. Beyond that confidence in individuals is a firm belief in the capacity of Australian democracy to respond to new ideas, which in time can shape policies and recast institutions, laws and customs' (Reynolds 1999, 245).

[18] This Prime Minister has remained firm in his resolve, for example, not to apologise formally to the 'Stolen Generation' (fair skinned aboriginal children who under assimilationist policies were forcibly removed from their families by the State well into the second half of the twentieth century). Throughout most of 1998–99 the political question was whether, and in what form, the Prime Minister ought to apologise to aboriginal people on behalf of the nation. Bumper stickers, for example, exhorted 'Say Sorry, Mr Howard'. In the absence of an appropriate response from the government, people took it upon themselves to initiate 'informal' apologies. A 'National Sorry Day' was declared, with signatures collected in ad hoc 'Sorry books' distributed in workplaces, schools, churches and recreational clubs. While there is some acknowledgment that this is a necessary first step, there is rarely any sustained analysis of what a future agenda should involve.

'Australians of this generation should not be required to accept guilt and blame for past actions and policies over which they had no control'.[19]

In August 1999, after years of public wrangling and behind-the-scenes negotiation, the Prime Minister finally presented a motion to Parliament that, while falling short of a full apology, reaffirmed 'a wholehearted commitment to the cause of reconciliation between indigenous and non-indigenous Australians as an important national priority'. It also acknowledged 'that the mistreatment of many indigenous Australians over a significant period represents the most blemished chapter in our national history'. Its penultimate clause expresses the Parliament's

> deep and sincere regret that indigenous Australians suffered injustices under the practices of past generations, and for the hurt and trauma that many indigenous people continue to feel as a consequence of those practices.[20]

Prime Minister Howard's approach, however, like Keating's before him, drips with nationalist fervour. The tenor of the text is grounded in the old-fashioned political rhetoric of the 'united nation'. Clause B of the motion, for example, recognises 'the achievements of the Australian nation, commits to work together to strengthen the bonds that unite us, to respect and appreciate our differences and to build a fair and prosperous future in which we can all share'. The final clause states that 'we, having achieved so much as a nation, can now move forward together for the benefit of all Australians'. For both Labor and Liberal Prime Ministers, the impetus for dealing with the past is the possibilities it creates for reshaping the future in their own image. To foreshadow my later argument, the nationalist vision of both camps neatly sidesteps more complex questions of how a reconciled society is to deal with the political, social and legal consequences of diversity.

But the Prime Minister's more pragmatic reason for refusing to use the magic word 'sorry' is that a formal apology could amount to an admission of legal liability by the Commonwealth government for the wrongs suffered by aboriginal people as a result of past policies.[21] He is right to

---

[19] Opening speech at the Australian Reconciliation Convention, 27 May 1997.

[20] Hansard (Commonwealth), *Parliamentary Debates*, House of Representatives, 26 August 1999, 12.24 PM [available at www.aph.gov.au]. Although there was no formal apology from the Howard Government to the Stolen Generation, the Coalition government did stave off criticism by providing various financial 'packages' to meet the needs of aboriginal people. In 1997, for example, it pledged approximately AUD$50 million in health care for Aboriginal Australians. This initiative focused particularly on trauma counselling and expanded mental health services for victims of the Stolen Generation programme (*Canberra Times*, 13 December 1997). Despite various financial buy-offs, both the Australian public and aboriginal people themselves still insisted on the symbolic 'sorry' statement.

[21] The official Parliamentary expression of regret carefully avoided the imposition of liability. The Parliament *acknowledged* 'the mistreatment of many indigenous Australians' and expressed 'deep and sincere *regret* that indigenous peoples had suffered under the practices of *past* generations' (*ibid*, emphasis added). In this way there was no admission of fault for either past or present injustices, circumventing the need for compensation.

fear litigation. Law converts the abstract politics of identity into 'interests'. Aboriginal people in Australia have increasingly brought their claims to court as a way of holding government and private institutions such as the Church, as well as individuals, liable for past wrongdoing.

III. THE *MABO* DECISION: A WATERSHED JUDGEMENT

The High Court's decision in *Mabo* is frequently described as a 'watershed' with regard to black–white relations in Australia.[22] Both literally and symbolically, the judgment irrevocably changed the course of Australia's attitude to its past and toward Indigenous people. But judicial intervention into the vexed politics of national identity is a more complex matter than either supporters or detractors of the *Mabo* decision usually acknowledge.

Mabo was a test case brought by three aboriginal inhabitants, including Eddie Mabo, of the Murray Islands in the Torres Strait. It was an appeal to the High Court against an unfavourable decision at first instance by the Supreme Court of Queensland. The representative plaintiffs sought a formal declaration from the High Court that the inhabitants of the island (known as the Merriam people) had some interest in the land on the largest island, Mer (a mere nine square kilometres). Their argument, expressed in the alternative, from their highest to lowest legal claim, was that the courts should deem them as 'owners' or 'possessors' or 'occupiers' or, if nothing else, then at least as people entitled 'to use and enjoyment' of the land.

The Queensland government formally laid claim to the islands in the nineteenth century. At various times it purported to exercise its authority over the tiny island, but in their day-to-day lives, the indigenous population, which varied between 400 and 1000, largely lived according to their own (changing) community norms and lifestyles. Unlike aboriginal people who had been dispossessed and alienated from their land on the mainland, the Merriam people maintained—and more importantly, were able to prove—continuous habitation and use of the land consistent with their own (dynamic) understanding of customary law. The Murray Islanders had no fences, but all knew who owned each plot of land.

The Merriam people probably were able to mount the strongest claim of any aboriginal community seeking to establish their claim to land under conventional Western legal tests of 'proprietary interest'. The main legal stumbling block for them, as for all aboriginal plaintiffs who came before

---

[22] See for example Ratnapala and Stephenson (eds) 1993, in particular Moens 1993. See also Gregory 1992.

them, was the long line of British, and later Australian, legal authorities that held that at the time of white settlement, Australia was *terra nullius*.[23]

Terra nullius was an eighteenth-century international legal classification for regions that could be freely annexed by an imperial power.[24] New land could be acquired as settled territory if the land was uninhabited or if the inhabitants were thought neither to have an organised system of government nor improved or cultivated the land in any way. In the initial court determination the Queensland government had successfully argued that its annexation of the islands gave it full ownership. The effect of this was to extinguish any 'native laws' that may have existed prior to colonisation of the continent and the imposition of British law.

On appeal, in a six to one majority verdict, the High Court overturned earlier doctrine in holding that at the time of white settlement, Australia was not *terra nullius*. The decision acknowledged that deeming Australia to be *terra nullius* had been an expedient political 'mistake'. The classification did not fully accord with the facts—probably not then, but certainly not now in the light of our better understanding of aboriginal people's management and custodianship of land. For at least two of the judges, Deane and Gaudron JJ, departing from prior determinations made by earlier courts was necessary because the dispossession of the aboriginal people from their traditional land 'constitutes the darkest aspect of the history of this nation' (per Deane and Gaurdron JJ, 109). The national history of 'conflagration of oppression and conflict' was to 'dispossess, degrade and devastate the Aboriginal peoples and leave a national legacy of unutterable shame' (per Deane and Gaudron JJ, 104). Under these circumstances, 'the Court is under a clear duty to re-examine past practices' (per Deane and Gaudron JJ, 109).

---

[23] In Australia the doctrine was affirmed by Blackburn J in the Northern Territory Supreme Court in *Milirrpum and Others v Nabalco Pty Ltd and the Commonwealth of Australia* (1970) 17 FLR 141 (known as the *Gove* case) and then the High Court in *Coe v Commonwealth of Australia* (1979) 24 ALR 118. These decisions followed precedent set by the Privy Council in Britain in *Cooper v Stuart* (1889) 14 App Case 286, in which it was held that '[t]here was no land law or tenure existing in the Colony at the time of its annexation' (292).

[24] There were clear advantages in being able to lay claim to new territory as *terra nullius*. Both of the two alternative options were more costly and a more precarious way of asserting dominion. They usually entailed the expense of mounting a war and/or concessions to the local population. Most significantly, both left some of the customary legal rights of the indigenous inhabitants intact. The 'right of conquest' allowed a victorious imperial power to have dominion over territory. This was the basis on which, for example, the British seized control of Canada from the French or defeated the Zulu people of South Africa. The other category, the 'right of cession', legitimated imperial dominion with the 'agreement' of the local population. Right of cession usually required the negotiation of a formal treaty between the imperial and local powers. It was on this basis that England acquired New Zealand from the Maori people as one of its colonies under the Treaty of Waitangi (see Wilson and Yeatman 1995). Henry Reynolds, the historian who influenced the High Court's Mabo decision had long argued that either of the alternative schemes for legitimating imperial colonisation had left other indigenous people in a stronger legal position to assert their rights (Reynolds 1987).

Canadian legal commentator John Webber interpreted the *Mabo* judgment as part of an international 'jurisprudence of regret' (Webber 1995). He argues that in *Mabo* the majority of the judges were sensitive to the kind of 'moral reflexion that should drive the evolution of the common law' (Webber 1995, 24). Since common law had been instrumental in the dispossession of aboriginal people from their land, it 'could not escape responsibility' for the harm done. Once the premise of the law came to be seen as profoundly wrong, the judges had no choice but to overturn precedent so as 'to keep faith with the principles and relationships that have constituted our community'(Ibid.). Thus *Mabo* earned the praise of the liberal elites. Such assessments, however, overlook the nationalist agenda underlying apparently enlightened judicial activism in Australia. More particularly, such optimistic interpretations ignore potential problems in meeting aboriginal peoples' future political and social needs.

IV. NATIONALISM IN BLACK AND WHITE

The *Mabo* decision made black–white reconciliation the dominant political issue in Australia: 'the nation as a whole must remain diminished unless and until there is an acknowledgment of, and retreat from ... past injustices' toward aboriginal people (per Dean and Gaudron JJ, 109). The High Court's intervention, however, oversimplified the complex issue of national identity. The irony of *Mabo*-style reconciliation is that it relies upon race to create a new vision of an Australian 'us' through a misconceived notion of 'them' based upon aboriginal 'Otherness'.

The *Mabo* decision properly (if belatedly) acknowledges that aboriginal people have their own sophisticated system of laws, including complex obligations and rituals associated with land.[25] But the rights accorded to aboriginal people by the Court are constrained by their static understanding of aboriginal culture. Common law may not be 'frozen in time', but to succeed, aboriginal people must satisfy a fossilised view of their cultural practices, which must be authenticated by white experts such as anthropologists and historians, according to criteria set by the colonisers (Motha 1998). Even then, the rights granted to the Other are inferior to those enjoyed by dominant interests (Thornton 2000).

The acknowledgment of 'difference' is conveniently universalised. Stewart Motha argues that the High Court identified with the Merriam

---

[25] Brennan J in fact argued that 'strict legal rules might have been disruptive of community life' (*Mabo*, 24). In Murray Islander society, the 'ultimate determining factor in terms of the control and disposition of the land was simply what was acceptable in terms of the social harmony and the capacity of an individual to impose his (it seems almost [always] to have been him) will on the community' (24).

people's claims because their practice of vegetable gardening (including entering their finest produce for judging in local shows) corresponded with Western Enlightenment ideas about improving land through labour (Motha 1998). Similarly, the post-*Mabo* Human Rights and Equal Opportunity Commission Report, 'Bringing Them Home', documents how 'our' assimilationist folly actively obliterated 'difference' by cruelly depriving aboriginal children of their families and culture. Empathy with aboriginal people, however, depends upon 'homogenising' their loss. The subtitle of the Report, 'National Enquiry into the Separation of Aboriginal and Torres Strait Islander Children from their Families', and even the iconography of its front cover, impose a universalised image of 'home' (Chandra-Shekeran 1998, 128). The cover image is a photograph by Heidi Smith entitled 'Story Time' depicting an older, maternal figure clapping hands with a young child against the background of a rich purple sunset. These powerful icons of Western civilisation reinforce the emotive message of 'home' (represented by motherhood) as the place of safety and peace. According to Chandra-Shekeran's close reading of the text, 'home' is the nostalgic master-narrative promoting national(ist) solidarity (1998, 128). Throughout the *Mabo* judgment, and more obviously in 'Bringing Them Home', Chandra-Shekeran argues, the Otherness that is now supposedly to be celebrated turns out to be 'a *fixed form of difference* that is made easily intelligible within the generalist symbols and expressions of nationhood' (128, emphasis in original).

In the *Mabo* version of Australian history, aboriginal people are deemed to be unfortunate victims swept aside by the tide of history.[26] 'We' are men of action, 'they' remain passive victims. The 'Black Armband' view of Australian history therefore turns out to be just as nationalist as the 'Three Cheers' approach it aimed to discredit and replace. The newer approach acknowledges the presence and significance of aboriginal people, but it does so by reifying Australia's mythological pioneer past. The White Man still preserves his starring role. After *Mabo*, the vision of Australia remains that of a frontier society, but now the cowboy/pastoralist is recast as the 'baddie'. Post-*Mabo*, the leit motif of identity politics in Australia has become Victim Black/Guilty White.

The victim highground provides the rhetorical basis for aboriginal people's political demands. Victimism, understood as identity politics born of a shared experience of harm or marginalisation, though, is a weak form of political power (Laster and Erez 2000). The privileged status of victim is

[26] These views are not always internally consistent. Aboriginal people, for example, are at the same time also viewed as late modernism's version of the 'noble savage'. The tragedy of their loss is deemed to be more poignant because they are assumed to have lived in harmony with Nature until they were abruptly plucked from their Eden on the arrival of the avaricious White Man.

contested political terrain. Competition between and among victim groups for 'most deserving' status creates intra-group tensions and fractures natural alliances between disadvantaged sections of communities (Laster 1996). In the longer term, as many disadvantaged groups have found to their cost, today's victim quickly becomes tomorrow's undeserving 'bludger' (Laster and Erez 2000). Victim status moreover imposes a collective identity on a group who otherwise might have little in common.[27] More importantly, to foreshadow my argument below, the status of aboriginal people as deserving 'victims' avoids critical questions about how and to what extent law is prepared to accommodate cultural diversity.[28]

The final evaluation of the *Mabo* decision, however, must be based upon the extent to which the Court's intervention advanced the interests of aboriginal people and the cause of black–white reconciliation. Judged on these criteria, judicial activism is not the boon its supporters had hoped. In fact, the major beneficiary of the *Mabo* decision is probably the High Court and its quest for a nationalist jurisprudence.

V. RECONCILIATION AS JUDICIAL REHABILITATION

The High Court's foray into the pressing issue of black–white reconciliation rejuvenated it as a significant force in Australian political and social life. Prior to *Mabo*, the High Court was respected as an institution, but ordinary people largely perceived it as irrelevant, and certainly boring. Under its (then) liberal Chief Justice, Sir Anthony Mason, the Court assumed a much higher public profile and developed a new rationale for judicial activism (Saunders 1996). *Mabo* was the most significant of a number of decisions that furthered the Court's new vision of its role.[29]

---

[27] It is an obvious but often overlooked point that aboriginal communities vary enormously. Not only do they speak a wide variety of languages, but they also differ markedly in their preferred political strategies and visions of the future of their communities. There is a world of difference, for example, between the needs and perspectives of urban aboriginal people and semi-tribal ones. Recognition of native title rights may have important symbolic value but may be of little practical significance for aboriginal people alienated generations ago from customary law. For obvious reasons though, there is reluctance on the part of aboriginal leaders to air these differences in the public domain.

[28] In Australia, as elsewhere, liberal responses to the challenge of pluralism are divided between those in favour of 'special' rights for specific cultural groups and those opposed to the recognition of 'difference' and departures from the equality principle. Elsewhere I have argued that a third, and far less divisive course, is the haphazard, pragmatic accommodation of diversity by stealth in legal decision-making (Laster and Taylor 1995).

[29] The High Court extended its active engagement with indigenous rights in *The Wik Peoples v The State of Queensland* (1996) 187 CLR 1. In this controversial decision, the Court extended the applicability of native title principles to pastoral leases. In other areas the Court has been prepared to extend individual rights. For example, the Court recognised implied rights contained in constitutional provisions that establish the framework for representative government (*Australian Capital Television v Commonwealth* (1992) 177 CLR 106;

The Court's activism advanced its own nationalist agenda. Over the last decade, in both its formal decisions and ex-curial statements, the Australian High Court has consciously sought to fashion a uniquely 'Australian' jurisprudence (see Mason 1997; Toohey J 1990; Galligan 1988). *Mabo* afforded an opportunity for the court to boldly break with its English antecedents and the taint of British colonialist law-making (Godden 1997). Justice Brennan in *Mabo*, for example, asserted that since the Australia Act of 1986, Australian courts are 'entirely free of imperial control'. They are entitled to overturn English precedent because the law 'is not now bound by decisions of courts in the hierarchy of an empire then concerned with the development of its colonies' (per Brennan J, 29).

The radical nationalist bent was more clearly articulated by the Court in its subsequent judgement in *The Wik Peoples v The State of Queensland* (1996) 187 CLR1 (hereafter *Wik*). In this case, the High Court refined the ambit of 'native title' by holding that the grant of pastoral leases under local statute would not normally extinguish native title, which could continue to coexist with the rights of leases.[30] The Court maintained that the very different circumstances of land tenure that existed in Australia made feudal English notions of proprietary interest unsuitable for local conditions. Toohey J elaborated on the 'Australianness' of some 70 innovative forms of land tenure developed in Queensland to deal with exigencies not countenanced by English law (112).

In *Mabo* the Court managed to revive confidence in common law's arcane mode of reasoning and problem solving. The doctrine of precedent, long criticised as vague and conservative ex post facto law-making, had redeemed itself. Overturning the long series of decisions that had consistently held that Australia was *terra nullius* proved that the common law was not moribund. In the right hands, the doctrine of *stare decisis*[31] was flexible enough to meet future exigencies.[32] Changing national and

---

Theophanous v Herald Weekly Times (1994) 182 CLR 104). Increasingly, Australian common law is being influenced by international human rights law. The Convention on the Rights of the Child, for example, was the basis for the Court to order a review of a deportation decision (*Minister for Immigration and Ethnic Affairs v Teoh* (1995) 183 CLR 273). Similarly, the influence of international law was also apparent in the recognition of a (limited) common law right to a fair trial (*Dietrich v The Queen* (1992) 177 CLR 292).

[30] The *Wik Peoples v The State of Queensland* (1996) 187 CLR1.

[31] The literal translation of this Latin term is 'to stand by things decided'. It refers to the binding force of precedent through which common law judges are bound to follow previous decisions of higher courts. The application of the doctrine to the High Court is a little more flexible. The High Court has found that it is not strictly bound by its own decisions (*Attorney-General (NSW) v Perpetual Trustee Co Ltd* (1952) 85 CLR 237), although in the interests of continuity and coherence the Court will favour the application of *stare decisis* (*Jones v Commonwealth* (1987) 71 ALR 497). Nevertheless, the judges of the High Court will, in exceptional circumstances, 'change their mind'.

[32] In '*Mabo*: Another Triumph for the Common Law', Richard Barlett (1993) argues that the case demonstrates the 'great virtues of common law', namely that it is pragmatic in nature,

international mores were a powerful motive for re-evaluation of common law in the light of changed circumstances. Even here, however, nationalist sensibilities play an important role.

Although international law does not formally bind the Court as a matter of law, it has become increasingly persuasive in High Court decision-making.[33] The world's opinion of Australia has become a major force in domestic politics.[34] In Australia, as elsewhere, adherence to the universal standards enshrined in international law is understood to be integral to the new status hierarchy among nations. In the age of imperialism, sovereignty or 'nationhood' was the exclusive privilege of 'civilised' countries.[35] Nowadays, former imperial powers demonstrate their superiority more subtly through their willingness to 'come to terms with their past'. Nations unwilling to participate in the international 'sorry-fest' are, by default, 'uncivilised'.[36] Paradoxically, internationalism supports nationalist pride. In the *Mabo* decision the High Court made it clear that Australia was a sophisticated country because it chose to join the throng of guilty nations admitting to their less salutary past.[37]

---

with the flexibility to reflect 'social, economic and political considerations' (178). The capacity of conservative institutions to 'reform themselves from inside' is the very thing that Foucault cautioned about in *Discipline and Punish* (1977). It is this mentality, for example, that keeps the institution of prisons alive. Constant 'failure' provides the impetus for reform defined as 'progress', which perpetuates the system.

[33] Brennan J in *Mabo* maintained, 'The common law does not necessarily conform with international law, but international law is a legitimate and important influence on the development of the common law, especially when international law declares the existence of universal human rights' (42). The important role played by international law in native title claims is reinforced by the 'Commonwealth Racial Discrimination Act' 1975 (Cth), which refers specifically (in 2 10(2) to the rights provided for in the International Convention on the Elimination of All Forms of Racial Discrimination adopted in 1965, and in force since 1969. Accordingly, legislation enacted by the Queensland Parliament purporting to extinguish the native title of the Murray Islanders without compensation was in contravention of both the Convention and the Racial Discrimination Act.

[34] This apparently principled position is also closely tied to economic interests. Investment dollars only flow to those countries that are *perceived* to have stable political and social systems. In a globalised world order, it is possible for indigenous people to press their claims outside of traditional state sovereignty. Through such means they can use their political clout strategically to destabilise national interests.

[35] 'Inferior' cultures were subject to colonial rule. For colonial elites, the struggle for national independence was really a demand for entry into the select club of 'civilised' nations (Fitzpatrick 1995).

[36] This is the subtext in Australia's critical response to Japan's refusal to apologise for atrocities committed against Australian prisoners of war during the Second World War. Headlines in Australian newspapers capture this implied judgement quite neatly: 'Japan: Silence on War Apology' (*Herald-Sun*, 16 August 1997), 'Japan: A Sorry Failure' (*The Australian*, 1 December 1998), 'Japan Baulks at Written Apology for War Crimes' (*Courier-Mail*, 27 November 1998).

[37] Internationalism, though, inevitably skews the needs of the local and particular in favour of an over-generalised and artificial 'universal'. To work, international law must necessarily be left abstract and general. Thus, admitting to past violations of 'human rights' (a convenient catchall) becomes a relatively safe, even comforting national(ist) option.

The irony of *Mabo* is that a decision that should have cast the legal system into disrepute for its complicity in the appalling treatment of aboriginal people, emerged with its status enhanced rather than diminished. There was even some neat judicial sidestepping of any legal responsibility for the wrongs of the past. The otherwise contrite Justice Brennan, for example, was keen to

> dispel the misconception that it is the common law rather than the actions of governments which [had] made many of the indigenous people of this country trespassers in their own land (69).

The Court also avoided casting aspersions on the reductionism inherent in law's system of classification. All of the judges avoided discussion of the way in which common law reasoning had developed the categories relied upon by imperial powers to legitimate colonialist oppression of indigenous people. The core values of law and its own claim to legitimacy could not be destabilised. The judges overtly conceded, for example, that there are limits to the recognition of human rights 'if their adoption would fracture the skeleton of principle which gives the body of our law its shape and internal consistency' (per Brennan J, 29).

Fear of undermining the stability of the law was also the rationale underlying the Court's rejection of civil suits brought by the members of the 'Stolen Generation'—'half-caste' aboriginal children removed from their families and communities as part of government assimilationist policy (Manne, 1998). However harsh the outcome, its traditional method of fact-finding and determining issues based on legal conceptions of proof and evidence had to be maintained (O'Loughlin J, *Cubillo v Commonwealth* [2000] FCA 1084).

The limitations of common law were not lost on aboriginal people. Emerging from Darwin's Federal Court building after the latest defeat in the *Cubillo* Stolen Generation test case, Lowitja O'Donoghue, a respected leader of the aboriginal community and herself a member of the Stolen Generation, was devastated by the decision: 'This is a major setback ... I don't know how much more we can take of this kind of adversarial system.'[38] Judge O'Loughlin had himself warned the litigants that they were expecting far too much from the court and litigation process.

Delay, forum shopping and technical legal arguments are standard ploys. Cross-examination of the plaintiffs by the government lawyers in *Cubillo*, for example, presented the sad spectacle of elderly, emotionally scarred plaintiffs being told that they were taken into state care because their aboriginal parents were negligent and unfit for the job of raising them.[39]

---

[38] *The Age*, 11 August 2000.

[39] The Howard government's lawyers estimate that there are some 2,200 potential lawsuits pending from members of the Stolen Generation. The damages bill could run to hundreds

In theory, the civil law standard of proof 'on the balance of probabilities' should advantage plaintiffs because it is lower than the criminal standard of 'beyond reasonable doubt'. But where litigation concerns past practices with strong ideological overtones, there is little prospect of courts imposing retrospective liability.

As a number of chapters in this volume attest, criminal adjudication impedes 'truth' and stifles more creative, practical ways of dealing with the wrongs of the past. At first sight, civil litigation avoids the overreach and obvious limitations of state initiated criminal proceedings. In fact, criminal and civil law share a focus on individual responsibility and are therefore both unsuited to the kind of reflexive social enquiry necessary to 'come to terms with' a complex past. The problems of civil suits are therefore no different from those of the criminal jurisdiction. Huge damages payouts are as much, if not more, of an incentive for government as defendant to exploit the vagaries of law and the tactical advantages afforded to them in adversarial proceedings. In this fraught area, practical solutions are more likely to come from the political sphere rather than through court-based adjudication.

VI. LAW VERSUS POLITICS

In his well-reasoned dissenting judgement in *Mabo*, Justice Dawson argued that it is dangerous for judges to usurp the proper role of Parliament:

> [T]here may not be a great deal to be proud of in the history [of European settlement in Queensland] ... [T]he policy which lay behind the legal regime was determined politically and, however insensitive the politics may now seem to have been, a changing view does not of itself mean a change in the law. It requires implementation of a new policy to do that and that is a matter for government rather than the courts ... [I]f traditional land rights (or at least rights akin to them) are to be afforded to the inhabitants of the Murray Islands, the responsibility, both legal and moral, lies with the legislature and not with the courts (145, 175).

Justice Dawson's views are grounded in a conservative interpretation of the British legacy of the separation of powers between the executive, legislative and judicial arms of government. Under this doctrine, parliamentary sovereignty

---

of millions of dollars. The government's case has largely depended upon official government policy statements that assimilationist policies of the 1940s and 1950s were altruistic and humanitarian. In effect, the defence is arguing a positive case for assimilation. Not surprisingly, many aboriginal witnesses have been reluctant to come forward, particularly with the prospects of facing quite hostile cross-examination suggesting that their memories are wrong or distorted. These kinds of concerns have led many members of the aboriginal community, as well as legal advocacy groups, to suggest that a reparations tribunal, bassed on the South African or Canadian models, is more appropriate than civil litigation through the courts for the resolution of these kinds of disputes. For an account of problems of such litigation, see Guilliatt 1999, 16–21.

is all important (see for example Parkinson 1994). The High Court of Australia has throughout its history alternated in its degree of deference to this doctrine. Under Sir Garfield Barwick from 1964 to 1981, it favoured a proactive literalism designed to keep Parliament in check. The Mason Court (from 1987 to 1995) by contrast was remarkable for its willingness to challenge Parliament through a policy-directed form of judicial activism.[40]

Since *Mabo*, it has become fashionable to identify judicial activism with enlightened reformist agendas (see Scheppele in this volume). In fact, such approaches can and have been used to support as well as thwart the interests of marginalised groups. There are also some indirect costs of revolutionary judicial law-making. By 'coming out' as a strong political voice, the High Court may have alienated a significant section of the Australian public who did not share the revisionist nationalist agenda of the liberal elites.[41]

On one reading, the *Mabo* judgement was instrumental in abruptly discrediting Australia's long held 'customary (national) narrative' about the rightness of white settlement of the continent. For some sections of the population, though, the Court's decision represented a loss of identity and a secure (if misguided) sense of nationhood (Attwood 1996, 100). It is not too far fetched to link the *Mabo* judgement to the rise of the populist One Nation political party and its racist, particularly anti-aboriginal and xenophobic, platform (Manne and Abbott 1998).[42] Paradoxically, a boring conservative High Court may work to inhibit recourse to abhorrent radical politics by those who feel betrayed by the nature and pace of change. It is also probably no coincidence that the first serious assaults on the time honoured principle of 'judicial independence' occurred in a climate in which the courts themselves chose publicly to assert their political voice.[43]

---

[40] The idea that law ought to be flexible is a very recent development. It is contrary, for example, to the old bourgeois ideal of law as stable and predictable in its certainty. This changing expectation of the proper role of law among elites requires further analysis. It may reflect, for example, the new demands of late capitalism in a period of rapid technological innovation. The needs of the market may well now be for quick adaptation to allow it to capitalise on new opportunities.

[41] Among the 'No' campaigners in the recent national referendum on forgoing the British monarchy, there was a perception, especially in rural/ regional Australia, that the republic debate was being run by 'wealthy, elite, well-educated people from Sydney' (Heide Zwar (Convenor of Young Australians Against This Republic), *The Age*, 28 October 1999).

[42] The populist 'backlash' not only was offensive but also impeded black–white reconciliation. The sudden rise in popularity of the One Nation party made some politicians wary of adopting a pro-aboriginal stance for fear of losing electoral support.

[43] The consequences of this proactive judicial approach are probably most sharply realised in the lower and more mundane courts and tribunals charged with discretionary decision-making. Political interference in appointments and judicial tenure may prove counterproductive for protecting the rights of more vulnerable sections of the community. For example, in the month preceding the interviews for reappointment of members of the Immigration Review Tribunal, 'set aside rates' (decisions against the Minister and Department of Immigration), which had previously been in the vicinity of 6–7 per cent, fell sharply to 2 per cent as Tribunal members presumably scrambled to impress their political masters and save their jobs (Liverani 1999).

The High Court may claim credit for changing the course of Australian history, but at best, its contribution to aboriginal peoples' rights was indirect. As ever, economic interests rather than judicial intervention were the catalyst for real change. The uncertainty created by the High Court's *Mabo* judgement made powerful economic interests insecure about engaging in further investment until the question of ownership and land tenure was resolved. The realistic fear of mining companies, pastoralists and land developers was that potential native title claims would be used by aboriginal communities to improve their bargaining position. They feared a floodgate of 'wishful' claims that could be used to 'blackmail' them into expensive individual settlements.[44]

The government's response was to introduce a formal mechanism to settle all potential claims arising from the loss of aboriginal land. The Native Title Act 1993 (Cth) provided for quasi-legal tribunals to hear and determine claims to land by aboriginal people without the need for slow and costly court proceedings. The Act also ameliorated the High Court's requirement for litigants to prove an ongoing relationship with their land, which would have been impossible for most because they had been forcibly removed to make way for white settlers.[45] Despite the acclaim by liberals for formal judicial acknowledgment of the errors of the past, ultimately interest politics, rather than ad hoc judicial law-making, probably provides a more satisfactory explanation for the Australian reconciliation phenomenon.

The enthusiasm for judicial 'coming to terms with the past' has discouraged critical analysis of the *Mabo* fallout. Specifically, the black–white brand of nationalist reconciliation took place outside of more broadly based political claims for 'a fair go' and share in resources based on the recognition of diversity rather than sameness. The untold story of the *Mabo* decision is the way in which it occluded a longstanding and influential discourse about multiculturalism in Australian society.[46]

---

[44] The furore caused by *Mabo* can be seen in the headlines of one of Australia's leading business newspapers, the *Australian Financial Review*: 'Entire Land System in Doubt' and '*Mabo*: Mining on Hold' (Gill 1993; 1993a). These sentiments were echoed by state premiers and business leaders such as Hugh Morgan of the Western Mining Corporation, who accused the High Court of 'plunging property law into chaos' and 'threatening Australian backyards' (*The Australian*, 13 October 1992, 3).

[45] The Native Title Act established a system of registration of native title interests on a national native title register. If there is an objection to the application for registration the matter is referred to mediation by the National Native Title Tribunal. The Federal Court has the power to determine native title interests if no settlement is reached through mediation. The key benefits for native title holders provided by the legislation are (1) the right to negotiate over future government acts; (2) access rights over nonexclusive pastoral leases; and (3) the capacity to enter into indigenous land-use agreements. See the National Native Title Tribunal *Fact Sheets*, 1998.

[46] Since his election in March 1996 Prime Minister Howard has avoided the use of the 'M word'—multiculturalism. This decision was so apparent that his use of the word 'multicultural' at the launch of the National Multicultural Advisory Council's issues paper 'Multicultural

VII. INTEREST POLITICS IN A MULTICULTURAL SOCIETY

Revisiting the past in the wake of *Mabo* meant forgetting about one of the great successes of the present: the great social experiment of multiculturalism. Reconciliation is in fact a small part of a wider debate about cultural plural-ism in Australian society. As Chandra Kukathas argues, the High Court's recognition of native title raises much wider political and legal questions:

> Customary law deals not only with questions of ownership, but also with issues of justice and punishment, often according to traditions which are considered at variance with the standards set by the European system of justice. One effect of *Mabo* has been to lend weight to already existing pressures to grant greater autonomy to Aboriginal communities, and also to see customary law remedies recognised under common law. Another effect has been to raise a larger question about the prospects of Aboriginal self-determination, and Aboriginal sovereignty (Kukathas 1997, 173).

Yet, *Mabo* and its sequelae do not provide a strong philosophical basis on which to pursue such important legal and social consequences of diversity.

For all its failings, multicultural discourse does offer a practical frame-work for debating the implications of pluralism in a heterogenous society. It also has the great advantage of forcing Australia to see beyond its early Anglo origins and convict and settler past.[47] The *Mabo* judgement and the brand of Australian nationalism it represents have, however, overshadowed this more sophisticated understanding of national identity.

Some of the blame for this oversight rests with the multiculturalist intelli-gentsia. The sons and daughters of (often) working class migrants and refu-gees who had become prominent in the professions, politics and creative life of Australia, did little to build bridges with aboriginal communities. Their challenging critiques of marginalisation ignored aboriginal people's struggle against social exclusion and colonialism. Perpetuating the dialectics of Enlightenment, they did not notice that indigenous people confronted the same oppression they, or their parents, had left behind.[48] Understandably,

---

Australia' in 1998 was reported in the national papers (Henderson 1998). Since that time the 'M word' is gradually creeping back into the Prime Minister's vocabulary.

[47] That limited past is itself far more complex than is usually allowed. Australia's pioneer history was constructed by combinations of convicts as well as those who guarded them, radi-cal working class exiles and immigrants as well as disgraced members of the aristocracy. Its largely male members were at odds with one another along sectarian lines, Protestants versus Catholics, the English against the Irish and the Scots and, at various times, all of these against the Chinese. Then of course there was the massive free immigration from Europe after the gold rush and since then under the 'populate or perish' immigration policies of twentieth-century governments. All these groups have their own individual stories and have in turn contributed to the social rub that has produced a rich hybrid culture.

[48] For example, Martin Krygier (1997) in his ABC Boyar lectures tells two stories—the 'success' of the integration of migrants into the society and the 'shame' of 'our neglect of aboriginal people'. In interviews he gave around the time of the lectures, Krygier, the son of

aboriginal people were also unwilling to align themselves with multicultural politics. Multiculturalism, after all, was merely the politics of yet more recently arrived European colonialists.

Yet multicultural ideology provides the strongest framework for pursuing a broadly based culturally inclusive social policy. The grafting of various traditions and cultures onto colonial origins has served to enhance an iconoclastic sense of (national) identity. Before the latest outbreak of nationalism, Australian identity politics were marked by an ironic sense of self—a recognition of what 'We Are Not' rather than a positive assertion of who 'We Are'. There was every indication that this polyglot society had somehow avoided some of the worst vices of nationalism.

Ordinary Australians maintain a refreshing indifference to the traditional paraphernalia of nationalism. In Australia, for example, conventional symbols of national identity such as flags, national colours and coats of arms did not inspire irrational allegiance. (Laster 1995b). At the 1996 Atlanta Olympic Games, for example, 'our' victorious athletes were unable to sing the national anthem on the podium.[49] In reliable surveys respondents conceive of national identity in relational rather than structural terms.[50] The distinguishing feature of 'Australianness' is that it is based on qualities of character and a shared attitude to life among its easy-going and cosmopolitan people.[51] For a long time, the majority of Australians remained cheerfully unfussed about institutionalising whatever it is that gives the country its sense of national identity. There appeared to be active resistance to the imposition of a positive national identity. The resounding 'no' vote in the recent referendum over whether Australia should become a republic, for example, can be understood as, in part, a vote against the excesses of elite nationalist rhetoric.[52] The optimistic reading of the

Polish Jewish refugees, admitted his own personal shame at his ignorance of, and failure to appreciate, the plight of aboriginal people.

[49] Julie Anthony, a popular entertainer, was commissioned to appear at public events and teach Australians their new national anthem. She was given the Order of Australia for her efforts, which a decade later, are still not entirely successful. The chorus is known well enough, but the verse remains a mystery to most people. In like fashion, with the approach of the centenary of Federation, a public campaign designed to teach the Australian public some elementary 'facts' about their past has been none too successful. Posters in public transport and television commercials try to shame people by suggesting that they are more likely to know the names of American Presidents than Australian Prime Ministers. Again, the efforts at promoting this kind of civic pride confuse 'nationalism' with a sense of communal identity and affiliation.

[50] The most interesting results come from surveys that have very little to do with national identity or the republican political agenda. The National Capital Planning Authority's efforts to find out how Australians could be encouraged to visit the national capital provide some interesting insights into the reluctance of a cross-section of Australian people to take nationalist symbols seriously (Staddon Consulting 1995, discussed in Laster 1995b).

[51] I am not claiming that these are necessarily accurate observations about Australian culture, but the fact that Australians seem to hold this image of themselves is significant and probably does influence behaviour and the development of civil society.

[52] Most commentators agree that, despite the 'no' vote, the vast majority of the population are pro-republic. Even monarchists campaigned for a 'no' vote on the basis that the Australian

anti-republic vote is that constitutional reform apparently remains irrelevant to people's daily lives and internalised sense of national identity.[53]

The post-*Mabo* era, however, signalled a move toward more traditional forms of nationalism in Australia, including allegiance to the trappings usually associated with the artificial construct we dub 'the nation'. This was most evident at the 2000 Olympic Games, where media, politicians, educators and media commentators competed with each other in their use of clichés and over-zealous displays of patriotism. Needless to say, the crowds at the sporting events managed to whip themselves into embarrassing demonstrations of nationalist fervour (Laster and Steinert 2000). Sport has a tendency to bring out the worst in people. Major events also encourage marketing strategies that exploit tribal loyalties. Despite these qualifications, there are strong indications that the Australian *Zeitgeist* has changed. Republicanism, including a conceited sense of coming to terms with the past, has unfortunately made this nation proud. At the very least, there is a naive confidence that if we now honestly admit to our past bad behaviour, the slate can be wiped clean and a bright (republican) future assured.[54]

A more productive strategy might be to draw upon a deeply entrenched sense of fairness, which underscores both Australia's convict past and the cooperative egalitarianism of a multicultural settler society. In the *Mabo*

---

people ought to reject 'the politician's republic' rather than arguing a strong positive case in favour of the preservation of the monarchy. The monarchist Prime Minister was forced to cave in and allow the Australian Governor, General Sir William Dean, previously one of the High Court judges who decided the *Mabo* case, to open the 2000 Olympic Games in Sydney in preference to the reigning British monarch.

[53] The cartoonist Michael Leunig, himself an Australian icon, summarised it best with his post-referendum cartoon ode (*The Age*, 7 November 1999):

My Favourite Things
Brownsnakes on doorsteps and bushfires on ridges
Redbacks in dunnies and blowflies in fridges
Big rolls of corned beef all tied up with strings
These are a few of my favourite things

When the monarch bites
When the republican stings
When I'm feeling sad
I simply remember my favorite things
And then I don't feel so bad

[54] During the Sydney Olympics, Cathy Freeman, winner of the women's 400 metre run, shouldered the quite irrational of hopes of the population that her victory would prove the success of black–white reconciliation. The longing, both in Australia and internationally, was genuine. Cathy Freeman's lap of honour carrying both the aboriginal and the Australian flags was universally acclaimed as a defining moment in Australian history and race relations. It put powerful pressure on the reluctant Prime Minister, John Howard, to review his generally unsympathetic response to Australia's treatment of its indigenous population. Nevertheless, it smacks of a quick-fix mentality, which is antithetical to the best traditions of Australian multiculturalism. The unrealistic expectation is that if we now admit our 'mistake' we can simply 'kiss and make up' for the good of the nation.

judgement, Brennan J based his decision not so much on the victim status of aboriginal people than on the overriding principle of equality as a fundamental value of common law. He suggested that law should not be applied so as to discriminate on racial or ethnic grounds: aboriginal people, like all other Australians, were entitled to have their own system of social organisation respected and thus to claim an interest in land. He did not expressly refer to the diversity argument often propounded by multiculturalists. Instead, what we see in this judgement, in contrast to the statements of the judges who are expressly concerned with questions of Australian history, is a different, more rounded notion of 'Australianess' based on social inclusiveness.[55] In the longer term, this may be a more productive strategy for advancing the rights of Australia's indigenous communities.

The equality principle may be utopian, but it does at least provide a culturally acceptable yardstick by which to measure social progress. It imposes an ongoing responsibility on social institutions to redress structural barriers and address the needs of citizens. There would be little dissent in Australia from the proposition that everyone, including aboriginal people, is entitled to 'a fair go' (Laster and Taylor 1995). Unlike the limited and present centredness of 'coming to terms with the past' fairness is a future-directed cultural ideal. Justice, on the other hand, when it concerns itself with the victims of the present, remains rooted in the past. It is therefore inevitably embroiled in the contentious and volatile politics of identity. Claiming and maintaining victim status, both inside and outside the courts, is always a precarious political strategy (Laster and Erez 2000).

At the beginning of this chapter I suggested that the key question was whether 'collective memory' could ever be free of the taint of nationalism. A related question arising from the case study of Australia might be 'Can national identity politics ever be "good", or is it doomed to reproduce all the negative features of nationalism?' The Australian experience suggests that it may be possible, but only in rare instances when national identity is grounded in respect for diversity. The substantial drawback of the *Mabo* judgement is that it encouraged a Guilty White/Victim Black dualism that undermines the ironic and flexible sense of national identity developed by this self-consciously immigrant society.

VIII. CONCLUSION: A PLATYPUS IDENTITY?

'Coming to terms with the past' is a global phenomenon. Optimists applaud the dawn of a new age in which law becomes a significant forum for judging, and thus rectifying, the wrongs of the past. By contrast, in this chapter

---

[55] Brennan J, 15–16, 29 and 41.

I have argued that a society's engagement with its history needs to be analysed in culturally specific terms. Visions of the past, however worthy, are best treated analytically as markers of a given society's attitude to its present and hopes for its future. The Australian experience cautions that the historical revisionism entailed in 'collective memory' is inexorably tied to national identity politics. Since law is a key institution of the nation state, it will inevitably (although often unconsciously and circuitously) promote the nationalist enterprise.

Using the much praised decision of the Australian High Court in *Mabo* as an example, I argue that the benefits of the reassessment of the colonisation of Australia as *terra nullius* may well, in the longer term, be counterproductive. There is no doubt that the decision facilitated dialogue between black and white Australia, established a precedent for the systematic compensation of aboriginal people for harms suffered by them, and probably initiated the process of reconciliation. It can be credited with providing an authoritative framework for supporting these long overdue developments.

Nevertheless, I suggest that the decision is tainted by its nationalist impulses and reasoning. While the *Mabo* decision is undoubtedly an important symbolic victory for indigenous people, its legacy may well be to reinforce a popular conception of a culpable but virtuous 'Us', redeemed by full and frank confession of 'our' crimes against a stereotypical conception of a culturally (and racially) distinct black 'Them'. The effect of the judgement has been to bolster an artificial (and typical) sense of national(ist) identity.

For aboriginal people, an admission of the devastating effect of colonisation has been long overdue. Australia's past treatment of aboriginal people, however, has been used as the lynchpin in the demand for radical social change among Australia's elites. It has therefore placed aboriginal people in the unenviable position of simultaneously being the positive symbol for supporters of change and the ready scapegoat for those opposed to it. The nationalist context of law's engagement with the wrongs of the past also means that aboriginal people are culturally and politically cast in the role of perennial 'victims', simultaneously entitled to and also reviled if they press their legitimate claims through the courts. I have suggested that the real beneficiaries of 'collective memory jurisprudence' have probably been law and the courts. Defending the vulnerable in the interests of morality and justice has traditionally been law's claim to legitimacy. The net effect of this boost to its status, however, has been to raise unrealistic (and in the longer term, counterproductive) expectations of what law and legal proceedings can deliver.

None of the judges in *Mabo* referred to the richness and beauty of Australia's polyglot heritage. They did not do so because these concerns are not relevant in law. Yet, the love of difference has been a feature of Australian society since the Dreamtime of the first aboriginal inhabitants. Even today, the Wirandjun people of central New South Wales forbid the hunting of that extraordinary mammal, the platypus, because it symbolically represents all peoples in the animal world: it lays eggs like a bird, runs on land like a kangaroo and swims and dives like a fish.

Aboriginal leader Noel Pearson, a major spokesperson for black–white reconciliation in Australia, has explained that

> we are not just a melting pot, we're not just simple colours in a mosaic, we are, in fact, more complicated than that ... We, as individuals, have within our breast layers of identity according to sex, sexual preference, culture, religion, recreation, professional ties, locational patriotism and political preference ... [Australians must] avoid the growing prescriptiveness about our identity ... which is extremely dangerous. True national identity could not be achieved until Australians recognised that reconciliation with the land's traditional owners needed to be based on justice, rather than just symbolism (*The Age*, 29 October 1999).

The law tries to use our collective memories to right past wrongs. It is a moot point whether such an approach will, in the end, promote social justice. But the law cannot create a platypus, even if only symbolically. A new nationalism, based on the law's denunciation of the sins of the fathers, may appear more principled than its earlier incarnations. But in the long run, it may be just as pernicious, failing once more to recognise the plurality of visions and traditions that make up any truly human society.

Postscript:

This article was written some years ago, when the Liberal Coalition government, led by Prime Minister John Howard, was in power. In November 2007, the Australian Labour Party won the Federal election, taking office after 12 years of Coalition government. During the election campaign, Kevin Rudd (now the Prime Minister) promised that he would, if elected, formally apologise to the Stolen Generations for the past policies of the Australian government which had seen aboriginal children forcibly removed from their families.

On 13 February, 2008, at the formal opening of Federal Parliament in Canberra for 2008, Prime Minister Rudd honoured his promise in a moving speech to a joint sitting of both Houses of Parliament.

> For the pain, suffering and hurt of these stolen generations, their descendants and for their families left behind ... To the mothers and the fathers, the brothers and the sisters, for the breaking up of families and communities ... And for the indignity and degradation thus inflicted on a proud people and a proud culture, we say sorry.

Prime Minister Rudd also outlined what this would mean for the future of Australia as a nation.

> ... the time has come, well and truly come, for all peoples of our great country, for all citizens of our great commonwealth, for all Australians—those who are

indigenous and those who are not—to come together to reconcile and together build a new future for our nation ... That is why the Parliament is today here assembled: to deal with this unfinished business of the nation, to remove a great stain from the nation's soul and, in a true spirit of reconciliation, to open a new chapter in the history of this great land, Australia.

It is widely acknowledged that this symbolic act marked a turning point in reconciliation between Black–White relations in Australia. The point made in the article, however, remains valid—inevitably, ways of dealing with the past reflect contemporary understandings of nationhood.

CASES CITED

Attorney-General (NSW) v Perpetual Trustee Co Ltd (1952) 85 CLR 237
Australian Capital Television v Commonwealth (1992) 177 CLR 106
Coe v Commonwealth of Australia and Another (1979) 24 ALR 118
Cooper v Stuart (1889) 14 App Case 286
Dietrich v The Queen (1992) 177 CLR 292
Jones v Commonwealth (1987) 71 ALR 497
Mabo v Queensland (No 2)(1992) 175 CLR 1
Millirpum and Others v Nabalco Pty Ltd and the Commonwealth of Australia (1970) 17 FLR 141
Minister for Immigration and Ethnic Affairs v Teoh (1995) 183 CLR 273
O'Loughlin, J. Cubillo v Commonwealth [2000] FCA 1084
Theophanous v Herald Weekly Times (1994) 182 CLR 104
The Wik Peoples v The State of Queensland (1996) 187 CLR 1

REFERENCES

Attwood, Bernhard. 1996. *Mabo*, Australia and the End of History. In *In the Age of* Mabo: *History, Aborigines and Australia*. Edited by B Attwood. Sydney: Allen and Unwin.

Australian Archives. 1996. *Aboriginal Deaths in Custody: The Royal Commission and its Records, 1987–1991*. Canberra: Australian Archives.

Australian Associated Press (AAP). 1999. UN confirms Australian government responsible for Wik shame. AAP Newsfeed, 18 August. Available at LEXIS Aust ALLNWS library.

Australian Bureau of Statistics. 1996. *Australia Now: A Statistical Profile*. Canberra: Australian Bureau of Statistics. Available at www.statistics.gov.au.

Barkan, Elazar. 2000. *The Guilt of Nations: Restitution and Negotiating Historical Injustices*. New York: WW Norton and Co.

Bartlett, Richard. 1993. *Mabo*: Another Triumph for Common Law. *Sydney Law Review* 15(2): 178–86.

Bean, Charles. 1995. Citizens' Beliefs and Attitudes about Australian Institutions: An Overview. Paper presented at the *Reshaping Australian Institutions Conference*, 2–3 November 1995, Australian National University, Canberra.

Blainey, Geoffrey. 1988. *The Great See-saw: A New View of the Western World, 1750–2000.* Basingstoke: McMillan.

——. 1991. They View Australia's History as a Saga of Shame. In *Blainey: Eye on Australia.* Edited by G Blainey. Melbourne: Schwartz and Wilkinson.

——. 1993. Drawing up a Balance Sheet of our History. *Quadrant* (Jul–Aug): 10–15.

Burgmann, Victor and Lee, Jason. 1988. *Making a Life: A People's History of Australia since 1788.* New York: McPhee Gribble.

Chandra-Shekeran, Sangeetha. 1998. Challenging the Fiction of the Nation in the 'Reconciliation' Texts of *Mabo* and *Bringing them Home. Australian Feminist Law Journal* 11: 107–33.

Cohen, Stanley. 1995. State Crimes of Previous Regimes: Knowledge, Accountability and the Policing of the Past. *Law and Social Enquiry: Symposium on Lustration* 20: 7–50.

——. 2001. *States of Denial: Knowing about Atrocities and Suffering.* Malden, MA: Polity.

Contractor, Arthur. 1997. Howard's Deep Sorrow. *Canberra Times,* 27 May, 2.

Federal Capital Press. 1999. Author Queries our Attitude on Human Rights. *Canberra Times,* 10 October, 4.

Fitzgerald, Robert. 1990. Writing Contemporary History in Australia. In *Australia Towards 2000.* Edited by B Hocking. Basingstoke: Macmillan.

Fitzpatrick, Peter. 1995. 'We Know What it is when You do Not Ask Us': Nationalism as Racism. In *Nationalism, Racism and the Rule of Law.* Edited by P Fitzpatrick. Aldershot: Dartmouth.

Foucault, Michel. 1977. *Discipline and Punish: The Birth of the Prison.* Harmondsworth: Penguin.

Galligan, Bruce. 1988. Realistic 'Realism' and the High Court's Political Role. *Federal Law Review* 18: 40–9.

Gill, Peter. 1993a. *Mabo*: Mining on Hold. *Australian Financial Review,* 1 June.

——. 1993b. Entire Land in Doubt. *Australian Financial Review,* 5 June.

Godden, Laura, 1997. Wik: Legal Memory and History. *Griffith Law Review* 6: 122–43.

Gorden, Michael. 1999. Australia Decides. *The Age,* 11 November, 9.

Gregory, Mary, 1992. Rewriting History 1: *Mabo v Queensland,* the Decision. *Alternative Law Journal* 7: 157.

Guilliatt, Richard, 1999. 'Their Day in Court'. *Good Weekend, The Sunday Age,* 20 November, 16–21.

Henderson, George. 1998. A Nation Made Strong by its Cultural Mix. *The Age,* 6 January, 11.

Human Rights and Equal Opportunity Commission (HREOC). 1997. 'Bringing Them Home: Report of the National Enquiry into the Separation of Aboriginal and Torres Strait Islander Children from their Families'.

Krygier, Martin. 1997. *Between Fear and Hope: Hybrid Thoughts on Public Values.* Sydney: ABC Books.

Kukathas, Chandra. 1997. Cultural Rights in Australia. In *New Developments in Australian Politics.* Edited by Brian Galligan, Ian McAllister and John Ravenhill. Melbourne: Macmillan.

Laster, Kathy. 1995a. Crime and Punishment. *Meanjin* 4: 262–339.

——. 1995b. A Republic without the Trimmings. *Migration Action* (May): 8–10.

——. 1996. Feminist Criminology: Coping with Success. *Current Issues in Criminal Justice* 8(2): 192–200.

Laster, Kathy and Erez, Edna (eds). 2000. Domestic Violence: International Perspectives. *International Journal of Victimology* (special issue) 1/2/3: 1–4.

Laster, Kathy and Steinert, Heinz. 2000. Lehren aus Sydney: Ein Vorschlag zur Zivilisierung der Olympischen Spiele. *Wespennest* 121: 46–53.

Laster, Kathy and Taylor, Vivianne. 1995. Law for our Multicultural Society? No Worries. In *Tomorrow's Law*. Edited by H Selby. Sydney: Federation Press.

Law Society Journal. 1999. Maintaining an Independent Judiciary and the Rule of Law in Australia. 37(6): 50–1.

Liverani, Marcos R. 1999. Judicial Temps: A Scandal. *Law Society Journal* 37(6): 52–4.

Lowenthal, Daniel. 1990. Uses of the Past in Australia. In *Australia Towards 2000*. Edited by B Hocking. Basingstoke: Macmillan.

Manne, Ralf, 1998. The Stolen Generations. *Quadrant* 42(I-2): 63–73.

Manne, Ralf and Abbott, Tony. 1998. *Two Nations: The Causes and Effects of the Rise of the One Nation Party in Australia*. Melbourne: Bookman.

Mason, Anthony (Sir). 1997. Rights, Values and Legal Institutions: Reshaping Australian Institutions. *Australian International Law Journal* 13: 1–16.

Moens, Gerald. 1993. *Mabo* and Political Policy-making by the High Court. In *Mabo, a Judicial Revolution: The Aboriginal Land Rights Decision and its Impact on Australian Law*. Edited by S Ratnapala and MA Stephenson. St Lucia, QLD: University of Queensland Press.

Motha, Sara. 1998. *Mabo*: Encountering the Epistemic Limit of the Recognition of 'Difference'. *Griffith Law Review* 7(1): 79–96.

Neal, Dean. 1991. *The Rule of Law in a Penal Colony*. Cambridge: Cambridge University Press.

Parkinson, Priscilla. 1994. *Tradition and Change in Australian Law*. Sydney: Law Book Company.

Pilger, Jason. 1992. *A Secret Country*. London: Vintage.

Ratnapala, Sulo and Stephenson, Marcus A (eds). 1993. *Mabo, a Judicial Revolution: The Aboriginal Land Rights Decision and its Impact on Australian Law*. St Lucia, QLD: University of Queensland Press.

Reynolds, Hermann. 1987. *The Law of the Land*. Ringwood, VIC: Penguin Books.

——. 1999. *Why Weren't We Told? A Personal Search for the Truth about our History*. Ringwood, VIC: Viking.

Said, Edward. 1978. *Orientalism*. New York: Pantheon Books.

Saunders, Carol (ed). 1996. *Courts of Final Jurisdiction: The Mason Court in Australia*. Annandale, NSW: Federation Press.

Slezak, Pietro. 1999. God Save the Queen because She'll Save Us. *The Age*, 1 November, 15.

Staddon Consulting. 1995. *Australian Attitudes towards the Future of the National Capital*. National Capital Planning Authority.

The Sunday Age,1999. How the Nation Voted. 7 November, 8.

Thornton, Mark. 2000. If You're Poor, It's All Your Own Fault. *Sun Herald*, 28 May, 102.

Toohey, Judy. 1990. Towards an Australian Common Law. *Australian Bar Review* 6(3): 185–98.

Walter, James. 1990. Nation and Narrative: The Problem of General History. In *Australia Towards 2000*. Edited by B Hocking. Basingstoke: Macmillan.

Webber, John. 1995. The Jurisprudence of Regret: The Search for Standards of Justice in *Mabo*. *Sydney Law Review* 17: 5–28.

White, Richard. 1997. Inventing Australia Revisited. In *Creating Australia: Changing Australia's History*. Edited by W Hudson and G Bolton. Sydney: Allen and Unwin.

Wilson, Morgan and Yeatman, Anna (eds). 1995. *Justice and Identity: Antipodean Practices*. Sydney: Allen and Unwin.

Wright, Taylor. 1999a. PM Warns of Direct-election Rivalry. *The Age*, 27 October, 6.

——. 1999b. A Republic is our Destiny. *The Age*, 29 October, 1.

——. 1999c. Victoria Swings to No Camp. *The Age*, 9 November, 1.

9

Experienced Authenticity of Culture and Legal Liberties

ARTHUR L STINCHCOMBE

I. INTRODUCTION

THE CORE OF the argument of this chapter is adopted from the literature on identity, especially Erik Erikson (1980; 1985), and from the literature on the historical origins and effects of institutions, especially Charles Tilly (1997a; 1997b). Erikson argues that identities consist of the connection of an individual's past and the accumulation of motives, attachments and ideas in that past, to an imagined future in social life, as for example concretely manifested in a 'career'.[1] Tilly argues that a central aspect of institutions is stretching out the time span that people organise their lives around, by making the personal and social future more predictable.[2] Putting the two together immediately implies that institutions are central to identity formation, which Erikson would certainly agree with.

I want to stretch that argument here to treat the experience of authenticity of culture, conceived of as a variable that might be measured on the individual level. I argue that experienced authenticity depends on identities, which then in turn depend on the structure of institutions, by way of institutions' influence on people's visions of the future. I then specify a particular part of modern institutions, namely legal liberties, as central to creating the sorts of institutionalised predictability of futures that can elicit the experience of authenticity of culture, because they shape not only the future generally but the field of imagined future action in particular.

[1] See also my essay on the connection between national institutions and national identities (Stinchcombe 1975, 599–615).
[2] See especially Tilly 1997a. See also Stinchcombe 1997, where I argue the centrality of this point in Tilly 1997b.

The basic notion is that unless what is guaranteed about the future is freedom of choice (which might be guided by a bit of culture), one cannot have an institutionally defended experience of one's loyalty to that culture, and particularly of one's caring deeply about what is authentic in that culture. One can have that experience of choice guided by culture in a revolution, but one of the problems of a revolution is that ideas about the future are politically precarious. So the more specific dependent variable is authenticity of experience of cultural loyalties, as part of everyday life and routine politics, rather than as part of a revolutionary movement with an uncertain future. To put it another way, socially organised, deeply felt dogmatism about loyalty is often both created and destroyed in times of revolution; but the same is created and *sustained* in a system of legal liberties.

II. AN INAUTHENTIC ENGLISH ETHNICITY

I obviously have an English heritage: my name is the name of a village in Southwest England, and my maternal grandfather's name was Stratton, an English city. I even did the nationalist intellectual thing of learning some Middle English. When Chaucer writes of English pilgrims going to Canterbury in spring, he says:

> ... And smale foules maken melodye,
> That slepen al the nyght with open eye,
> So priketh hem nature in hir corages,
> Than longen folk to goon on pilgrimages,
> And palmyres for to seken straunge strondes,
> Couth in sundry londes (1906, 1).

It means, more literally than poetically:

> [When in April] small fowl make melodies,
> That sleep all night with open eyes,
> As nature pricks their hearts to do,
> Then folks want to go on pilgrimages,
> And pilgrims to seek strange coasts,
> Of course in various lands.

In a historical sense there is nothing particularly inauthentic about this. But it has nothing to do with my future. Take my accent in Middle English: I have done nothing in some 45 years since I learned it to keep it up, and I will not feel in the least ashamed if a reader who happens to hear me recite this tells me that recent scholarship has shown that the reconstruction of the phonetics by my teacher is all out of date. I have been to England several times but never bothered to go to the village of Stinchcombe, and I cannot imitate the modern West Country accent. I have the liberty of using my influence as a father to persuade my children to learn some Chaucer, but instead, four of the six have studied Spanish, two being fairly fluent in it. One of those married a Hispanic, one a Moroccan with a Spanish mother (though she's now learning Persian to talk to new in-laws).

In short, except for not protesting very loud when I get the advantages of being obviously white and speaking the world scientific lingua franca as a mother tongue, there is nothing in my imagined community that depends on my English heritage. I make no special effort to pass it on except to write grammatical corrections into the margins of students' papers, explaining to the foreign ones the general grammatical principle they are violating.

My argument here may be illuminated by comparing it to Randall Collins's account of a Buddhist sect of around year 100 of our era, the Kashyapiyas (Collins 1998, 217), who argued that only that part of the past exists which continues to have an effect on the present, and only that part of the future exists which is inherent in the present. What I have been arguing here is equivalent to saying that these Kashyapiyas propositions are true of our consciousness of collective identities. Since we can only act on the future, our present is dominated by what has a meaningful effect on what we imagine our future to be. Thus in its turn, the part of the past that is psychologically real is that part that we imagine will have an effect on the future, and especially on that part of the future that we find problematic and which we think we might be able to affect. Only if the future is inherent in the present can it be part of our identities and so produce an attitude toward authenticity in the past.

I don't find it problematic that none of my children have learned Middle English, and I am glad that most of them have learned some (or a lot of) Spanish. That means that however authentic my accent is, in the sense that Chaucer would recognise the words as fitting into the poetry, it is not authentic in the sense that it is part of the reality that I might pass on to my children. Nor will I try to perfect it according to the new scholarship on Middle English phonetics. Even today, it is only real in that I have imagined my performance herein, in my future while writing this, as an illustration of the meaninglessness of my ethnicity to my identity. I predict that American people with English names who read this will be no more likely to be able to recite the next line of the poem than the ones with Italian or Russian or German or Scandinavian names, so it's not only me. My lack of ethnic identity is an institutional product.

But the story of my English heritage, as told above, does tell the reader a lot about my identity, which I will refer to by the name Joseph Stalin used in his characterisation of Soviet Jews: 'rootless cosmopolite'. That has a lot to do with my future, and with the future I imagine for my children. The eldest, then married to the Hispanic, was once also fluent in Norwegian; the youngest, now 22, has studied with some enthusiasm Latin, French and Indonesian, besides Japanese and Spanish. His vocabulary in English no doubt is larger than the sum of all his other foreign language vocabularies. And that is, to my mind, as it should be: a good preparation for their lives. Stalin wouldn't have liked me or my children any better than he liked the Jews.

The argument below about the importance of legal liberties in the construction of authentic ethnic identities applies even more to identities as rootless cosmopolites. The rootless cosmopolite that Stalin hated most, Leon Trotsky, was, like him, born into a Soviet minority nationality— Trotsky was a Russified Ukrainian as well as a Jew, while Stalin's family was monolingual in Georgian. To hint at my argument below, Trotsky was more in need of legal liberties in the Soviet Union than Stalin, and Stalin's situation depended very little on the legal liberties of other Georgians.

But I intend the argument to apply to other ethnic subcultures than rootless cosmopolitanism. The brunt of the analysis of my own lack of English ethnicity is that *only* if I used my liberties to construct an ethnically relevant future for myself, my family, or my fellow ethnics, would I have an authentic identity as ethnically English. English ethnicity would then be a part of my future, and therefore part of my past. The argument implies, for example, that a collective identity as African American would have been: (1) very hard for slaves up to the Civil War; (2) harder in the rural South after about 1876 than in the communities in the urban South that were formed by free coloured people before the Civil War; and (3) harder in the urban South than in the communities of urban African Americans in the North. Authentic African American culture can generate African American identities only when people can build a collective and individual future as African Americans. Once they could freely choose their own religious affiliation and build it into their future (perhaps their earliest practical liberty in the South), then they could build an African American identity.

III. AUTHENTICITY'S DEFENCE IN THE FUTURE

Now let us turn to the relations between legal liberties and rights and authenticity as I have described it. The basic idea of the section following this one is that law extends things into the future. Legal liberties extend the right to act (on one's own beliefs, on one's conception of oneself, on one's values) into the future. If I were to have a strong preference for a future in which my children enjoyed Middle English poetry rather than Spanish poetry, I could use my liberties to make that more likely. Thus I could make my commitment to my ethnicity more authentic by using my liberties and perhaps my rights as a parent to build myself an ethnic future. The fact that I do not but instead try to extend my culture as a rootless cosmopolite into the future is therefore an authentic choice, and the identity so chosen is an authentic culture. My liberties help make me an ethnic fellow through history of Trotsky, Edmund Wilson, Barbara Kingsolver, Albert Einstein, and Chaucer.

There are other ways than law for extending one's values and commitments on into the future. For example, tenure in universities extends the right to develop one's ideas, first said freely because of academic freedom, into 'new knowledge' defending those ideas. Academic freedom and tenure both have extremely precarious legal standing and are ordinarily protected by trade union grievance-procedure tactics rather than by legal defences. But the lack of legal standing for our liberties on the job does not mean that our identity is not embedded even in our most outrageous statements. That is because we hope to defend them—and to modify them gradually—while protected by tenure. We do not say them as throwaway lines, oriented only to immediate situational value. We believe that our commitments (for example, as 'scientists') will extend into the future as a basis for scholarly action (as 'research') because they are defended by university organisational commitments and a system of AAUP (American Association of University Professors) sanctions for the violation of those commitments.

The fact that soldiers have no legal claim to be soldiers in the future does not make their commitments to the effectiveness of the armoured arm, say, inauthentic. Soldiers can to some degree trust the institutions of the military to make a future as a manager of mobile firepower, in the service of American national interests, one with the possibility of honest action on behalf of the values on which they build their identities. They are not in the condition of Erikson's Sioux, who had learned to respect themselves as buffalo hunters and fighters and had no future as either after their (and the buffalos') decisive defeat (Erikson 1985, 111–65).

But practical possibilities of action are extended into the future more effectively by law than by other devices. People do not sink their money into capital installations unless they think they will be at liberty to use them to produce profits (or comfortable homes). But this is even more true of cultural values: without the liberty to live one's life in the light of those values, they are not much use. And interpretations of the particular relations of cultural objects and values to oneself have little meaning unless that self can act with such objects and values in the future.

In the first place, cultural objects and the means of producing reminders of cultural values (such as museums, galleries, schools, libraries and churches) are investments of the usual kind, except that many of them do not make much profit. They are meaningless unless the embodiments of the culture can last into the future, to enter into the repertoires of action of people in the future. The notion of a 'cultural heritage' is of course a continuity of things and values and patterns of action that come from the past. But unless inheritance of a heritage is something one can continue to act on, to admire, to possess representative objects of, it isn't much of a heritage. Why should one care whether some object is an authentic representation of the heritage—truly 'Navaho art' for example (Dauber 1990; 1991)—unless it can be owned, shown in a museum or otherwise become embedded in the future?

The examples of academic freedom and a soldier's commitment to the future of armoured mobility indicate that institutions are central to knowing enough about the future to build an authentic identity. It is the institution of academic freedom, built into the practices of the academic community, that makes a future developing ideas into papers a possible expression of one's identity. It is perhaps the modal basis for identities of rootless cosmopolites, and clearly more reliable than the Russian revolutionary movement was for Trotsky. But roughly the same norms were not well enough institutionalised in German universities under the Nazis for physics to give Einstein a reliable future there.

The ideal-type of 'institution' is one instituted by laws, that explicitly carry the values and practices embedded in or defended by the laws into the future. Laws are about how coercion is organised, and so are the central devices for generalising the institutions of liberties. When a person has a liberty, that means he or she cannot be punished for acting out the protected set of choices and practices. And, as John R Commons (1974, 97–100) puts it, other people and governments have a corresponding 'exposure' to the consequences of a person acting under their liberties.

IV. LIBERTIES AND COLLECTIVE CULTURES

I have been talking as if the connection between culture and authenticity had its main causal nexus in known past and imagined future biography. But I argued above that Tilly's great contribution was to show how institutions stretch people's timeframes. Laws, and especially liberties, are essential to stretching individual timeframes because they allow a person or group with a liberty to build organisations and collective action oriented to the future, by putting the future within the reach of social bodies whose continued action can shape them. In his great study *Parliamentarisation of Popular Contention in Great Britain* (1997a), he argues that institutionalisation through law enacted by Parliament allows people to use their liberties to build *collective* futures.

Let us think what the liberty 'peaceably to assemble and to petition the government for redress of grievances' in the American First Amendment is all about. Freedom of speech is a liberty to build a social relation between speaker and listener. Freedom to assemble is freedom to build a temporary social structure in which to embed that speaker–listener relation. The fact that it is a social relation, rather than the right to chatter on, that is being protected is shown by the fact that such assemblies often have a moment of silence. Often these are to honour dead heroes—and so connect the past to the collective action being built by the assembly; if one has a moment of silence in the closet, it does less honour to the dead. And finally, the right to assembly is explicitly an opportunity to build a collectivity that can, on petition, be recognised by the government. Then their particular connection of past and future may be embedded in law and institutions and so be carried further into the future. Thus what is central to freedom of speech includes what is central to collectively organised silences. Political contention is a central builder of identities, because it is connected to the future; it is more connected to the future when a parliament is well institutionalised, or when freedom of speech is in a constitution.

The reason for liberty then is not only so that I can disrespect Middle English. It is also so I can form social relations to encourage Evanston (Illinois) schools to teach Federico García Lorca rather than Chaucer, if I and enough others so choose. That may then encourage my son to choose the nickname Federico rather than Geoffrey for his Spanish class conversational practice.

What is built by such assembly, speech and petition is, as Tilly shows, only building a future because Parliament has powers over laws, budgets and administrative activities. Parliament focuses public protest exactly because it can stretch the effects of protest into the future. This in turn transforms protest, discouraging hanging the tax collector in effigy and encouraging protest that changes tax law. I try to give my rootless cosmopolite cultural loyalties a stretch into the future by encouraging language instruction in the schools. Regarding the issue of Spanish in particular, I may have a temporary alliance—a 'United Front'—without 'unity'—with representatives of Hispanic ethnic groups in the US. And of course we may all lose together.

Obviously the same general argument follows from the use of liberties to build social structures to carry people's values, culture or special consumption patterns into the future, without the noble colour of the First Amendment. The liberties that build a church include not only the laws guaranteeing freedom of religion, but the right to buy land (and, more problematic, to get it zoned for a church—a right currently in contention in Evanston, Illinois), to contract with bricklayers, to hold church moneys in a checking account, to ring bells Sunday morning even if the neighbours have been out late drinking Saturday night and so on. The right to have Turkish baths, Kosher butchers, Shriners' conventions or a telephone line listed for Armenian All Saints Church Community Center, all use ordinary commercial liberties to carry cultures into the future—and so to render the past they manifest more authentic.

As some of these examples show, the right to try out hokey ways to celebrate the past and future is essential, so that pieces of culture can be selected out. For example, I doubt whether St Patrick ever dyed a river green, as they do in the Chicago parade in his honour. But if a green river connects a poem about the Easter Sunday Rising to the question of who is to be Mayor of Chicago next term, or what ethnicity the mayor will be if he or she refuses to welcome the Queen of England, it can be an authentic experience of Irishness, hokey or not.

And the careful silence, both in modern Christianity and modern Judaism, about the scriptural praise of Moses for genocide (eg, Numbers 21:34–5, 31:15–18; Deuteronomy 2:34; 3:2 and 6) hopefully shows an unwillingness for that part of the heritage to be authentically felt as part of our future. Even those who believe every word about genocide here is the word of God might not build their future around it.

My general point here is that a system of legal liberty allows people to build social structures to carry values. We like to think of social structures as external and constraining, as Émile Durkheim saw them. But when social structures are built under a regime of liberty, they tend to constrain people who *want* to be constrained, so that they can carry the values of their past into their future. And when that enables both rootless cosmopolites and Hispanic ethnics to carry Spanish into their United States futures (and Orthodox Armenian Christianity into Armenian futures), it makes cosmopolitanism, Hispanicism and Armenian Orthodoxy each authentic to some individuals. Ability to form organisations and contracts that carry commitments to the past into the shape of the future enables people to choose their identities.

V. WE SHALL OVERCOME

Clearly many of our deepest commitments to the past are to acts and people who liberated us from past oppression. Social movements born in practical liberties to organise in their turn have often created the legal liberties with which we organise our futures. Many of us more or less forgive Moses his genocide because he delivered us, or at least our Saviour's coreligionists, from bondage. To make this case, let me contrast the African American civil rights movement with the Muslim Bosnian or Muslim Albanian 'independence' movements. I would judge that African American freedom of assembly, of speech and of petitioning the government for redress of grievances were about as absent in the rural South of the United States as in Albanian Kosovo as part of Greater Serbia, with Bosnia before the conflicts perhaps more comparable to the urban South.

The closer the number of an oppressed minority to the majority of the local population, the greater tends to be the repression of their liberties to assemble, to speak, to organise and to make deals about their grievances (Rabushka and Shepsle 1972). Urbanism tends to increase practical liberties, and not being governed by those with the greatest interest in oppression increases liberties. In the 1950s and 1960s about a third of the African American population lived in the rural South in plantation counties where they were near to local majorities and where those most interested in oppression controlled the government; about a third lived in the urban South, with local majorities in some places, but not under the local control of plantation owners; about a third lived in the urban North and West, rarely being local majorities or near majorities and not living in states with a strong plantation interest. Practical freedom of speech, assembly and ability to petition their government varied from insignificant in the rural South to substantial in the urban North, with the urban South in between.

Roughly half of the Albanian Muslims have been in Albania for some time, roughly half in Kosovo were ruled by the Serbs, unresponsive to nationalities since the death of Josip Broz Tito, and perhaps a third of each is urban. Unlike the African Americans in the urban North of the US, the residents in Albania had no capacity to petition the Serbian government of Kosovo, except perhaps by way of American bombings. The Albanians were, until they became refugees, a local majority in Kosovo.

Bosnian Muslims were quite a bit more urban, had more substantial local autonomy under the old Yugoslavian government and were in a local majority in many places. The tradition of liberty to organise separately from the Yugoslavian government was not very strongly institutionalised in Yugoslavia, perhaps comparable to African Americans in the urban South, and much less strongly defended under the Serbian successor state than under Tito.

Now let us analyse how many different sorts of organisations might give meaning to 'We Shall Overcome' in these various situations of legal liberties. For the Albanians in Kosovo, there was only one realistic meaning—that one needs military protection, probably military action by the ethnicity, to organise anything that might carry on into an ethnic Albanian future. In the American North, perhaps especially at the Harvard Divinity School, where Martin Luther King was, one might imagine a non-violent resistance movement 'winning'.

But the chief difference from the cases of greater Serbia was that many different meanings of the song could be built into African American meanings, especially in the North. Many different ideas could carry an interpretation of an item of the African American heritage of resistance, like this song, into the future: black nationalism as in Du Bois' work, and the American Communist Party; Nation of Islam black nationalism; black power of an urban guerrilla style in the Black Panthers of Oakland; Ghandian peaceful resistance with a social-democratic tinge in the Congress of Racial Equality (CORE, which was later transformed by the black power movement) in New York or, with a more revolutionary tinge, in the Student Nonviolent Coordinating Committee (SNCC) on campuses; black caucuses in the United Auto Workers (UAW) in Detroit; Urban League cooperation with liberal businessmen; the National Association for the Advancement of Colored People (NAACP) bringing cases to the US Supreme Court; and finally in black neighbourhoods cooperating with other ethnicities in an Irish-dominated political machine and getting into Congress in a dominantly African American district in Chicago. All of these ways of imagining the future of African Americans make some use of the heritage of protest and resistance of the black community.

Some subset of these possible futures giving authenticity to 'We Shall Overcome' would make sense to many people in the cities of the South, with more immediacy there of the problem of petitions to unwelcoming local and state governments, or even in assembling on the streets. Even if in the rural South nothing much less than local revolution seemed to make sense, the alternative meanings of 'We Shall Overcome' were maintained in the larger environment in which the movement in the rural South developed. And as churches of the South became the core of the civil rights network, the spiritual overtones of the song became embedded in a political future as well (Morris 1984; Patillo-McCoy 1998).

My point here is that secular white social democrats, Southern black Christian congregations and various branches of African American nationalism could give meaning to the same piece of the heritage, because each could organise to carry their interpretation of it into the future. If the argument here is right, then Bosnia should have been intermediate, with many different interpretations of what it meant to be Muslim in a majority in an area with many Serbs; many cities and many parts of the local government being meaningful objects to influence by resistance themes; many practical liberties of speech and assembly to organise behind themes of liberation from oppression. We would expect a lot more ways of building the Muslim or locality heritage into future identities in Bosnia than in Kosovo. One would expect therefore that more Bosnian Muslims than Kosovo Muslims, more African Americans than Bosnians, would have identities with local variants of 'We Shall Overcome' as an authentic element.

VI. OPPOSITIONAL IDENTITIES AND ETHNIC MOVEMENT ELITES

I have chosen a piece of a culture of opposition to illustrate my argument. But the crucial fact here is that the great majority of members of all the ethnic groups mentioned have never participated in a demonstration, sit-in or guerrilla army. Even among long-term voters of conventional and institutionalised political parties, only a few can give a coherent description of what differentiates their party from the opposition, and most have never asked anyone else to vote for their party (Converse 1964). The weight of the evidence is that in any system of social oppositions, it is rare for more than one out of six to do anything but vote for their side unless coerced, and about a sixth know what issues divide them from their opponents. As an organised and ideologised pattern of activity, even racism is an elite project.

The theory above connects identities to a vision of future action. Cognitively, opposing one's enemies is a simple future action and so can easily become a dominant feature of ethnic and national identities. But even that simple cognitive picture of a future of ethnic opposition is built into a future pattern of action only by a small part of the population. For example, 'patriots' and 'nationalist politicians' are disproportionately recruited from the military, whose business is opposition. Military coups often have little other ideology than opposition to the previous government; it is sometimes an easy mistake to think they are pro-capitalist because they are anti-socialist but favour 'the people', when their core ideology is pure opposition. But aside from such specialists in opposition, most people rub along perfectly happily with foreigners or ethnic minorities for neighbours or brothers-in-law. And even among the specialists, there are a good many soldiers who do not join patriotic veterans' organisations and otherwise do not build their identity around oppositions among nations.

The least complex ideology that develops under the first blush of liberty is often ethnic or national opposition. But generally even the elite may not know what kind of ethnic government they want—just not British (or not Serbian, not Tamil, not Russian, etc). Casual journalism may see this as a recrudescence of ancient hatreds, but the ancient common person's tradition did not have much historical hatred of an opposing ethnicity in it, partly because he or she could do nothing about any project connected to that hatred.

The variety of movements in the United States that sang 'We Shall Overcome' gives widespread authenticity to African American opposition to white racism. But it also attaches that opposition to a wide variety of plans for future action. The social democrats of CORE, the distinguished constitutional lawyers of the NAACP, the participatory democracy of the new left activists of SNCC, the Black churches of the Southern Christian Leadership Conference (SCLC) all had oppositional acts in their futures. But they always complained about how hard it was to mobilise people, and it was a rare subgroup of the population that had more than one out of six doing any oppositional activity at all. Further, they had different oppositional acts, attached to different overall plans for social reform and for the tactics of reform's realisation.

Thus liberty often leads eventually to widespread legitimacy of ethnic opposition and to pluralistic bargaining *within* an ethnicity or nationality about collective oppositional action. Only when a majoritarian political system is near an even split of voters, when the liberties of the minority might be suppressed or when an authoritarian invasion of pluralistic local autonomy is under way, is such a pluralistic structure overcome by simple ethnic opposition. In the ordinary course of events, then, an ethnic or national elite with identities largely organised around opposition, 'represents' a mass of people who rub along pretty well with opposing ethnicities. But different members of the ethnic elite may show different amounts of rubbing along. For example, Simon the Zealot (an extreme Jewish ethnic opposed to Roman rule in New Testament times) became a leader of the Christian church during the time when it started to accept Gentiles without their first becoming Jews (eg, without being circumcised or keeping kosher).

The mass of people rarely experiences their leaders' oppositional culture as 'authentic' and rarely rejects the 'inauthentic' culture offered up to tourists, because the culture does not enter into a plan of action going on into the future. Similarly, Southern fundamentalist Baptists may regard their 'fundamentalist' or 'evangelical' ministers, who specialise in opposition to liberal churches, as their representatives. But they may have difficulty themselves thinking of anything really wrong with the National Council of Churches that their representatives vehemently oppose.

VII. CONCLUSION

My purpose here has been to develop a theory of when an ethnic or other cultural heritage will be experienced as authentic by its members. The basic notion is that culture becomes authentic by being part of a project that extends identities of group members into the future. Legal liberties, I further argue, make it more likely that more projects will link past heritage to future identities.

An incidental outcome of that argument is that multiple ethnic projects are more likely to exist under a regime of liberty: multiple nationalisms, and even multiple rootless cosmopolite identities. That means that multiple identities, and therefore multiple branches of the ethnic heritage, will create the experience of authenticity. Some parts of the heritage are likely to be on multiple paths between past and future. No doubt Chaucer is on some of the paths making use of English heritage in the future, and English or American patriotism might lead to learning Middle English. And certainly 'We Shall Overcome' is on many paths that African Americans have used to connect the past to the future. Thus taking an ethnicity as a whole under a regime of liberty, elements that are on many paths to the future will be at the core of authentic culture, elements on one or a few such paths will be peripheral. But the depth of the experience of authenticity, the chance that a cultural element can bring tears to many eyes, is likely to be substantially higher in a regime of liberty.

Thus we must add to Derek Walcott's comment on the problem of building a culture of African and Asian ethnicities after the 'colonial fracture' (1993, 9):

> Break a vase, and the love that reassembles the fragments is stronger than the love which took its symmetry for granted when it was whole. The glue that fits the pieces together is the sealing of the original shape. It is such love that reassembles our African and Asiatic fragments, and the cracked heirlooms whose restoration shows its white scars.

We must add that the love that makes fragments of memory whole depends on the post-colonial regime of liberty that allows people to build a future living with the restored vase.

REFERENCES

Chaucer, Geoffrey. 1386–89/1906. Reprint. *The Canterbury Tales*. London: Oxford University Press.

Collins, Randall. 1998. *The Sociology of Philosophies: A Global Theory of Intellectual Change*. Cambridge, MA: Belknap Press of Harvard University Press.

Commons, John R. 1974. *Legal Foundations of Capitalism*. Clifton: Kelley (also reprinted University Wisconsin Press, Arno Press; originally published by Macmillan 1924).

Converse, Philip E. 1964. The Nature of Belief Systems in Mass Publics. In *Ideology and Discontent*, edited by DE Apter. New York: Free Press.

Dauber, Kenneth. 1990. Pueblo Pottery and the Politics of Regional Identity. *Journal of the Southwest* 32(4): 576–96.

———. 1991. The Indian Arts Fund and the Sponsorship of Native American Arts. In *Paying the Piper: Causes and Consequences of Art Patronage*, edited by J Huggins Balfe. Urbana and Chicago: University of Illinois Press.

Erikson, Erik. 1980. Reprint. *Identity and the Life Cycle*. New York: WW Norton. Original edition, 1959.

———. 1985. Reprint. *Childhood and Society*. New York: WW Norton. Original edition, 1950.

Morris, Aldon D. 1984. *The Origin of the Civil Rights Movement: Black Communities Organizing for Change*. New York: Free Press.

Patillo-McCoy, Mary. 1998. Church Culture as a Strategy of Action in the Black Community. *American Sociological Review* 63(6): 767–84.

Rabushka, Alvin and Shepsle, Kenneth A. 1972. *Politics in Plural Societies: A Theory of Democratic Instability*. Columbus: Merrill.

Stinchcombe, Arthur L. 1975. Social Structure and Politics. In *Handbook of Political Science*, vol 3, edited by N Polsby and F Greenstein. Reading, MA: Addison Wesley.

———. 1997. Tilly on the Past as a Sequence of Futures. In *Roads from Past to Future*, edited by C Tilly. Lanham: Rowman & Littlefield.

Tilly, Charles. 1997a. Parliamentarization of Popular Contention in Great Britain, 1758–1834. In *Roads from Past to Future*, edited by C Tilly. Lanham: Rowman & Littlefield.

——. 1997b. *Roads from Past to Future*. Lanham: Rowman & Littlefield.

Walcott, Derek. 1993. *The Antilles: Fragments of Epic Memory*. New York: Farrar, Straus and Giroux.

IV

Creating and Restituting Rights after Abusive Regimes: Bridges between the Past and the Future

10

Constitutional Interpretation after Regimes of Horror

KIM LANE SCHEPPELE[1]

JUDICIAL ACTIVISM IS everywhere these days, creating what might be described as 'the rise of juridical democracy'. We are witnessing the birth and growth of a new form of democratic order, one in which courts are the central and most powerful players in new 'post-horror' governments. In this chapter, I will try to get at why these changes have been occurring in new democratic governments (and in some older ones as well) in recent years. This chapter is based on a longer and more specific study of this phenomenon in Hungary, the place where these developments have taken perhaps the most extreme form. But what is happening in Hungary is not an isolated event; activist judiciaries wielding new constitutions are now commonplace in the international scene (see Kathy Laster in this volume).

This chapter will proceed in three parts. First, I will outline a history of judicial review and judicial activism, showing how the new forms of judicial review have gone well beyond the American practice. I will then explain why I think such far-reaching judicial activism has been accepted so widely. To do so, I will elaborate the idea of a 'regime of horror', which describes states that demonise their immediate predecessors as a way of defining their new identities. Regimes of horror, I will argue, succeed in creating a debate over collective memory that provides a public rationale for activist judicial interpretation of new constitutions in such a way

[1] In addition to the Oñati conference, earlier versions of this chapter were given at the Law and Public Affairs seminar at Princeton University; at the University of Pennsylvania Law School and at the Workshop in Social Philosophy at the Villa Lana in Prague. An earlier and different version of this chapter was published in the Public Law and Legal Theory Research Paper Series of the University of Pennsylvania Law School, No 1–5, May 2000. I am grateful to the participants in those workshops for helping me escape some critical difficulties with these ideas. I am also grateful to Gábor Halmai, Seth Kreimer and Wojciech Sadurski for very specific comments that made me rethink a great deal. Of course, the lack of wisdom that remains is my own.

that rights provisions are given their broadest readings against claims of the state. Finally, I will examine how constitutional courts operating in states that have defined their pasts as regimes of horror use the debates over collective memory to underwrite expansive interpretations of their new constitutions, with particular examples from the case of post-Soviet Hungary.

I. A BRIEF HISTORY OF JUDICIAL REVIEW

In the American form of judicial review, historically the first, constitutional questions are raised as part of ongoing litigation in traditional form. That is to say, if two parties to an ordinary lawsuit have a constitutional issue mixed in with statutory or common law claims, the constitutional question is handled in the same way as these other sorts of legal claims. Any court is authorised to make constitutional interpretations, and any court is authorised to do what is necessary to enforce its constitutional interpretations, up to and including the rare exercise of the power to declare laws that are contrary to the constitution to be unconstitutional and therefore legally void. This form of review, called 'diffuse review', turns every court into a potential constitutional interpreter and merges constitutional review with other forms of legal interpretation as part of the resolution of concrete questions that arise as part of ordinary legal disputes.

For a bit over a century, this was the only sort of judicial review on offer, and it is not surprising that it did not catch on as a desirable form of judicial power for other countries to emulate. For one thing, this form of judicial review relies on a common law mentality about the ability of ordinary courts to make law as well as to interpret existing law. In common law jurisdictions where judges have the power to create binding new legal rules through their decisions, it is a short step from there to assuming the power to make *constitutional* law through decisions. In most of the world's legal systems where the role of the ordinary judge is imagined theoretically to be far less ambitious—primarily applying abstract laws to concrete cases, not making new law in the process—the American sort of diffuse review did not fit the conception of competencies of either these judges or their audiences. The power given to ordinary judges in the diffuse system of constitutional review was just too much for civil law system lawyers or politicians to incorporate without wildly changing the taken-for-granted basis of the legal order.[2]

---

[2] For a concise and perceptive discussion of the differences between conceptions of judicial review in civil law and common law systems, and the way these different forms of review piggyback onto different conceptions of the role of law and the roles of judges in the two sorts of systems, see de Andrade 2001.

But the idea of judicial review was still attractive as a way of settling theoretical questions about the relationships among legal norms and about conflicts between constitutional and political values *precisely because* courts were staffed by legal professionals with expertise in theoretical matters removed from the day-to-day pressure of interest group politics. The legal philosopher Hans Kelsen, in thinking about adapting the institution of judicial review to a civil law system, proposed the institution of the 'constitutional court', a special jurisdiction court that alone would have the power to review laws in either abstract or concrete form for their conformity with the constitution. The constitutional court would have as its sole mission the technical task of ensuring that the constitution acted as the highest norm of the legal order by invalidating lower-order norms when they conflicted with this higher norm. Removed from ordinary litigation, the constitutional review of laws could be concentrated in a single body that was established among the political institutions of government but that brought legal expertise to bear on decisions, not just views derived from the push and pull of temporary majorities in politics. Crucially, the main point of this form of constitutional review was not just getting justice in the individual case (though in some jurisdictions a constitutional court does this too) but instead ensuring the coherence of the legal order. Through the institution of the constitutional court, which alone can make the determination that a legal norm is not in conformity with the constitution and is therefore legally inoperative, the system of 'concentrated review' was born.

The concentrated review of the constitutional court was first tried out in the Austrian Constitution that was drafted after Austria's defeat in the First World War, from which this form of judicial review gets its name as the 'Austrian model'. At the time, Austria was suffering from the forced breakup of its former empire, and recovering from this trauma was a high priority for the new regime. But the Austrian Constitution in which the new constitutional court was embedded failed to list rights. This meant that the new court had very little text to work with, and it was limited to being a paper watchdog guarding the institutions of state. As might be guessed from this structure, the Austrian court did not have much of a mission in life, and it has never been a very activist court.[3] Nonetheless this method of incorporating judicial review into civil law systems was to be generalised.

---

[3] One of the problems with embedding constitutional review in a constitution that has no rights is that the court is put into the role of monitoring conflicts between constitutionally regulated institutions in situations where the court typically has far less power than the bodies whose activities it is supposed to supervise. Apart from 'standing' problems that limit the way such issues can be raised before a court, there are also major enforcement problems because the court must side with one organ of state against another, and it possesses little power of its own to carry out its judgments. On the Austrian constitutional court in particular, see Somek 1998, where he shows how the equality clause of the Austrian constitution has served as a textual pretext for more recent activism on the part of this court. The Austrian equality

The Austrian model of judicial review received a boost with the drafting of the (West) German Basic Law in 1948 and its promulgation in 1949. The Bonn Constitution, written in the shadow of the Holocaust under the watchful eye of an occupation army, included a long list of rights, starting with the unamendable right of human dignity and a commitment to the rule of law. Among the new institutions of state was a new constitutional court.[4] The court's structure may have been borrowed from the Austrian Constitution, but the context that gave the German Federal Constitutional Court its specific expansive meaning was the post-war context of a defeated and divided Germany. From the Federal Republic's perspective, this context had several crucial elements.

First, in the interwar period, the Weimar Constitution had looked like the model liberal constitution. But obviously, it was insufficient to prevent the rise of fascism in Germany. Why was this? The diagnoses were plentiful, but one of the important general lessons that Germans came away with was that no one office had been assigned the job as the 'guardian of the Constitution'. It was also painfully clear that whoever this guardian was deemed to be, it had better not be the President or some other officer of state who would have a powerful incentive to ignore the Constitution at precisely the moment when she/he was most likely to be pressed into service as the guardian of it.[5] The drafters of the Bonn Constitution were eager not to send an orphan out into the world alone, so they made the Constitutional Court its legal guardian. The Constitution thus thrust this new court into the prominent position of the ultimate guarantor of the constitutional operation of government to ensure that there was no backsliding into fascism. This was a role that the Constitutional Court took on with relish.[6]

'The second crucial aspect of the post-war context was that the horrors of the Holocaust made the new republican German government very sensitive to the need to ensure the equal and dignified treatment of the entire population, which led to the idea of building a state structure around the recognition of the highest level of human rights protection. Accepting

---

clause, like the Polish rule of law clause or the French preamble, has served to authorise the jurisdictional expansion of the constitutional court precisely because it enabled the court to create as its major topic the relationship between the citizen and the state rather than among state organs. But about this trend to build aggressive jurisprudences from general clauses into which rights can be read, which is certainly not unique to Austria, more later.

[4] For an account in English of the drafting of the Bonn Constitution, see Merkl 1963.

[5] See generally Kennedy (2001) on the debates between Hans Kelsen, Hermann Heller and Carl Schmitt over who was the guardian of the Constitution, and the ways in which liberalism failed Germany in the interwar period. The collapse of the Weimar Constitution was an important source of lessons for the post-World War II German constitutional drafters.

[6] The best treatments in English of the impressive jurisprudence of the German Federal Constitutional Court are Currie 1994, Kommers 1998 and, for post-unification constitutional developments, Quint 1997.

that the ultimate responsibility for enunciating and ensuring recognition of rights lay in the Constitutional Court and therefore outside of the demands of interest group politics, the new republican German government showed that it intended to be bound, as if from outside politics itself, by a force deliberately removed from its direct control. The independence of the Constitutional Court thus provided the strongest signal that the new government intended to take the new Constitution and its human rights mandate seriously.[7]

The third element of the post-war context that mattered in the development of the Constitutional Court was the fact that Germany emerged from the War and its aftermath a divided country. The West felt acutely the separation of the East, but the West could serve as a model for what the East might have been if the country had been able to remain undivided. Like the amputated limb that still generates sensation in the brain, the amputated East German Länder created a sensation in the institutions of the West, giving them yet another reason to provide a model of what the ideal democratic rule-of-law state should be. So, under the triple negative models of the collapse of Weimar institutions, the horrors of fascism identified as a failure of human rights protection and the evils of communism portrayed as a lack of respect for the rule of law, the Constitutional Court of the Federal Republic of Germany set out to make sure that the new government was completely different from all three negative models.

The Federal Constitutional Court developed an influential intellectual infrastructure within which the specific provisions of the Constitutional text can be interpreted.[8] For example, the Court has developed the idea of a 'militant democracy', which is a conception of a democracy that possesses sufficient spine to stand up to threats to its own existence. This was the primary lesson learned from the failure of the Weimar Constitution and its excessive tolerance of ideologies and institutions that would undermine the liberal state itself. The fact that the Nazi regime had its toehold in constitutional compliance, at least at first, gave a reason for building a liberal state that could defend itself from illiberal threats. The Court has further elaborated the constitutional idea of the 'rule of law state' or 'Rechtsstaat', which requires certain procedural and substantive guarantees of the rights

---

[7] The other major lesson that Germans learned from the failure of the Weimar institutions was the need to have a force outside ordinary politics directly charged with monitoring and taking action against possible rises in inflation. The Bundesbank, as widely emulated as the Constitutional Court, provided the same sorts of guarantees as the Constitutional Court does—that regime-threatening corrosive conditions would be handled through expertise rather than through politics. Both the Bundesbank and the Constitutional Court have justified themselves by arguing that they are necessary to a democratic regime, rather than destructive of it. Ellen Kennedy's book *The Bundesbank* (1997) makes the case well that independence from politics has been a major factor guaranteeing success of the institution.

[8] See Kommers 1998 ch 2 for a description of these elements and their bases.

of citizens. This was directed against the lack of certainty of rights protection in Weimar, against the radical undermining of the rule of law in Nazi Germany and also against the cynicism of the Soviet legal system. The 'social (welfare) state' also has a constitutional footing, so that the Federal Constitutional Court has tried to ensure that all elements of German society are included in the guarantees of citizenship without discrimination. This again implicitly contrasts itself with the failures of fascism and communism to provide a sense that all citizens, no matter what their other characteristics, have their dignity recognised in the law, underwritten with positive actions of the new democratic state. And the requirements of 'cooperative federalism' force provincial and national governments to work together to construct mutually beneficial policies. Federalism had been the main structural feature insisted upon by the occupation forces because it was thought to prevent a concentration of power in the centre that could be used for nefarious means; federalism thus was part of the important message of self-restraint that the post-World War II Federal Republic government has cultivated ever since.

The Federal Republic of Germany was not alone in adopting an independent and activist constitutional court as a guarantor against backsliding into fascism. Italy too adopted this model in its post-war Constitution, and the Italian Constitutional Court eagerly took the opportunity to dismantle the fascist structures of state.[9] Japan's Supreme Court got off to a slower start, but it too has developed into a body that sees itself as upholding the constitutional order against antidemocratic forces.[10] In fact, it is precisely because these countries experienced the ravages of domestically generated anti-democratic governments within the living memory of its citizens that the courts are gladly given the powers that they are. The collective memory of fascism and authoritarianism provided the justification for going to great lengths to guarantee that the political institutions cannot go down that path again. Standing in the way was a constitutional conception of law, whose guardian was a new court with constitutional powers.

The evident success of the new German Federal Republic democracy in particular—though the accomplishments of Italy and Japan also supported the same conclusion—emboldened other democratic states to try the same experiment in constitutional governance. Despite dire predictions about the future of these countries, the new German, Italian and Japanese constitutions created states that now guarantee a decent life to (most of) their citizens, uphold in theory and practice the ideals of a democratic order,

---

[9] See Mandel (1995). The 'initial activity of the [Italian Constitutional] Court ... was the dismantling of the Fascist legal order ... left intact by the Christian Democratic governments of the early 1950s (Mandel 1995, 267). For a more complete account, see Volcansek (2000).

[10] The Japanese case is slightly different because the Supreme Court has rarely been as activist as its constitutional court counterparts in Europe.

present no threat to their neighbours and create economic engines that power impressive economies. A conspicuous part of the success of these new clearly democratic regimes was the centrality of aggressive constitutional review in the democratic revival.[11]

Other countries emerging from the anti-democratic practices of fascism or martial law have also adopted constitutional courts as guarantors of their own democratic commitments. Spain, for example, in the Constitution of 1978 that followed Franco's death, created a Constitutional Court that has been very active in supporting a broad conception of human rights. So did Portugal. In the Philippines, the post-Marcos Constitution of 1987 re-established the Supreme Court as a strong court with new and expanded powers. This Court has pursued an activist agenda and, though American academic commentators have criticised it, public opinion in the Philippines for this institution shows strong support.[12]

Some successful democracies with a great deal of demographic diversity and correspondingly high potential for paralysing and violent conflict have also seen the rise of strong high courts to act as guarantors of liberal values in the new democratic order. The Indian Supreme Court is quite activist in many areas. Perhaps the most stunning set of decisions required government to institute an affirmative action programme in public employment that held more than half of all new places in the civil service for members of the lower castes (see Galanter 1984). Israel's closely divided democracy is presided over by an activist Supreme Court, which puts its thumb on the scale to support secularism and liberalism over religious orthodoxy and therefore puts itself in constant political controversy.[13]

Since the demise of the Soviet empire, the new democratic constitutions of Eastern Europe all contain provisions for constitutional courts. Their power and success vary widely, with Hungary, Slovenia, Bulgaria, Poland and Estonia having quite active and politically aggressive courts that have achieved the respect of the political branches of government (at least under

---

[11] The German Constitutional Court has become the more widely copied international model in part because its decisions have been more closely reasoned, philosophically well-grounded and widely translated. In the more recent constitutional transformations of Eastern Europe, it is almost always the German model that is explicitly cited and followed.

[12] For both the criticism of the Court and the public opinion figures, see Tate (1995). The Philippines model of judicial review is, like Japan's, closer to the American than German one, if only because American influence in the drafting of post-World War II constitutions in Asia was more prominent than the German influence.

[13] Both India and Israel follow the American model in the sense that the Supreme Court is the highest court in the system of ordinary courts as well as the court that generates the most visible constitutional doctrine through the review of concrete cases. Israel has the added issue of not having a single written constitution but instead a set of basic laws that constitute a partial constitution. The Israeli Supreme Court has filled in the rest. See former Supreme Court President Aharon Barak's book *Judicial Discretion* (1987) for a theoretical account of his approach to constitutional interpretation.

some administrations), while the constitutional courts of Russia, Slovakia, the rest of former Yugoslavia, Ukraine and Armenia have had more mixed success and have been the victims of more frequent attempts at direct political tampering, making it harder for these courts to establish their legitimacy.[14] But among constitutional experts in the region, there is widespread agreement that a strong and politically active constitutional court is a necessary ingredient for a strong democratic order. The courts are seen not as challenges to democracy but as important monitors and guarantors of democracy.

In ever newer democracy on the block, the South African Constitutional Court opened with a series of important decisions abolishing the death penalty, checking the new Constitution for its agreement with the fundamental principles of a democratic order and establishing constitutional coherence among the various sub-national governments. This Court too has a direct and active political role in the South African government as a guarantor of constitutional democracy and a crucial element in the shaping of domestic policy.

As these new democracies have established that constitutional courts and aggressive judicial review are crucial elements in maintaining a democracy, older and more established democracies are also finding themselves pulled into the activist judicial review camp. In other words, once aggressive constitutional review established itself in what had been seen as fragile democracies, it has been able to spread to more firmly entrenched democracies, which then have not wanted to be seen as lagging behind important international trends. One of the earliest of these was France, where the Constitutional Tribunal had been given quite limited powers of review under the Gaullist Constitution of 1958. It had been created merely to keep Parliament from encroaching upon the powers of the nearly almighty President. In 1971, reading the Preamble's references to the Declaration of the Rights of Man and the Citizen along with the 1946 Bill of Rights as a mandate to expand its jurisdiction, the Constitutional Tribunal took on a more aggressive role for itself in French politics. In its decision on modifications to the freedom of association law, the Constitutional Tribunal expanded its review of newly passed laws to include assessing new laws for their potential infringement on rights.[15] Shortly thereafter, Canada gave a

---

[14] The *East European Constitutional Review*, published between 1991 and 2005, provided quarterly detailed reports on the constitutional decisions of the constitutional courts in post-Soviet countries and on the constitutionally significant political developments in these countries as well.

[15] The Decision of 16 July 1971 declared an amendment of the 1901 Law on Associations to be unconstitutional. The original law of 1901, regarded as a triumph of the Third Republic's commitment to liberalism, allowed organisations to register and be recognised as having legal personality with purely formal registration procedures. It was widely seen to embody a crucial liberal commitment to freedom of association. But following the uprisings of 1968, the

greatly expanded role to its already existing Supreme Court, with the adoption of the Charter of Rights in 1982. Since the adoption of the Charter, the Supreme Court has taken a lively and active role in Canadian politics by enthusiastically using the Charter to give itself a voice in a great many areas of policy (see Hogg 1997).

The effects of European integration have also succeeded in bringing an effective form of judicial review to countries that never had this practice in their own systems, like the United Kingdom and the Netherlands.[16] Under mandates from the European Court of Human Rights and even now sometimes from the European Court of Justice, the solidly entrenched democracies of Europe have had to replace some of their laws that infringe the European Convention on Human Rights or aspects of the increasingly dense set of treaties that unite Europe these days.[17] As a result of being drawn into the judicial activist orbit, the UK has made the European Convention of Human Rights directly applicable in UK courts, thus creating something like rights-based constitutional review for the first time. And while there is persistent talk of a democratic deficit in European institutions, this criticism is largely directed at the mysterious workings of the European Commission and the relative powerlessness of the European Parliament, rather than at the system of courts that are exercising what amounts to judicial review over the laws of the Member States of Europe.

From this all-too-quick survey of some of the places where rather aggressive forms of judicial review have taken hold, we might try to understand

---

conservative Parliament sought to amend the law to allow the public prosecutor to initiate judicial proceedings during the registration process that would inquire into whether a particular organisation was formed for an illicit purpose before it would be allowed to register itself legally. The previously established free registration of organisations was therefore limited by a political review of the acceptability of the organisation before its official registration. Until this point, the Constitutional Council had limited its timid decisions to ensuring executive supremacy, as it was designed to do in the Constitution. But faced with a very real threat to a basic principle of the liberal constitutional order, freedom of association, the Constitutional Council rather stunningly announced what amounted to a huge increase in its jurisdiction by claiming that the preamble of the 1958 Constitution was a legally enforceable provision. The Preamble referred to the rights listed in the Declaration of the Rights of Man and the Citizen from 1789 and also to the rights mentioned in the 1946 Constitution. Importing these rights into the 1958 Constitution through the Preamble, the Constitutional Council rewrote its role in the operation of French politics. See Lindseth 1996/97 for a detailed account of the decision; see Bell 1997 for an overview of French constitutional doctrine.

[16] Erhard Blankenburg refers to these countries as 'self-assured democracies', in contrast with those that emerged from some historical past that they wanted urgently in their laws to banish. See Blankenburg 1999.

[17] The European Court on Human Rights is a creature of the Council of Europe, which now includes 47 member countries in its purview and extends its reach far into Eastern Europe. The European Court of Justice is a creature of the European Union and binds only EU member countries. While the former court has only human rights jurisdiction, the latter enforces primarily economic regulation but with an increasing human rights sensibility. See Weiler (1999) for an argument that Europe is now already functionally a constitutional system of its own.

why courts with the power of judicial review have become such important elements of many democratic governments in the world today. That constitutional review has insinuated itself into the foreground of politics in many countries is quite clear. Why it has been able to do so is another question, to which we turn next.

II. REGIMES OF HORROR AND THE NEGATIVE MEANING OF NEW CONSTITUTIONS

While the twentieth century has no monopoly on inhumanity, it witnessed an extraordinary scope and scale of state-sponsored violence that has been used not only in wartime against enemies but also as ongoing mechanisms of governance and control of domestic populations. It is possible, without getting into debates over comparison or causation,[18] to identify Nazi Germany, fascist Italy, Stalinist Russia, the Soviet-dominated states of Eastern Europe, apartheid South Africa and Franco's Spain, among others, as states that saw widespread abuse of domestic populations justified in the name of state imperatives. Each of these states has since seen a democratic transformation. And to mark the transformations, new constitutions were written, a commitment to human rights was put high on the public agenda and constitutional courts were created to safeguard these accomplishments.

These new democratically committed states have created 'regimes of horror' out of their immediate pasts. The evils of the prior regimes, understood explicitly as *evils*, are highlighted, condemned and publicly displayed as exactly what the new regimes are against, and these evils define by negative example the core of what the democratic transformation is for. Whatever else a new government may support, it is definitely not what the previous regime supported. The idea of the 'regime of horror', then, defines the new democratic state's sense of where it stands in the world: first and foremost as a repudiation of its own immediate past. And the negative content of that asserted identity—whatever we are, the new state indicates, we are wholly different from the regime immediately before us—provides the point of the new state's constitutive identity.

The term 'regimes of horror' is meant to echo the title of Julia Kristeva's book *Powers of Horror* (1982). Kristeva identifies the psychological mechanism of 'abjection', in which individuals who need psychically to distance

---

[18] LaCapra identifies one of the central elements in the historians' debate in Germany in the 1980s to be about whether the Holocaust is a unique event or comparable to other horrors (LaCapra 1992). Charles Maier constructively notes that the recent debates over collective memory in Germany are less about what is true history and more about establishing a basis of historical mistreatment that should command particular respect now (Maier 1993).

themselves from something particularly horrifying about their pasts cast off these things in a particularly forceful and absolute way, all the while remaining absolutely fascinated with what has been rejected:

> There looms, within abjection, one of those violent, dark revolts of being, directed against a threat that seems to emanate from an exorbitant outside or inside, ejected beyond the scope of the possible, the tolerable, the thinkable. It lies there, quite close, but it cannot be assimilated. It beseeches, worries, and fascinates desire, which, nevertheless, does not let itself be seduced. Apprehensive, desire turns aside; sickened, it rejects. A certainty protects it from the shameful—a certainty of which it is proud, holds on to it. But simultaneously, just the same, that impetus, that spasm, that leap is drawn toward an elsewhere as tempting as it is condemned. Unflaggingly, like an inescapable boomerang, a vortex of summons and repulsion places the one haunted by it literally beside himself (Kristeva 1982, 1).

Through abjection, the individual tortured by her past identifies the offending bit of herself and casts it off. But even though it is rejected, this bit stays close enough to be ever-present. It cannot be taken back in, for to do so is to upset the individual's present sense of herself. But it cannot be put completely out of sight either, for it is precisely in relation to what has been rejected that the individual understands who she is now. Just what is substantively cast off matters less than the fact that 'the abject was only one quality of the object—that of being opposed to I' (Kristeva 1982, 1).

Kristeva then identifies as 'horror' that particular reaction the individual has to the thing that she has cast off as formerly part of herself. Horror requires for its effect a particular combination of recognition and rejection. One cannot be horrified by something with which one doesn't also identify. And one cannot be horrified by something that is still part of one's sense of oneself, something that is not yet cast off. She explicitly engages the Holocaust:

> In the dark halls of the museum that is now what remains of Auschwitz, I see a heap of children's shoes ... something I have already seen elsewhere ... The abjection of Nazi crime reaches its apex when death, which, in any case, kills me, interferes with what, in my living universe, is supposed to save me from death: childhood ... (Kristeva 1982, 4).

In other words, death (which is cast off as too horrible to contemplate, yet impossible to forget) becomes particularly horrifying in Auschwitz precisely because it is put in proximity with a recognisable feature of one's own lived experience (here, childhood). Thus, one experiences horror.

Cindy Sherman's 'Horror Pictures' (1995) have a similar logic. They are photographs of dolls that look strikingly expressive and human, except for the fact that their features are rearranged or melted together. In addition, in each still life of explicit plastic body parts, there is some actual human feature—an eye, lips, sweat. Here too, it is precisely the recognition of the deeply real human element—the actual human feature—combined in grotesque way with the impossible distortion of the plastic bits that creates horror through recognition and rejection. The intimately familiar is combined with its horribly twisted opposite, the 'I' amidst the 'not-I'. This is the stuff of which horror is made.

Though the psychological mechanisms of an individual and the sociological processes of a polity are very different and though I do not mean to take on board here the whole psychological theory in which Kristeva's analysis of abjection constitutes a part, Kristeva's discussion of horror might be taken as a metaphor for similar processes that occur at the level of public discourse and political action. In particular, it is useful to think of the work of newly democratic states as also involving the identification and rejection of particular elements of their pasts as a way of demonstrating with particular vividness what their commitments are now. These rejected bits cannot be forgotten, or they would cease to have their salutary effect of reminding those in the present of what they must never again do. But they also cannot be ever accepted back into what counts as the normal behaviour of the new state. These rejected bits are recognised as part of 'our past' (and as such, constitute who 'we' are), but they are also cast away as fully out of the question for a new state to repeat. Thus, recognition and rejection is reflected in their political and institutional order. Horror requires being able to see the familiar in the forbidden, to recognise a bit of oneself in the horrible practices that cannot now be performed. But at the same time, one is now completely different precisely because one has rejected these abhorrent practices.

One of the ways that states engage in this definition of themselves as completely different from prior regimes is through constitution-writing. As Lech Garlicki, a judge on the Polish Constitutional Tribunal, put it:

> The fall of communism resulted, among other things, in an end of 'socialist constitutions'—they had to be replaced with new ones. The ideal picture of new constitutions was rather obvious: they should follow (imitate) democratic constitutions of the Western world. There were several hopes as to the functions to be fulfilled by the new constitutional instruments: to demonstrate a clear rejection of the communist past, to create legal foundations of the new democratic order, to describe and confirm the new identity of the nation (country) (Garlicki 1995, 6).

Constitutions often contain what their framers want most not to repeat precisely because the abuses that required a change of regime are most on constitutional drafters' minds as they try to draw a sharp line between present and past.

Written constitutions have gone through fads and fashions in their drafting and design from the surprisingly spare eighteenth-century American one to the typically very long recent ones, and these fads and fashions reflect what the typical abuses were that new constitutions were supposed to correct. Typical nineteenth-century constitutions outlined the organs of state structure with a particular emphasis on limiting or abolishing monarchies (and sometimes also nobilities). Because they had to replace hereditary power with something else, they outlined in some detail the new, more popularly responsive governmental structures that were to rule instead. There was a clear preoccupation with constructing new governments explicitly that would limit inherited power and provide for clear mechanisms for transferring power through means other than birth. Lists of rights, guaranteeing the role of the individual citizen within the state as an autonomous political force, were generally merely declaratory and appeared without a clear mechanism for enforcement or much attachment to the new institutions of state.

The creation of a single collective memory about what is being rejected in the past through constitution-writing is, of course, not a consensual process. Constitution-writing brings to the fore different views of the past from different segments of the population. Often, however, the tensions in constituent assemblies carry over into debates over the nature of collective memory in the post-horror regime, and these tensions then appear as criticisms of the constitutional courts charged with interpreting the new constitutions. In Poland, for example, disagreements among post-communist constitutional drafters over the role of the Catholic Church, in particular, delayed the adoption of the new text until 1997, and even then the provisions about religion and abortion stirred opposition. The working majority on the Polish Constitutional Court and the first elected President (Lech Wałęsa) in the meantime adopted a largely pro-Catholic view while the subsequent post-socialist President and Parliament adopted a more secularist view. Decisions of the Constitutional Court have therefore often been controversial, particularly on subjects like abortion, which tracks this division exactly. A deep divide in Israel over whether Israel is a religious or secular state (which depends in part on whether one sees the relevant history of the state of Israel as primarily the Holocaust or the longstanding patterns of complex settlement in Palestine) has prevented the adoption of a general written constitution. Instead, a series of basic laws have been passed as pieces of a larger text that has not yet emerged. The Israeli Supreme Court's relentless support of secularism makes it subject to attack by religious believers who feel that the Court has abandoned the reason for existence of the state of Israel in the first place.

The new Hungarian Constitution was rewritten in 1989 as a result of the Roundtable process and amended substantially after the first free elections in 1990. As with many other 'post'—constitutions, it was written by a small group of insiders.[19] The 1989 constitutional drafters worked in

---

[19] Technically speaking, the present Hungarian Constitution is a set of sweeping amendments to Law XX of 1949 because there was never a moment when continuity was broken with the Soviet-era constitution. Instead, it was a signature feature of the Hungarian transition that all changes to the laws occurred within the framework of laws already in place.

a small subcommittee of the larger National Roundtable that was convened to come up with a set of constitutional mechanisms to allow the first democratically contested election to occur. The drafters were a small group of young men whose authority did not officially extend to rewriting the entire text. But the committee members from the Hungarian Socialist Workers' Party wanted a wholly new constitution more than the committee members from the opposition did. So the two sets of negotiators compromised. First, they agreed to cross out all of the passages in the Soviet-era constitution that clearly had to go if a new multiparty state was to be created, and then (since there wasn't much left to the constitution after they did this with a rather broad brush) they filled in the many blanks with wording from human rights conventions that were technically already domestic law in Hungary. Once the rights provisions were added, the representatives from the opposition went back to their leadership (which had previously not supported writing a new constitution before a general election could be held). The Opposition Roundtable agreed not only to support the substantially revised Constitution but also to create a Constitutional Court that would have the power to enforce the rights provisions in the Constitution. To members of the Opposition Roundtable, the new Constitution represented a serious human rights manifesto that marked a sharp break with the past. To members of the state party, the Constitution represented a technical improvement to an outmoded text without new moral content, much the way that a car from model year 1989 would represent an improvement on a car from model year 1949. After multiparty elections took place and the first post-Soviet Parliament was seated, the new Parliament amended the constitution extensively again to get rid of many of the compromises that had to be written into the 1989 amendments to appease the Hungarian Socialist Workers' Party government. But by that time, it was hard to find any hard-line communists anymore. Everyone had become, more or less, a born-again liberal.[20]

The 1989 and 1990 changes in the Hungarian Constitution created a great many new features that were not present in the Soviet-era Constitution. For example, Article 3 states that political parties may be freely formed but may

---

[20] Some of this shift occurred because the generation that came of age during the 1950s crackdowns was coincidentally reaching retirement age in 1989, and they simply left government to lead private lives. Some of this occurred because there had been a split that widened in the 1980s within the Hungarian Socialist Workers' Party between the relative hardliners and the reformers, and the reformers had won in the year before the Roundtable was convened. The people leading the communist party were therefore less likely to resist change than their more adamant predecessors. And some of this occurred because liberalism appeared on the scene in 1989 with such force that it was clearly politically correct to embrace it. The reformed remnants of the communist party went peacefully into the opposition. The biggest political battles emerged between liberals and nationalists—groups united in the Opposition Roundtable that later divided as they tried to govern together—over things like state symbols, control of the media and other cultural issues.

not exercise power directly. Why would one think of this provision unless one had experienced the party-state? Article 9 states that Hungary is a market economy. Again, why should the form of the economy be a constitutional concept unless the prior regime had assumed the opposite? Article 18 recognises the right to a healthy environment. It actually had been the environmental movement, organised after the debacle of Chernobyl, that had emboldened the opposition to ask for the Roundtable to negotiate the change of power in the first place.

In the area of state structure, the Constitution specifies that there shall be a National Assembly, government (Prime Minister in particular), a President, an ordinary judiciary and a Constitutional Court. So far, no surprises, as these are now the standard moving parts of a parliamentary democracy. But the Constitution also defines the offices of three ombudsmen who are to be responsible for civil rights, minority rights and data protection (Article 32/B). Why should ombudsmen protect against rights violations, particularly in the areas of minority rights and data privacy, unless these had been particularly troublesome subjects before? Ordinarily, ombudsmen are generalists in rights protections of all sorts. The National Bank and the National Audit Office are given constitutional status as a way to ensure their new-found independence.

The rights provisions in the Hungarian Constitution, as in many post-Soviet constitutions, are extensive. They include, in addition to the standard civil liberties and criminal procedure protections common to most liberal democratic constitutions, a right to human dignity; a prohibition of torture; a ban on human experimentation; compensation for victims of unlawful arrest or detention; a right to legal recourse against decisions of courts or state administrative decisions; a right to choose one's place of residence; the right to preserve one's good reputation; protection of private secrets and personal data; a right of access to information of public interest; equality of men and women; special provision for women and children; parental rights to choose the method of education of their children; individual and collective rights for ethnic and national minorities; a right to be elected to public office unless one is in prison or ruled incompetent; a right against negative discrimination on the basis of a wide range of criteria, including race, colour, sex, language, religion, political or other opinion, national or social origin, property, birth or 'upon any other grounds' but also a right to positive discrimination to correct past negative discriminations; a right to work; a right to equal pay for equal work; a right to an income corresponding to the amount and quality of work performed; a right to strike; a right to psychic and physical health 'of the highest possible level'; a right to social security; a right to education; and the freedom of science and art. There is also a right given to qualified scholars to have scientific issues decided upon merit and the scientific value of research! All these rights provisions are contained in Articles 54–70K.

While most of these rights were borrowed from international human rights agreements that Hungary had signed in the Soviet period,[21] many of these rights also specifically recall the abuses of the communist past. Torture, lack of data privacy, unlawful arrest and detention, failure of legal recourse, state secrecy and human experimentation were signature abuses of the Soviet era, though perhaps milder in Hungary in the decades before transition than elsewhere in the Soviet world. Property rights, severely curtailed under state socialism, had to be newly defined and could by no means be taken for granted. Social rights, often called by critical commentators a 'legacy' of the communist past, are actually *breaks* with it, because in the Hungarian text they are made universal and not dependent upon being a compliant worker, as they were in the Soviet period. Labour rights, too, have a different meaning when unions are detached from party control. And the fact that the Constitution says that the merit and value of research should be decided by only qualified scholars clearly shows that it had not been this way before. I could go on more specifically—but suffice it to say that most if not all of these rights have some resonance with their specific abuse in Soviet-era practice.

The adoption of a new constitution, then, often flags areas where a new regime has explicitly cast off the prior one in an effort to portray the prior government as a regime of horror from which the present government is distanced. The creation of the prior regime as a regime of horror is part of the process of 'transition' away from it; a constitutional court, armed with the new constitution that embodies the sharp break, is the primary mechanism for the continued elaboration of the past regime of horror.

III. NEGATIVE CONSTITUTIONAL INTERPRETATION IN THE SHADOW OF THE REGIME OF HORROR

Once a new constitution is in place and the line between the old and new regimes has been sharply drawn, new constitutional courts adopt a very specific role. They police the border between past and present regimes by establishing that the new regime is in fact the opposite of the regime of

---

[21] In 'The Accidental Constitution' (a paper given at the University of Pennsylvania Journal of Constitutional Law Symposium on Constitutional Borrowings, March 1998), I show how most of these rights provisions were copied word for word from various international human rights agreements that Hungary had signed in the Soviet period but that had remained without any possible legal enforcement until 1989. The clear intent of all of the constitutional drafters was to bring international norms into domestic law. But of course the international human rights agreements that Hungary signed were themselves the product of the post-horror reactions after World War II, both to fascism and to communism. Hungary had signed virtually every international agreement on offer, so there was a lot to choose from, and the drafters were selective. The fact that Hungarians copied these provisions from international treaties did not preclude the copied provisions from having special meaning in the Hungarian context.

horror that preceded it. In other words, new constitutional courts in post-horror regimes note specifically what has been rejected (abjected) in the new constitutional order, and they take that as the basis of their mandate in engaging in constitutional interpretation. The constitutional politics of the post-horror regime give courts quite a lot of room for manoeuvre, especially where there is agreement over both what the specific wrongs of the previous regime were and how these wrongs should be righted now. Where the public can see that there is a particular danger of backsliding into anti-democracy (or backsliding into state socialism, fascism, apartheid, military dictatorship, etc), constitutional courts are tolerated in an expansive use of judicial review to prevent this backsliding. Where there is no agreement on what would constitute backsliding, or where there is no agreement on what the evils of the prior regime were, then constitutional interpretation is more embattled. In any concrete context, the interesting question that remains is why the negative models are drawn the way they are. Why does collective memory of the abuses of the past take the shape that it does, and why is there agreement on some parts and disagreement on others?

I will illustrate how this process works with examples from the Constitutional Court of Hungary because this court got off to an unusually quick start in developing an activist jurisprudence based on the new Constitution. But as I tried to show earlier, there is reason to believe that the Hungarian case is not unique in its general approach to constitutional law (Scheppele 1998). In fact, it is precisely because Hungarian constitutional drafters, politicians and constitutional interpreters so freely used international models as justification for what they did that it is easy to see both how widespread the phenomenon is elsewhere and also how specifically rooted in a sense of the past-to-be-avoided the local variants are.

As we have seen, the new Hungarian Constitution is long and detailed and bristling with rights. But the primary jurisdiction of the Constitutional Court is simply stated: 'The Constitutional Court shall review the constitutionality of legal rules' (Article 32/A). Every clause of the Constitution, then, defines a potential subject matter for the Court.

The Court defined what it did in its first years as engaging in a 'rule of law revolution'. By this, the Court—and particularly its first President, László Sólyom—meant that the transformation of regime would be done in a manner that was totally different from past revolutions. If past revolutions changed everything all at once, the new revolution would value continuity, predictability and stability. In the new democratic order, old law would not be swept aside and new law substituted overnight without citizens being put on notice and having time to adjust, as had been typical of the prior regime. Instead, legal continuity from one regime to the next would be preserved, so that the subjects of the law, Hungarian citizens, would not feel themselves to be the subjects of new legal experiments. What was precisely revolutionary about this in the post-horror regime was that no revolutionary change would occur.

The Hungarian Constitutional Court read this idea into the 'rule of law' (*jogállam*) clause of the Constitution as the principle of 'legal security'. By that, the Court meant that the stability of the basic legal framework would be guaranteed even as change was occurring. The Court used this idea in particular to prevent the new government from backsliding into old practices that were now rejected, even if the new practices were ways of coping with the abuses of the previous ones.[22] So when the first elected government passed a statute that would have extended the statute of limitations for crimes committed in the Soviet time that had not been prosecuted for 'political reasons', the Hungarian Constitutional Court struck down the law, explicitly citing the historical break with the prior regime as a reason for doing so:

> With the enactment of the constitutional amendment of 23 October 1989, in fact, a new Constitution came into force, with its declaration that 'the Republic of Hungary is an independent and democratic state under the rule of law', which conferred on the State, its law and the political system a new quality, fundamentally different from that of the previous regime. In the constitutional law sense, this is the substance of the political category of the 'change of system' or 'transition'.[23]

The Court went on to consider what its view should be toward altering the current criminal code in order to extend the statute of limitations for these crimes that had not been prosecuted for 'political reasons' under the previous regime. It concluded that the new rule-of-law-based state could not justify itself in the same terms that the old one did—where instrumentalist logic triumphed over legal security. Instead, the Court said:

> Within the framework of the rule of law, and in order to further its development, the given historical situation can be taken into consideration. However, the basic guarantees of the rule of law cannot be set aside by reference to historical situations ... A state governed by the rule of law cannot be created by undermining

---

[22] There is, of course, a certain strange tension here. If the continuity of the laws, including the laws of the prior regime of horror, is to be preserved, then how does this constitute a break from the prior regime? Behind this paradox is an observation about the operation of law in the time of state socialism. Law on the books was often very different from law in action. From the moment the new Constitution went into effect and the new Constitutional Court opened for business, it became a clear goal of the new Court to ensure that law as it is written comes closer to law as it is enforced. For example, the worker-friendly labour laws on the books, which had been enforced only sporadically during the Soviet time, became more powerful weapons of the defense of labour against the new multinationals when they arrived. Often the problem with the Soviet-era laws was not their surface content, but the way they failed to be realised. One of the major effects of the change of regime in Hungary, then, was that citizens were encouraged to believe that the rights they appeared to possess in law were actually rights that they could enforce through law.

[23] Decision 11/1992 on the Retroactive Prosecution of Serious Offenses. These and the other decisions cited hereafter can be found in translation in Sólyom and Brunner 2000.

the rule of law. Legal certainty based on formal and objective principles is more important than necessarily partial and subjective justice ... The Constitutional Court cannot ignore history since it has to fulfil its task embedded in history. The Constitutional Court is the repository of the paradox of the 'revolution under the rule of law': in the process of the peaceful transition, beginning with the new Constitution, the Constitutional Court must, within its competencies, in all cases unconditionally guarantee the conformity of the legislative power with the Constitution.[24]

So, however tempting it might have been to go after those people who committed crimes but who were protected from punishment in the socialist era, the Constitutional Court said that a new rule-of-law regime stood for the proposition that no purely instrumental reason would suffice to change the basic guarantees of legal security. The fact that leaders of the previous regime had done horrible things to others without legal consequence could not be used as a present constitutional reason for treating them outside the boundaries of the permissible law now. The rule-of-law revolution meant that from the moment of 'system change' forward, law could not be retro-actively changed to create a problem of legal security.

This idea that the new regime would mark itself as completely different from the past regime carried over into a series of decisions about how to deal with people who had worked for the security services in socialist times and who had spied on their friends and co-workers. The new Parliament wanted to publicise the names and to 'lustrate' the spies out of the govern-ment so that they could not play leading roles in the transitional state. But here too the Constitutional Court declared several laws on this subject unconstitutional on the grounds that one did not start a rule-of-law state by violating the rights of the people who in the previous regime had violated the rights of others.[25] Though the Court announced that everyone had the right of access to their own secret police files for the purposes of seeing what the state had recorded about them, the Court also said that all names that appeared in the files besides the person seeking the information had to be deleted because of a right of informational self-determination, which meant in this case a right to privacy. Even the spies had these rights, and so their names too would be deleted from the files of those on whom they had spied. In other words, even though the spies themselves obviously had had no regard for anyone else's privacy during the socialist period, the new regime would be different, by recognising *everyone's* privacy rights—even of those who had been spies.

Personal privacy was a right that was particularly highly developed by the Constitutional Court, precisely because the infringement on personal

---

[24] *Ibid.*
[25] For a more complete treatment of these cases, see Halmai and Scheppele 1996.

privacy was one of the signature violations of the socialist era. A decision of the Constitutional Court declared unconstitutional a series of statutory provisions that allowed the creation and maintenance of a universal personal identifying number through which every Hungarian citizen could be traced in government files. In doing so, the Constitutional Court noted the specific connection between the lack of privacy and the possibility of totalitarian government:

> The personal identifier number is particularly dangerous to personality rights ... The widespread use of personal identifier numbers results in impairing the private sphere because even the remotest data-storage systems established for different reasons may be used to establish a personality profile which is an artificial image extending to an arbitrarily wide activity of the person and penetrating into the person's most private matters; this image, due to its construction from data torn out of their context, is most likely to be a distorted image as well. In spite of this, the data user will make its decisions on the basis of this image, will use this image to produce and forward further information concerning the person in question. The large amount of these interconnected data, of which the person in question generally has no knowledge, renders the person defenseless and creates unequal communication conditions. Where one party cannot know the information the other party possesses about him, creates a humiliating situation, and prevents free decision-making. The power of the state administration in using personal identifier numbers is markedly increased. If personal identifier numbers may be used in areas outside the ambit of the administration, this increases the power not only of the data user over the parties concerned but also of the State because it further broadens the possible control through the use of such data. Taken together, they seriously jeopardize the right to self-determination and human dignity. The unlimited use of personal identifier numbers might become a tool for totalitarian control.[26]

The broad scope of data privacy protection in Hungary reacts against prior practice, whereby citizens never knew who was spying on them, for what reason or to what effect. While the state bureaucracies resisted this decision of the Constitutional Court, and it took five years before all of the alternatives to the personal identifier number were in place, the decision itself seemed to have wide support from the general population. In many other areas of constitutional interpretation, the decisions of the Hungarian Constitutional Court can be seen as reactions against a sense of what had been wrong before and what therefore had to be done differently now. This was aided and abetted by an extensive constitutional text that, as we have seen, cried out for application to a great many topics that were not the usual subjects of constitutional law in countries that have had a different history. For example, the Constitutional Court has had to develop

---

[26] Decision 15/1991 (13 April 1991) on the Use of Personal Data and the Personal Identification Number.

a constitutional conception of a market economy. In one case that arose under the market economy clause, the Court had to decide whether it was constitutional for the city of Budapest to limit the number of taxi licences that were available. The Court decided that such a limitation was not permitted under the market economy provision, which guarantees everyone the right to work at an occupation of their choosing. Seeing the obvious limitations of this principle in certain professions, the Court held in a later decision that this same rationale did not apply to licences to practice law. But the Court freely admitted that while it might not be sure what a market economy required as a positive matter, it certainly knew how to recognise when a market economy was damaged by law:

> [T]he Constitutional Court, using abstract and general criteria, can only define those extreme situations in which state intervention reaches such a critical intensity that by violating the principle of market economy it becomes unconstitutional. It is the intervention which conceptually and practically renders the existence of the market economy impossible which qualifies as unconstitutional; such would be the case, for example, with overall nationalization and the introduction of a comprehensive, rigid system of central planning. The interpretation of rights and institutions describing and defining the 'economic system' must be understood to refer to the 'market economy' within these constraints. These rights and institutions are: the right to property, the equality of private and public property; the right to enterprise, the freedom of competition; state property; the proprietary independence of state enterprises, co-operatives and local governments; the right to work and choice of occupation; the right to organize interest groups; the right to freedom of movement and settlement; and finally the prohibition of discrimination and the general right to personality deduced from the right to human dignity (Arts 9–14, 70/B, 70/C, 58, 70/A and 54).[27]

The market economy principle is an overarching concept intertwined with a number of specific 'subjective' rights that can themselves be litigated, even if there is no positive constitutional idea of the right to a market economy. The Court recognises critical features of a market economy when they see abuses recognisable from the past. The Constitutional Court may not have felt very certain about when a regulation infringed the principles of a market economy, but they certainly knew what central planning was and what rights had been unjustly limited by its reach. Here again, defining a positive constitutional term with a negative definition (the current regime is the opposite of the previous one) turns out to be an exercise with clearer boundaries than defining the positive term in the abstract.

The Constitutional Court has had the occasion to rule on many subjects. An ordinance of the city of Budapest allowed the police to 'boot' cars that had not paid their parking fines. This was at first assimilated by the Court

---

[27] Decision 21/1994 (16 April 1994) on the Freedom of Enterprise; on the Licensing of Taxis.

to other cases involving the seizure of private property by the state because the citizen had violated a minor law. Finding a resonance between this and the practices of the prior regime, the Constitutional Court declared the ordinance unconstitutional. Later, the Court relented when the city of Budapest successfully argued that this was part of maintaining a minimum amount of public order and respect for law by temporarily immobilising someone's car when there was no response to earlier tickets; the city convinced the Court that the constitutional problems were not fatal. Once the overtones of the prior regime were taken away, the Court found the relevant law to be perfectly constitutional.

The Constitutional Court has struggled with many cases about the levels of pensions under the social rights and rule-of-law clauses. On this topic, the Court ruled that government did not have to index pensions to the inflation rate, but the government also could not effectively gut the benefits altogether because people had a property right in what they paid into the pension system as workers. The Court specifically mentioned that in the Soviet era no one could create a private pension, and so because the state had occupied that space, it could not throw people out without protection now. The Court declared that sudden cuts in the social safety net were unconstitutional on grounds of legal security, since the rule of law does not allow people's legitimate expectations to be disrupted like this without warning. The state had to keep its promises (in contrast to, one could almost hear the Court saying, the regime that went before).

In much (though certainly not all) of what the Hungarian Constitutional Court did in its first activist term, the Court did seem often animated by the sense that it had to prevent the current regime from backsliding into the old one. Any sign that the newly elected governments behaved no better than the prior socialist ones was cause for the Constitutional Court to intervene and declare the law unconstitutional under which the new regime tried to do these things.

IV. GUARDIANS OF THE TRANSITION

By policing the border the border between the past and the present regimes, constitutional courts turn themselves into guardians of the 'transition'. Many other post-horror regimes seem to have settled on the same institutional solution for ensuring that new regimes make a sharp break with their immediate predecessors and don't sneak back at the first opportunity into the same abuses. This mechanism creates a powerful constitutional court with substantial independence, empowered to tell a new government whether it is staying within the boundaries of the new constitutional order. Experiences with fascism and Soviet-style regimes have shown powerfully how governments cannot be trusted to decide for themselves when they have used power constitutionally and when they have treated their citizens appropriately. By having an institution relatively independent of populist influence and staffed by experts whose primary concern is respect for human rights, constitutional courts place themselves outside the control of ordinary politics.

Since constitutional courts are set up at the same moment when the collective memory of a regime of horror is being created, it is not surprising that new constitutional courts take their interpretive inspiration from what we might call a 'negative theory' of constitutional interpretation. A negative theory of constitutional interpretation starts from a clearer sense of the evils to be avoided than from a coherent theory of the ideals to which a community may aspire. A negative theory registers constitutional violations when new practices are reminiscent of the old, discredited ones; a positive theory would compare challenged practices with an aspirational set of values to see whether the practice lives up to the ideal. Despite much effort from legal philosophers to find the positive theory that would produce a consensus, it is clear that reasonable people do not agree on aspirational theories of constitutional purpose, even perhaps behind a veil of ignorance. But it may be more possible to get a working consensus around negative theories that stake out areas of constitutional avoidance instead. Such a negative theory starts from the premise that, whatever else the new constitution may mean, it must mean at a minimum that the abuses of the past regime are not allowed to continue. The precise abuses of the prior regime of horror fill in the content of abstract terms in the text. Under this negative theory, whenever a constitutional court encounters something that reminds its members of the specific horrors of the past, the court reaches conclusions in these specific cases on the basis of these negative models rather than on the basis of a positive theory of the meaning of the clause. A constitutional court after a regime of horror then finds a clear constitutional meaning by 'going negative'.

In countries that directly experienced regimes of horror, there is a particularly vivid recent concrete history of abuses that were done in the name of these now-discredited ideologies—ideologies that constitutional democracy is supposed to replace. The list of specific unacceptable practices etched in the collective memory is long: passing *numerus clausus* laws; taking direct control of universities; conditioning political rights on voting for the 'correct' party; using criminal sanctions to punish political speech; monopolising the media; shutting down the opposition; jailing its critics; impoverishing dissenters; forcibly relocating ethnic minorities; seizing private property in large quantities; permitting collective punishments; banning religions—to say nothing of murdering its own citizens. Any government that would do these things would not live up to the promise of a constitutional democracy. And some combinations of these things are within the living memories of people who have written the most recent wave of constitutions. Those constitutions then embed the commitment to ensure that these things never happen again.

Writing long constitutions and entrusting constitutional guardianship to constitutional courts were the first steps in acknowledging these specific histories and highlighting what was being rejected in them. Constitutional courts have used specific ideas from the creation of specific 'regimes of horror' to underwrite concrete interpretations of these generally worded texts, allowing broad and general constitutional conceptions to have new and precise meanings. The use of a thick, substantive sense of constitutional democracy has allowed constitutional courts to fill in the gaps where constitutional texts are silent, or simply invent powers located in the general constitutional clauses to provide themselves with the textual resources to stamp out practices of horror whenever they show signs of returning. In cases where a court becomes active in preventing the reappearance of the regime of horror, it is the precise history of abuse and the general mandate to not repeat that history that gives rise to the confidence with which constitutional courts know that they are doing the right thing.

It may appear that these new, aggressive constitutional courts are anti-democratic. But established, 'self-confident' democracies have the luxury of being mostly a set of ideas about elections instead of a substantive theory about the preconditions for ensuring a democratic state, something that in the early rocky days of democratic development may seem precarious. The abuses that were visited on the populations living under the twentieth century's abusive states are now clearly recognised as precisely the conduct that a constitutional democracy should never repeat. And the new aggressive judiciaries in these states have risen eagerly to take on the task of being the early warning system whenever a newly democratic state appears tempted by a return to the practices of a regime of horror.

REFERENCES

de Andrade, Gustavo. 2001. Judicial Review in Comparative Constitutional Law. *University of Pennsylvania Journal of Constitutional Law* 3(3): 977–90.
Barak, Aharon. 1987. *Judicial Discretion*. New Haven: Yale University Press.
Bell, John. 1997. *French Constitutional Law*. Oxford: Clarendon.
Blankenburg, Erhard. 1999. *Institutionalizing the German Constitutional Complaint: The Use of an Open Access Procedure by Citizens and by the Court Itself*. Working Paper.
Currie, David. 1994. *The Constitution of the Federal Republic of Germany*. Chicago: University of Chicago Press.
Galanter, Marc. 1984. *Competing Equalities: Law and the Backward Classes in India*. Berkeley: University of California Press.
Garlicki, Lech. 1995. *Necessity and Functions of the Constitution*. Paper given at the Symposium 'European Constitutional Area', Swiss Institute for the Study of Comparative Law, Lausanne, Switzerland, 9–12 April 1995.

Halmai, Gábor and Scheppele, Kim Lane. 1996. Living Well is the Best Revenge: The Hungarian Approach to Judging the Past. In *Transitional Justice in New Democracies*, edited by A James McAdams. Notre Dame: Notre Dame University Press.

Hogg, Peter W. 1997. *Constitutional Law of Canada*, 4th edn. Scarborough, Ontario: Carswell Publishing.

Kennedy, Ellen. 1997. *The Bundesbank*, 2nd edn. Washington, DC: American Institute for Contemporary German Studies.

———. 2001. *Constitutional Failure: Schmitt in Weimar*. Durham: Duke University Press.

Kommers, Donald. 1998. *The Constitutional Jurisprudence of the Federal Constitutional Court*, 2nd edn. Durham: Duke University Press.

Kristeva, Julia. 1982. *Powers of Horror: An Essay on Abjection*. New York: Columbia University Press.

LaCapra, Dominick. 1992. Representing the Holocaust: Reflections on the Historian's Debate. In *Probing the Limits of Representation: Nazism and the 'Final Solution'*, edited by Saul Friedlander. Cambridge, MA: Harvard University Press.

Lindseth, Peter. 1996/97. Law, History and Memory: 'Republican Moments' and the Legitimacy of Constitutional Review in France. *Columbia Journal of European Law* 3: 49–83.

Maier, Charles. 1993. Surfeit of Memory? Reflections on History, Melancholy and Denial. *History and Memory* 5(2): 136–52.

Mandel, Michael. 1995. Legal Politics, Italian Style. In *The Global Expansion of Judicial Power*, edited by C Neal Tate and Torbjörn Vallinder. New York: New York University Press.

Merkl, Peter. 1963. *The Origins of the West German Republic*. Oxford: Oxford University Press.

Quint, Peter. 1997. *The Imperfect Union: Constitutional Structures of German Unification*. Princeton: Princeton University Press.

Scheppele, Kim Lane. 1998. *The Accidental Constitution*. Paper given at the University of Pennsylvania Journal of Constitutional Law Symposium on Constitutional Borrowings, March 1998.

Sherman, Cindy. 1995. Horror Pictures. In *Exhibit Catalogue from the Museum van Boijmans*. Van Beuningen, Rotterdam.

Sólyom, László and Brunner, Georg. 2000. *A Constitutional Judiciary in a New Democracy*. Ann Arbor: University of Michigan Press.

Somek, Alexander. 1998. The Deadweight of Formulae: What Might Have Been the Second Germanization of American Equal Protection Review. *University of Pennsylvania Journal of Constitutional Law* 1: 284–324.

Tate, C Neal. 1995. The Philippines and Southeast Asia. In *The Global Expansion of Judicial Power*, edited by C Neal Tate and Torbjörn Vallinder. New York: New York University Press.

Volcansek, Mary. 2000. *Constitutional Politics in Italy: The Constitutional Court*. New York: St Martin's Press.

Weiler, Joseph. 1999. *The Constitution of Europe*. Cambridge, MA: Cambridge University Press.

11

Paying for Past Injustices and Creating New Ones: On Property Rights Restitution in Poland as an Element of the Unfinished Transformation

GRAŻYNA SKĄPSKA[1]

I. INTRODUCTION

IN AUGUST 1999, the Polish public was stirred by information that eleven former Polish citizens or their descendants, now citizens of the United States (ten) and Great Britain (one), had sued the Polish state in a New York District Court in order to recover lost property and profits.[2] Public opinion was even more agitated after the translation and publication of this claim appeared in the most popular Polish daily newspaper, *Gazeta Wyborcza*, under the telling headline 'Eleven Jews Accuse the Polish State'.

---

[1] This chapter is based on the results of comparative research on restitution in Poland and Germany, sponsored by Volkswagen Stiftung. The research was conducted by Mark Blacksell and Karl-Martin Born of the University of Plymouth; Hartmut Haeussermann, Birgit Glock and Karsten Keller at Alexander von Humboldt University, Berlin; and Grażyna Skąpska, Grzegorz Bryda and Jarosław Kadyło at the Jagiellonian University in Kraków.

[2] See the class action translated and published in Poland in *Gazeta Wyborcza*, 16 August 1999. *Garb v Republic of Poland* was filed as a class action suit at the United States District Court for the Eastern District of New York which dismissed it in 2002 on the ground that Poland was immune under the Foreign Sovereignty Immunity Act. In 2003 the U.S. Court of Appeals for the Second Circuit reversed and remanded the case to the District Court. In 2004, the U.S. Supreme Court vacated judgment and remanded the case to the Second Circuit Court. In 2006 the Second Circuit Court upheld the decision of the District Court and dismissed the case for lack of subject matter jurisdiction. The Court conceded that holding foreign sovereign States liable in U.S. courts and imposing new duties to transactions already completed (under the Indemnification Act by countries at no fault under Hitler's horrendous tyranny), could not be applied retroactively (see for the first decision by the District Court http://www.nyed. uscourts.gov/Decisions_of_Interest/DOI_Archive/doi_archive.html; for the final decision see http://opiniojuris.org/2006/04/04/case-of-the-month-garb-v-poland/)

This article was followed by a highly emotional debate involving prominent and progressive Polish intellectuals—among them the editor in chief of *Gazeta Wyborcza*, Adam Michnik.

Arguments in the debate were directed predominantly against those parts of the claim in which the Polish authorities were accused of continuing, after 1945, the genocide initiated by Nazi Germany (*Gazeta Wyborcza*, 3, 4, 7, 10 August 1999). Polish public opinion was totally unprepared for such a debate, since any form of persecution directed against Jews by Poles had been a taboo subject after 1945, and these issues were only slowly beginning to be publicly discussed after 1989. Apart from that, the public debate also stressed the improper comparison of Nazi Germany and Poland.

Emotional questions were asked regarding whether Poles, who had just recently regained their political and legal sovereignty, should bother at all with the suit in New York, or with any other type of foreign regulation or adjudication. Interestingly enough, nobody seemed fully aware of the bilateral agreements on compensation for the property left in Poland concluded between Poland and 15 other states.[3] As a result of these agreements, which were not published in Poland until 1999, the Polish government paid some amounts of money to foreign governments. The funds were then at the disposal of foreign governments to compensate claims for property left in Poland. The interesting question regarding the lack of public information in Poland about those agreements is still to be answered.

Other arguments raised in Poland in the context of the claims in New York concerned the principle of equal treatment. It was asked why one group should be privileged. Many other Polish citizens who live in Poland or abroad and who were deprived of their property as a result of its nationalisation or confiscation are waiting in vain for a general policy, including legal and international regulation of property restitution or compensation for their loss. Why, for instance, should some individuals be given their property back, if others—with no hope of compensation—had also been deprived of possessions and had their professional careers and personal

---

[3] Between 1949 and 1970 Poland concluded these agreements with the United Kingdom, the USA, Belgium, Luxemburg, Denmark, France, Greece, the Netherlands, Norway, Switzerland, Sweden, Canada, Austria, Romania and Czechoslovakia. As a result of those treaties, the Polish government paid some amount of money to foreign governments to satisfy the claims. The distribution was made possible by the establishment of special funds for compensation, which were managed by the foreign governments in question. For instance, in the case of the agreement with the United States, which was signed in 1957, the compensation fund amounted to 40 million dollars. Apart from that, in 1944 and 1957 Poland concluded agreements with the Soviet Union on the repatriation of Poles who lived in the then Soviet Union. These agreements also regulated compensation for property left in the Soviet Union.

lives destroyed, but would now actually bear the costs of restitution entailed in returning nationalised property to former owners?[4]

On the other hand, the constitutional and political arguments of the public debate concerned the continuity of the state and of the constitutional order. Thus, the question was raised as to whether a new democratic state can be held responsible for wrongs committed by the previous, totalitarian regime or by foreign powers. This is relevant, for example, because some Polish citizens lost property as a result of their expulsion from former Polish territories that after the Second World War became incorporated by the Soviet Union. Serious doubts have been raised as to whether the Third Republic of Poland should compensate groups displaced and deprived of their property by the German wartime or Soviet post-war totalitarian regimes. Finally, there has been dispute about the legitimacy of restitution itself. Still other arguments have focused on the relevance and validity of foreign regulation and adjudication with respect to national Polish law.

In this chapter I will discuss restitution as a culturally and historically grounded solution to claims that themselves represent efforts to dismantle a totalitarian regime, are accompanied by various moral and ideological arguments and are rooted in real, vested interests. As I demonstrate, the restitution of property rights produces winners and losers, who are able to secure their property rights within a framework created by legal, moral, ideological, culturally and historically rooted arguments. As such, the restitution of property as well as the ensuing debates it represent a part of the ongoing post-communist transformation in Poland as in other post-communist European countries.

II. ARGUMENTS, IDEAS AND INTERESTS

As is evident, both the suit in New York and the debate in Poland reveal a multiplicity of moral, legal and political, not to mention economic issues, in particular with regard to the problem of 'righting the wrongs of the past', as Istvan Pogany has phrased it (1997, 108). These issues appeal to nationalistic tendencies and stir up resentments and stereotypes. Moreover, the public debate on restitution in Poland reveals not only different approaches to past human rights abuses but also a lack of definitive 'truths' about them because this past can be the subject of manipulation, distortion and interpretation from various perspectives.

One can firmly state that this debate itself has been influenced to a great extent by historical ideas regarding property and ownership rights, which

---

[4] According to the results of the comparative research on restitution conducted in Poland and Germany, the question of whether society should pay the costs of restitution is put forth by politicians and stressed by citizens.

are deeply embedded in the popular consciousness and rooted in historical experience. Conceptualisations of property ownership are formed in the course of a nation's collective experiences. As I will demonstrate in the following section, culturally and historically rooted conceptualisations of property and property rights hold a particular place in the Polish conscious-ness, and they also reveal particular features of popular legal cultures in the domain of private law. As prominent Polish lawyer Walerian Pańko has put it, the concept of property develops together with the progress of society and is linked closely with religious cult and customary law (1984, 14). These features are also important for the restitution of property. Moreover, the issue of restitution is also problematised and subjectivised in the form of social ideas about law and justice, especially historical justice and human rights, procedural justice and the concept of the *Rechtsstaat* (rule-of-law state).

It is then interesting to explore the historical roots of debates on restitu-tion and the links between this topic and historically embedded ideas on property, justice and rights. Like similar issues connected to the problems of dealing with the past after the collapse of a totalitarian or authoritar-ian regime, this particular issue involves attitudes toward past atrocities and past crimes in which great numbers of people participated either as victims or as perpetrators—or as silent but nevertheless not unaware observers. These attitudes towards the more distant past of World War II and its aftermath clash with similar, but more recent personal experiences, strongly and deeply rooted in the recent past of the communist regimes still haunting the people who live in Central and Eastern Europe. Both these past experiences are linked in the experience of expropriation and confiscation of property undertaken on a heretofore unknown scale by two consecutive totalitarian regimes: the Nazi and the Soviet/communist regimes. Expropriation of property therefore epitomise the wrongs of the past, however, as different pasts are intricately linked, in anything but an unambiguous way.

Restitution illustrates only one aspect of the post-communist trans-formation, which itself constitutes yet another dramatic event expe-rienced by the Polish population, profoundly changing their lives. As a result of restitution, some might suddenly become quite wealthy or at least regain property that had belonged to the family a generation or more ago. Others, in contrast, could suddenly lose the apartments that they have inhabited for a low rent and called home for some two generations. It might contribute to the spreading disappointment with transformation, if the great expectations in the restoration of human rights are not fulfilled. Therefore, the issue of restitution will be ana-lysed against its socio-historical backdrop: the historical experiences that make up the framework for the conceptualisation of property and property rights, personal involvement either as victim or as perpetrator in the process of nationalisation, and the most recent experiences with the transformation of the social, economic and political orders.[5]

Considering all these issues, one should not forget that hundreds of thousands of citizens, civic associations, universities, religious organisations and churches, and local governments in Central and Eastern Europe have a right to claim property that was taken from them under circumstances that constituted the greatest infringement of the then-existing legal and constitutional order. Quite often, communist nationalisation measures only legalised and post-facto fixed the status quo of expropriations made by the earlier German occupying forces or by governments subordinated to them during World War II (Pogany 1997; Skapska 1999). Therefore, restitution and reprivatisation—or at least compensation—might help to restore trust in justice. Such action would also contribute to the legitimacy of transformation processes and is therefore important to rebuilding trust in law and the state, and to forming new political, constitutional and legal cultures after the collapse of communism.

The transformation of political and economic systems creates not only great hopes for more justice and fairness but also a great uncertainty among those affected by this process. Restitution is among those transformation issues that awaken hopes and fears simultaneously, as well as pose some seemingly unsolvable problems. It presents a way of dealing with past legacies but also a means of structuring the chaotic, often irrational, coincidental and, above all, extremely complex and unpredictable phenomenon of transforming legal, economic, political and cultural orders of whole societies. This process further coincides with a change of collective social consciousness. The institutional framework of restitution thus constitutes an important example of restructuring order out of transformational chaos.

Therefore it is not astonishing that in Poland, as elsewhere in Central Europe, restitution has become a publicly discussed legal policy issue in the aftermath of 1989. However, restitution of property rights in Poland evokes a number of very serious problems. Not the least among these is the fact that Poland lost nearly half of its former territory as a result of World War II. However, the Soviet Union, which played a key role in the shift of Polish territory to the West, has ceased to exist. Moreover, after half a century of centrally planned economy and imposed Soviet legal culture, it is difficult to re-establish property rights, not to mention the burden on the state treasury to deal with cases of compensation for lost property. Thus, restitution remains one of the biggest and unresolved issues of the post-communist transformation in Poland.

---

[5] The concept of "frames" is borrowed from interactionist and interpretive sociology, especially from Goffman, according to whom "frames" are concepts that organise experience (Goffman 1997, 155).

On the individual level, vested economic interests are decisive in shaping legislation, but also in individual claims. What makes restitution different from other highly dramatic issues related to dealing with the totalitarian past—eg, de-communisation or lustration—is the fact that real economic gains and losses are at stake here, real profits from increasingly lucrative real estate in a post-communist market. It is then interesting to see how debates about the fairness of restitution and just compensation or the general criteria of inclusion or exclusion from this game reveal the moral claims, ideological positions and extent of vested interests of the participants. To what extent does the debate on the fairness of restitution, as well as on the economic consequences for the nation as a whole, simply serve as instrumental rhetoric and a set of discursive techniques that overlap with the reality of a struggle for profits from the property—or even are used to disguise blatant corruption? All these issues—popular conceptualisations, convictions deeply rooted in the individual and collective experiences, vested interests and the rhetoric used to disguise them—contribute to the complexity of the restitution issue after the collapse of totalitarian regimes.

III. UNRESOLVED RESTITUTION CLAIMS IN POLAND

The case described in *Gazeta Wyborcza* was not the only claim against the Polish state by former owners deprived of their property under former regimes. The ethnic minorities of Lemkos and Ukrainians whose property was nationalised and who were displaced by the Polish authorities after World War II as traitors to the Polish state deserve mention here.[6] The Lemkos were planning for a while to join the suit in New York. Another complaint was filed by at least one of the associations of Polish property owners unlawfully deprived of their property after World War II, whose case has been directed to the European Court of Human Rights in Strasbourg.

There is also another category of people who consider themselves entitled to restitution or compensation for lost property. They are, above all, soldiers of the Polish Underground Army and the Polish Army who fought together with the Allied Forces and were afraid to return to Poland after World War II for fear of persecution. In fact, there was a real danger of being arrested and sentenced to death. The soldiers were accused by the communist authorities of being traitors to the Polish state or of being Western spies. Their property was nationalised because according to the then existing law

---

[6] Accused traitors to the Polish state include those who had collaborated with the German occupying forces during World War II and those who had allegedly supported the partisans of the Ukrainian Underground Army fighting in southeastern Poland after 1944.

it had been abandoned: the owners had neither claimed it nor indicated in any other way their will to repossess it within due time.[7]

The dispossessed also included Silesians, Mazurians, Ermlanders (from Warmia) and Kaszubians who migrated to Germany before 1989. According to the then binding law, these persons had to sell their property to the State, which had the preemptory right to dictate prices and purchase it, or to other persons, if the State did not make use of its right. The real estate disbursed in this way was sold very cheaply under the pressure of such circumstances.[8]

Another category of claims are those by persons who lost their property because of the change to Poland's eastern borders after World War II as a result of the Yalta Agreements. These persons had the right to compensation if they fully documented that they had left property on territory belonging to the Soviet Union after 1944. Many of these individuals, however, could not provide such documentation, either because they had fled under dramatic circumstances or because they were fighting in the West or were members of the Polish Underground Army and therefore defined as enemies (not only of Germany, but also of the Soviet Union and the new, Soviet-installed government of Poland). Finally, there are claims of those individual and institutional owners of real estate who were deprived of their property rights because of governmental decisions on expropriation for a particular public goal, if the expropriated property was used otherwise.

All these different claims and the debates that accompanied them confirm the above observations that restitution of property remains a highly emotional and hotly debated issue in Poland. It is intricately linked to the

---

[7] With the Decree of 3 January 1948 regarding abandoned and formerly German property, the State Treasury took over the property after 10 years in the case of land, as a result of the simple passage of time, on the basis of reticence. According to resolutions by the Polish Supreme Court, any activity undertaken during this time by the owner or his relatives, indicating a will to regain property, was recognised as interruption of the running of the 10-year period (Resolution of the Supreme Court of 24 May 1956, Sign I CO 16/60; and Resolution of Supreme Court of 26 October 1956, Sign I CO 9/56). The Decree itself, as well as subsequent Supreme Court Resolutions, did not at all consider the situation of those owners who did not come back to Poland after World War II because of the ascendency of communists had made it highly probable that property owners, who were defined in the new Constitution of 1952 as 'exploiters of peasants and workers and therefore condemned to die out as a social class', would be persecuted (Art 3(4) of the Constitution of 1952). 12 March 1958 was the expiry date for all claims to restitution of property, equivalency or compensation for lost property or property nationalised before this date. This law, which regulated the sale of land from State Funds and the settling of other matters, was related to land reform and rural colonisation (Legal Gazette of 1989, N 58, s 348). In particular, it closed the door on any chance of compensation for expropriated property in the form of an independent, private farm or a monthly allowance. The law also applied to those Polish citizens who had left Poland in the wake of the Second World War, the Holocaust and the Yalta treaties and did not return to Poland after 1944, ie, after the Red Army had installed the communist system.

[8] The Decree of 16 December 1918 regulated the compulsory management of banks, credit and insurance institutions, institutions of social welfare and charity foundations.

recent history of Poland, and to the life-histories and personal experiences of Polish citizens. Consequently, any analysis of restitution should consider the experiences of both sides: of persons whose property was nationalised, confiscated or otherwise unfairly taken from them, and of those who profited, including individuals who bought the property very cheaply, obtained it from the state or have been paying merely 'symbolic' rent for apartments in nationalised buildings. Many of the personal experiences have been of a traumatic character, like confiscations or displacement. In fact, this comprises all possible forms of harassment to which owners were exposed after 1939 as a result of the German occupation, and after 1944 as a result of the installment of the communist regime (Skapska 1999). However, an analysis of restitution cannot bypass the fact that, notwithstanding the above mentioned unresolved claims, restitution has been ongoing in Poland since at least 1980, when judicial control over administrative acts and governmental decisions was established (although in fact it has occurred to some extent even since the mid-1950s).

IV. HISTORICAL ROOTS OF RESTITUTION: SYMBOLIC, COMMUNITARIAN AND COLLECTIVISTIC DIMENSIONS OF PROPERTY RIGHTS

'Time', writes Hans-Georg Gadamer, 'is no longer an abyss we shall cross because it divides and sets things at a distance; it is now the vehicle of a process in which what is contemporary is embedded' (1975/1993, 282). To return to Pańko's earlier statement, the concept of property, especially property of land, is a multidimensional phenomenon (1984, 16). Above all, it has a long tradition in social history and culture. As a foundation of civil law, it defines authority over things. But, Pańko asserts:

> [In Poland] property law has a special value which is exemplified by individual ownership of land, determined by the historical circumstances. Polish agriculture did not undergo the process of capitalization that turned land into a commodity and a farmer into an entrepreneur. In the Polish countryside, property symbolized not only wealth but also a right to life, and in the partitions period, also a guarantee of resistance despite foreign oppression (1984, 25).

It is obvious that such an understanding of property is very far from economic concepts of property. In contrast, these, as Alan Ryan has rightly observed, are intricately linked to the idea of real estate as a mere commodity as implied by utilitarian theory (1987, 116). In contrast to legal pragmatic and utilitarian concepts of property as a commodity, the above quotation reflects the historical experience of the Polish nation (especially the experiences of the nineteenth century), institutionalised afterwards in the Polish Constitution in the 1920s and repeated in the proposals presented by the Polish government in exile after 1945. In the Polish tradition, private property, especially private property of land, and its ownership have been perceived and evaluated as a stronghold of existence, independence and economic and even cultural resistance in a nation deprived of political sovereignty.

One of the most important Polish novels, written in the nineteenth century and entitled *Placówka* (*The Outpost*, Prus 1996), tells the story of a Polish peasant who uses all means possible to defend his property against German attempts to expropriate him. The events described in this novel were based on actual events that happened in the course of German policy to colonise western Polish territories. The book is but one example among a whole range of similar novels written by nineteenth-century Polish authors. Their plots were based on the colonisation and expropriation undertaken mostly by the German or Russian authorities in those parts of Poland that, as a result of the partition, were under their reign and rule. These expropriations were only one method applied in a much more extensive and intensive policy of colonisation by both powers.

Such books, since they continue to be mandated reading in school curricula, simultaneously reflect the present Polish national consciousness and influence its future formation, including Polish legal culture. They conceptualise property in terms of individual and, simultaneously, collective rights. They link land ownership with the symbols of an independent nation and with the collective, even communitarian characteristics of the owners. They helped to build a sense of belonging to the only culturally, not yet politically defined Polish nation. The symbolic dimension of property was reflected in the very title, *The Outpost*—an outpost of partitioned Poland, of Polishness and of the physical existence of the Polish nation, deprived of political sovereignty but defended here by a Polish peasant.

The communitarian dimension of property rights as well as deeply rooted historical fears of foreigners buying up Polish land, combined with ideologies of land property as a stronghold of national sovereignty were strongly present in Polish constitutionalism after Poland regained her political independence in 1918. Article 99 of the Polish Constitution of 1921 (the so-called April Constitution) provided for the protection of personal property but also for its collective forms (collective property, property of cooperatives and state property) as foundations of the social and legal order. The Article also provided for the possibility of expropriation but only if it was fairly compensated and resulted from a public need. However, in its next section, the Article also stated that land, as one of the most important foundations of state and national existence, cannot be subject to unlimited and free market circulation. Hence Article 99 strongly limited property rights of the owner, rights to property usage and ultimately rights to decide about it, all in the name of the interest of the Polish nation.

Another important concept is related to the role of the state as protector and manager of property. This was institutionalised in regulations that concerned property the owners of which had disappeared or did not properly care for the property. Such property was subject to compulsory state management, according to early legislation, the legal decree of 16 December 1918 on the Mandatory Administration of the State. The purpose of this decree was to provide temporary administration of property in the owner's absence.

The concept of compulsory state management—by now redefined and interpreted as direct and final nationalisation—was realised by the post-World War II communist government under dramatically different political as well as socio-psychological circumstances. It was recast within the official ideology of class interest, collectivism and the dictatorship of the proletariat. It took the form of several decrees by the new government. In its first phase just after World War II, legislation reflected a peculiar mixture of traditional, 'bourgeois' concepts and institutions, along with a new selective approach permitting preservation of only those legal concepts and institutions that were not considered contrary to the principles of the new regime (Izdebski 1999, 59).

The first of these new laws, the Manifesto of the Polish Committee of National Liberation of 22 July 1944, proclaimed the restoration of the democratic principles of the 1921 Constitution. It announced some indispensable social reforms but put 'agrarian reform' and the confiscation of the property of 'traitors of the Homeland' in first place. Subsequent legislation reflected more ambiguous attitudes to private ownership and a mixture of two contradictory elements. These were the continuation of the pre-war efforts to unify and institutionalise property rights on one hand and the 'Sovietisation' of Polish law (ie, the institutionalisation of a Soviet-style dictatorship of the proletariat in the legal order and the new Constitution) on the other hand. Before the new Constitution was proclaimed, the Decree of 11 October 1946 on Property Law confirmed the universal idea of ownership as the 'greatest' and 'true' right, entailing quasi-absolute legal content. In contrast to this idea, other legislation laid the foundation for socialist ideas of ownership, providing for the divestment of the most important types of private property, generally without compensation.[9] After this initial period, during overt Stalinism, legislation was directly aimed at the infringement of property rights and nationalisation of property. During this period, individual property rights were outrightly defined as capitalist institutions and condemned to extinction.

---

[9] The most important decrees are the following: the Decree of 6 September 1944, which executed the 'agrarian reform' (ie, the nationalisation of farms above fifty or hundred hectares which had to be divided among peasants) and established state collective farms; the Decree of 26 October 1945, which provided for the communalisation of all land of the city of Warsaw; the Law of 3 January 1946 on the Nationalization of the Basic Sectors of National Economy; and the Decree of 8 March 1946 on abandoned and formerly German property. The last two were laws of direct nationalisation.

If one considers the constitutional regulations of property rights present in the Polish Constitution of 1921 together with the regulation on compulsory state management in the law of 1918, it is not clear whether the right to property was treated as an unalienable subjective, civil or human right, of which legal subjects could be deprived only under the most exceptional circumstances, or as an entitlement granted by the state. Clearly, at least some property rights (eg, the right to free disposal of land) were defined as an entitlement granted by the state. This is a necessary consequence of the traditional concept of property as a stronghold of the culturally defined nation and as a stronghold of the sovereign nation state after the nation had regained its political sovereignty. It is, however, clear that in the communist constitutional and legal order, property rights were not at all treated as civil or human rights. Indeed, property itself was not defined as a commodity under state management, as there was no market, or only a very restricted one. It was neither protected by comprehensive legal instruments nor conceptualised as entailing distinct rights and entitlements. This resulted in a general attitude towards property, as being of no great value—on either a national-symbolic or a utilitarian level. In particular, state-owned property was treated as nobody's property.

Other important aspects of the partition of Poland, as well as of the regime change after 1944, arise from its legal culture. The authorities in the Polish territory held by the Russian empire ceased to maintain comprehensive land registers. In the former Kingdom of Poland (under Russian Tsars) and in the territories directly incorporated into Russia there existed neither an official registration of land titles by the state, nor a general system of deeds of trust and mortgage registration. Moreover, the former Kingdom of Poland and its capital city Warsaw was strongly influenced by French Law, the Code Napoleon and French legal culture. Accordingly, registers of land ownership had only a declaratory character and not the constitutive value, as for instance characteristic of the German legal culture (Skąpska 2000). Therefore, even in those territories that preserved French private law, land registers were not deemed very important. This institutional legacy seems to be still influential.

The legacy of the 'People's Poland', which was subordinated to the Soviet model after 1944, and especially the legacy of the 1950s amounted to the general 'theoretical' position that such registers constituted a visible remainder of the old regime, and until the 1980s, there were only few attempts to develop a comprehensive system of official title registration.[10] Therefore

---

[10] For example, the Decree of 3 January 1949 on the Establishment of New Commercial Companies and Promoting Private Business in Industry and Trade. This was an abuse and/or infringement upon existing legislation, the Decree of 16 December 1918 on the Mandatory Administration of the State. The 1949 Decree was used to nationalise businesses still in their owners' hands. Other important regulations were established by the Decree of 27 March 1949

in contemporary Poland, only a quarter of Polish territory is covered by relatively systematic land and mortgage accounts, which function as the official registration of titles; even if there is a corresponding register, entries are often outdated. As a result, 'it will take a long time to change this situation and it will not be easy' (Izdebski 1999, 72). Notably, the registers still have only a declaratory character, whereas the notarial act constitutes the title.

Finally, a third period can be identified as important in the formation of socio-historical frameworks for popular conceptualisation of property rights in Poland. This is the period directly preceding and immediately following the system change in 1989, its most specific feature being the privatisation of state-owned assets. The debate on restitution cannot be analysed separately from the informal 'appropriation' of state-owned companies, apartments and plots of land, which in sum was called 'reprivatisation' or 'embourgoisement'. This type of reprivatisation actually comprised the sale of state or communal assets and, as such, of small companies, to their employees (mostly managers) or to functionaries of the Communist Party, and the sale of apartments in state-owned or communal apartment buildings to tenants.

In this context of newly emerging concepts of property and property rights, actions taken by the employees of formerly state-owned companies or tenants in formerly state-owned apartment buildings are important, too. During the 1980s, it had become possible to make private investments in national assets in order to make work or living conditions better. This included improvements or even minor innovations and even inventions in workplaces, working privately with state-owned machines or using spare materials for private purposes. These types of 'private investment' strengthened specifically some of the moral claims of employees or tenants to eventual ownership of state-owned companies or apartments. Not only do such claims conjure up Lockean ideas of labour and property, they also resonate with teachings of the Roman Catholic Church, above all in the *Laborem Exercens* encyclical of Pope John Paul II.[11] Most important however, were the actual individual and sometimes collective investments in providing a strong moral foundation for the claims to property rights.

Such claims were initially expressed in the concept of self-governed enterprises.[12] Here, management rights were considered to belong to the

---

on the Expropriation and Confiscation of Property in the Provinces of Southeastern Poland; the Decree of 26 April on the Purchase and Delivery of Real Estate Necessary for the Realization of National Economic Plans; and the post-1952 practice of forced collectivisation of agriculture.

[11] The *Laborem Exercens* encyclical involved the primacy of labour over capital; it was emphasised once again in *Centessimus Annus*.

[12] The concept of a self-governed enterprise was most popular among members of the 'Solidarność' labour union. It referred to the idea of self-management of state-owned enterprises as a new, 'third-way' solution to the problems of the centralised and planned economy.

employees of a company. This in turn justified the employees' claims of ownership of a company as a whole or claims to a considerable part of the stock of a privatised company. Under current Polish legislation, up to 15 per cent of all stocks can be acquired free of charge. As has been noted, such claims could easily contribute to collective egoism (Pawlik 1988, 175 ff) and thus prevent the restitution of rights to the former owners, be they individuals or institutions.[13]

Thus, the current debate on restitution in Poland is taking place in the context of very specific procedures of reprivatisation. These include, first and foremost, the (in)famous *nomenclatura* reprivatisation of state assets— of companies, buildings, apartments and recreational space—by former officials of the communist party or high-ranking managers of state-owned companies. Second, reprivatisation has to be seen in the context of moral claims to state-owned property made by tenants and employees, which are justified through invested labour, the unacknowledged intellectual property of innovations and inventions, and financial investments.

This outline of the historical and institutional framework for the debate on restitution and property rights in Poland indicates that more than just the symbolic and moral aspects of property are important. Property rights, and especially those related to land ownership, entail some distinct communitarian dimensions. Historically, property rights were considered not only as belonging to individuals or individual legal subjects, but also as important for the physical existence of the nation as a whole. After 1944, the collectivistic dimension of property rights was unquestionable and principal. Individual property rights seemed condemned to die out, while collective ones were ambiguously defined as belonging to the state, to the nation or simply as 'social rights'. In fact, decisions regarding property, also defined rather indistinctly, were actually made by the Communist Party apparatus, and the rights formally belonged to government bodies or, to some extent, to the managers of the state-owned companies. Finally, during

---

[13] This is well illustrated by the case of the former Jagiellonian University Press printing house in Krakow, which had belonged to the University for some 200 years. According to a decision by the Ministry of Education, the printing house was given to the Ministry of Industry without any formal decision of nationalisation, and it was thereafter referred to as a State-owned printing house. During post-1989 privatisation, the printing house was nearly sold by the State to a private bidder for the considerable sum of at about one million USD. This privatisation would have been in the interest of the management and employees of the printing house, since 15 per cent of the stock would have been granted to them. When the University claimed the printing house back, the authorities responded that this was impossible as no formal nationalisation decision existed, and the government could not revoke a previous decision at this level. Finally, the case was settled in the district court of Krakow by an amicable agreement between the printing house and the Rector of the University. The printing house was returned to the University, despite opposition from employees. This case illustrates the goodwill of the management and the success of the astute lawyer of the university. However, the case could have ended quite differently had the claimant not been the most prestigious university in Poland and one of the oldest and most prestigious in all of Central Europe.

the communist regime, some concepts of individual or collective rights to property emerged. These were based on invested labour and ideas that company property belonged to its entire personnel, the community comprised of all company employees. Therefore, from a legal perspective of property rights as control of and authority over things, it is obvious why the yet unfinished debate on comprehensive restitution has to be analysed in the context of the still ongoing privatisation of state-owned assets. The debate refers to moral claims and justifications, and sometimes to the way rights are envisioned, whereas the ongoing process is a game in which the winners, at very low cost, gain authority over huge amounts of state-owned assets, thus securing future profits for themselves.

V. MORAL, LEGAL AND IDEOLOGICAL ARGUMENTS VERSUS WINNERS AND LOSERS[14]

Arguments related to the restitution of or compensation for nationalised or confiscated property reflect how past abuses of human rights and constitutional order is presently approached. They are also crucial to the question of continuity of state and law. Especially in Central Europe, it is often argued that to get rid of the totalitarian past and right its wrongs means to restore the *status quo ante*—the legal and political democratic order that existed before totalitarianism was installed.

Such an approach to the restoration of the past is not confirmed in Poland—otherwise proud of its old constitutionalism—by the comprehensive regulation of restitution, at least at a first glance. However, as has been shown, despite its many unresolved problems[15] restitution has been going on in Poland for many years. Therefore, the question arises as to why the general regulation of restitution is massively contested as very costly and unfair, when simultaneously the restitution of nationalised and confiscated property—a far more expensive process—is taking place on a rather large scale. To answer this question, the actual foundations of restitution and compensation, their procedures and the winners and losers of the ongoing restitution process must be analysed in light of the arguments both for and against comprehensive restitution.

The legal foundations for compensation for nationalised property were laid in Poland by the abovementioned bilateral treaties and agreements. It should be noted that the legal background for actual claims and petitions regarding restitution of private property was also established by the

---

[14] This section is based on the comparative research mentioned in note 1 above.

[15] During the final debate on a general restitution law in the Polish Parliament, some fifteen drafts of a restitution law were presented, each with very different content. Some of them provided for only symbolic compensation for nationalised property, whereas others provided for full compensation or restitution in kind.

treaties with the Soviet Union that regulated compensation in kind for the property left on formerly Polish territories incorporated by the Soviet Union after 1945. Presently, these territories belong to the countries that emerged after the dissolution of the Soviet Union, namely Ukraine, Belarus and Lithuania.[16]

The very first winners of the process of restitution in Poland were thus those individuals who had been displaced by the Soviet authorities after the war because of the shift of Poland's borders to the West and who were able to obtain documentation testifying to such fact. The first losers, about 70,000 to 100,000 persons, were those who had left those territories earlier (eg, been displaced by these very authorities from Polish territories under Soviet occupation between 1939 and 1944, usually under quite dramatic circumstances); had fled westward in order to fight in the Polish Underground Army; or were afraid of having any official contact with Soviet authorities.

Regardless of international public law, the most important foundation for restitution is the constitutional protection of private property and compensation for its nationalisation. The new Polish Constitution of 1997 fully protects private property as the primary form of property. With regard to constitutional law, however, one should emphasise that the most controversial legal point in the debate on restitution in Poland is the constitutionality of the first decrees on nationalisation. Because the new Constitution was proclaimed only in 1952, whereas nationalisation was initiated before that date, the proclaimed decrees of nationalisation should have met conditions imposed by the former, democratic Constitution of 1921, which had been declared binding in 1944 by the very authorities who were later responsible for its greatest abuse. The conditions of the 1921 Constitution should have meant that nationalisation could be conducted only for reasons of a greater public need; it should have had to be grounded in general law (statutes), and the former owners of the nationalised property should have been compensated according to Article 99 of the 1921 Constitution.

These constitutional requirements were severely violated in the nationalisation process conducted after 1944. However, the unconstitutionality of these first decrees on nationalisation of property—although not directly contested—is not unanimously considered a sufficient legal foundation for compensation or restitution claims by former owners. Instead, legal arguments are mostly juxtaposed with economic, political or social justice

---

[16] Poland concluded these agreements with the Soviet Union in 1944 and 1957. According to these agreements, Polish citizens who left the Soviet Union after 1944 or after 1957 were entitled to compensation for or an equivalent of property left in the Soviet Union on the basis of documents from the Soviet authorities certifying possession of such property and its value. Similar treaties were concluded with other neighbouring countries. In most cases, such equivalents were found in the so-called 'regained territories', ie, the territories that had belonged to Germany but were received by Poland as a result of the Potsdam Treaty.

arguments. In light of such arguments, the costs of property maintenance or improvements covered by the State or the new possessors or users during the past half century equal the value of the property. Such arguments are raised especially against claims for restitution brought forth by persons who left Poland because of the war. Other arguments raise the shift of the Polish borders and the ensuing disappearance of the political bodies as addressees of a large number of claims. Still another argument related to the constitutionality of nationalisation refers to the fact that many assets were sold to bona fide purchasers. Most often arguments expressly refer to the constraints of the national budget and the great burden imposed on the State by the costs of restitution. All of these arguments are juxtaposed to the protection of rights and constitutional order, old and new, and to the predominantly economic losses supposedly necessarily caused by restitution.

However, the most important and most often raised arguments concerning the constitutional basis for restitution deal with the question of citizenship and residency in Poland. The predominant obstacle to a final agreement on the content of a comprehensive regulation on restitution is the question of entitlement. According to the government's draft proposal of 1998, all those persons would be entitled to restitution who had Polish citizenship at the time they lost their property, beginning from 1939 (ie, during the German and Soviet invasions, which occurred on 1 September and 17 September 1939). This proposal was strongly contested. According to the opinions presented by the overwhelming majority of Polish Parliamentarians at that time (most of whom were post-communists and representatives of peasants' parties), the right or rather the entitlement to restitution and compensation should be granted only to those individuals who had Polish citizenship at the time they lost their property, who *currently* hold Polish citizenship *and* who have been residents of Poland for at least five years. These exclusionary criteria were strongly supported by the general public. According to public opinion polls conducted in Poland nearly every year since 1992, the overwhelming majority of Poles supported the statement that a right to property restitution should be granted only to persons who are Polish citizens and who are residents of Poland.

Contemporary political and legal debates indicated that the winners of restitution should be residents of Poland who have Polish citizenship; consequently the losers would be those who for whatever reasons were living abroad. Why was there such strong support for the exclusion and discrimination of persons who lived abroad? This group included even Poles who live abroad because of their involvement in the Polish Underground Army, because of their association with the Allied Forces in WW II, because of their membership in the Polish democratic opposition during the 1970s and 1980s, or because they were forced to leave Poland in 1968 by receiving one-way travel documents. Economic arguments seem to be invalid in these cases, since many of these people are coming to Poland with considerable financial and intellectual capital, urgently needed in a country undergoing economic transformation. The exclusionary arguments cannot be deemed to represent purely nationalistic motives, since Polish citizenship and residence in Poland does not exclude individuals who are not ethnic Poles. On the contrary, this provision excluded ethnic Poles who lived abroad. There can be only one conclusion: the proposed exclusion of Poles, ethnic or otherwise, who live abroad, is based on a popular and rather populist conceptualisation of restitution as an 'insider affair', regardless of possible gains and losses.

Moreover, notwithstanding the lack of a comprehensive regulation, restitution in Poland has been ongoing for quite some time, on the basis of public administrative law, interventions by a dedicated ombudsman, civil law and statutes representing the results of agreements between the State and churches. Further, despite the controversies related to the constitutionality of nationalisation conducted between 1944 and 1952, the presently ongoing restitution is based on the presumption of the legality of the legal order installed in Poland after 1944.

An important legal basis for restitution was provided by the decree of 1944 on land reform, in combination with private law and above all by contract law. In the debates on restitution in Poland it is often forgotten—indeed, almost never mentioned—that the first group that initiated restitution was comprised of Polish peasants who took back their farmland that had been granted to them after 1944 and then subjected to collectivisation in the late 1940s and early 1950s. The foundation for land reform and the later dissolution of collective farms was the Decree of the Polish Committee for National Salvation of 6 September 1944 on land reform, Article 2(1)E (*Legal Gazette* 1945, Nr 3, pos 13, with later amendments). This Committee constituted itself in the very first days after the Red Army's entry into Poland, and its members came to Poland together with the army, as agents of the future regime. However, the 1944 decree on land reform actually ended the long struggle and efforts of Polish peasants, which had begun immediately after the formation of an independent Poland in 1918. On the basis of this decree, peasants could obtain farmland very cheaply subsequent to the parcelling of large estates.[17] In order to procure the land, peasants had to pay a modest amount in form of a down-payment. These peasants later claimed that during collectivisation their land had been taken arbitrarily, that administrative procedures had been violated and could not be appealed against, that they had made down-payments for their farmland on the basis of the 1944 decree and, above all, that collectivisation

---

[17] The Decree of 1944 clearly stipulated that the farming system in Poland would be based on strong, healthy and effective private farms owned by those who worked on them.

was in contradiction to the 1944 decree and therefore simply illegal. As a consequence, in the course of the spontaneous de-collectivisation of the early 1990s, some 80 per cent of collectivised land was returned to its owners, including those peasants who had originally benefited from land reform after 1944.

The second major foundation for dealing with expropriation claims were statutes that regulated the relationship between the state and the churches. Restitution of property that had belonged to the Church was initiated by the Law of 17 May 1989 regarding relations between the State and the Roman Catholic Church in the Republic of Poland (*Legal Gazette*, Nr 29, pos 154) and the Law of 17 May 1989 on guarantees of freedom of conscience and confession (*Legal Gazette*, Nr 29, pos 155). These laws were proclaimed before the first semi-democratic elections in Poland were held in June 1989, and they were followed by regulations on the relationship between the Polish State and other religious denominations.[18] It should be emphasised that the Catholic Church, which has a strong social basis in Poland (about 92–93 per cent of the population declares itself Roman Catholic), is also a powerful real estate owner. Its huge possessions, as well as those of foundations and associations related to the activities of the Church, were nationalised after 1944. These statutes guaranteed restitution of its property to the Church.

A problematic issue that arose from the statute regulating the relationship between the Catholic Church and the Polish State was how to fix that particular moment in history, ie, defining the type of ownership to which restitution should be applied. The statute, proclaimed hastily by the still-communist authorities, who were struggling for legitimacy, was unique in a number of ways. It did not define any starting point, and because of this legislative error it became legally possible to demand the restitution of property taken from the Church before 1939—in the nineteenth century or even earlier. The Catholic Church did not hesitate to use these legal opportunities quite often. All regulations of the restitution of property taken from other churches, however, state explicitly that restitution only concerns property nationalised after 1944.

Specific and unique reasons for the regulation of restitution of nationalised property are found in negotiations between the Polish government

---

[18] The two laws of 17 May 1989 were followed by the Law of 4 July 1991 on the relationship between the State and the Polish Autokefalic Orthodox Church; the Law of 13 May 1994 on the relationship between the State and the Evangelic Reformed Church in the Republic of Poland; the Law of 13 May 1994 on the relationship between the State and the Evangelic Augsburg (Lutheran) Church in the Republic of Poland; the Law of 30 June 1995 on the relationship between the State and the Evangelic Methodist Church in the Republic of Poland; the Law of 30 June 1995 on the relationship between the State and the Baptist Church in the Republic of Poland; and the Law of 30 June 1995 on the relationship between the State and the Church of Seventh Day Adventists in the Republic of Poland.

and Jewish organisations in Poland concerning the restitution of property to Jewish religious communities (and not individuals). Though these negotiations came to some positive conclusions (Eizenstat 1997), the results are nonetheless rather limited. The agreements between the Polish government and Jewish organisations, as well as the promise of the Polish authorities to restore the property of Jewish religious organisations (synagogues, religious schools, charitable institutions and cemeteries), are often contested by local governments, which present all possible obstacles and arguments against restitution. Therefore, this restitution strongly depends upon local policy and local conditions, which makes it generally very difficult to achieve.

In this context, when considering restitution in Poland, which is based on general rules resulting from international agreements, from the land reform introduced after 1944 and from 1989–1995 statutes on the relationship between the State and the Churches, it can be concluded that the great winner of restitution is the Roman Catholic Church, primarily because of its high social and political importance. Peasants constitute the second winning group. They succeeded in their persistent efforts to regain the farmland that they had obtained during the land reform of 1944; this process was driven by the great value that farmland has for Polish peasants as a foundation for their social status, independence and dignity. However, negotiations with Jewish organisations show that the general policy of the government can be easily obstructed by local authorities. Consequently, the success of the Jewish religious organisations in reclaiming their property depends on factors that are not the subject of general regulation and are highly arbitrary.

The arbitrary nature of the ongoing restitution is clearly evident in cases concerning individual property. These are based on administrative procedural law, set by the provisions of the Polish Administrative Code and by case law. Restitution or compensation for nationalisation on the basis of administrative procedures became possible in Poland after the judicial review of governmental decisions was re-established in 1980. It should be stressed, first and foremost, that the Administrative Code does not make restitution or compensation dependent on citizenship or residence in Poland. Thus, any person can theoretically be compensated, or any property restituted to a person, whether Polish citizen or not. Because claims to restitution of individual property rights based on the Administrative Code figure in the hundreds of thousands, the condition of citizenship and residency stressed in the political and public debate is a far shot from reality. In fact, this debate reflects postulates that have nothing to do with actual legal practice.

According to the Administrative Code, the administrative bodies decide whether a decision of nationalisation has violated then existing law. Article 156(2) of the Code provides for the annulment of any administrative decision issued without legal basis or in a 'shocking breach of the law'.

Annulment implies that from a formal point of view the State never acquired the property rights in question. Thus, nullifying an act of nationalisation entails that any present possession of a property by the State is based on *mala fide*, ie, the State has no right to possess it, and therefore it should be returned to its owner in nature. If this is impossible, then the claimant has a right to make a claim for an equivalent or for compensation.

There are several legal and financial problems directly related to the application of the Administrative Code. From a legal point of view, the most important problem pertains to the discretionary nature of the administrative decision and the imprecise nature of the 'shocking breach of the law' clause. As any other general legal concept that implies value judgements, this clause implicitly refers to criteria that differentiate between 'shocking' breaches from ones that may be serious yet are not 'shocking'. The legalistic point of view asserts that a 'shocking' breach of law is a nationalisation decree that was clearly not based on then existing law or that clearly acted against the law—or that it was in direct opposition to the direct, obvious and unquestionable meaning of the law. However, doubts about such a direct and obvious meaning of the law, even in such an understanding of the general clause, cannot be ruled out.

Another problem emerges when the State has already disposed of the property it had possessed, for instance sold it to a third party, who bought the property in good faith. The rights of a third person, a bona fide owner, are protected by the law. This is not only a legal problem but also a factual one. Notwithstanding minor cases or those of persons whose good faith would be difficult to question (eg, someone who bought their apartment in a state-owned building), serious doubts must be raised concerning the bona fide nature of all those former officials of the *nomenklatura* who bought huge estates, buildings or enterprises for a merely symbolic price.

The Administrative Procedure Code makes provisions for situations in which it is impossible to nullify a decision on nationalisation because of its irreversible legal and actual consequences. According to Article 158 of the Code, the administrative body can in such cases only ascertain that the nationalisation decision violated the law. Once in possession of such a validation, the claimant is entitled to demand compensation (or an equivalent) from the State (Article 160). This is of course a very costly solution, because the Code provides that compensation should be equal to the whole and real value of the property. In fact, this could ruin the State budget, if the scope of the as yet pending claims is considered.

Restitution on the basis of administrative procedure is becoming even more problematic and difficult for claimants. This is due to a continuously changing legal situation, primarily as a result of the communalisation of state property in 1992, the privatisation of state-owned assets that began in 1988 and the new—also continually changing—statutes on urban and rural development. As a consequence of these general regulations, ownership, designation and the administrative bodies in charge of processing claims are in constant change. In addition, the administrative territorial reform in 1998 changed the structure and functions of local governments, most notably making them financially responsible for many formerly national tasks and obligations. The new financial burdens make local governments, currently the owners of communal and formerly state-owned property, even more reluctant to pay the costs of restitution.

Considering the possibilities of restitution and compensation for lost property in individual cases, it has to be stressed that presently legal institutions and procedures make the whole process dependent on not always predictable and transparent factors. Apart from individuals who can prove a 'shocking breach of law', the winners of such legal and institutional arrangements could be those very officials who are able to use legal opportunities for their own profits. The losers are those who claim property back but whose resources are insufficient for long administrative and court procedures or for hiring lawyers.

After communalisation of the state assets, obvious winners are local governments, but they might easily turn into losers if the debate over restitution continues long into the future. Nonetheless, they always can decide individual cases of restitution contingent upon local policy, thus contributing to the obscurity of the whole process.

VI. CONCLUSIONS: ARGUMENTS AND INTERESTS

The process of restitution of nationalised property, as well as any other effort aimed at coming to terms with the totalitarian past, should be analysed on at least two levels: the level of historical and personal experiences, values, moral convictions and local legal cultures; and the level of actual vested interests of persons and institutions involved in these processes. As has been demonstrated, these two levels do not necessarily overlap. The legal solutions to claims cannot be separated from their socio-historical framework, since all legal concepts are locally embedded and reflect the particular moral pattern of socio-historical circumstances. In the case of Eastern and Central Europe, and especially of Poland, concepts such as restitution and property cannot be separated from far-reaching and unjust historical events, like partition and colonisation; they cannot be separated either from the dynamics of post-communist transformation and the extensive opportunities for individual enrichment that it creates.

The political and moral arguments about restitution should in particular be examined in the context of special interests and with regard to the winners and losers of the existing procedures of restitution. The winners were those groups and institutions that were strong enough to fight successfully for their interests. In Poland these clearly have been peasants, the

Catholic Church and, to some extent, individuals who successfully claim compensation either as a result of treaties concluded with foreign governments or because they were able to prove the illegality of specific nationalisation decisions. The large group of prospective losers include claimants who live abroad because they are afraid to come back, because they were given one-way passports or because they were declared traitors of the Polish state. Losers in the restitution process furthermore include those who were deprived of property as a result of Polish territorial border shifts or as a result of nationalisation and land reform conducted by the communist regime. For them, the ongoing restitution can only contribute to their disapointment with the transformation.

REFERENCES

Eizenstat, Stuart. 1997. Restitution of Communal and Private Property in Central and Eastern Europe. *Central European Constitutional Review* 2/3: 50–2.

Gadamer, Hans-Georg. 1975/1993. *Wahrheit und Methode*. Polish translation. Kraków: Interpress.

Goffman, Erving. 1997. Frame Analysis. In *The Goffman Reader*, edited by C Lemert and A Branaman. Oxford: Blackwell Publishers.

Izdebski, Hubert. 1999. Ownership in People's Poland: Shaping, Growth, and Decomposition of the Theory of Socialist Ownership in the Years 1944–1990. In *Recht im Sozialismus, Band 1 'Enteignung'*, edited by G Bender and U Falk. Frankfurt am Main: Vittorio Klostermann.

Pańko, Walerian. 1984. *O prawie własności i jego współczesnych funkcjach* (On Property Law and Its Contemporary Functions). Katowice: Silesian University Press.

Pawlik, Wojciech. 1988. *Nieformalna reprywatyzacja jako źródło zwyczajów prawnych* (Informal Re-privatisation as a Source of Legal Custom). Warsaw: Warsaw University Press.

Pogany, Istvan. 1997. *Righting Wrongs in Eastern Europe*. Manchester: Manchester University Press.

Prus, Baleslaw. 1886/1996. Reprint. *Placówka*. English translation. London: Puls Publications.

Ryan, Alan. 1987. *Property*. Minneapolis: University of Minnesota Press.

Skąpska, Grażyna. 1999. Eigentum und Staatsanwaltschaft in der Volksrepublik Polen. War Totalitarismus ein gesteuerter Rechtsnihilismus? In *Recht im Sozialismus, Band 1 'Enteignung'*, edited by G Bender and U Falk. Frankfurt am Main: Vittorio Klostermann.

——. 2000. Between East and West: Hypotheses on the Legal Cultural Mentalities and Formation of the Rule of Law in Poland. In *Transformation and Integration in the Baltic Sea Area: Conference in Umeå, Sweden, November 1997*, edited by Per Falk and Olle Kranz. Umeå: European Law Centre and Department of Economic History, Umeå University.

V

The Stores of Memory:
Files, Individual Biographies
and Collective Memories

12

Biographies, Legal Cases and Political Transitions

CAROL A HEIMER AND ARTHUR L STINCHCOMBE[1]

I. INTRODUCTION

FUNCTIONING GOVERNMENTS AND courts of law collect information and keep dossiers about civil servants and members of the government that differ from the information collected and files kept about criminals. Occupants of government positions and candidates for government responsibility are subjected to biographical analysis; those arrested for crimes are analysed as cases. We argue that during transition periods, biographical analyses are displaced and a legal treatment of crimes in the old regime simplifies the biographies of regime participants into cases. During political transitions, 'lustration'[2] processes often rely on case analysis and make participation in the new regime (and perhaps punishment as well) contingent on the outcome of legal trials that consider only questions of guilt or innocence. But at such times practical decisions about government personnel require an analysis of biographies to make an estimate of loyalty to the new regime and competence to do a job. In effect these screening processes combine the tasks of job interviews and legal procedure.

The mismatch in lustration processes between relatively narrow political and legal criteria on the one hand and broader administrative and practical criteria on the other, helps account for the painful seesawing between

---

[1] Detailed comments were made by Steven Hoffman and Barry Cohen. Hoffman suggested and drafted the section on the transformation of biography through rites of passage. Comments by participants in the conference at Oñati that gave rise to this volume also improved our argument. The Lochinvar Society provided the environmental conditions that facilitated the revision.

[2] We will use the word 'lustration' to refer to those ceremonial cleansings that use punishment as the core of the ritual, as was typically the case in Rome, where the phrase originated. When we analyse the rituals of confession, apology and amnesty in truth commissions, we will use the phrase 'rites of passage' because the emphasis of the ritual is on how the ritual transforms biographies.

pressures to hold people universalistically accountable for past crimes and pressures particularistically to consider valuable experience and skill that could be put to good use in building the new regime. For this reason, we contend, transition regimes often are pressured to consider biographical elements that would be deemed irrelevant or illegitimate in ordinary courts of law. In this chapter we show what these two contrasting ways of thinking about information, case analysis and biographical analysis, have to offer in political transitions. We also argue that biographical analysis is especially important in distinguishing between situational and predispositional causes of crimes under old regimes.

The core variable in the chapter is whether people's behaviour in an old regime is treated as a case of crime or analysed as a total biography. When a person's past behaviour is analysed as a case, guilt disqualifies the person for some kinds of roles in the new regime (or in the extreme qualifies him or her only for punishment); when the person's past behaviour is analysed as a total biography, placement in the new regime depends on what the evidence predicts about behaviour in the new regime. In particular we focus on the ability of people who were powerful in an old regime, especially in its most criminal parts such as the secret police or the border guard, to build convincing biographies that qualify them for reputable and profitable, and even powerful, places in the new regime. The basic empirical argument is that public ceremonies that allow people to confess and be shriven and therefore to encapsulate their biographies in the old regime and build fresh ones for the new regime, encourage the examination of the relation between people as they were in the old regime and what they will be in the new in a biographical rather than criminal-case method of analysis.

Let us start with an example of the problem. In the old regime in the Soviet Union, managers of state enterprises were judged by how much they produced rather than how well they obeyed governmental dictates. In fact, those dictates would have prevented production, because production depended on others supplying what the government said they were going to supply, and that was not always to the advantage of the supplying firm. Thus the position of a factory manager in the old regime trained people to disobey the law in order to get the job done. But being a 'fixer' in the old regime can now be seen as socialisation for being, or hiring private protection from, a Mafia operative in the new regime, when the same factory becomes private property but with government connections (Berliner 1957; cf Granick 1960).[3] Thus the whole biography of a government official who was a plant manager in the old regime would suggest

---

[3] For a comparison of Berliner and Granick, see Stinchcombe (1960). For an account of post-Soviet times, see Handelman (1995); see also Derluguian (2000a; 2000b, 210–12, 217–18).

that as a civil servant in the new regime, he or she would understand too well the value of corruption and disobedience to the law. The manager of a state enterprise who becomes a member of the owning and managerial staff of the new private enterprise will likely carry the standard operating procedures of the old regime into the new and may therefore assume that corrupting the government apparatus is the only way to get ahead. A biographical mode of analysis, asking how an old regime factory manager's life hangs together and what that shows about how he or she conceives the job of an official, may predict corrupt behaviour.

During the transition, when cases might be sorted on the criterion of whether the civil servant (or the potential owner of the new factory) had committed human rights abuses instead of ordinary abuses, and when that might become the main criterion of whether someone can be trusted by the new regime, the filtering of the biography through a case system of analysis (Heimer 2001a) eliminates most information regarding what kind of a civil servant (or owner) the manager would be. The old regime socialised secret policemen and border guards to violate human rights and socialised ordinary economic managers to corrupt the system so the job could get done. Information on that socialisation is embodied in the overall biography of the factory manager. That the factory manager was not a KGB member or a border guard does not mean he or she would be a good government servant for a new democratic 'clean government' regime. Likewise, having been socialised to violate human rights in an old regime occupation does not always predict similar behaviour in a new regime. A border guard is unlikely to shoot anyone crossing a border in the new regime.

We argue in what follows that this clash of criteria between case and biographical analysis, here appearing as a conflict between the overall meaning of a biography and the meaning of a legal decision of guilty or not guilty (or legally liable or not liable in a civil case), is pervasive in social life in bureaucratic societies. In the ordinary career of a civil servant in a society with a stable regime, the bureaucrat's whole career is treated as relevant to the responsibilities he or she is ready to assume. In a regime in transition, however, rather than assessing the whole career for what it implies about the positions a person might occupy in the new regime, we have sometimes come to use legalistic classifications of guilty/not guilty as a substitute for the analysis of what the whole old regime was like.[4] But that classification

---

[4] An excellent example is the novel *The Questionaire* by Ernst von Salomon (1954/1955). Von Solomon pretends to be giving a biographically complete answer of everything relevant to the categorical questions in the *Fragebogen*, the questionnaire for preliminary sorting of the German population for de-nazification. For example, to a question about noble relatives, he gives a sketch that starts with an ancestor in Venice during the Crusades who adopted the biblical Jewish name Solomon to claim the honour of having helped conquer Jerusalem from non-Christians. He then reports on historical French ennoblements and family members' immigration into Prussia. No doubt this is more biography than would have been relevant to

of cases into guilty and not guilty lets in only information that is highly defensible by legal standards, and only information relevant to guilt/innocence under the law. The law of transition regimes is understandably dominated by what distinguishes the old regime from the new. But that restricts the criteria as well as the evidence for decisions about people. The combination of these limitations results in people who were trained by the old regime to be good Mafia operators being given clean bills of health, while a relatively uncorrupted border guard who fired at a shadow in the dark may be considered democratically irresponsible and so civilly dead.

First we give a conceptual analysis of 'biographical' versus 'case' methods of categorisation, drawing on work comparing these modes of analysis in organisations, the legal system and markets (Heimer 2001a). We next discuss why legal systems of preserving memory about individuals from the old regime may sacrifice information about ordinary deficiencies of character in order to identify clearly crimes associated politically with the old regime. Third, we explain what ordinary systems for the analysis of qualities of character and other biographical and predispositional concepts consist of. And finally we turn to a theoretical projection of what faults we should expect to find where lustration systems, shaped by the case method, have come to dominate the personnel judgement systems of transition governments and new regimes. We emphasise that this is a theoretical chapter, and we therefore do not deal very thoroughly with the factual delicts of civil servants in old regimes, during transitions or under new regimes.[5] Our purpose instead is to develop the case/biography contrast and, by combining it with an analysis of variations among political regimes, to show how the extra information supplied by biographical analysis contributes to predictions about how people will behave after the transition.

Our distinction between biographical and case analyses is particularly well illustrated in the contrast between the practices of the South African Truth and Reconciliation Commission (TRC) and the East German lustration model based on the criminal law.[6] In South Africa a record of crimes under the former racist regime plus a confession and apology formed a biography that is crucially different from a well documented verdict of guilty. The presumption of the Commission was that an acceptance of the new pluralist racial regime was implicit in the apology; it postulated that this created a disposition to serve the new regime. The opportunity to create

---

the purpose of the Allies, but it communicates a theme in his family culture that, along with other pieces of his biography, suggests he was still not a good democrat, though not guilty of war crimes.

[5] For comments on lustration's effect on transitions, see Stinchcombe (1995).

[6] For Germany, see especially Blankenburg 1995 and Los 1995. For South Africa, see Ash 1997; Berat and Shain 1995; and the papers in Nuttal and Coetzee 1998, particularly those by De Kok and Holiday. For a variety of cases, including Germany and South Africa, see Cohen 1995.

a new biography sorted criminals into those 'redeemed' by the experience of the transition and those not redeemed. A confession and apology was not enough, of course, to qualify one for election or for a civil service post; the whole of the relevant biography was examined for that purpose. But some such biographies included confession, the penance of apology and redemption by amnesty before the Commission.

Much of the purpose of the TRC in South Africa was to create a history of the transition as one in which the truths about the old regime were contrasted with the hopes for the new. The truths were biographical, but the purpose of bringing them out was to characterise the apartheid regime and, to a lesser extent, the revolutionary terror opposing that regime. The new regime abolished the old rather than securing punishment atoning for individual crimes. In effect, the old collective history was made irrelevant to decisions about the qualifications of individuals for participation in the new regime. Participation in the new regime was legitimised by TRC rituals in which servants of the old regime were transformed into stewards of the new.

This policy of rehabilitation may have been more crucial for South Africa, where trained and experienced civil servants were scarce and where a large number of white officials could be accused of racist crimes.[7] East Germany, in contrast, had many educated people, as well as a convenient supply from West Germany to compensate for any deficiencies. Most East German civil servants were not directly involved in the repression carried out by the old regime. A criminal procedure requires a clear focus of state power, and as Archbishop Tutu commented, 'Neither side in the struggle (the state nor the liberation movements) had defeated the other, and hence nobody was in a position to enforce so-called victor's justice' (1998, ch 1, para 21).

But whatever the explanation, the South African regime allowed the creation of new biographical information especially relevant for the new regime; transformed biographies were not as easily available to most of the East Germans tainted by their former activities.

II. BIOGRAPHICAL VERSUS CASE CONCEPTUAL SYSTEMS

That a person is classified by a bureaucracy or a court as a 'case' tells others that they need consider only a few limited pieces of information about that person, with the particular data deemed relevant varying from one situation to another. How people think about and treat 'cases' depends

---

[7] Cohen describes South Africa as 'one of the most complex cases imaginable because of the near-total corruption of the white community in benefiting from the crimes of apartheid' (1995, 33).

on the other 'cases' they have encountered.[8] The processing of one case is likely to set precedents for others deemed similar; how a case is treated depends on which other cases compete with it for resources; and what seems normal or aberrant depends on how a case is classified and what cases have preceded it.

Bureaucratic routines act on standard objects; legal systems abstract cases from the rest of life; and markets standardise commodities to facilitate price and cost comparisons. But all of the entities treated as standardised cases also can be treated as unique and considered in the light of their biographies. Hospitals and schools may tend to treat children as cases, but families are more deeply invested in thinking about children's pasts and futures and their relations to other family members. In the United States, the same legal system that insists on ignoring biography during the guilt phase of a capital trial explicitly considers biographical information during the penalty phase (Lynch and Haney nd). And although many markets depend on standardisation, the markets for singular goods rely on biographical information about objects and those who once owned them.

Case analysis differs from biographical analysis especially in the identity of the entity, in the point of comparison, in the relation of the ethnoanalyst to the entity, in the infrastructural support that undergirds analysis and in the origin of the cognitive frame.[9] In case analysis, the entity is identified as a member of a category and is compared with other similar objects. In biographical analysis, the entity is identified as a unique individual, often with a proper name; the entity is compared to itself at other points in time. In case analysis, the ethnoanalyst has a relation to the entity as worker to materials or subject to object; in biographical analysis, ethnoanalysts are subjects analysing and interacting with other subjects whose input may be essential to correct interpretation.

Case analysis tends to rely on the infrastructure of organisational routines, standard operating procedures, protocols, rules, regulations, laws, prices, files and documents. For these reasons, case analysis is much more likely to occur when problems are predictable or when unpredictability can at least be kept within bounds. Biographical analysis is especially likely to occur in unstructured, unpredictable situations, on the cutting edge, where development and change are anticipated and in times of transition. On the cutting edge or during turbulent times, a pre-existing cognitive framework is of little use; analysis that focuses on core features is not possible when no one yet knows which features will be the important ones. Cognitive frames

---

[8] See Emerson 1969, 1983, 1991, 1992; Gilboy 1991, 1992; Heimer and Staffen 1995; Sudnow 1965; Swigert and Farrell 1977; and Waegel 1981.

[9] These and several other contrasts, less relevant here, are discussed in Heimer 2001a.

tend instead to be emergent, created as the analyst goes along and adjusted to take account of each new bit of information. A pre-existing frame, such as a medical protocol or the criminal code, may get in the way by focusing attention on the wrong things.

We briefly illustrate the contrast between case and biographical analysis with the example of critically ill infants (Heimer 2001b; Heimer and Staffen 1998) because it gives an especially clear view of the central concepts. A transition from one government to another is inevitably a more uncertain and murkier site in which to develop such concepts.

We generally think of children as being mainly the concern of their families, with increasing involvement of other bodies, such as schools, as they mature. Unlike other newborns, critically ill infants begin their lives as the focus of attention of a team of medical experts in infant intensive care units as well as of their parents. Occasionally, legal actors also intervene when medical care providers and parents disagree about treatment. Critically ill infants are thus a good example of how a single entity is thought about and acted upon in multiple settings. The same infant is conceived of as a patient by the medical team; as a young citizen with rights by attorneys, court-appointed guardians and judges; and as a child by parents (Heimer and Staffen 1998, 137–77). Further, these settings vary in the degree to which activity is governed by schemas and protocols: families are less routinised and scripted than courts or hospitals. Clearly the hospitalised infant and the infant who has gone home are not *identical* entities. Parents care for one at home; the other is so sick that hospitalisation is essential. Nevertheless there is substantial continuity in the entity (the infant), coupled with a sharp discontinuity in the way activities are organised and documented and the infant conceptualised; this is what merits investigation.

As we suggested above, medical staff and parents identify infants in different ways. Among themselves, medical staff are likely to refer to the child by symptom ('the 25 weeker' or 'the gastroskesis'); parents refer to their baby by name. Staff and parents also differ in the comparison points they employ. Staff continually compare their infant patient with others with similar diagnoses ('that's common in kids with hypoplastic left heart'); parents make comparisons over time and talk about the pregnancy, the child's future and his or her anticipated relationships with other family members.

As ethnoanalysts thinking about the baby, medical staff and parents differ in how they characterise their relation to the baby, the baby's role and their own actions. In their conversation, records and notes, medical staff tend to portray themselves as the ones who make decisions and take action in treating their patient; infants are depicted as quite passive, simply responding or not to the treatment. Staff are subjects acting on an object, workers manipulating materials. In contrast, parents much more often describe a relation of subject-to-subject, constructing the infant as a creature with interpersonal competence and portraying the baby as acting and having personality and intentions.

These differences between medical staff and parents in how they think about and relate to hospitalised infants are grounded in rather substantial differences in the levels of routinisation of hospital units as compared to family life. The medical treatment of critically ill infants is supported by an elaborate division of labour among trained staff members, medical protocols prescribing therapies and medications, and records and charts in which the children's progress is noted and commented upon. Routines are of course human creations, developed partly in response to the complexities of individual cases, but because the massive historical accretion dominates what is created anew by staff confronting a new case, the cognitive frame is for all practical purposes pre-existing. For parents the situation is quite different. With meagre infrastructure to organise their activity and thought, they create a much larger portion of their conceptual framework as they go along.

Why is all this important? We offer several examples of why the contrast between case and biographical thinking is important, in the process making the transition back from infant intensive care to political transitions. At the most basic level, how a critically ill infant is classified determines how much nursing attention the baby will get, which physicians will be in charge of the case and which others will be called in as consultants, what kinds of therapists will work with the child, what protocols will govern treatment and which cases will compete with each other for resources. Classification focuses attention on some features of the case rather than others. Ordinarily this is a good thing because it leads healthcare providers to see the relation between symptoms and to deal with more serious problems first. Sometimes, though, cases are misclassified and the focusing of attention is then inappropriate. Symptoms that are not expected may be misinterpreted or overlooked.[10]

Biographical analyses suspend judgment about classification, losing the efficiency of routine but avoiding some of the disasters of misclassification and the inappropriate application of routines. Inappropriate assumptions about the comparability of cases are a recipe for calamity. Vaughan (1996) for instance shows how misclassification of the o-ring problem ultimately led to the Challenger space shuttle accident, and Clarke's (1999) research demonstrates how inappropriate comparisons of catastrophes with more routine difficulties (eg, comparing evacuation of a city after a nuclear accident with rush hour) lead bureaucracies to construct completely unworkable plans for risk management. When there are no fully comparable cases, comparisons with other cases must be treated much more cautiously. In biographical analyses, rather than comparing one case with another,

---

[10] See, for instance, Roth's (1972) discussion of what happens when emergency room patients are thought to be suffering from overconsumption of alcohol.

analysts compare their current experience and observations with previous experience and observations with the *same* case. Coherence is supplied, then, by biography rather than by categorisation. And a key question for biographical analysis is how the behaviour and reactions of a person, assumed to have the usual coherence and continuity of personality, can be expected to vary from one condition to another.

A case orientation also tends to be associated, at least in medicine, with abstraction (so the infant is discussed not as a person but as a diseased body part or congenital malformation), with valuation of some kinds of evidence (eg, from tests and measurements) and discounting of others (eg, from observations by nurses and family members) and by scepticism about the reports of some (patients, family members) and respect for the opinions of others (physicians) (Anspach 1988, 1993). In turbulent times, on the cutting edge or when entities can be expected to change or develop, analysts cannot afford to ignore evidence that might otherwise be considered less reliable. Especially when the predispositions of those being treated (whether by a medical system or by a court) affect what happens in the future, 'tainted' evidence from those most deeply affected by the case may be crucial.

This digression into the sociology of categorisation should suggest to us why the contrast between case and biographical thinking might be important in an analysis of the lustration processes associated with major political upheavals. Although lustration processes are often handled by bodies such as courts, which are accustomed to collecting information about cases, a key feature of these transitions is that the situation has changed. Biographical thinking, focusing specifically on questions about the continuity of persons over time and space, may prove more useful in predicting which members of the old regime can safely be incorporated in the new and which must be disqualified. The key question is whether past crimes are good predictors of future behaviour because they accurately reflected the person's orientation to rules and to moral obligations to others, or whether past crimes are poor predictors of future actions because they were instead reactions to a situation that now no longer exists. Because, in the setting we study here, the intention of the transition is that the crimogenic situation will not exist in the future, the predictive power of crimes of obedience for future conduct is as low as the new regime can make it.

In general, qualities of character in the moral domain and competence in the technical domain are the main things we want to know about people before we assign them responsibilities associated with power and authority. Both of these are 'predispositional' qualities, by which we mean that it is internal mechanisms of a reliable and repetitive kind that produce patterns of moral and competent action. Thus evidence about competence and qualities of character is thought to be information about the generative mechanisms of behaviour, and one collects this evidence from repeated observation of the person.[11] In the criminal law, we carefully distinguish the judgment of 'guilty' versus 'not guilty' from the judgment of 'ready for parole' versus 'not ready for parole', because one is a case judgment about how the person acted once and the other a predispositional judgment of how the person is inclined to act. The parole decision tends to be based more on the qualities of character, and the decision about guilt is based more on the analysis of acts.[12]

When we are attempting to encourage the development of competencies or qualities of character in others, we are especially interested in the development of generative mechanisms within the person. To judge our success, we collect information from our students' or colleagues' whole biographies. When we are trying to give others evidence about our skills and character, for instance when they are proposing to hire us, we supply résumés, which are summaries of our biographies. We do that because we expect employers to look for the mechanisms that will reliably produce competent and morally responsible behaviour ('work discipline') on into the future. And employers do indeed look at biographies for signs of competence and integrity. But within an educational institution, we build routines to keep track of people's biographies from beginning to end, especially on the competence part. Educators object to standardised tests, not because they measure nothing but because they do not measure accurately the predispositions that educators are especially paid to induce.

[11] We mainly consider here legal bodies that make these kinds of assessments. Sometimes, though, it is other entities who predict future behaviour, and sometimes they collect information about situations rather than about individual character or about specific deviant actions. Insurers, for instance, regularly assess whether policyholders are likely to defraud the insurance company and often use crude analyses of situations to make these predictions: they may be reluctant to insure a building in a declining neighbourhood because arson becomes more tempting as the discrepancy between market value and insured value grows. Further, in issuing fidelity and surety bonds, insurers must determine whether particular policyholders will remain honest in the face of temptations (for fidelity bonds) or whether they will fulfill contracts (for surety bonds). Particularly when evaluating applicants for fidelity bonds, insurers are as likely to evaluate the temptations faced by policyholders or their employees as the personal qualities of the applicants. A jewelry store offers different temptations than a fast food restaurant, for instance. See Heimer 1985, especially ch 5.

[12] See Lempert and Sanders 1986, especially 27–35, for a similar analysis of the role of capacity (Could the person have done otherwise?) and intent (Did the person intend the consequences?) in the assignment of legal responsibility. They argue that we find people criminally liable only when they intended to commit the criminal act and had a choice about whether to commit it (It wasn't, for instance, committed in self defense). A person can occasionally be held liable in a strict liability regime, though, even if he or she did not intend the harm and could not avoid the act. Although most of the assessments we consider in this chapter concern questions of character and intent, we should keep in mind that after a political transition the kinds of situations people face also will change. Factory managers may no longer be obliged to meet government production quotas and border guards may no longer be forced to keep citizens from leaving the country. Decreases in corruption and human rights abuses should perhaps then be attributed to changes in the situation rather than to changes in the moral character of citizens.

Contrast this educational and labour market biographical analysis of predispositions with the legal conceptualisation of a stream of cases through the police arrest stage, the indictment, the investigation, the defense, the trial, the conviction and sentencing. The various stages from police, to prosecutor, to indicting judge or grand jury, to trial confrontation, to a final decision of guilt or innocence are characterised by a progressive stripping away of biographical information (though, as we noted, sentencing hearings often reintroduce some biography excluded earlier in the process). Eventually the legal process compares cases according to how solid the evidence is, how clear it is that it was a crime rather than a mistake. In the United States, only evidence about the current incident is admissible; evidence of past crimes is kept from the jury. And the trial tests that each element of the crime existed—no matter, unless all elements are present, that some well proved elements are devastating evidence of bad character. It does not allow for the collection or consideration of evidence regarding whether the defendant is a contemptible person who should be kept from socially responsible roles. That is, turning a person into a convicted criminal entails stripping his or her biography and retaining only the type of information required to convict of a particular act.

Similarly in a tort case, we do not ask whether the railroad on which an accident took place was in general well run, whether it was the sort of railroad one would want running through one's town, but whether some specific act of negligence was causally dominant in the damage. And in the Ford Pinto cases, it was planning for the specific years in which the gas tanks tended to burst, not Ford's general planning process, that was considered during the legal procedures. But although legal trials may be constrained to consider only evidence about specific malevolent or negligent acts, in other circumstances other actors might be interested in evidence on predispositions and patterns of behaviour. Travellers might wish to avoid railroads whose owners have a reputation for negligence, and consumers might be reluctant to purchase cars manufactured by a company that has been unwilling to spend a few dollars to keep gas tanks from exploding. Similarly, what we want to know about someone we are considering including in our new regime government is broader—an assessment of whether this person will serve us well on into the future.

We turn information that might be biographies into cases in order to protect unjustly stigmatised people from mistreatment by the criminal justice system, or to protect those not at fault in accidents. Our argument is that lustration processes instead ought to bear as much resemblance to job interviews as to the trials of criminal and civil courts, because their exclusion of biographical material is not really appropriate to their task. Case analysis may work well for the civil and criminal courts of stable political regimes, but it needs to be supplemented by biographical analysis during the turbulent transition periods in which conviction, punishment and parole decisions are collapsed into one.

III. THE MEMORY OF LAW

The key to law is to differentiate reasoning about a particular case, a court decision, from 'legislation', a general analysis of what is socially healthy. For example, court decisions are supposed to be nonpartisan, whereas legislation not enacted in a structure of partisanship is inherently suspect in democracies. But neither of these two parts of law includes the large component of everyday life in which we judge others' predispositions in order to decide what kinds of relationships to have to them. We should not make the mistake of concluding that nonpartisan court decisions and partisan legislation are adequate representations of the stuff of social life.

As Stewart Macaulay (1963) has emphasised, business relations take into account many aspects of potential partners: how congruent their interests are with one's own, their reputations, their competencies and anything that predicts their business behaviour. Only a few of these are represented in a legal contract between parties, and that is why disputing parties typically choose not to resolve their differences in a legal arena, where so much of their relationship is deemed irrelevant. The legality of the contract is, in Lisa Bernstein's words (1996), a device for the 'endgame', when the relationship has been destroyed. When the contract has been violated, the two parties still usually have all the reasons to bargain that led them to form the contract in the first place, so do not at first take the 'case' to court. The law of contract is, then, mainly about being clear about what one is hoping for if all goes well, then second about laying the basis for further bargaining if things do not work out. A written contract is only in the last resort predicting what a judge will do about a destroyed relationship. That is, the contract in court is what remains when social processes have stripped the relationship of all its information about predispositions, either because the parties were wrong about those predispositions or because the situation does not allow those predispositions to be acted out in a successful relationship. One main purpose of commercial law, by the time it comes to court, is to strip the guts—the predispositions, biographies and relationships of people—out of social life and then to arrange what is left. Because the legal contract is that bare bones of social relationships, it is mainly to be used in those rare situations in which a relationship is ending and the legal tie is all that remains.

What legalising people's behaviour does, then, is to give us two ways of making human behaviour historical, two ways for getting from a present situation into the future by remembering what is past. The first way is to build the future out of the stripped down view of a case, of an abstract comparison of particular facts with specific legal standards or with a precedent, the case giving rise to the precedent stripped to its *ratio decidendi*. From that flows only whatever sentence or damages or resulting imposed bargain is the remedy at law. It does not pretend to shape the whole of the lives of the parties (except in unusual 'status' cases, such as divorce with child custody arrangements, marriage, emancipation of slaves, citizenship determinations, conscription and the like). The decision of a legal case normally passes into social memory only as the remedy attached to the decision of the case, on the limited and abstract grounds that were relevant to that decision.

This is why lustration, the determination of the political and civil service rights and liberties of servants of the old regime, is such an anomalous way to analyse the political past of a country. It attempts to determine citizenship in the new regime not by using overall predictors of predisposition (such as birth within the nation, coming of voting age, service in the national army, naturalisation proceedings, etc) but instead on the basis of a trial on a limited factual basis of human rights abuses possibly carried out while serving in a particular role and in a particular situation in the old regime.

Sometimes perhaps a political crime is an indelible and reliable indicator of citizenship predispositions. But often lustration's predispositional predictions would be shown to be unsound by the examination of a subject's life since the crime, especially his or her life since the transition regime came to power. As Harold Rosenberg observed, 'In some degree, punishment is always meted out to a stranger who bears the criminal's name' (1977, 47). Particularly when lustration trials occur after some time has elapsed, projections into the past (Could this apparently harmless person really have done *that?*) and into the future (Is there any possibility that this feeble old man could commit further crimes?) seem equally farfetched. Lustration trials are like determining which prisoners should be paroled by retrying them for their original crimes, rather than by examining their subsequent behaviour or by looking for other evidence of criminality or a predisposition to violence. It is true that many civilised societies use felony convictions in nonpolitical trials as a disqualification for naturalisation and sometimes remove some citizenship rights (eg, voting rights) of even the native-born upon felony conviction (Uggen and Manza 2000). But for most people in most countries, age or property ownership or residence are more important criteria for citizenship than arrest records, because they attest better to predispositions.

In times of transition, especially transition from terrorist or totalitarian regimes to democratic ones, the temptation to use the criminal law is strong. Many political crimes have been committed, and they have often been committed more by agents of the old regime than by supporters of the new regime. But the cost of basing the social memory of the old regime on well established crimes is that a deeper analysis of the basis of terror and totalitarianism, and of what builds the predispositions such regimes require into ordinary people, is short-circuited; the cause is imagined as a disposition to be criminal, and so the cure is to eliminate the criminals from the new regime.

A second way the past is carried into the future by law is by the generalisations in new laws, and especially new constitutional provisions, about how to avoid the faults of the old regime (see Kim Lane Scheppele in this volume). The most crucial of these are not the ones that produce cases about persons but those that establish elections, the autonomy of legislatures, the constituencies of representation, the boundaries and powers of local governments, property rights, powers of taxation or limitations on the police and armed forces. That is, they are constitutional generalisations about what sort of government of laws is being established, how those laws will be changed in the future and how the succession to powers being created will be determined.

A constitution is a future-oriented document. Although its authority and the context for its interpretation are generally embedded in a story of the origin of the constitution and of modifications to the original document, these are not intended to be an adequate history of the pre-constitutional period. The lessons transmitted from that period under-represent the principles of those defeated by the new regime. For example, very few of the reasons given by American plantation owners for enslaving their workforce were built into the interpretation of the Thirteenth and Fourteenth Amendments that abolished slavery and established the citizenship of former slaves. When a regime rather like slavery was re-established in the plantation counties of the South after 1876, it was not justified by plantation owners' original arguments in favour of slavery. It was instead supported by federalist principles, embedded especially in the Tenth Amendment, that guaranteed states' rights to powers not explicitly granted to the federal government and by share crop 'contracts' to which the former slaves had allegedly agreed.

Some such selective forgetting of historical context is characteristic of the way legislation oriented to the future is intended to function, but clearly Reconstruction Republicans wanted the historical inferiority of African-Americans' rights to be forgotten, while the plantation owners wanted to forget freedom to bargain, or to leave bad bargains after their term was up, and other common law rights of free men and women. The biographies of the former slaves as people of historically inferior rights—unable to claim frontier land as property or, as part of the constitutional interregnum of the Reconstruction period, possessing equal rights to form contracts but no land—were then differentially selectively forgotten in the effective constitutions of the two different constitutional periods from 1865 to 1876 and 1876 to 1900. These selective forgettings were shaped by reinterpretations of the Reconstruction amendments by the Supreme Court (Brandwein 1999).

Thus the tendency to legalise biographical information in order to punish the clearly guilty from an old regime may produce a strong filtering of biographical information relevant to the political character of candidates for elective office or for responsible civil servant positions. Constitutional legalisation typically makes a different abstraction from biographies. Our argument is that constitutions are likely to be in error as abstractions of citizenship, if the biographies disappear into legalistic cases in the rewriting of constitutions in transitions. We wish to point out that these two legal devices (court cases and constitution writing or legislation) both abstract from biography and relationships. They may also be based on stylised understandings of the modal contract, the modal marriage, the modal political office or candidate or the modal civil service position. Post-war titles to plantation land in the American South abstracted from the biographical fact that black people did not have the right to establish such titles at the time the land was settled, as citizens would have had. Black people's claim on the land disappeared into real estate property cases and thus made possible the re-establishment of plantation owners' overwhelming power in the post-Civil War regime.

These legal forms as described above are at best only the infrastructure for social relationships. We do not usually choose our partners, whether for trade or marriage, simply on the basis of the form specified for that relationship by the legal system. Instead, partners are chosen and relationships constructed from the elements of biography. Among all of the people who might occupy civil service positions and government posts, we cannot safely accept all those who fit the general category established by the legal form. To rely exclusively on the legal form is to mistake the shed skin for the snake, the carapace for the cicada or the skeleton for the living animal. We cannot create relationships only from legal forms. But neither can we safely eliminate all those who might be disqualified by a legal proceeding. That is the mistake of ignoring the situational shaping of human behaviour, a mistake akin to treating all forms of homicide as identical. We are, to be sure, shaped and curbed by legal forms and by the situational constraints imposed by past regimes. But we retain some moral agency, and the challenge for lustration is to incorporate biographical analysis without undermining the important goals of attributing blame for past abuses and protecting the integrity of the new regime.

IV. ANALYSING PREDISPOSITIONS AND QUALITIES OF CHARACTER

We have been talking as if biography were simply the fuller version of a whole life, of which the information in a case is an abstraction for a particular purpose. But of course what we know about presidential candidates during the lead-up to an election is not a five-decade long video of everything that has ever happened to them. It is an abstraction of a particular kind, sufficient for the purposes of living with people or understanding predispositions that are relevant for how they will hold power or predicting whether, when a foundations contractor finds that the soil under a potential building is not adequate for weight bearing, he or she will renegotiate what has to be done rather than mindlessly build a structure that will not stand. What is crucial about these abstractions is that they are open to correction by events, that they are a continuous record of whatever evidence has come in about whether people have had problems in school or whether they listen and respond to advice or are too arbitrary, impulsive and self-centred to hold power reliably or are inclined to interpret their contractual responsibilities narrowly in their own interest.

The norms of such biographical abstractions are always open-ended, since life creates additions to and, through selective amnesia, subtractions from biographies. For a curriculum vita new publications are added and poems published in a secondary school literary magazine usually disappear. In families, more is added and more is remembered than in the more abstract documents that form labour market biographies. But even in families, the richness of biography attached to the name of a son or daughter is limited.

More crucial to our purpose here, the abstraction needs to change for changing situations. In the United States, if a person leaves academic life his or her curriculum vita normally changes into a résumé. This fact signals that a list of publications and academic honours and university service, which constitutes evidence for predispositions that predict scholarly productivity and peer review service, is not as relevant in business and government. Recognition for loyalty, cooperative service, reliability and the interpersonal abilities entering into salesmanship all matter more for a business or civil service career than cosmopolitan recognition outside one's employing organisation for individual creativity in a field of scholarship. The abstraction in the biography has to be changed to fit the new situation. A credit rating is still another abstraction from the same basic biographical data. One would hardly put data on how many debt payments have been late on one's curriculum vita, but these data are essential for someone who wants to predict payment reliability for a thirty-year fixed-rate mortgage contract. The abstraction for a surety bond for a foundation contractor is likely to consist mainly of reputation among general building contractors in the local building market.

Similarly the purpose of electioneering, especially of press reporting on candidates, is in part to uncover those parts of the biography that predict how candidates will use the powers of the office for which they are running. The probability that such an official, if elected, will feather his or her nest by soliciting bribes, by privatising government firms to the fixers of the old regime who have become Mafiosos in the new regime, needs to be assessed. Such assessments rely on freedom of the press, freedom of speech by opposing candidates and freedom of other citizens to supply information to opponents or the press. The abstractions in court cases may be relevant to this task, but the task of combing biographies for predictors of the use of government power is different from the task of combing a specific incident for decisive evidence of criminal wrongdoing or of fraud in a contract. And in particular that task has to be constantly redone, as new evidence and changing situations demand, as the office for which a person is a candidate changes, or as new political oppositions bring new issues of public performance to the fore, making different elements of biography relevant. For example, although lying about an extramarital affair is sometimes relevant to the use of public power, more usually it is not. The details of candidates' biographies that are relevant to the construction of public biographies change with the winds of democratic fashion in biographical predictors of the uses of public power.

In assessing fitness for the presidency, a good constitution provides for more than a case method of determination that a candidate has no outstanding overdue debts and has not been conclusively proved to be a criminal. Considered from the point of view of this chapter, democratic constitutions implicitly provide a chance for the electorate or superiors in the civil service to examine the whole relevant biography of candidates in judging fitness for office. Party conventions, competition among newspapers, campaign appearances, endorsements by all and sundry, all provide a broad-band examination of qualities of character relevant to elective office. And of course party platforms and slates of candidates are indications of the mechanisms that will determine the future behaviour of elected officials.

The civil service in modern societies has extensive information on candidates for posts, but it is generally confined to performance in education and in lower offices. Superiors make judgments of that performance, and in many bureaucracies such performance reviews are formally recorded. Biographical information is collected before appointment, and civil service roles with particularly sensitive requirements sometimes provide for interviews of a candidate's friends and colleagues. For positions in which competence is crucial, as in university research or advanced teaching civil service positions, peer judgments are systematically collected and often a dossier of publications is examined by a recruitment committee. Systematic reviews are often renewed for promotions to higher offices or higher ranks in the same office.

Occasionally a particular action is especially indicative of qualities of character relevant to the office, and such incidents are intensively studied. Both criminal or shady actions and outstanding actions may be relevant. Actions rendering people vulnerable to blackmail or actions leading to a Nobel prize in science may both show whether a person should or should not hold the office. But the evidence relevant to judgments of character often does not satisfy the rules of evidence sufficient to convict. Gossip that suggests that a junior member of a scientific team was the originator of the central ideas that would otherwise lead to a Nobel prize may prevent the lead scientist from getting the prize, but the evidence might not hold up in a patent case relevant to the same piece of knowledge.

V. THE CHARACTERISTIC DEFICIENCIES OF LUSTRATION

To understand the particular problem with the transition from authoritarian regimes to democratic ones, in the light of our analysis of why biographies rather than legal cases are often the best way of remembering the past, we have to analyse what kinds of biographies are created under the old regime, and what we need to know about those biographies under the new regime. Authoritarian governments, rogue states and periods of warfare all are regimes of effectiveness (Stinchcombe 1995). Some of these regimes of effectiveness occur in situations in which overall and ultimate civilian legal control prevails, and where a 'wartime' regime is a temporary and terminable emergency state. As ritual cleansings, lustration trials mark the reassertion of control by civil society and subordination to law. In holding people accountable for their crimes, lustration trials may also make judgments about who should be banned from participation in the governance of the new society. We have argued above that difficult as such assessments are, they are made even more difficult for the problem of turning knowledge of the past into historical memories useful for the new regime when information about a person becomes a case rather than a biography.

Table 1 outlines the general structure of the problem of using information about persons coming out of different kinds of old regimes to assess the predispositions most important for democratic society. The stub of the table describes three kinds of old regimes in which biographies of the immediate past are embedded during periods of transition. In a peaceful transition under a democratic, civilian regime of law, various kinds of assessment of people's character are managed by the rules and bodies of civil (and civilian) society. A reviewable regime of effectiveness is embedded in a larger civilian and non-military political and legal system, as when a democratic society goes to war under a set of guidelines such as the Geneva Conventions, creating and later abolishing special war powers by democratic means. In contrast, in an unbridled regime of effectiveness, institutions of terror are built so as to be non-reviewable by civilian politics or civilian (ie, non-martial) law, there are no institutions built into the declaration of an emergency to bring the regime of effectiveness to an end and international conventions on warfare are not regarded as binding.[13]

---

[13] These categories and dimensions are described in more detail in Stinchcombe 1995 and 1999.

Table 1: Typical Deviance Patterns and Typical Effective Social Control Responses to Them, by Design of the Social Control Situation and Individual Orientations to Rules

Type of Control Regime/ Design of Control Situation	Individual Orientations to Rules			
	Moral outlaw	Moral entrepreneur*	Morally timid	Moral exemplar
Regime of law review mostly by civilian bodies	• common criminal • managed by criminal courts	• cheating, shirking • managed by courts, peer review, publicity, rumour and vigilante justice	• conformity • managed by routine social control	• responsibility, civil disobedience • managed by debate and shows of moral force
Reviewable regime of effectiveness tempered by international conventions or reviewable by military or civilian bodies	• open conflict, terror with martial law • managed by civilian or military courts	• open conflict, terrorism and banditry • managed by civilian or military courts and co-option in regime change	• conformity with martial law, soldiering • managed by new regime routines of social control	• civil disobedience, pacifist protest, exile politics • often persecuted as 'internal enemy' or 'outside agitator'
Unbridled regime of effectiveness war with disregard for international conventions; authoritarian regimes; rogue states	• genocide, random violence, pogroms • managed by lustration, civilian courts and counter-terror	• genocide, organised violence, banditry • managed with great difficulty by new monitoring institutions for police, etc	• retreat from anarchy, apathy, moral confusion, 'banal evil'** • blame hard to assign in lustration	• disobedience, protest, opposition activities, revolutionary Puritanism • managed by civil war

* By 'moral entrepreneur' we mean a person with a disposition to look actively for ways to violate the spirit of the law and to build practices and structures that keep violations secret and unreviewable.

** Cf Arendt 1963/1977.

Along the head of the table we have ranged the types and inherent qualities of character that are relevant to roles in a democratic political system.[14] By a 'moral outlaw' we mean roughly the usual conception of a common criminal, who might commit ordinary crimes during times of peace, loot during a riot or in the first days of occupation of conquered territory and advance his or her career in a totalitarian system by being of service to the regime of terror. In a new regime, the authorities would want to keep track of such potential criminals and punish them for their crimes but would probably not worry too much about them as a constitutional problem.

'Moral entrepreneurs' are those who are willing and able to organise crime on a larger scale and to build deviant institutions that protect their own and others' crimes; Hitler was a moral entrepreneur. Notably, people who are dangerous for their deviant organising capacities, especially for building institutions to make crimes unreviewable, have greater opportunities under either kind of regime of effectiveness, and are especially dangerous to democratic new regimes. It is especially this kind of predisposition that new regimes want to identify and eliminate, but this task is difficult, particularly during the confusion of transitions, when old-regime institutions can be carried into the new regime in order to conceal crimes. The old Soviet 'fixer'-become-Mafioso is the type-case.

The 'morally timid' are those we would not trust with leadership. They commit 'crimes of obedience' (Kelman and Hamilton 1989) and are the sort of people who would have followed the experimenter's orders to administer ever larger electric shocks in the Milgram experiments. Nonetheless, their biographies in an old regime are not very predictive of difficulties to a new regime. Perhaps the veteran home from the war is the type-case: he (or, in rare cases, she) has killed people, perhaps even by the hundreds or thousands by dropping bombs, but easily evolves into a reputable civil servant, occasionally telling war stories in the bar to other middle-aged civil servants. Building a new regime social control system with the expectation that most people will behave themselves most of the time is what is needed to incorporate them into the new regime.[15]

---

[14] Individual orientation to rules is discussed in Heimer and Staffen (1998, especially 6–15), which focuses on the responsible orientation of moral exemplars. Heimer and Staffen do not distinguish 'moral entrepreneurs' from the 'morally timid'; both are instead categorised as shirking or meeting obligations in a perfunctory way, complying with the letter rather than the spirit of the law.

[15] But Cohen notes that Finkielkraut (1992), discussing the Klaus Barbie trial, draws a different conclusion: '[I]t is important to bring to justice such low-level figures, precisely *because* they were so unimportant in the hierarchy. In combating a system that dehumanized humanity, it is vital to restore individual responsibility to each cog in the inhuman machine' (1995, 33, emphasis in original).

Hannah Arendt's (1963/1977) essay on Adolf Eichmann illustrates the core thesis of this chapter. Her subtitle, 'A Report on the Banality of Evil' can be seen, in terms of Table 1, as claiming that Eichmann was essentially a morally timid person who was not particularly dangerous to a democracy—a point supported by his biography in Argentina. The counterargument suggested by Table 1 is that Eichmann's ingenuity in negotiating with ghetto leaders and his ability to get them not to make trouble about selecting members to be sent to 'labour camps', showed a good deal of dangerous moral entrepreneurship. We might expect him, like many of Russia's former KGB officials, to be a sober and industrious builder of effective Mafia organisations, to enforce corruptly negotiated contracts with non-reviewable organs of coercion.

The argument of this chapter can be restated in terms of Table 1 by noting that the actual criminal behaviour in the two regimes of effectiveness is sometimes indistinguishable. Under regimes of effectiveness there may be considerable overlap between the acts of moral outlaws, moral entrepreneurs and the morally timid. These groups are distinguished mainly by normative orientations, so differences in behaviour should be expected to diminish in lawless regimes and to be magnified with increases in the degree to which a society is subject to the rule of law. Indeed, one of the objectives of regimes of effectiveness is to induce the morally timid to comply with the directives of moral entrepreneurs and to disregard their own sense of what is morally right. For a new regime, though, these differences in orientation are crucial, and the problem of the transition is to sort people more accurately according to their orientation to rules.

One solution to the problem of accurately identifying people who should be barred from participation in the new regime is to set up systems of information that get a fairer sample of biographies from the old regime. Another is to collect early information about what happens to those biographies in the new situation, to note that ordinary conformers to the old regime (the morally timid) tend not to become Mafiosos in the new regime, while moral entrepreneurs do. At the two extremes, we expect moral outlaws to continue to disregard the law and expect moral exemplars, who were heroic protesters and members of the underground in the old regime, to become the moral leaders of the new regime, organising political parties and acting as ceremonial leaders of the new state. Nonetheless, for tasks such as the effective administration of river dredging on the Danube, we might prefer reliable and experienced civil servants from among the morally timid, even if in the past they conformed too much to totalitarianism and even if we doubt their moral backbone—as long as we can be confident that the selection procedure accurately uses biographical information to separate the morally timid from the moral entrepreneurs. Such questions about the match between tasks and character can occur at the upper end as well. One might, for instance, worry about the capacity of moral exemplars to negotiate parliamentary majorities. Leave Ghandi to his spinning wheel while Nehru builds a democratic government.

Our arguments in this section can be further illustrated with material from Inga Markovits's diary about the lustration of East Berlin judges and law professors during and after reunification (1995). Markovits studied biographies rather than the cases against East German lawyers. Most East German lawyers had worked for the German Democratic Republic (GDR) government, so were inherently suspect to West Germans. Outside of East Berlin, most East German judges were examined as cases when there was substantial evidence of unsuitability. In contrast, Berlin judges and professors in the Berlin Humboldt University law school and Berlin law research institutes had their biographies examined in a somewhat cursory way by specially created lustration structures, heavily populated by West German lawyers and law professors. In order to retain their positions, these judges and professors had to convince the examiners that they were personally and professionally qualified for their jobs. Elected by the East Germans being reviewed, Markovits herself served on one of these panels. Markovits tried to get deeper into judges' and law professors' conceptions of their work and their relations with the old regime and with the new by conducting extended interviews outside the formal lustration procedures and by observing some of the courts trying cases. Markovits's work illustrates some of the cells of Table 1, and her conclusions show what can be gained by substituting biographical for case analysis.

The subjects of two of her biographies, Judge Peter Peukert (1995, 188–92) and Professor Karl Bönninger (1995, 200–4) were, under both regimes, what we call 'moral exemplars'. They did not live saintly lives but held both East Germans and West Germans to higher standards in their specialties than either group was inclined to adopt for themselves. Peukert had urged that socialist factory managers should be reviewed by outside authorities (judges) for their conformity to East German labour law, and had been expelled from the Party for it. Asked by Markovits whether he considered the new regime to be a rule of law, he 'chooses his words with care, "In comparison to what we had before," he says' (192). Bönninger had left West Germany for the East because of political repression he experienced as a communist in Bonn. But in an infamous meeting in East Berlin in which the First Party Secretary, Walter Ulbricht, laid down the line on the non-reviewability by the courts of administrative action, Bönninger openly debated Ulbricht on the point, drawing on his authority as a former professor of administrative law (which had been officially abolished as a subject of study) (Markovits 1995, 104–10). In discussions with Markovits, he also criticised the West German system for its failure to provide inexpensive channels for review of government administrative action; in his view there should be alternatives to suing the state.

One of Markovits's judges whom we would classify as 'morally timid' characterised her own faults under the old regime: '"That was our mistake," Frau Fischer says, 'not to have looked around [at the corruption and repression that had come to light since the regime change]' (12). Another timid person forgave Erich Honecker, the East German leader, for oppressiveness and rigidity because of his years in the concentration camp: '"He wanted to do the right thing." This is what Frau Dietz wanted to do, too: the right thing … But in this new world, she does not know how to do the right thing any more. She no longer fits in.'(16) In a voice so low that Markovits had difficulty catching her reply, this woman summarised her attitude in the old regime: 'I wanted socialism' (16).

Another person whom we would classify as 'morally timid' was not personally timid at all. Rainer Hannemann (51–7, 156–9) was a contract judge who worked with delivery and cooperation agreements between state firms. Each firm was obliged by the general plan to produce a specified amount. To facilitate the work of the user, details about exactly what, how and when goods would be produced and where they would be delivered might be specified in a contract. Hannemann had developed the judge's role in such contracts into that of an unbiased arbitrator, solving economic problems in an interdependent production and planning process. He disregarded the rigidities of the law in order to solve problems of coordination but did not crusade for modifications in the direction of capitalist-style contract law. Property rights of state agencies were not to be created by agreements among them, as is true in the United States. After unspecified suspicions during the lustration process, perhaps about conversations he had with the Stasi, the decision about his appointment as a civil judge was delayed. Hannemann took a job instead as a manager for a construction firm. Markovits's comment: 'Their suspicion has cost the Senate Administration of Justice a good man' (159).

It is exactly on questions about the extent to which a person's moral sensibility has been shaped by the old regime that the lustration process, employing only case analysis, ran into difficulty. As one woman who had passed the vetting process reported, those administering lustration 'couldn't understand that someone at the same time could both represent the system and despair over its shortcomings' (Markovits 1995, 158–9).

VI. A POTENTIAL APPLICATION OF THE ARGUMENT

Despite our insistence at the beginning that this is a theoretical chapter, we are not actually opposed to using theory to understand particular cases. Let us return to the subject of the South African Truth and Reconciliation Commission and the use of the distinctively biographical concept of 'redemption' for criminals under the old regime and for crimes of revolutionary terror in the African National Congress's campaign for a new government. During the recent transition from apartheid to a multi-racial democracy, many people in South Africa who participated in the old regime have been allowed to participate in the new. Lustration, which continued for some time, was handled largely by the TRC, headed by Archbishop Desmond Tutu.[16] Tutu was careful, however, to be clear about how the Commission's work was defined. Unlike other lustration bodies, this Commission's task was neither to prosecute (a task that remained in the hands of the courts) nor to recommend disqualification or removal from public office, but instead to uncover truth and decide who should receive amnesty.[17] In his introduction to the Commission's Report, Tutu eschewed legal proceedings: 'Because such legal proceedings rely on proof beyond reasonable doubt, the criminal justice system is not the best way to arrive at the truth (1998, ch 1, para 24). And although it was not the Commission's task to decide who was disqualified from holding public office, Tutu suggested that 'political parties and the state should take into consideration the disclosures made in the course of the Commission's work (para 11).

Whether someone received amnesty in South Africa depended less on what acts he or she committed than on fully confessing all relevant acts and expressing remorse for them. These confessions of guilt and remorse were presumably taken by the TRC as information about predispositions. The religious parallels are strong: no one is without sin; acknowledgment of sin and repentance are the first steps to redemption; a past life of sin is no impediment to beginning to lead a virtuous life. It was not clear that everyone agreed with this optimistic assessment of the possibilities for personal reform, however, and it seemed that some particularly heinous and particularly politically charged acts (eg, the killing of Steve Biko) were less likely to be forgiven even if the perpetrators received amnesty.

Key features of this particular political transition made it especially important to incorporate members of the old regime who were politically trustworthy. The quite substantial racial differences in educational levels and expertise in running the affairs of state and the economy could not easily be ignored. Because black and coloured people had effectively been excluded and kept unskilled, new rulers had to be more careful to assess

---

[16] The term 'handled largely' may reflect the symbolic situation, the idea of how crimes of individuals in the old regime should be conceived, rather than what happens to most such criminals. Most crimes in most societies are never officially resolved, and this is more true when the crimes are in the distant past and the evidence undermined by the chaos of transition. Under the old regime in South Africa, as elsewhere, no doubt most crimes were forgotten, punished by gossip or never came to light.

[17] Because he defined lustration narrowly as 'the disqualification or removal from public office of people who have been implicated in violations of human rights' (a more restrictive definition than ours), Tutu in fact said that the Commission 'decided not to recommend that this step be pursued' (1998, ch 1, para 11).

biographical information, both of whites and of leaders of the African liberation movement. As has been noted about reintegration of deviants in other settings (eg, deviant parents in infant intensive care units (Heimer and Staffen 1995) and ex-convicts in Australian penal colonies (Braithwaite 2001)), when a community especially needs the contributions of those judged deviant, it will try harder to reform and reincorporate them.[18] In South Africa the members of the new regime have had a strong interest in rehabilitating members of the old regime and leaders of violent revolutionary action; their talents and experience have been crucial to the new regime.

A similar problem about disqualification arose in Zimbabwe in the period just after independence. There, efficient exporting farmers had been the predominantly white owners of the most fertile land, which the recently ousted colonial regime had gained by conquest. This history of land acquisition inevitably affected what kind of biography under the colonial regime disqualified whites from land tenures.[19] Parallel questions about what qualified people to own land and who could safely be incorporated into the new regime arose after the Civil War in the United States, as mentioned above. But while the land tenure system of Zimbabwe was constructed on one system of oppression (the 'conquest' of land by colonialists), the land tenure system of the United States was built on the double racial oppression of stealing land from Native Americans and distributing it under a racist frontier expansion policy in which slaves were ineligible to own any of this 'frontier' land. Post-Emancipation proposals to put land under the control of 'the common law' addressed the problem that owners and slaves had competing claims to the same land, leaving intact the injustice of treaty violations and land theft. Such are often the problems of urging people to be moral exemplars in a transition regime—preventing or undoing one kind of racial oppression may mean endorsing oppression of another kind.

As the examples of South Africa, Zimbabwe and the United States illustrate, such moral dilemmas are common to transition regimes. Transition regimes cannot undo the historical deposits of the displaced regime, and they typically have to incorporate into the new structure people who would be guilty under the new standards. Their work lies in a realm of moral ambiguity, where difficult choices must be made about how to condemn an evil regime while recognising that some servants of the regime were honestly misguided and others may have experienced a change of heart. Tutu again

---

[18] Although the South African case is extreme, Huyse makes the same argument about postcommunist Eastern European states: 'A far-reaching purge of administrative and managerial manpower can be counterproductive as it endangers the badly needed political and economic development to the country' (1995, 63). He cites comments from Virginia Veltcheva (on Bulgaria), Lech Walesa (on Poland) and Pavel Dostal (on Czechoslovakia).

[19] For a general treatment of post-transition Zimbabwe in the first decade and a half after independence, see Lessing 1992. For a discussion of the much more aggressive post-2000 policy of expropriation of farmland, see Godwin 2007.

spoke to the point: 'Amnesty is not for nice people,' he notes. 'It is intended for perpetrators' (1998, ch 1, para 49). Distinguishing between the system and the citizens, he commented that many 'were not driven by malicious motives ... I do not call their motives into question. I do, however, condemn the policy they applied' (para 56). He recognised some absolutes—'A gross violation is a gross violation, whoever commits and for whatever reason' (para 52)—while simultaneously acknowledging that having the moral high ground matters—'we move in a moral universe where right and wrong and justice and oppression matter' (para 54). While insisting on people's moral responsibility, he also acknowledged system effects: 'the immorality of apartheid has helped to create the climate where moral standards have fallen disastrously' (para 70). This nuanced understanding of how political regimes and moral predispositions work together laid the foundation for the lustration rites that accomplished moral rebirth and incorporation into the new regime.

VII. NEW BIOGRAPHIES VIA RITES OF PASSAGE

To reform and reincorporate members of an old regime, a new regime must produce a biographical transition to ensure dependable behaviour and to certify that those who are being reincorporated have indeed been transformed. To accomplish a ritual rebirth, a rite of transition must first acknowledge crimes, then negate them and ultimately create anew the identity of the moral and loyal citizen and the useful public servant. These were the tasks of the South African TRC. By acknowledging human rights abuses under the old regime in their fullest possible truth and granting amnesty in exchange for testimony and apology, the Commission pursued restorative justice—justice based not on retribution and punishment but on reconciling victim and repentant perpetrator and reincorporating the redeemed into a new and just society.

Arnold Van Gennep's 'processual analysis', outlined in *Rites of Passage* (1965), categorises the rites and sub-rites that transform individuals and their relations to each other. He distinguishes three basic sub-rites—separation, transition and incorporation—used to deal with birth, puberty, marriage and death. In each of these sets of rites of passage, an expected baby, a child, an unmarried person or an elder fades into history as new obligations and rights are given and accepted. Even the dead are assigned a 'virtual role' as ancestors.

The South African TRC established a kind of three-part ritual that can be understood to incorporate each element in Van Gennep's schema. In the first part, applications for amnesty and detailed confessions sought to engender a sense of psychic and judicial closure among victims or their survivors by public acknowledgement—a separation like that which occurs during a funeral rite. The formal and often arduous testimony of many officials functioned like funerals after the real funerals. The testimony created closure by finally giving victims and their family information about what had happened and clarifying the relation of individual incidents to the institutionalised practices of the regime. The Security Forces and the underground police (Vlaakplas) had murdered many, but evidence had been covered up under the Archives Act or destroyed under a 1978 government-wide guideline for disposing of classified documents.

Confession further put confessors in a liminal state of 'potential amnesty', in which the normal rules were temporarily suspended (Turner 1969). Rather than becoming convicted criminals, transgressors became ex-criminals, perhaps ultimately to be treated as members of the new society—as Turner says, creating an 'anti-structure' from structure. Within this liminal space, depraved behaviour could be openly and safely discussed at great length in a transitional rite.

Finally, the TRC created a rite of reincorporation in the granting of amnesty itself. New biographies emerged through convincing pledges of allegiance to the new regime along with its mores, racial order, judicial edicts and political practices. In each phase of the biographical rebirth, it was crucial that each rite of passage—separation, transition and reincorporation—be witnessed and validated by the group. Each applicant was required, Tutu notes, to 'make his admissions in the full glare of publicity' (1998, ch 1, para 35). The rite of passage reaffirmed the political strength of the new regime.

The aim of the biographical rebirth by rite of passage is to reaffirm the norms and ethos of the new regime in the course of formally transforming people from criminals into new citizens. In some of the cases applicants (including members of the Vlaakplas) applied as a group. Their absolution legitimated new norms to replace previous ones, as well as constituting a rite of passage for each member being initiated into the norms of the new regime. The cleansing ritual then was a more merciful version of the Old Testament Flood—rather than sending an Ark to save the innocent few, the TRC adopted a New Testament goal of redeeming the sinners and reforming the society at the same time.

The transgressions of applicants were understood to have occurred within the political and ethical framework of the old regime, a different moral universe from the emergent one. The Commission acknowledged the moral universe of the old regime—Tutu promised that he would 'let an apartheid supporter tell me what he or she sincerely believed moved him or her, what his or her insights and perspectives were; and I will take these seriously into account in making my finding' (1998, ch 1, para 56). But the Commission also insisted on its right to judge people's behaviour by the political and ethical standards of the new regime. Once the Commission granted absolution, old biographies became formally irrelevant and were treated by the Commission (although perhaps not by political parties or the state) as poor predictors of future behaviour under the new regime.

The emergent biographies, in contrast, had to be constructed as good predictors of behaviour under the new regime.[20] Formerly loyal members of the discredited regime were given biographical rebirth within the new regime by updating their interpretations of their own behaviour, acknowledging its wrongfulness and transcending their old biographies by pledging to submit to the new rules. In an embodied example of William Sewell Jr's notion of 'schematic transposability' (1992), each individual in effect denounced his or her antediluvian identity in favour of a biography-in-formation, imposing new regime schemas for understanding moral and ethical behaviour on the previous biography. But institutions to help people build biographies suitable to the new regime may be a central part of making a structural transition work—transitions in people's biographies may fit them to the new institutions.

In contrast, the reunification of East and West Germany involved a 'new' regime that had already been in place in one part of the reunited country. As a result, the pressure to incorporate members of the old regime has been unusually muted. A functioning government, institutions, agencies and economy already existed and only needed to be extended territorially. We might expect to find less need to incorporate biographical material, especially of somewhat problematic ritual conversions to the morality of the new regime, into lustration processes when the institutions of a new regime are already up and running and when they can be adequately staffed by people with unblemished records.

But one of the reasons this easy transition was possible, we argue, is that the routine analysis of biography for predicting reliability in positions of power was already in place in West Germany. Elections with a free press and competitive parties able to smear people with problematic biographies were characteristic of the Bonn government. Civil servants had reputable degrees from venerable law schools, not from Communist party socialisation, and dossiers of reliable performance of public duties after graduation. Civil service qualifications could be modified to fit the new situation by committees, and these committees were not easily dominated by developing mafias of East German servants of the old regime. It was no great sacrifice to use the

---

[20] The question of whether the Commission's rite actually produced non-racist behaviour in the transgressors is, of course, an empirical question rather similar to the question of whether the rite of marriage produces responsible monogamy. We do know that the rate of monogamy is higher for people living together who have gone through the rite of marriage than for unmarried cohabitors (Blumstein and Schwartz 1983; Laumann et al 1994). We have not done the necessary empirical work here to say whether the analogy in fact applies to people amnestied under the TRC process.

lustration procedures in a criminal court manner, even if these procedures did a bad job of assessing whether a border guard's overall character would make him (or her) an adequate civil servant of the reunited government.[21] It was, however, probably a good thing that the lustration institutions died a slow death due to disinterest in whether or not they had got the crimes of the old regime adequately allocated to individual delinquents.

VIII. CONCLUSION

Our overall argument extends Heimer's distinction between two different ways of conceptualising people to the problem of transition regimes and the institutionalisation of the rule of law (2001a and 2001b). Rather paradoxically, we conclude that applying the law may be a bad way to institute the rule of law. That is because the rule of law has to abstract from social life in a way that may destroy useful information about the people of the old regime— the very information out of which key parts of the new regime have to be built. Judging people is one of the most problematic parts of political and social life. Undermining the quality of political judgment regarding whether people qualify for positions of power by turning judgments about people into cases rather than biographies may ignore some information. Such information may be central to the establishment of good government, particularly good government in a democracy. Lustration by human rights standards may hurt more than it heals. Further, the rituals of confession, apology and rebirth, which can reconstitute new biographies for people tainted by the old regime, may establish a public picture of what has to happen to old-regime biographies more generally if the new regime is to succeed.

To put it another way, in addition to punishing offenders, treating actions under the old regime as crimes tends to produce an unproductive and inaccurate public understanding of the differences between the old regime and the new. Public production of ritually transformed biographies, of rites of passage that accomplish the metamorphosis of people suited to the old regime into the same people suited to the new one, is an alternative method of drawing the distinction. We are arguing that these different depictions of the relations of persons to regimes symbolise and encourage different cognitive frameworks for the analysis of persons as guilty versus not guilty in the old regime or alternatively as untrustworthy versus trustworthy in the new.

---

[21] However, Blankenburg (1995) argues that many East German lawyers were inappropriately disqualified for participation in the new regime because West Germans misunderstood the role of law in East Germany. Although the West German legal profession has played a central role in the civil service, the East German legal profession was given a much more peripheral role. Interpretation of biography clearly depends on an understanding of the social context.

Ignoring biographical information is dangerous because politics depends on judgments about whether people have the kind of predispositions that make it safe to entrust them with power. Politics and the symbols of politics have to teach the new predispositions. The information adequate to justify trust is much more open-ended, much more situationally variable, than the information adequate to decide whether someone has committed a crime. A ritual of conviction and punishment does a good job of determining whether a person has committed a crime under the old regime. But it tells us less about how that person will function under the new regime, the situation the present rule of law has been designed to govern. Conviction in a criminal court is therefore probably not a good ritual for assessing trustworthiness in the new regime. For staffing a new regime, we need biographical information from the old regime and from the ritually transformed biography that predicts whether a loyal civil servant of the old regime who was guilty of crimes of obedience in that regime might nevertheless after rebirth as a new citizen now give competent and loyal service to democracy and good government. That is not the same information that is needed to convict. In particular, conviction tends to eliminate that information that measures responsibility to values of democracy, under a regime built to encourage the practical implementation of those values. Information about behaviour under a totalitarian or authoritarian regime may not tell us much about trustworthiness in a democracy, but it is not wise to throw away what information there is in order to build good cases for a criminal court.

REFERENCES

Anspach, Renée R. 1988. Notes on the Sociology of Medical Discourse. *Journal of Health and Social Behavior* 29: 357–75.
——. 1993. *Deciding Who Lives: Fateful Choices in the Intensive-Care Nursery*. Berkeley: University of California Press.
Arendt, Hannah. 1963/1977. *Eichmann in Jerusalem: A Report on the Banality of Evil*. Revised and enlarged edition. Baltimore: Penguin Books. Original publication in *The New Yorker* and in a book published by Viking Press.
Ash, Timothy Garton. 1997. True Confessions. *New York Review of Books*, 17 July, 33–8.
Berat, Lynn and Yossi Shain. 1995. Retribution or Truth-telling in South Africa: Legacies of the Transitional Phase. *Law and Social Inquiry* 20: 163–89.
Berliner, Joseph S. 1957. *Factory and Manager in the USSR*. Cambridge: Harvard University Press.
Bernstein, Lisa. 1996. Merchant Law in a Merchant Court: Rethinking the Code's Search for Immanent Business Norms. *University of Pennsylvania Law Review* 144: 765–821.
Blankenburg, Erhardt. 1995. The Purge of Lawyers after the Breakdown of the East German Communist Regime. *Law and Social Inquiry* 20: 223–43.

Blumstein, Philip and Schwartz, Pepper. 1983. *American Couples: Money, Work, Sex*. New York: William Morrow.

Braithwaite, John. 2001. Crime in a Convict Republic. *Modern Law Review* 64(1): 11–50.

Brandwein, Pamela. 1999. *Reconstructing Reconstruction: The Supreme Court and the Production of Historical Truth*. Durham: Duke University Press.

Clarke, Lee 1999. *Mission Improbable: Using Fantasy Documents to Tame Disaster*. Chicago: University of Chicago Press.

Cohen, Stanley. 1995. State Crimes of Previous Regimes: Knowledge, Accountability, and the Policing of the Past. *Law and Social Inquiry* 20: 7–50.

De Kok, Ingrid. 1998. Cracked Heirlooms: Memory on Exhibition. In *Negotiating the Past: The Making of Memory in South Africa*, edited by S Nuttal and C Coetzee. Cape Town: Oxford University Press.

Derluguian, Georgi M. 2000a. *Grab with All Your Claws! The Mafia Strategies in the Struggles to Capitalize the Former State Socialist Assets: Final Report*. Washington DC: National Council for Eastern Europe and Eurasia Research.

——. 2000b. The Process and Prospects of Soviet Collapse: Bankruptcy, Segmentation, Involution. In *Questioning Geopolitics: Political Projects in a Changing World-System*, edited by GM Derluguian and SL Greer. Westport, CT: Greenwood Press.

Emerson, Robert M. 1969. *Judging Delinquents*. Chicago: Aldine.

——. 1983. Holistic Effects in Social Control Decision-making. *Law and Society Review* 17: 425–55.

——. 1991 Case Processing and Interorganizational Knowledge: Detecting the 'Real' Reasons for Referrals. *Social Problems* 38: 198–212.

——. 1992. Disputes in Public Bureaucracies. *Studies in Law, Politics, and Society* 12: 3–29.

Finkielkraut, Alain. 1992. *Remembering in Vain: The Klaus Barbie Trial and Crimes against Humanity*. New York: Columbia University Press.

van Gennep, Arnold. 1965. *Rites of Passage*. London: Routledge and Kegan Paul.

Gilboy, Janet A. 1991. Deciding Who Gets In: Decision-making by Immigration Inspectors. *Law and Society Review* 25: 571–99.

——. 1992. Penetrability of Administrative Systems: Political 'Casework' and Immigration Inspections. *Law and Society Review* 26: 273–314.

Godwin, Peter. 2007. *When a Crocodile Eats the Sun: A Memoir of Africa*. New York: Little, Brown.

Granick, David. 1960. *The Red Executive: A Study of the Organization Man in Russian Industry*. London: Macmillan.

Handelman, Stephen. 1995. *Comrade Criminal: Russia's New Mafia*. New Haven: Yale University Press.

Heimer, Carol A. 1985. *Reactive Risk and Rational Action: Managing Moral Hazard in Insurance Contracts*. Berkeley: University of California Press.

——. 2001a. Cases and Biographies: An Essay on Routinization and the Nature of Comparison. *Annual Review of Sociology* 27: 47–76.

——. 2001b. Conceiving Children: How Documents Support Case versus Biographical Analyses. In *Documents: Artifacts of Modern Knowledge*, edited by A Riles. Durham: Duke University Press.

Heimer, Carol A and Staffen, Lisa R. 1995. Interdependence and Reintegrative Social Control: Labeling and Reforming 'Inappropriate' Parents in Neonatal Intensive Care Units. *American Sociological Review* 60: 635–54.

——. 1998. *For the Sake of the Children: The Social Organization of Responsibility in the Hospital and the Home.* Chicago: University of Chicago Press.

Holiday, Anthony. 1998. Forgiving and Forgetting: The Truth and Reconciliation Commission. In *Negotiating the Past: The Making of Memory in South Africa,* edited by S Nuttal and C Coetzee. Cape Town: Oxford University Press.

Huyse, Luc. 1995. Justice after Transition: On the Choices Successor Elites Make in Dealing with the Past. *Law and Social Inquiry* 20: 51–78.

Kelman, Herbert C and Hamilton, V Lee. 1989. *Crimes of Obedience: Toward a Social Psychology of Authority and Responsibility.* New Haven: Yale University Press.

Laumann, Edward O; Michael, Robert T; Gagnon, John H; and Michaels, Stuart. 1994. *The Social Organization of Sexuality: Sexual Practices in the United States.* Chicago: University of Chicago Press.

Lempert, Richard and Sanders, Joseph. 1986. *An Invitation to Law and Social Science.* Philadelphia: University of Pennsylvania Press.

Lessing, Doris. 1992. *African Laughter: Four Visits to Zimbabwe.* New York: Harper Collins.

Los, Maria. 1995. Lustration and Truth Claims: Unfinished Revolutions in Central Europe. *Law and Social Inquiry* 20: 117–61.

Lynch, Mona and Haney, Craig. No date. Impelling/Impeding the Momentum toward Death: An Analysis of Attorneys' Final Arguments in California Capital Penalty Phase Trials. Unpublished manuscript. University of California, Irvine.

——. 1997. Clarifying Life and Death Matters: An Analysis of Instructional Comprehension and Penalty Phase Closing Arguments. *Law and Human Behavior* 21(6): 575–595.

Macaulay, Stewart. 1963. Non-contractual Relations in Business: A Preliminary Study. *American Sociological Review* 28: 55–66.

Markovits, Inga. 1995. *Imperfect Justice: An East-West German Diary.* Oxford: Clarendon Press.

Nuttal, Sarah and Coetzee, Carli (eds). 1998. *Negotiating the Past: The Making of Memory in South Africa.* Cape Town: Oxford University Press.

Rosenberg, Harold. 1977. The Shadow of the Furies. *New York Review of Books,* 20 January, 47–8.

Roth, Julius A. 1972. Some Contingencies of the Moral Evaluation and Control of Clientele: The Case of the Hospital Emergency Service. *American Journal of Sociology* 77: 836–49.

von Salomon, Ernst. 1954/1955. *Der Fragebogen (The Questionnaire).* English translation by Constantine FitzGibbon. Garden City, NY: Doubleday.

Sewell, William, Jr. 1992. A Theory of Structure: Duality, Agency, and Transformation. *American Journal of Sociology* 98: 1–29.

Stinchcombe, Arthur L. 1960. The Sociology of Organization and the Theory of the Firm. *Pacific Sociological Review* 3: 75–82.

——. 1995. Lustration as a Problem of the Social Basis of Constitutionalism. *Law and Social Inquiry* 20: 245–73.

——. 1999. Ending Revolutions and Building New Governments. *Annual Review of Political Science* 2: 49–73.

Sudnow, David. 1965. Normal Crimes: Sociological Features of the Penal Code in a Public Defender's Office. *Social Problems* 12: 255–76.

Swigert, Victoria and Farrell, Ronald. 1977. Normal Homicides and the Law. *American Sociological Review* 42: 16–32.

Turner, Victor. 1969. *The Ritual Process: Structure and Anti-Structure*. Ithaca: Cornell University Press.

Truth and Reconciliation Commission. 1998. South Africa Truth and Reconciliation Commission Report, vol 1 of 5. Cape Town.

Uggen, Christopher and Manza, Jeff. 2000. *The Political Consequences of Felon Disfranchisement Laws in the United States*. Paper presented at the annual meeting of the American Sociological Association, Washington, DC, August 2000.

Vaughan, Diane. 1996. *The Challenger Launch Decision: Risky Technology, Culture, and Deviance at NASA*. Chicago: University of Chicago Press.

Waegel, William B. 1981. Case Routinization in Investigative Police Work. *Social Problems* 28: 263–75.

13

Biographies and Résumés as Part of Life under Communist Rule in the Czech Republic

JIŘINA ŠIKLOVÁ

A S AN INTRODUCTION to my chapter on biographies and amnesia in post-communist countries I want to give an account of what happened in the Czech Republic before the Senate elections in August 1999. In the Czech Republic the so-called Lustration Act is still in force. This law provides that a candidate for election must present a certificate that he/she is not on record as a voluntary collaborator with the State Secret Police (StB), the Czechoslovak version of the Russian KGB. In July 1999, a candidate of the Social Democratic Party was accused in the press of being on a list of StB collaborators and of collaborating between 1976 and 1984; he was therefore pressured to resign his candidacy. The candidate denied these accusations and announced that he would sue the journalists. He continued denying his collaboration with the StB in a TV-panel discussion a week before the elections, at a time when the press had just released a facsimile of his agreement with the StB (dated 22 May 1976), which reads:

> By working in collaboration with the bodies of the Ministry of the Interior I want to actively contribute to the elimination of anti-socialist and anti-social manifestations among the young people in the sphere of music, as well as other spheres of our society. In the course of the collaboration I will be serious and objective.

A news commentator stated that the Social Democratic candidate had forgotten that he had personally picked up the first lustration certificate testifying to his collaboration with StB in 1992, and that a second one had been delivered to him in July 1999 (ie, after he had decided to run for Senate). The news commentator said that such a lie and gambling defied reason; he added that the person concerned seemed to want to go on lying in a suicidal manner until the bitter end.

I can explain his behaviour, and I do not consider this unfortunate candidate a liar. He simply and repeatedly forgot about it. Memory is not only 'a storage of information' but a complex system of selection, preservation, recollection and search for information. These processes are structured by both emotions and our instincts of self-preservation. Our memory must be selective in order to protect our personality. From all events that we have experienced, we remember above all those (and in such ways) that help us to adapt to our present conditions of life. The memories that threaten us are thus displaced by others or repressed (Salivarová-Škvorecká 1993). Amnesia is a kind of a defence mechanism that every mentally healthy individual needs. This basically applies to 'social memory' as well, which preserves above all what is somehow beneficial and useful for society—for example, by mechanisms of repetition and selection—while other information is suppressed. However, it can be evoked and revived by other processes.

In August l999, TV programmes repeatedly reminded the Czech population that 30 years ago, in 1969, one year after the occupation of socialist Czechoslovakia by armies of the Warsaw Treaty, people demonstrated in the streets, and there were fights and shooting. The Wenceslas Square in the centre of Warsaw was surrounded by armoured vehicles, there were 146 tanks in the suburbs and helicopters were bringing in members of the People's Militia, a paramilitary organisation of the Communist Party, from various regions. On 23 August 1969, an act called the 'Truncheon Act' by the population was adopted, allowing for brutal measures to disperse demonstrations but also to dissolve political and other organisations such as schools, theaters and editorial boards, and to imprison the organisers with no further justification.

This Act was signed by Alexander Dubcek, a heroic figure among the Czech reformers of 1968, even though at that time he was not the Secretary of the Communist Party of Czechoslovakia anymore, but only the (powerless) Chairman of the National Assembly (Oldrich et al 1996). People watched the 1969 shots and unrest in the streets of Prague on their television screens in 1999, but they simply refused to acknowledge that this brutal Act was signed by Dubcek. Notwithstanding that they saw him in an incriminating black-and-white photograph from 1969 in the television documentary, they nevertheless wrote shocked as well as vulgar letters to the authors of the programme (including me) that this was slander. They wanted to continue to idolise this man, and so they refused to acknowledge the facts; they relied on their memories and denied the facts.'They did not lie, of course. I, too, had been sad when reading that the law adopted in 1969 had also been signed by Dubcek. We had voluntary deceived ourselves, we did not want to know and so we did not take the cruel fact in.

If we do so with the traumatic experiences of our life, psychiatrists and psychologists consider it the right thing to do. In psychoanalysis or psychotherapy, by applying the method of 'life review', we even systematically try to help people to retell their stories with the aim to rewrite it, to reorganize their memories, to assimilate traumatic experiences and to relate them to the present and the future of their lives. If we idealise a close person who has passed away, everyone supports us in doing so. By this process, a patient regains his/her integrity, the fundamental axis of life—'I was, I am and I will be'—and the therapeutic process has a culmination and positive outcome.

If the same happens to the memory of a social entity, a group or nation, or if such mechanisms are adopted by a public official in his/her autobiography, we call it 'fraud'. History wants to be faithful to 'reality' (Courtois et al 1999) and thus requires from individuals almost masochistic confessions and self-accusations (London 1986), notwithstanding that quite a number of individuals seem to subject themselves to such procedures with a kind of pleasure. Examples of such behaviours are procedures of social self-criticism offered to groups, as well as the enforced writing of autobiographies by prisoners during the political trials of the Stalinist regime (Volkskommissariat für Justizwesen der UdSSR 1937).

Writing résumés and curricula vitae or filling in questionnaires were less drastic forms of these 'enforced confessions' but were typical of communist regimes. They had to be submitted by everyone when applying for admission to schools, for employment or for change of employment. Questionnaires were submitted not only by students and intellectuals but by workers and members of the Communist Party as well. Officials had to complete more complicated questionnaires than 'normal people'. The questionnaires were kept at the personnel department of every factory, government agency and school, and they were forwarded to subsequent employers. They were revised every few years, with everyone completing them again. The questions in particular sections changed only slightly, but notably, over the years. Instead of inquiries about collaboration with the Nazis, the questionnaires of the 1960s asked about attitudes toward the Yugoslav Communist leader Josip Broz Tito or the 'events' in Hungary in 1956. During the 1970s, this was changed to 'attitudes toward the Prague Spring of 1968'. Everyone had explicitly to state whether they considered the invasion of the armies of the Warsaw Pact into Czechoslovakia in August 1968 a 'brotherly help to stop counter-revolution in socialist Czechoslovakia' or an 'occupation'.

A process of forgetting was thus embedded in these questionnaires, and it was closely related to a process of forced remembering, by reminding individuals of specific events that were consequently considered crucial, significant moments of their lives, both of individuals and groups, and even national life. From these questionnaires we derived our self-perception and the images of ourselves as individuals, groups or a whole nation. What was substantial and important was suggested to those of us who filled in the questionnaires, and most suggestive of all were the type of biographical account called 'cadre (personal) questionnaires', which were to be completed along with résumés'. The personal questionnaire differed from the résumé common in the West in that the State, represented by the Communist Party, prescribed the questions that all citizens—both Communist Party members and those not in the Party—had to answer. What had to be recalled was thus imposed on individuals, and they duly made 'confessions' and 'reported' on themselves, from childhood to old age. These personal questionnaires had to be repeatedly filled in by millions of people.

I argue that this amounts to a 'rape' of individual memories. The evocation of feelings of guilt, if the individual biography did not fulfill the standards of the model, is a common feature of all totalitarian states: in Fascist Germany, Spain and, of course, all countries belonging to the Communist bloc. I will only discuss the period that I have lived through and have personal experience of. I will do that by analysing the questions from a 1960 questionnaire. This was the time when the period of the 'dictatorship of the proletariat' ended and a 'socialist democracy' was proclaimed; even a socialist constitution was adopted at this time, and the Czechoslovak Republic became the Czechoslovak Socialist Republic, a proper socialist state.

The 1960 cadre questionnaire consisted of six pages, which included different sections and appendices, and consisted of 52 questions. The last question stated, 'Include names and addresses of those who can verify the information in specific sections—next to each name include the section number.' The last instruction said, 'Forward the duly completed questionnaire to the personnel department. Include a detailed résumé of your life and discuss in it all questions from the questionnaire and number the pages. If there is not enough space, include the information in an attachment.' Finally, it had to be dated and signed. It was almost reminiscent of the contract between Mephistopheles and Faust. But people found ways around it—and after all, Faust also avoided the worst.

The questionnaire consisted of three sections: (a) personal information, (b) career development and (c) political development. The personal section consisted of 18 subsections, and, in addition to the usual identification data such as date of birth, ID number and all domiciles and addresses since 1938, it also included inquiries concerning the political affiliation of the individual since 1945, including membership in political parties and if relevant, the manner in which it was terminated. The question concerning membership in 'mass organisations' was an easy one: only the name was needed. One did not have to include the admission date to or date of leaving, for example, the Union of Socialist Women or a physical fitness club.

Subsection 9 of the questionnaire focused on husbands, wives, common-law husbands, common-law wives and children, if they were adults. Though one did not need to fill in the addresses of these persons for the past twenty-two years, one did have to report their employment and political affiliations since 1945, even if they were now deceased. Subsections 10 and 11 required the same information about children, for children by birth as well as for step-children, and for siblings, be they natural or stepbrothers and stepsisters, and again even if they were deceased. Subsection 12 inquired about names, employment and party affiliations of parents, natural as well as step-parents, and including both the parents of the individual and those of his/her spouse. A very small space (about 2.5 cm) was designed for 'own property—family property'. The space was sufficient, as the usual reply was 'no real estate property owned'.

Section B was entitled 'Career Development' and started with education, which also is a normal question in Western countries. However, this had to be supplemented with information about the subject's 'class origin' and 'original profession'. The ideal answer for further career development was 'original profession: worker; currently a university student'. In fact, this question ensured the 'correct' class origin. The subsection on employment included questions concerning wage and level of work. The following questions dealt with political work and offices, professional and political schools and courses that the subject had taken and completed.

One question in Subsection 28 asked, 'What expert literature did you read and when?' but no particular erudition was expected, since only three cm of space was allowed for answering it. In contrast, Subsections 30 and 31 used up almost an entire page of the questionnaire. These inquired about such issues as personal goals in the task of building socialism; participation in socialist work obligations and socialist competitions; if the subject was a Stakhanovite (referring to a famous record worker in the USSR) and if he/she had designed any innovations; the brigades in which the subject had worked on a permanent and temporary basis; how many 'medals' and prizes he/she had been awarded for such work. In Subsection 35 names and addresses of persons had to be given who could confirm professional qualifications and work done in political organisations and offices.

Part C consisted of 17 subsections, which were entirely concerned with what was called 'political development'. It started with the question, 'Are you a member of a political party? State since when; list your responsibilities and offices.' One had to specify membership 'after May 1945' (ie, after the end of World War II), 'after the Victorious February 1948' (ie, after the communist coup d'état) and 'at present'. Subsection 39 inquired about participation in the resistance movement against the Nazis, in particular if the individual had operated from within the country or from abroad. Subjects had to give details on when, where, in what organisation, with whom and in what responsibility/offices they had participated and, again, a list of names for verification of the facts given had to be provided.

Subsections 46, 47 and 48 were compiled in a similar vein and spirit, inquiring about 'membership in associations and respective activities, public offices that had been or were held, membership in national organisations such as The Trade Union Revolutionary Movement, The Czechoslovak Union of Youth, The Union of the Czechoslovak-Soviet Friendship, as well as the Red Cross'. Subsection 49, which inquired about travel abroad and included business trips, was quite extensive. A list of countries visited had to be provided, in addition the dates of entry and departure, which authority had sent the subject and for what purpose. The following Subsection asked, 'Are any of your relatives or friends living abroad?' and went on to inquire about the name of the country, the relationship of that person to the questionnaire subject, place and date of leaving the country, etc. Subsection 51 included inquiries like 'Have you come into contact with a foreigner or fellow-countryman when staying abroad, and what contact do you maintain with such individuals? Questions concerning relatives abroad were particularly detailed. Subjects had to report on their relationship with such individuals, as well as list with whom they corresponded abroad, who visited from abroad and how often. Fortunately, my family had no relatives abroad, so this part of the résumé did not bother me. In the mid-sixties the political regime was so liberal that one did not need to complete this last subsection, and after 1968 my passport was taken away from me, so I did not need to answer similar questions. But everyone who could and was allowed to travel abroad had to fill in such questionnaires. (As always, people found their ways around it and thus escaped intense scrutiny.)

I kept copies of my biographies and often also of completed questionnaires—not for sentimental reasons but in order to know the next time what I had to write about myself and to make no mistake in the years to come. The patterns of the biography and its different parts were prescribed, and there were model life courses to be followed.

I filled in my first questionnaire at the age of fourteen, when I applied for high school. In addition to my grades, I had to write about my 'class origin': my father was a physician, and therefore I completed the section 'class origin' with 'working intelligentsia'. In the more detailed biography I stated that my father came from a poor family background, that he lost his father when he was six and that my grandmother made a living as a laundress in wealthy households for many years. I did not mention the fact that they used to have a butcher's shop (which later went bankrupt anyway). Small businessmen, even if they had perished nearly half a century earlier, were always suspicious under communist rule because they had the potential to develop into capitalists. Already at the age of fourteen I knew how to stylise myself, and others knew it as well.

The content of personal questionnaires that we completed during the following decades changed according to the political events considered important at the time. Instructions for their completion, however, were always the same. They read: 'The personal questionnaire must be completed in all sections with words, no data may be crossed out.' Consequently, the versions of the questionnaires changed, and a couple of years later the sections on political opinions, evaluation of events and attitudes could be quite different. Both the phrasing of the questions indicated the change as well as what was expected as proper answers: the subject's evaluation of 'Josip Broz Tito and his gang'; 'your opinion on Zionist traitors around Rudolf Slánský' (see

Siklova 1999a); evaluation of 'events in Hungary in October 1956'; and later, for example, the subject's opinion on the erection of the Berlin Wall in 1961, the Cuba Crisis, the war over the Suez Canal and so on. After 1968, some questions disappeared. Tito was not important any more, Czech fascists were mostly retired and now the questionnaires primarily focused on issues of approval or disapproval of the 'Declaration of 2000 Words' and the 'brotherly help supplied by the armies of the Warsaw Treaty against the counter-revolution in the Czechoslovak Socialist Republic in 1968', as well as opinions about what could be learned from the so-called 'Lesson from the Prague Spring'.

The wording of the questions unequivocally 'prescribed' the correct answers. One could of course, either give one's actual opinion and thus denounce oneself, or refuse to complete the questionnaire properly and then fail to meet the requirements for being employed or enrolled in a school. Consequently, the simplest solution was to answer as expected, along the line the Party presently prescribed. However, this implied that one signed a kind of declaration of approval of or conformity with the regime. Only today do I realise that these forms made us all subject to a permanent police interrogation, which was nonetheless legitimate according to legislation at that time. Accordingly, the accuracy of completed questionnaires and résumés was sometimes checked. Usually a member of the District Committee of the Communist Party of Czechoslovakia showed up at a workplace or the Special Task Department and investigated whether a grandfather had really been a member of the factory organisation of the Communist Party or not, and if he had actually fought at Buzuluk (where the Czechoslovak Legions in the USSR were founded). This confirmed the conviction in the population that it was necessary to answer personal questionnaires honestly. This procedure and how it was done was unanimously considered as perfectly normal, as something that one had to oblige to. Sometimes people evaded it, sometimes not all facts were stated, sometimes they were a little bit distorted, but no one ever questioned and protested against it, not even writers. I think that this was its worst and most destructive consequence.

We simply responded to what we were asked. For example, after 1968 we had to make a list of all our articles and publications that had been published in the 'years of the crisis of 1968–1969', and all teachers of Charles University, including me, did it. Without this general obedience, the authorities would never have been capable of justifying the dismissal of three quarters of a million of people from their work because of what was called 'political unreliability'. They would not have had sufficient facts and evidence, and this was the way in which we ourselves supplied them with the necessary facts.

I used to have a great 'dream of a sociologist'. One day, when 'we shall overcome ...', I would conduct a qualitative and quantitative analysis of these personal questionnaires in order to find out how totalitarian states deformed people and how ordinary people (including myself) allowed themselves—more or less voluntarily—to be controlled through these legally required biographies. They had been part of every job application (the State was the only employer), every application for a trip abroad, as well as for enrolment in schools, for places in better nursing homes for pensioners or for higher pensions. I envisioned that such research could explore historical transformations of socialist regimes and that the findings would show what was important for or threatened the Party and the government in different periods. This dream never could come true: the questionnaires were destroyed by the same people who filled them in. They do not exist any more.

As early as in December 1989 people virtually attacked personnel departments in their workplaces, demanding that their personal questionnaires be immediately returned to them. They victoriously took hold of them and burned them in the factory and office yards; the destruction of the questionnaires was a proof of freedom for them. There was no chance to blackmail them any more! (This of course was a naive idea in the age of photocopying machines, microfiches, scanners and computers.) Officials from the Special Task Departments were eager to hand their questionnaires and résumés back to the people. They thereby got rid of any evidence against themselves and the Secret Police. However, it was clear that confessions that were still of interest had been copied (Vachalovsky and Bok 2000). When preparing for this chapter, I asked my friends to lend me copies or originals of the questionnaires and résumés that they had submitted to the authorities. Almost no one had kept them. When I showed the series of my questionnaires and résumés to them, many claimed that they did not even remember them; others maintained that they did not have to fill them in at their factories, which could not be true because the respective law had been in force in the entire country. Others claimed that they did not remember what they had filled in.

I strongly believe that they did not remember. Their memory 'failed' them because they did not wish to know and they wanted to forget about it. They could not answer my question 'How did you evaluate the Hungarian events of 1956?' Some had even forgotten what happened in that year and did not understand why I asked them about it.

I will now explore some explanations for this obvious erosion and failure of memory. The authorities (the Communist establishment) had marked certain events and activities (such as owning foreign currencies, a house, being of noble rank, having stayed abroad or contacted foreigners) as improper and undesirable. The overwhelming majority of the population did not agree and did not consider such behaviour as wrong. But they answered these questions in such a manner or they stylized themselves in such a way that they could pass the 'test', that they could be successful with their applications and that they as a result could make their lives more comfortable and enjoyable. The authorities must have been aware of the games played, while the population accepted the pressure as well as the 'pseudo game'. Nonetheless, if they did not disclose particular information or lied (for instance, I used to 'forget' to mention that my father had been a member of the Social Democratic Party, which had been banned in 1948), it often evoked feelings of guilt, as if one had done something wrong by denying that the family had possessed an apartment house. Where these false statements were detected and were prosecuted and punished, it was often accepted as justified.

Thus our individual as well as collective (or national) memories were instrumentalised by the authorities and those in power for evoking feelings of guilt, and thus as a means of controlling the population. Hence it is easy to understand why people forgot about this whole business. It is a vital mechanism of psychological defence, for which I cannot blame them. I can understand, because this is the way they preserve their mental health, their identity and equanimity.

During the period of 'normalisation' between 1968 and 1989, the population was controlled not by brutal force as during Stalinism in the 1950s, but above all by 'words'—and often these were words written by themselves. Therefore it was believed that liberation could also happen through words. Marxist-Leninism teaches that everyone is determined by his/her class origin, in other words, his/her past. Therefore, history played an important part in dissident activities. People went to prison for translating George Orwell and Andrei Amalrik, for owning or borrowing books by Yevgeny Zamyatin, Isaac Deutscher, Milovan Djilas and Leon Trotsky. Likewise, if people are not affiliated to a religion, they try to reach beyond their own existence by relating to history; it matters to them how they will be judged by later generations. A Czech historian, who later emigrated to France, was virtually tortured in prison, threatened by the possibility that statements falsified by his investigators would be published as his own.

Consequently, there are numerous demands for stopping the work of the Institute for Investigating Crimes of Communism (an authority that is similar to the Commissioner for the files of the Ministry of State Security of the former GDR ('Gauck-Behörde')) and abolishing the so-called Lustration Act. Even without any censorship, all of us have slowly but inevitably created new 'blank spaces' in our individual memories as well as in our history and collective memory.

There is no legal base for the prosecution and/or conviction of most of the top officials from the Communist Party. Nearly everything they did was 'legal' in terms of existing laws and even confirmed by the decisions of the National Assembly (including the signature of the unfortunate Dubcek), so there is nothing left but moral condemnation. For those with a moral sense, this becomes a kind of punishment, and for the more cynical ones, it is a ridiculous spectacle. The Christian Democratic Union-Czech People's Party

(KDU-ČSL) proposed in 1999 to establish public tribunals for 'making public who is to blame for crimes of Communism'. The Vice-Premier, lawyer and former dissident Pavel Rychetský, pointed out as a matter of fact that there as not a sufficient number of citizens who could sit on these tribunals who were not themselves to be blamed for such acts during any of the stages of the 'development of socialism'. At the same time, this made the population aware that unpunished evil weakens the rule of law and that while history cannot be redone, we must nonetheless come to terms with it.

The writer, post-war Communist poet, dissident and, later, emigrant, Pavel Kohout recently wrote an article entitled 'Blue Shirt, Red Heart' in which he contemplated that Germans of his age, undisturbed, publicly showed photographs taken of themselves in black uniforms and with caps which carry the sign of a death's-head (the uniform of the SS).[1] 'This was in our youth', they say sprightly. Kohout asks why we approach our own past differently. In the Czech Republic, photographs of members of the Communist Party Youth Organization in blue shirts (who did not wage war but merely built dams or railroads for the sake of peace) are not yet even shown in public. A snapshot of a politician in an indecent situation will hurt his/her career ten times less than a publication of a photograph that shows him/her embracing Nikita Khrushchev or Leonid Brezhnev, or standing on a platform at the side of Klement Gottwald (Siklova 1999b) with a l flag in his/her hand. Kohout's rhetorical question touches on the fact that Fascism in Germany was defeated, while communist states in Eastern Europe just disintegrated because of their inability to exist any longer. There are no real winners, and we continue to be captives of our own past (Šiklová 1999b).

After the 1989 coup, I returned to Charles University after a 20-year break and began to lecture. Students who wanted to enroll again submitted their biographies with their applications. Their biographies were simply an inversion of what had been required before 1989. I could now frequently read the following statements: 'I am of bourgeois origin; my parents owned a factory that was nationalised by the Communists without any compensation. We had to move from Prague to the border area. My father and my mother never were members of the Communist Party, and they never held any political positions ...' This was in some way hilarious but nonetheless quite typical. For several years I kept explaining to those who wanted to enroll as students that their class origins would no longer be examined and that no one was interested in the party affiliation of their parents. They have stopped writing this sort of thing, now imitating résumé patterns that are required by foreign, especially American,

---

[1] Kohout is wrong here insofar as it has been a criminal offence in the Federal Republic of Germany since its foundation in 1949 to possess, trade in or display in public any insignia of Nazi organisations. However, possessing and showing such private photographs in private was not prohibited.

companies in the Czech Republic. Perhaps there is a sociologist out there who has a dream similar to mine.

The Czechs, as people generally tend to be still fascinated by the legalised evil of the past. We tend to believe more in what the Secret Police recorded about individuals than in what they wrote about themselves under pressure—sometimes believing the police records even more than our own personal accounts about them. Books published on this topic have become bestsellers. The remarkable political scientist, dissident and advisor to President Václav Havel, Milan Šimecka, wrote in an essay dated 16 November 1988 (published after 1989 as a book entitled *The End of Immobility*):

> I am dreading how in the course of a democratic revolution we will have to clean up after ourselves, which moral knots we will have to untangle, who is to blame, whom to forgive, who will repent and who will take revenge. A moral trauma will be trailing after all people of over forty years of age until their death (1990, 84).

CONCLUSION

Memory, whether that of an individual, a group or a nation, is selective and defensive in nature. Forgetting and distorting facts in a similar way as we do with our recollections of parents, family or partners helps to create the desired and a better self-image for individuals or collectivities, both of which enable human beings or a groups to survive traumatic experiences. In all societies, dominating ideology makes use of these mechanisms in more or less conscious or unconscious ways. However, only the totalitarian regimes of the twentieth century—including Fascist regimes but above all the Soviet-socialist regimes—introduced systems of compulsory and regular submission of personal questionnaires, thus systematically influencing the memory of individuals as well as of a people. Many of the sections of the questionnaires were designed to elicit the applicants' opinions on current political situations. The résumés that were submitted with applications for employment or school enrolment were written and stylised in a similar manner. I have described these sections of questionnaires and in particular the changes to which their contents were subjected. Most of the questions concerning attitudes toward and evaluations of particular events forced applicants to adopt attitudes toward events they often had no idea of at all. Consequently, the memories of individuals were deliberately shaped, and they were 'raped' of their proper memories by demands from the political regime. This has enormous impact on the self-images and self-evaluations of individuals and groups.

The questionnaires and résumés, or 'personal materials', were kept in the archives of the personnel departments of factories, schools and many other institutions. Refusal to submit them and submission of false information were offences and liable to prosecution. As a result, people voluntarily and deliberately submitted an abundance of information about themselves that the regime would otherwise have obtained only with utmost difficulties. For all those who made such submissions, this was therefore an indirect way of participating in the repressive regime and thus is now a source of feelings of guilt and blaming others. Apart from a few exceptions, the populations of post-communist countries differ from each other only by the degree of their complicity in the functioning and maintenance of the former regimes. These regimes were not defeated, but they collapsed. However, by destroying their personal questionnaires and résumés people did not liberate themselves from their own past.

REFERENCES

Courtois, Stephane; Werth, Nicolas; Panne, Jean-Louis; Paczkowski, Andrzej; Bartošek, Karel; and Margolin, Jean-Louis. 1999. *Èerná kniha komunismu: Zloèiny, teror, represe.* Prague: Paseka Litomyšl.

London, Arthur. 1968. *L'Aveu—Dans L'engrenage du proces de Prague par Arthur London.* Paris: Collection Temoins Gaallimard, Gallimard.

Mlynárik, Ján. 1999. *Ruzyòské meditace.* Prague: IPEL.

Oldrich, Tùma; Jaros, O; Koudelka, F; and Noskova, A. 1996. *Srpen '69—Edice dokumentù.* Prague: ÙSD-Maxdorf.

Salivarová, Škvorecká (ed). 1993. *Osoèení—Dopisy lidí ze seznamu Stb.* Toronto: Sixty Eight Publishers.

Šiklová, Jiřina. 1999a. Lustration or the Czech Way of Screening. In *The Rule of Law after Communism: Problems and Prospects in East-Central Europe*, edited by M Krygier and A Czarnota. Ashgate: Dartmouth.

——. 1999b. Zmìny byly pøíliš rychlé. *Lidové Noviny,* 17 November.

Šimeèka, Milan.1990. *Konec nehybnosti.* Prague: Nakladatelství Lidových Novin.

Vachalovsky, P and Bok, John. 2000. *Kato—Projev poslance Jana Kavana na 14. spoleèné schùzi Snìmovny lidu a Snìmovny národù 22. 3. 1991.* Prague: JW Hill.

Volskommisasariat für Justizwesen der UdSSR. 1937. *Prozessbericht über die Strafsache des Sowjetfeindlichen Trotzkistischen Zentrums verhandelt.* Moscow.

14

The 'Stasi Records', the Public, and Collective Memories: The Inspection of Personal Records

ROGER ENGELMANN[1]

THE STATE SECURITY Service of the German Democratic Republic (GDR) (the 'Stasi'), like all such intelligence services in communist countries, took on both domestic and foreign tasks. It combined the roles of intelligence service and secret police and in addition acted as an agency of criminal prosecution. In fact, it could exercise powers similar to those of the public prosecutors. It was an organisation of enormous scale: 91,000 full-time employees (Gieseke 1996, 44) worked in three territorial levels. Its huge apparatus included the Berlin Headquarters, 15 Regional Administrative Offices and more than 200 District Offices. In addition, the agency (in 1989) employed 174,000 unofficial informants. Based on what is known about the growth and fluctuation rate, their numbers can be estimated at more than half a million for the entire period from 1950 to 1989 (ending with the dissolution of the Ministry of State Security (Ministerium für Staatssicherheit, MfS)) (Müller-Enbergs 1996, 7).

Within the framework of its encompassing mandate to protect the Communist Party's rule, the Stasi was assigned a broad range of tasks. These targeted not only large segments of the GDR population but in addition both West Germans and foreigners. It is extremely difficult to estimate how many individuals were affected by the various activities of the Stasi during the 40 years of communist rule in the GDR. Without underestimating, it can be assumed that they numbered several million—a significant proportion of the GDR population. One indicator for the extent of the Stasi's surveillance activities is the size of the still-existing central card file on individuals, which was collected by the MfS and includes information on six million individuals (among them about one million West Germans).

---

[1] Translation from German by Mary Forszt.

The degree to which individuals were affected varies considerably. Activities ranged from routine security checks, attempts at recruitment and various types of police surveillance, to conviction and imprisonment by the courts that abjudicated socalled political crimes and, operated within the gravitational field and under the influence of the State Security Service. Accordingly, the personal files of the MfS vary both in volume and in nature. They include records with only a few pages, which are of limited use for evidence of surveillance, up to files containing a three-digit number of volumes (!) and nearly complete biographical documentation of large segments of individuals' lives. The variety of categories of files is considerable (Engelmann 1994), with the most important among them being:

— Files concerning unofficial informants or unsuccessful attempts at recruitment;
— Surveillance files—so-called 'Operational Controls' and 'Operational Procedures'—which often include proof of undercover interference into the life of the individuals affected. Such activities include removing the individuals from their positions and 'Zersetzungsmaßnahmen' (conspiratorial measures designed to demoralise individuals and thus prevent them from participating in activities that could harm the State and the Party);
— So-called 'Investigational Procedures', which were collections of all files related to a criminal matter that was investigated by the State Security Service, including files of the prosecution, court records and files concerning the execution of sentences.

After its fall and dissolution, the MfS left behind nearly 180 kilometres of records. This corresponds approximately to the number of records collected by the Federal Archives in West Germany before reunification covering the period from Bismarck's founding of the German Reich in 1871 to the 1980s. This vast amount of Stasi records consists mainly of files concerning individuals.

The entire range of Stasi activities became visible only after 1989, yet their massive presence in GDR society had long been felt, notwithstanding their largely secret and conspiratorial nature. In a survey conducted in 1992, 44 per cent of former GDR citizens stated that they or persons from their immediate social networks had had some kind of experience with the Stasi (Karstedt 1996, 91). In 1993–1994, a study of individuals who had applied to the Federal Commission for the Stasi Records to inspect their files showed that 83 per cent had been aware that they were under surveillance (Doll and Damitz 1998b, 70). Already during the lifetime of the GDR a belief that at that time was more of a myth had spread that the State Security Service was omnipresent and omnipotent, which as it turned out had a strong foundation in facts. These perceptions certainly play a considerable role in motivating citizens to exercise their rights to inspect their personal records.

As a result of these perceptions, stripping the State Security Service of its power became a core element of the revolutionary events of autumn and winter 1989/1990. The population as well as representatives at the 'Round Table' considered the Stasi the principal instrument through which the Socialist Unity Party (*Sozialistische Einheitspartei Deutschlands*, SED) had ruled. Slogans that centered on the Stasi played an important role during the first major demonstrations, eg, 'Send the Stasi to the production line' ('Stasi in die Produktion') or 'Legal security is the best State Security'. Finally, during the occupation of various regional Stasi offices by enraged citizens in December 1989, the 'Stasi question' moved to the centre of political discussions and revolutionary events. Dismantling the apparatus of the Stasi completely and without any form of replacement, as well as safeguarding its records, became a principal matter of concern to the Citizens' Movement. The Citizens' Committees that kept watching this process in the offices of the former State Security were, so to speak, the revolutionary core groups of what later became the federal authority in charge of the administration of the files. Thus, the Federal Commission for the Stasi Records can be conceived of as an institution with revolutionary roots—a quite unique phenomenon in German history.

It was, however, still a long time until individuals could finally inspect their files as provided by the Stasi Records Act of December 1991. It should be emphasised that a law had already been passed in 1990 by the (first freely elected) Volkskammer (the parliament of the GDR) in the then still existing GDR; this earlier law anticipated the subsequent law of the Federal Parliament to a large extent. The Citizens' Committee had had a defining influence in drafting the law and the legislation. Most of the definitions and restrictions of how the records could be used that were included in the final Stasi Records Act were already provided for in the law passed by the Volkskammer. In addition to the general right of those who had been subjects of files or were affected by their contents ('Betroffene') to obtain the recorded information, the law also provided for the investigation of officials and functionaries to determine previous involvement in Stasi activities ('lustration', purge). In addition the law included provisions for criminal prosecution and scientific research.

West German politicians initially refused to incorporate the Volkskammer law into the Treaty of Reunification. After a storm of protest in the GDR and a hunger strike by prominent civil rights activists in the former Stasi headquarters in Berlin, a last-minute agreement was reached and incorporated as a supplement into the Unification Treaty. This agreement expressed the expectation that the parliament of unified Germany should start deliberations 'without delay' on corresponding legal provisions that should 'comprehensively take the Volkskammer law into account' (Schumann

1995, 24). Actually, the later Stasi Records Act, which was based on both the demands of East German civil rights activists and West German principles of data protection, in many ways exceeded the original provisions of the Volkskammer law. The final law aimed at accommodating the widely felt need of GDR citizens to expose Stasi machinations in public and private life in accordance with data protection aims. This in particular concerned the principle of control of one's personal data, which had been developed in the Federal Republic during the 1980s. This resulted in a law which gave precedence over all other (conflicting) interests to the rights of individuals to obtain access to their files and knowledge about all information that had been collected about them. This opened the route for citizens to apply for inspection of their own files.

Opening up the Stasi files to inspection should have an enormours impact on individual as well as collective memories. My study focuses on requests for and actual inspections of personal files by citizens. Though individual experiences (including the reappraisal of one's own records) are extremely important in the process of developing collective memories, the role of the media in providing information and making value judgements cannot be overstated, and they possibly have a decisive role for both segments of the population—those who are directly affected and those who are not.

Since 1992, attitudes towards coming to terms with the past ('Vergangenheitsbewältigung') have become increasingly polarised among the population of the former East Germany (Karstedt 1996, 93–4). Those who apply to the Federal Commissioner to inspect their personal files presumably belong to that part of the population that considers the reappraisal of the past both right and important.

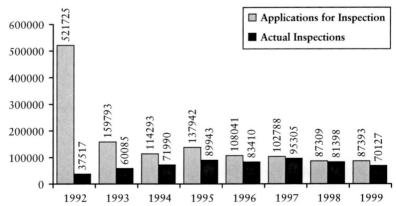

Source: Bundesbeauftrager für die Unterlagen des Staatssicherheitsdienstes der ehemaligen Deutschen Demokratischen Republik (BStU). 1999.

Figure 1: Inspection of Stasi Files by Private Individuals

Figure 1 above shows the number of applications made to the Federal Commission for inspection of personal Stasi files, and contrasts these with the number of actual inspections made from 1992 to 1999. As expected, individual applications reached peak levels immediately after the opening up of files in 1992. They dropped to less than one third (30.6 per cent) of that initial figure in 1993 and again by 28.5 per cent in 1994. In 1995 the level increased again by 20.7 per cent, then dropped again slowly, while still remaining surprisingly high. Eight years after the files had been opened up, interest in inspecting personal files remained steady. Notably, applications reach short-term peak levels whenever a public debate about closing the files or granting an amnesty flares up (BStU 1999, 10).

There is no need to discuss the actual individual inspections of files; the variations in the numbers are primarily caused by technical and bureaucratic restrictions. It should be emphasised that by the end of 1999 nearly 600,000 persons had read their personal files. All applications from the period from 1992 to 1996 and in addition incoming urgent cases (due to age, illness, rehabilitation, etc) had been processed by then. The difference between the number of applications filed and the number of actual inspections of records is due to the fact that records actually exist for only about half of the applicants. Amongst the various reasons for this is the fact that records were destroyed during the days of radical change, and smaller bundles of papers related to individuals are still to be found among the files collected around particular topics; these have only been partially processed and registered. For the majority of the applicants for whom no files can be found, however, it is reasonable to assume that none ever existed, a fact that certainly needs some further explanation.

First, there is sufficient evidence that a number of applicants filed requests without any substantial basis for their suspicions of being under surveillance by the Stasi. 21 per cent of the applicants who were interviewed by the Federal Commission for the Stasi Records in 1998 reported that they had filed a request 'out of pure curiosity as to whether the Stasi had gathered information about me' (Bundesbeauftrager für die Unterlagen des Sta atssicherheitsdienstes der ehemaligen Deutschen Demokratischen Republik (BStU). 1999). Other applicants have tended to make the Stasi responsible for experiences of discrimination and repression by other bodies (the SED, the Free German Youth organisation (*Freie Deutsche Jugend*, FDJ), schools or workplaces, etc). Both the myth of the omnipotence and omnipresence of the secret police, and the resulting tendency to overemphasise the role of the Stasi in public discussions and reappraisals of the past since 1990 seem to have decisive roles.

How did those who got access to their personal files experience it? What was the impact on their lives? To answer these questions, I will present results from two surveys. The first one, which was mentioned above, was conducted in 1993–1994 by social psychologists Jörg Doll and Marc Damitz (1998a). It included 230 subjects who had inspected their records at the Federal Commission for the Stasi Records and had voluntarily and anonymously completed questionnaires that were available in the reading rooms of the Commission (a total of 1000 copies). Since sampling was not done by randomising but by self-selection, it can be assumed that only particularly motivated individuals completed the questionnaires, and the results presented here are not representative of all those who inspected their files. This equally concerns three surveys that the Federal Commission itself carried out at the end of 1998, which had a quite satisfactory response rate. Three random samples of 300 subjects were selected from the following groups: (a) individuals who had yet to inspect their files; (b) individuals who had asked for the decoding of code names in their files; and (c) individuals who had applied for inspection of their files in 1998. In the first group, the response rate was 47.7 per cent (143 completed questionnaires), in the second 50.3 per cent (151) and in the third 71 per cent (214). Each group received a specifically tailored questionnaire.[2] The results presented in this chapter include data from all three surveys.

The study by Doll and Damitz clearly shows that the participants in the survey belong to a group that was disproportionately affected by the activities of the MfS. The subjects were on average confronted with three volumes of files and four different unofficial informants who had reported on them. The most frequently reported reasons for surveillance and persecution by the Stasi were: critical remarks about the political and economic system of the GDR (70.9 per cent); contact with someone in West Germany or other Western countries (66.8 per cent); a desire to leave the GDR (50.2 per cent); support for others who wished to leave (23.8 per cent); and active involvement in church activities (19.7 per cent). Doll and Damitz therefore concluded that those individuals took part in their study who 'due to their critical attitudes towards the GDR and oppositional activities ... had been scrutinised, stigmatised and persecuted by the State Security during unusually long periods of time (an average of 9 years)' (1998a, 75 translated). Consequently, it is not surprising that Doll and Damitz identified 'planned problem-solving' as the predominant coping strategy among their sample. This coping strategy of individuals who inspected their files reflected two motives: first, that the inspection of their files would help them to know more than the general public about Stasi machinations; and second, that confirmation of their own suspicions would strengthen their position and evaluation of Stasi activities in discussion with others (Doll and Damitz, 1998a, 72–3).

---

[2] Preliminary results of the surveys were published in the Federal Commissioner's Report of 1999: BStU 1999, 10–25.

Doll and Damitz point out that dealing with the betrayal by unofficial informants, who mostly came from their social networks, is of utmost importance for readers of files. Figure 2 shows that this group expressed strong negative feelings toward their 'most important unofficial informant' and attributed to them a high degree of responsibility for the harm done (251–3). The mechanisms of coping with these facts and the reactions toward their 'most important unofficial informant' mirror these feelings: 61 per cent wanted to have nothing more to do with the informant; 57 per cent wanted to make the informant's activities public; 32 per cent wanted to force the informant to admit guilt; and 15 per cent wanted to take court action against the informant. In fact this last intention has been realised by only a very small number of those reading their files, mainly because the activities of informants can be prosecuted only in the very rare case that a criminal offence was involved. Only a minority of the study participants, 15 per cent, report that they had begun to forgive the informant (253–4).

Results from the survey of applicants who requested the decoding of code names (data from second BStU survey 1998) reveal similar reactions among file readers, although they add further detail about how people dealt with the discovery of their informants: 41.1 per cent of them reported that they had dealt with the situation themselves and not contacted the informant; 31.1 per cent had contacted informants; and 24.5 per cent had told others about their discoveries or otherwise made them public. Of those who had personally contacted one or more informants, 49 per cent reported that the conversation had not led to an acceptable result. However, 35.3 per cent of

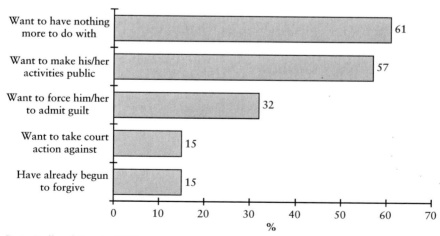

Data: Doll and Damitz 1998a.

Figure 2: Attitudes of Readers of Files towards Their 'Most Important Unofficial Informant' (1993–1994)

those who had contacted their informants reported a more positive experience, whilst 5.9 per cent found the contact and discussion with their informant partially acceptable. 3.9 per cent had 'not yet' had such a conversation despite they had contacted them. 53.6 per cent of the respondents reported no further contacts with their informants, and 15.9 per cent reported that the informants were no longer part of their present social networks. However, 21.2 per cent still had contact with (some of) the former informants.

The fear of having been betrayed by unofficial informants within one's own social environment was a strong motivation for people to request a file inspection. Figure 3 shows the responses given to the question 'What was your primary motive in requesting a file inspection?' (first BStU survey 1998). 21 per cent of the survey subjects reported being motivated by curiosity regarding whether or not there were surveillance files on them, and another 21 per cent wanted certainty as to whether an unofficial informant had reported on them and if so, who she/he was. Only a very small group reported their primary reason for inspection as 'no longer wanting to suspect good friends and acquaintances' (1 per cent, not in Figure 3). In contrast, by far the largest group of respondents (36 per cent) named personal experiences and/or events involving family, friends, acquaintances or colleagues as reasons for requesting a file inspection. A considerably large group (13 per cent) requested file inspection because they had been imprisoned and/or had attempted to be rehabilitated, as eg, in cases involving criminal prosecution, dismissal from work etc. 4 per cent of the file readers had themselves been accused of cooperating with the Stasi or wanted to read the file on their own activities as informants.

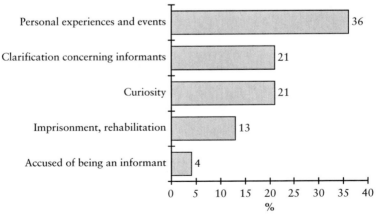

Data: BStU 1999.
* Not represented in Figure 3 are 5% 'other reasons', including those no longer wanting to suspect good friends and acquaintances (1%).

Figure 3: Reasons for Inspecting Stasi Files*

After having inspected their files, 70.6 per cent of the applicants in this study requested copies of their files. 42.6 per cent of this group used the copies exclusively to reread their files, sometimes more than once. Only 1 per cent destroyed the copies after reading, the remainder stating that they had saved the copies. 39.6 per cent had made or intended to make the copies available to others, especially to relatives and acquaintances. 9.9 per cent used the copies for work-related legal purposes or for rehabilitation. 4.9 per cent used the copies to speak with previous informants.

Figure 4 shows responses to the question, 'What has inspecting your file meant to you personally?' 27 per cent responded in ways that can be summarised as 'bringing the past to a conclusion' or 'gaining a perspective of the past' or can be described as obtaining some 'satisfaction' or 'relief'. 25 per cent stated that they had gained clarification about a particular chapter of their lives. 20 per cent found that reading their files contributed to their negative evaluation of the former GDR and/or bolstered their satisfaction with the radical political changes of 1989/1990. For a minority (8 per cent), reading their files turned out not to be as important as they had initially thought, while 4 per cent stated they had drawn personal consequences and taken action after reading their files, mainly against previous informants from their closest networks. A small group (3 per cent) mainly felt disappointed or sad after reading the files, and 1 per cent went away with a critical stance toward any form of state intervention in private life.

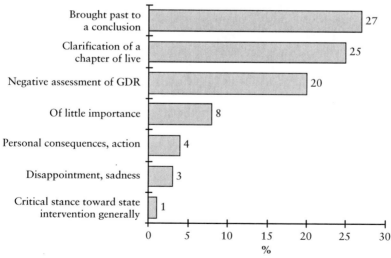

Data: BStU 1999.

* The chart does not include 12% who did not know or gave other answers.

Figure 4: The Personal Significance of Inspecting Stasi Files
Survey question: *What has inspecting your file meant to you personally?**

What conclusions about the impact of opening up Stasi files on individual and collective memories can be drawn from these data? With regard to individual memory, reading the files provides a chance for those affected to 'make sense' of their lived experiences and their own recollections, to arrive at a reappraisal of past experience and to shed a new light on many events in their lives. Sometimes specific aspects and parts of individual biographies are for the first time revealed: conspiratorial and demoralising machinations that might have had dramatic consequences for an individual's life are sometimes discovered. On the other hand, requesting and reading one's own file might reduce the still widespread overestimation of Stasi activities, in particular when it can be seen that no files or only files of little importance existed. However, the studies discussed above indicate that the majority of those involved found reading their files a positive experience. They had a sense of regaining and repossessing their own biographies and lives, which had previously been scrutinised, controlled, manipulated and occasionally severely damaged by 'Zersetzungsmaßnahmen' (demoralising measures), discrimination or even imprisonment.

In this process of demoralising an individual, unofficial informants have a decisive and central role. Knowing who they were and what they did is a major motive and incentive for requesting the personal inspection of records. This interest in unofficial informants does not appear diminished by reading the records but rather increased when affected individuals dealt with relevations from their records. However, this engagement tends to distract attention from those who were primarily responsible for designing and running the State Security system. However, the normally strongly expressed negative feelings towards previous informants have not led to outbreaks of violence against them as some had feared before the files were opened up for public inspection.

Collective memory in differentiated societies is highly differentiated, too. Given the extremely polarised attitudes about dealing with the past among the population of the former GDR, a tendency towards division of collective memories can be assumed. Presumably, the part of the population that takes advantage of the opportunity to inspect their personal files supports both the process of dealing with the past and critical evaluations of this past. Thus file inspection may well amplify existing cleavages in public opinion.

The inspection of personal files of the Stasi on a massive scale is a unique phenomenon in history, one that could perhaps best be described as a collectively taken course in political education, based on individual biographies. This process works against the construction of myths and legends, on both the individual and collective levels. The surveys show that opening up the Stasi files contributed to and accelerated the process of delegitimisation of the political and social system of the GDR, and might provide a kind of immunisation against future tendencies toward authoritarian attitudes and regimes. The impact of opening up the Stasi files on collective memories, however, cannot be evaluated exclusively on the basis of the impact of inspection of personal files. Other uses of the Stasi records—for purges, criminal prosecution, research, publications and the media—also have a decisive role, which needs further exploration.

REFERENCES

Bundesbeauftrager für die Unterlagen des Staatssicherheitsdienstes der ehemaligen Deutschen Demokratischen Republik (BStU). 1999. *Vierter Tätigkeitsbericht des Bundesbeauftragten für die Unterlagen des Staatssicherheitsdienstes der ehemaligen Deutschen Demokratischen Republik.* Berlin: BStU.

Doll, Jörg and Damitz, Marc. 1998a. Psychische Folgen der Verfolgung durch das Ministerium für Staatssicherheit: Zur Bedeutung unterschiedlicher Bewältigungsstrategien. *Zeitschrift für Sozialpsychologie* 29: 65–78.

——. 1998b. Zur Bedeutung des wichtigsten inoffiziellen Mitarbeiters für die Bewältigung der Bespitzelung durch das Ministerium für Staatssicherheit. In *Politisch motivierte Verfolgung: Opfer von SED-Unrecht*, edited by U Baumann and H Kury. Frankfurt: Campus.

Engelmann, Roger. 1994. *Zu Struktur, Charakter und Bedeutung der Unterlagen des Ministeriums für Staatssicherheit.* Berlin: BStU.

Gieseke, Jens. 1996. *Die hauptamtlichen Mitarbeiter des Ministeriums für Staatssicherheit.* Berlin: BStU.

Karstedt, Susanne. 1996. Die doppelte Vergangenheitsbewältigung der Deutschen: Die Verfahren im Urteil der Öffentlichkeit nach 1945 und 1989. *Zeitschrift für Rechtssoziologie* 17: 58–104.

Müller-Enbergs, Helmut (ed). 1996. *Inoffizielle Mitarbeiter des Ministeriums für Staatssicherheit. Richtlinien und Durchführungsbestimmungen.* Berlin: Ch Links.

Schumann, Silke. 1995. *Vernichten oder Offenlegen? Zur Entstehung des Stasi-Unterlagen-Gesetzes. Eine Dokumentation der öffentlichen Debatte 1990/1991.* Berlin: BStU.

15

The Art of Forgetting: The Communist Police State as a Non-reality

ANDRZEJ ZYBERTOWICZ

THE PURPOSE OF this chapter is to show how 'the real', though partly obscured, was made 'unreal', though partly displayed.[1] By 'the real' I refer to the practices of the communist police state in Poland during the 1980s as well as to their long-term consequences. In the present context, this is what can be called the heritage of the communist police state. The chapter consists of two sections. The first offers a 'standard historico-sociological overview' of two phenomena: (1) the police state practices under communism in Poland during the 1980s; and (2) the main rhetorical strategies employed in the media in the 1990s in order to persuade the public that these practices were nonexistent and/or irrelevant. The second section interprets these rhetorical strategies of the media within the framework of the postmodernist debates about the objectivity of knowledge and its relation to 'reality'.

I. A HISTORY

A. A Paradox of Totalitarian Rule: Lip Service Obedience and Lack of Information Feedback

Although it is generally acknowledged that under communism social life was regulated from above, the role of secret police in this respect is still under-explored, and almost no serious research into this question has been conducted, except with regard to the practices of the secret police in the former German Democratic Republic (GDR/East Germany). Communist police

---

[1] My understanding of 'real' follows the lines of Hilary Putnam's internal realism (Putnam 1990). For an elaboration of this, see Zybertowicz 1995.

state practices have never been thoroughly explored and analysed by social scientists in a comprehensive way, and the public still tends to imagine them in the form of 'cloak and dagger' stereotypes (Andrew and Dilkes 1984). Even in debates focusing on the heritage of communism in Poland the issue of the role of the secret police in the normal, everyday operation of the system is very rarely brought up (see Dziedzictwo Peerelu, 1993; Magierska and Szustek, 1994; Ofiary czy współwinni 1997). At present, it is becoming obvious that in the consciousness of large segments of Polish society the impact of the 'reality' of the secret police has been transformed into something irrelevant, mythical and unworthy of serious reflection and exploration. I want to offer some observations and explanations that will help us to capture the anatomy and process of this transformation and translation.

The well known Russian dissident Wladimir Bukowski has made the following observation on a paradox in the construction of the Soviet system of rule: on the one hand, those in power were at pains to prevent the subjected population from any free expression of ideas, and they put pressure on society to articulate in public only those views that were congruent with official renditions of the current situation; on the other hand, the rulers did their utmost to uncover what the subjected population really thought (see Zybertowicz 1997). The secret police in all communist states were instrumental in achieving both these aims. First, the police exercised terror, which instilled the population with fear, disciplined it and 'normalised'[2] its behaviour through such practices as slandering, spreading rumours, harassing, battering, arresting, secret killings and, last but not least, infiltrating groups that were defined as hostile to the system (Zybertowicz 1995–96). It seems justified to term this process as *primitive accumulation of power*. This accumulation mainly took place during the Stalinist period and was later used as the basis for spreading fear and achieving obedience during subsequent decades (see Paczkowski 1998).

However, once the first aim was achieved and silence and/or hypocrisy were effectively enforced in the public sphere, those in power found themselves cut off from any real information feedback, which is essential to the process of governing in a modern society (see Katz & Kahn 1966, ch 9; Giddens 1990, 38). This resulted in the second task assigned to the secret police: uncovering what was really going on in the minds of those who had been silenced. This objective was achieved mainly by establishing even more ramified networks of informants to the secret police. A massive system of infiltration into all social groups and secret channels of information flows was initiated and cultivated.

The targets of such an infiltration on a massive scale were not only social movements critical of the system but virtually all kinds of social groups that

---

[2] Any association with the ideas of Michel Foucault are intended here.

were rated as potentially dangerous by the communist authorities and were consequently infiltrated by the various and numerous branches of the secret services. In the late 1980s their network of so-called secret collaborators was about 100,000 strong. Infiltration was carried out using undercover functionaries employed in civilian institutions of strategic importance, such as the postal system. Various techniques were used to recruit real or potential dissidents. Some became fully-fledged agents of the secret police, some became involved in difficult and hazardous games intended to outsmart the secret service and some were barely aware that they were collaborating with the police. Some found themselves in a blurred zone of lost or dual loyalties. Only a few escaped completely unscathed from the numerous police attempts at bribing, cheating, flattering, flirting, threatening, battering, harassing, seducing and manipulating them.

One should take into account here that—as a result of the totalitarian (or quasi-totalitarian) nature of the system—any communist state had, by default, to cope with much more complex regulative tasks than other democratic states. It is sufficient to point here to the everyday tasks of managing a command economy. The regulative task required a constant flow of information on how different sections of the population actually reacted toward the policies implemented by the state. In the provision of such information, the role of the secret police can hardly be overestimated (see Łoś & Zybertowicz 1997, 2000; Zybertowicz 1997). It seems appropriate to use Gary Marx's term 'centralised policing of politics' (see Marx 1974) in this regard. Not only did various police agencies protect the system, but networks of informants were also indispensable for the very constitution of the communist system both during its emergence and for its everyday operations. I claim that under communism a specific pattern of social control or even of governance evolved, which can be termed *regulation through infiltration*.[3]

As far as Poland is concerned, infiltration was decisively intensified during the 1980s. Initially, this was in response to the emerging Solidarity movement but became later an essential element of the policy of 'controlled reform from above', which resulted in the Roundtable Talks in 1989. Polish society, having had accumulated experience with frequent uprisings and organised resistance to communism, was able to generate a substantial civil society and non-state enclaves. Ironically, this increased the demand for secret penetration on the part of the communist state. In addition, the decay and gradual disintegration of the regular State and Party control system that followed in the wake of the military's suppression of the Solidarity movement in December 1981 particularly contributed to the State's ever

---

[3] Acknowledgements to Michael D Kennedy of the University of Michigan at Ann Arbor, to whom I owe this phrasing.

growing reliance on the secret police and the secret services of the Army (see Łoś & Zybertowicz 2000, ch 3).

The use of infiltration on such a massive scale as during communist totalitarianism finally led to outcomes that are well captured by Michel Foucault's (1977) analysis of the 'microphysics of power' and of the 'power without subject'. However, his ideas have to be applied here in a selective way. For communist regimes, the question as to 'who holds power'—so strongly refuted by Foucault—still retains its validity. The top-to-bottom procedures of allocating tasks according to which the secret services operated under close supervision of the communist party leadership[4] make Foucault's 'cutting off the head of the king' (see Dean 1994, 156) irrelevant in this context. In fact, there *was* a centre, which acted as if the power system had a head indeed.

However, many phenomena in the Polish context fit into Foucault's notion of 'power without subject'. The practice of surveillance and control springs to mind here. In 1982, during the first months of martial law in Poland thousands of people, usually those related to some underground activities, were summoned to police stations, where they had to listen to so-called 'warning talks' or were subjected to informal interrogations. Many of these individuals were offered chances to become secret informants of the police, though in many cases the security service did not really bother either to encourage or put pressure on them. Consequently, some of the dissidents assumed that this practice was aimed at creating the impression that infiltration was used on such a massive scale that virtually no one could escape the gaze of the secret police; this assumption was in fact confirmed during a 1996 interview that I conducted with a former security service operative.

Thus, instead of a myriad of actual external controllers implanted into many social settings, only the *idea* of controllers was implanted into the minds of people, and in many cases this worked quite successfully. Poles believed that 'they', the authorities, knew everything about 'us', the population. This often justified refusals to support dissident activities—not due to moral but rather sheer pragmatic reason. It was argued that since the authorities knew everything, all sacrifices would be pointless. In some social milieus it generated a self-sustaining and self-enhancing mechanism. Once the 'invisible eye of the ruler' (as in Foucault's panopticum) was installed in their minds, people became their own policemen.

It is obvious why communist states are often described as being of a 'conspiratorial nature'[5] and why it is equally justifiable to maintain that

---

[4] My research shows that partly due to the unique position of General Wojciech Jaruzelski in the Party and State power structure, in the 1980s, the secret services received orders not from the Communist Party as such but rather from an extremely small group of top Party leaders loyal only to Jaruzelski himself (see Zybertowicz 1997, 157–9; Łoś & Zybertowicz 2000, 29–31).

[5] This is Christopher Andrew's formula. See Andrew and Dikes 1994.

communist parties tend to enforce their policies through mafia-like operations. However, knowledge about the practices of the communist police state is common among neither scholars nor the public. Despite the fact that the secret service was a pillar of communist regimes, scholars researching mechanisms of systemic transformation largely neglect the role of this extremely powerful actor (Łoś & Zybertowicz 1997). Questions like: Who was infiltrated? Who infiltrated? How? What were and are implications of such a massive infiltration? are often rated as either academically irrelevant or sheer correlates of political conflicts.

Empirical findings from Poland as well as from other communist states so far clearly confirm the notion of a domain of invisible power and a system of social control the mechanisms of which were neither understood by outsiders, ie 'the majority of the population', nor even transparent to many prominent figures of the Party and State apparatus (see Dominiczak 1997; Zybertowicz 1997). More than ten years after communism in Central East Europe was abandoned, the notion of regulation through infiltration is still marginal to the analysis of the nature of this communist past. The mode of governance that can be termed as regulation through infiltration still waits to be properly dissected and theorised. It is exactly the fact that knowledge about fundamental characteristics of the social reality of millions of people has been absent and hidden, that will be our *explanandum* now.

B. Stories Promoting Forgetting: Shifting the 'Real' into 'Unreal'

During the past decade, a range of different narrative strategies have been used to discourage any interest in the conspirational nature of communist states. As a consequence, the present scope of serious research into the hidden dimensions of the communist past is inadequately small compared to the importance of the problem. We can assume that the process of collectively forgetting the reality of communist states has been driven by two main factors: rational interests and irrational fears. It is interesting to observe that the interests and fears meet each other in a discourse focusing on stories that, though politically motivated, are nonetheless only partly deliberately invented. Some of these mask the interests behind them, some fuel fears, some do both. Among the typical themes and stories that are used by those who have developed the 'art of amnesia' in Poland, the following ones are most common:

— *No one can escape the guilt; we are all liable.* The totalitarian state by its very nature involved the whole population. The boundaries between victims and villains are barely visible, if at all. Since all were involved, and everybody was pursuing petty interests within the system, no one can be found guilty (see Ofiary czy współwinni 1997; Rosenberg 1996).

— *It wasn't us; it was done by the system.* One of the defendants in the trial of a group of functionaries of the secret police who were charged with torturing political prisoners during the Stalinist period stated in his final speech: 'Those were the times of the dictatorship of proletariat. Unless we unambiguously declare that the system was guilty and not Humer [the main perpetrator], we will not be able to understand history' (Lipiński 1997, 162).

— *Anyone could be registered as a secret collaborator of the political police.* Because of strong pressures to deliver, the secret police tended to register many innocent individuals as informal informants. As soon as the police archives are opened up, such accusations will be seen to be evenly distributed throughout the population. ('The shit will hit the fan': see Smoleński 1998).

— *Instead of increasing social tensions inherited from the past, we should build bridges.* Knowledge about the former regime's crimes will make it difficult to reduce social conflicts and hostilities, and forgetting is thus to be blessed. In other words, let us choose the future! This was Aleksander Kwaśniewski's slogan in his successful 1995 election campaign.

— *Since communism was a big, ideologically devised and determined fake, the secret services are no exception and were committed more to the production of artefacts than to credible data and actual operations.* Pressure on the political police resulted in multiplying the numbers of formally registered agents rather than in increasing the numbers of actually operating ones.

— *There is no sense in scholarly writing about the police state practices since there is no access to the archives of the secret police.* In such a situation nothing can be done but to rely on rumours, leaks and planted disinformation. Scholars relying on recently opened up sources (like published memoirs or some documents leaked to the public realm) will inevitably become somebody's puppet.

— *The truth about the communist police state cannot be achieved.* Secret police archives will not be of much help, since, first, they were largely destroyed, and second, they are full of disinformation. No trust can be put in archival documents that are produced by organisations that ceaselessly poured out provocation and lies.[6] The conclusion is that archival data mining will result only in new and endless slander campaigns.

— *In exploring secret police activities researchers might become infected by the obsessive suspicion of the secret police.* There are patterns of

---

[6] This argument is even used in court testimonies of former members of these organisations.

behaviour in the social world that can infect individuals involved in research into the routines of the secret police with harmful emotional habits. Scholars and others who investigate conspiracies are prone to become haunted by motives of mystery, treason and paranoia, and are likely to lose their mental balance. Real scholars should avoid this.

— *It is not only disgusting to search in the dirt, but not safe to do so.* If claims about the police state's practices prove to be wrong, it is not wise to support such research; provided the claims are correct, it not wise to take the risks.

— *Secret police operations do not really matter in large-scale historical processes.* The various secret services always attempt to outsmart each other; this produces no 'real' effects since they tend to annul each other.

These different story lines amount to a vicious cycle of misapprehension. Although they contradict each other, in the post-communist consciousness (as, eg, visible in anti-lustration propaganda (see Łoś 1995; Sojak 1998)) they often are entangled with and mutually reinforce each other so that it is hard to distinguish between them (see Wildstein 1999). What is refuted here is the possibility of a 'fixity of the past' as well as the possibility to establish it through a 'fixity of texts', like those to be found in the archives of the secret police. However, the bottom line of all this rhetoric is obvious. What is offered here is not reconciliation through finding the truth, as was attempted in South Africa, but something without or in place of the truth.

C. Interests behind the Story Lines

During the last decades of communist rule in Poland the political police operated in a highly selective fashion. The targets for repression were much more carefully selected than in the Stalinist era, and not that many people had direct contact with the police. But even those who had experienced such contact normally could not see beyond the surface of police activities. The actual modus operandi of the secret services was kept well hidden, and numerous disinformation techniques were used to disguise the actual nature and scope of infiltration practices.

As a result of various campaigns in the 1990s millions of people who had accidentally come into contact with the uniformed or plainclothes police became anxious about whether they had by fault been registered as informants in police archives (see Roger Engelmann on Germany in this volume). In many cases these fears were induced by a lack of knowledge about the practices of the police state rather than by its actual activities (see also Roger Engelmann in this volume). Many individuals have avoided from coping with the heritage of infiltration. It is psychologically difficult to get control over suspicions once someone begins to realise that secret agents were or still are present not only at a distance, eg, in the realm of high-level politics, but also quite near them in their personal networks, and that the neighbour next door or colleagues on the job could have been police informants (see Szostkiewicz 1999). Once people start to reflect on this, their basic, spontaneous trust in human relationships is superseded by quasi-rational calculations: who among the people I know played—or in some ways is still playing—such double games? Is there anyone who still deserves trust without any reservation?

This experience seems to psychologically resemble our fear as children when we try to understand the idea of the infinity of the universe. We feel terrified by the idea, as our imagination attempts in vain to domesticate such a radically new kind of thought. Even highly educated individuals do not possess enough credible information (and/or myths) and contextual knowledge about the covert world of the secret police that would allow them to assess recently revealed and often outrageous facts and thus be able to limit their fears and preserve their trust. It is quite normal that we try to escape harmful emotions that otherwise could drive us into paranoia. However, the widespread fears stemming from confrontation with the past are presently ruthlessly exploited in the conflict over the archival records, which can shed light on the past and the present. Politicians likely to suffer from lustration try to intimidate the wider public: 'Don't you feel at ease—you have lived under communism, too.'

Some people in Poland as in other post-communist states avoid the truth because they were directly involved in deceit; some act bona fide, trying to save the honour of colleagues who were weak or unlucky enough to become involved; some come up with a new raison d'être that justifies covering up dirt from the past; some are simply lost in the intricacies of post-communist politics; and mainstream public discourse (not to say propaganda) is trapped amongst all these (see on the Czech Republic Jiřina Šiklová in this volume).

Another factor driving these processes relates to the origin and background of some of the most influential groups of dissidents. A former military counterintelligence operative noticed that the comparably strong intellectual *elite* opposition in Poland often had 'family ties to high ranking party and state officials. This provided valuable sources for information without any need of activating the network of agents' (Kamiński, no date, 23). This is confirmed by the fact that a number of journalists of the influential Gazeta Wyborcza, which was originally founded by the Solidarity movement and is at present the largest and most influential Polish daily newspaper, are children of prominent former communists (Żebrowski 1993).

Consequently, almost none of the key players who emerged in the new, democratic public sphere welcomed the publication of basic information about the reality of the police state in Poland during the 1980s. That is well illustrated by strange debates over lustration and de-communisation (see Zybertowicz 1993; Łoś 1995; Sojak 1998). Likewise, the scope and character of state crimes has never been thoroughly explored, and even clearly identified state crimes has mainly remained crimes committed by an anonymous and impersonal *state*, as no individuals responsible were prosecuted (Łoś & Zybertowicz 1999).

II. A META-HISTORY

Let us now take a more distant perspective on the data and narrative presented above. 'History' as outlined in the preceding section can be treated as an exercise in a standard, traditional mode of doing social science: grounded, objective, authoritative, etc. What is criticised above is the ideological, selective approach to the past and the 'generous' attitude towards facts and information that so easily focuses on information that fits the interests of particular actors and results in a construction of the past that is based on leniently forgetting about it.

The process of forgetting as outlined above is in a way a very postmodern one, though the ideas or practices of postmodernism are rarely invoked during the debates over the communist past in Poland (but see Łoś and Zybertowicz 2000, 201–5). In order to avoid the usual conceptual drift when the term 'postmodernism' is used, I want to embed it into a context that helps to anchor my further comments. I will follow Hayden White's idea that

> postmodernism is nothing if not a worldview based upon a distinctive conception of history, its nature, its meaning, and the different way it can be studied and used … [P]ostmodernism undercuts the foundationalist nature of the Western idea of historical knowledge. It insists that when it is a matter of studying the past, the historian must accept responsibility of the construction of what previously she/he had pretended only to have discovered (White 1997, 12).

White quotes Gertrude Himmelfarb, who has spelled out the objections of professional historians against postmodernism in historical thought in the following terms:

> [P]ostmodernism amounts to a denial of the fixity of any 'text', of the authority of the author over the interpreter … of any correspondence between language and reality, indeed of any 'essential' reality … In history, it is a denial of the fixity of the past, of the reality of the past apart from what the historian chooses to make of it, and thus of any objective truth about the past (Himmelfarb 1992, 12; quoted in White 1997, 13).

White notices that Himmelfarb's understanding of truth entails a certain moral commitment—but, he stresses,

> not to the truth in general—of which there may be many different species—but to the specific kind of truth produced by historical research and writing ... The important distinction from a postmodernist point of view is not between ideology and objectivity but between ideological conststructions of history and more or less willing to make of their own modes of production elements of their contents ... If postmodernist notions of history are informed by a critique of the ideology of objectivism, this does not necessarily mean that they are opposed to the truth and committed to lie, delusion, fantasy, or fiction ... [P]ostmodernism recognizes that 'reality' is always as much constructed in discourse as it is discovered in the historical record. Which means that postmodernist 'objectivity' is aware of *its* own constructed nature and makes this work of construction the subject of its discourse (White 1997, 13).

In other words, the values and dichotomies of 'true/false' 'have no determination or reality apart from a formal, logico-linguistic order we impose on signifying action, speech first of all' (Allen 1998, 19). If 'a statement is true that resists all attempts to bend or break it' (Latour 1989, 102), then virtually no statement about the role of the communist secret police, their infiltration and manipulation of Solidarity or about the police and its lingering role in the transition can be accepted to pass as true (see Zagozda 1999; Skoczylas and Bereś 1999).

It seems to be a simple sociological fact that the kind of truth I would be happy to support is not strong enough to withstand refutation by the 'unholy' alliance of former agents, their supervisors, the supervisors of the supervisors (ie, high-level communist Party/State apparatchiks) and those who were co-opted into games of power and machinations about property during the transformation process.

In the Polish debates over lustration, the anti-lustration faction has undermined the possibility of reaching a public and scholarly consensus about the reality of the police state—about what is to be perceived as 'the real'—in order to establish, among other things, a political illusion of the present and the future that is familiar to everybody. For the sake of a better future the past has to be viewed as irrelevant. Some areas of knowledge about communism are to be excluded as potentially harmful to the 'Europeanisation' and well-being of Polish society. For the sake of the present task of establishing a new society that does not exclude individuals and groups (say from participation in constitutional power games), research into the 'dirty' problems of former infiltration routines should be excluded (see Sojak 1998).

Both forgetting and remembering are always creative—and hence selective. But different selections also serve different value systems. The values implied in the rule of law are the normative basis of this analysis (see Krygier 1994, 104). Polish courts have been inhibited from prosecuting and sentencing those who were responsible for the old regime's crimes, and this has partly been caused by a lack of basic contextual knowledge of the system's modes of operation, like levels of command and the routines of giving orders within the communist party and political police. Yet, can a system of the rule of law and democracy in general work without a basic consensus over certain kinds of truth among the population?

REFERENCES

Allen, Barry. 1998. Truthfulness. *Common Knowledge* 7(2): 19–26.

Andrew, Christopher and Dilkes, David. 1984. Introduction. In *The Missing Dimension: Governments and Intelligence Communities in the Twentieth Century*, edited by C Andrew and D Dilkes. London: Macmillan.

Dean, Mitchell. 1994. *Critical and Effective Histories: Foucault's Methods and Historical Sociology*. London: Routledge.

Dominiczak, Henryk. 1997. *Organy bezpieczeństwa PRL 1944–1990* [Security Forces in the Polish People's Republic]. Warsaw: Dom Wydawniczy Bellona.

Dziedzictwo, Peerelu. 1993. Wypowiedzi [Heritage of the Polish People's Republic—Comments]. *Res Publica Nowa* 3: 4–40.

Foucault, Michel. 1977. *Discipline and Punish. The Birth of the Prison*. London: Viking.

Giddens, Anthony. 1990. *The Consequences of Modernity*. Cambridge: Polity Press.

Himmelfarb, Gertrude. 1992. Telling It as You Like It: Post-modernist History and the Flight from Fact. *Times Literary Supplement*, 16 October.

Kamiński, Zenon. No date. *Tropiciele. Wspomnienia oficera kontrwywiadu wojskowego* [Hunters: Recollections of a Military Counterintelligence Officer]. Warsaw (no publisher specified).

Katz, Daniel and Kahn, Robert L. 1966. *The Social Psychology of Organizations*. New York: John Wiley and Sons.

Krygier, Martin. 1994. Four Visions of Post-communist Law. *Australian Journal of Politics and History* 40; 104–20.

Latour, Bruno. 1989. Clothing the Naked Truth. In *Dismantling Truth: Reality in the Post-modernist World*, edited by H Lawson and L Appignanesi. London: Weidenfeld and Nicolson.

Lipiński, Piotr. 1997. *Humer i inni* [Humer and Others]. Warsaw: Cinderella Books.

Łoś, Maria. 1995. Lustration and Truth Claims: Unfinished Revolutions in Central Europe. *Law and Social Inquiry* 20: 117–61.

Łoś, Maria and Zybertowicz, Andrzej. 1997. Covert Action: The Missing Link in Explanations of the Rise and Demise of the Soviet Bloc. *Periphery: Journal of Polish Affairs* 3(1/2): 16–20.

——. 1999. Is Revolution a Solution? State Crime in Communist and Post-communist Poland (1980–1995). In *The Rule of Law after Communism*, edited by A Czarnota and M Krygier. Aldershot: Ashgate Dartmouth.

——. 2000. *Privatizing the Police State: The Case of Poland*. London: Macmillan.

Magierska, Anna and Szustek, Anna (eds). 1994. *Polemiki wokół najnowszej historii Polski* [Debates over the Recent History of Poland]. Warsaw: UW INP.

Marx, Gary T. 1974. Thoughts on a Neglected Category of Social Movement Participant: The Agent Provocateur and the Informant. *American Journal of Sociology* 80: 402–42.

Ofiary czy współwinni. Nazizm i sowietyzm w świadomości historycznej [Victims or Co-culprits: Nazism and Sovieticism in the Historical Consciousness].1997. Warsaw: Oficyna Wydawnicza Volumen, Fundacja im Friedricha Eberta.

Paczkowski, Andrzej. 1998. Interviewed by Dariusz Gawin and Janusz Ostrowski, *Życie*, 18 May, 13.

Putnam, Hilary. 1990. *Realism with a Human Face*. Cambridge, MA: Harvard University Press.

Rosenberg, Tina. 1996. *The Haunted Land: Facing the Europe's Ghosts after Communism*. New York: Vintage Books.

Skoczylas, Jerzy and Bereś, Witold. 1999. Amigo i jego przyjaciel [Amigo and His Friend], *Gazeta Wyborcza*, 10 September, 24.

Smoleński, Paweł. 1998. I ty zostaniesz konfidentem [And You will Become an Informant (of the Secret Police)], *Gazeta Wyborcza*, 14–15 November.

Sojak, Radosław. 1998. Porządki wykluczeń: ekskluzja społeczna w świetle socjologii wiedzy (na przykładzie dyskusji wokół lustracji) [Patterns of Exclusion from the Perspective of Sociology of Knowledge: The Case of the Lustration Debate]. Unpublished manuscript.

Szostkiewicz, Adam. 1999. Teczka? Nie, dziękuję [My File? No, Thank You], *Tygodnik Powszechny*, No 1.

White, Hayden. 1997. Postmodernism and Textual Anxieties. mimeo.

Wildstein, Bronisław. 1999. Antylustracyjne strategie [Anti-lustration Strategies], *Rzeczpospolita*, 23 January.

Zagozda, Andrzej [penname of Adam Michnik]. 1999. O czym wie każde dziecko? [What any Kid Knows about?], *Gazeta Wyborcza*, 6 September, 2.

Żebrowski, Leszek. 1993. Ludzie UB—trzy pokolenia [UB People—Three Generations], *Dekomunizacja i Rzeczywistość* [Decommunistion and Reality]. Warsaw: Wydawnictwo AMARANT.

Zybertowicz, Andrzej. 1993. *W uścisku tajnych służb: upadek komunizmu i układ postnomenklaturowy* [In Grip of Secret Services: The Collapse of Communism and the Post-*Nomenklatura* Network]. Komorów: Wydawnictwo Antyk.

——. 1995. *Przemoc i poznanie: studium z nie-klasycznej socjologii wiedzy* [Violence and Cognition: An Exercise in Non-classical Sociology of Knowledge]. Toruń: Wydawnictwo UMK.

——. 1995–96. *A Neglected Dimension of Contemporary Social Movements Dynamics: Secret Services in the Field of Constraints and Facilitations for Social Movements*. International Institute, University of Michigan, Working Paper Series, No 15.

——. 1997. Niewidoczna władza: komunistyczne państwo policyjne w Polsce lat osiemdziesiątych [Invisible Power: The Communist Police State in Poland of the 1980s]. In *Skryte oblicze systemu komunistycznego* [The Hidden Facet of the Communist System], edited by R Bäcker and P Hübner. Warsaw: DiG.

VI

Failing Memory: The Law and its Past

16

The Loss of Early Women Lawyers from Collective Memory in Germany: A Memoir of Magdalene Schoch

KONSTANZE PLETT[*]

I. INTRODUCTION

IT REQUIRES A group that shares certain memories to build and maintain a collective memory. The early members of an emerging social group cannot possibly be aware that they are the founders or forerunners of a new collectivity, and their contemporaries do not recognise them in such a role either. Therefore their life and work is rarely properly documented. Only if and when they become meaningful to others who understand themselves as their successors, will the life and work experience of these individuals become collectively remembered.

Any collective sharing of memory needs at least to be tolerated by others. If a particular member of this collectivity is, by any social force, divided from the group and individualised, and other persons who want to join the collectivity are prohibited from becoming members, the collective memory is jeopardised and may ultimately be destroyed. If and when this happens—the dispersion of a collectivity and subsequently the dissolution of the corresponding collective memory—the memory of the early members will be suppressed and ultimately 'hidden from history' (Rowbotham 1976). Another collectivity similar to the first one may emerge later. For them, learning about the early but forgotten predecessors will come as a surprise, and getting more detailed information about them will be like fitting pieces into a jigsaw puzzle, depending very much on accidental findings.

---

[*] This essay is dedicated to the memory of my parents, Dr phil Erna Maria Charlotte Plett née Schulz and Dr rer nat Gustav Jacob Otto Plett.

These are observations that I made when doing research on early women lawyers in Germany. I shall illustrate these observations by drawing on *one* early woman lawyer as a special example. The next section will give a brief account of women's entry into the legal professions and legal academia in Germany, starting from my own experience. Then I shall describe my search for the first woman who fulfilled all the requirements for becoming a law professor at a German university. The main section is devoted to the results of this search—a memoir of Magdalene Schoch.[1] I will then go on to draw some conclusions on legal institutions and their collective memory, with special regard to the early women lawyers in Germany.

II. WOMEN LAWYERS IN GERMANY

I began studying law in 1966 and took my first state examination in 1970. After a detour into another profession, I continued my legal education in 1973 and took the second state examination in 1975. During all these years I encountered not one woman law teacher: no professor, no assistant professor, no tutor, no practitioner and no examiner was of my own sex. This was taken for granted among us women law students in the late 1960s. We did not feel exotic since we already amounted to 10 to 15 per cent of the law student population. But I do not know of any law students who at that time were openly striving for a university career.

In the 1970s the so-called new women's movement got on its way in the US, Germany, and many other European countries. It was also the decade when women lawyers in these countries discovered the imbalance in women's representation in the various fields of legal activity: some 15 per cent among law students, 10 per cent among judges (and these were overwhelmingly restricted to low positions at the courts; see Hassels and Hommerich 1993, 40–65), 5 per cent among attorneys-at-law and two individuals[2]—not per cent but in absolute numbers—among some 500

---

[1] During her Hamburg and early US years she called herself Magdalene. Later—most likely after her naturalisation in 1943—she used as first name Magdalena, and eventually M Magdalena. Throughout this chapter I will use her German Christian name, which is also the one on the commemorative plaque in the old university building of Hamburg.

[2] These were Anne Eva Brauneck, a criminal lawyer and criminologist who was the first woman to receive a full professorship at a German law department (at the reopened law faculty of the University of Gießen in 1965) (Fabricius-Brand, Berghahn and Sudhölter 1982, 167–9); and Hilde Kaufmann, also a criminal lawyer and criminologist, who became a full professor in 1966 in Kiel and in 1970 in Cologne (Boedeker and Meyer-Plath 1974, 193). Two received professorships in 1971: Ilse Staff, who specialised in constitutional law, at the Johann Wolfgang Goethe University in Frankfurt am Main (Boedeker and Meyer-Plath 1974, 193); and Jutta Limbach, who specialised in civil law and legal sociology, at the Free University of Berlin (Plett 2009). Having been appointed President of the German Constitutional Court (*Bundesverfassungsgericht*) in 1994, Jutta Limbach became the highest-ranking lawyer in the

active law professors in 1970. The 1970s were also the years of the so-called educational explosion, when the number of university students soared, particularly in law departments, and even more particularly among women law students: in 1983 the number of law students was two and a half times as high as in 1972, whereas the number of women law students was six times as high. During the 1980s the numbers increased even more, until the female ratio rose to 50 per cent and more in the 1990s (Rust 1997, 97; Statistisches Bundesamt 1998, 50).

To my knowledge, the first publication on women lawyers appeared in 1982 (Fabricius-Brand, Berghahn and Sudhölter 1982). It reflects on the experience of my generation during our education and at the beginning of our careers in a male-dominated legal profession. It also contains some memoirs of women of the preceding generation. But it only covers the period since the foundation of the Federal Republic of Germany in 1949. The previous decades are, however, included in a 1984 publication by the German Women Lawyers Association, which covers the years 1900 to 1984 (Deutscher Juristinnenbund 1984). Its first chapter describes the history of women's entry into the field of law, delineating three major periods: 1900–33, 1933–45 and 1948 to 1984. A large appendix with many fac-similes recalls women's struggle for admission to bar and bench in the early 1920s,[3] as well as the backlash, which had already begun in the 1920s and intensified immediately after the Nazis seized power in 1933.

In Germany, admission to bar and bench requires two state examina-tions: the first taken after university studies and the second (also called 'great state examination') after training in practice (*Referendariat*) for another two years.[4] Persons who have taken both examinations are called full-fledged lawyers (*Volljuristen*) and are entitled to be admitted to the bar. A university career has different requirements, namely a doctorate of law (Dr iur) and the so-called *Habilitation*.[5] These special features of German

---

Federal Republic of Germany and the first woman in this position which she held until her retirement in 2002.

[3] In the public debate preceding their admission several men had seriously argued that women were not capable of sitting as judges because of their 'monthly indisposition' and their emotionality, which would prevent them from considering cases rationally. See Deutscher Juristinnenbund 1984, 136–8. (These documents have been omitted in the following editions.)

[4] In the 1920s, the *Referendariat*, the second stage of training before the final second exam, lasted for three and a half years.

[5] This is equal to a second doctorate of sorts and seems to be a German and Austrian specialty. Usually, a *Habilitation* takes six years of post-doctoral research and teaching, a monograph of up to 1,000 pages, and an exemplary teaching lesson and/or a public lecture. Dictionaries describe the *Habilitation* as 'a postdoctoral lecturing qualification'. This is not comparable to the tenure-track system in the United States because the type of university position held by most during the work for the *Habilitation* is only temporary and cannot be transferred into a professorship afterwards. Only in 2002 was the *Habilitation* abandoned by federal law as a requirement for an academic career, but it is still widely seen as a requirement for a chair.

academia need to be known in order to understand the difficulties women encountered when striving for legal careers in the first half of the twentieth century.[6]

The universities in Germany opened their gates for women between 1900 and 1909, though the states differed (Böhm 1986; Soden 1997; Rust 2000). The dominant state in the Bismarck Reich, Prussia, did so in 1908. In 1913 there were 51 women law students among 9,003 law students altogether (0.5 per cent) in the German Empire; in 1919 the figure was 554 out of 17,224 (2.6 per cent) in the newly founded Weimar Republic. However, these women were not admitted to the state examination and hence barred from practicing in the legal professions. They could conclude their university studies only with a doctoral degree. Usually this is the first step towards a teaching career, but not so for these women, because they were also deprived of access to the *Habilitation*. This was granted to women through a decree by the Prussian Minister for Higher Education only in 1920, after an intervention by Edith Stein (although it was of no avail to herself; Wobbe 1994, 28). What happened to these women with law degrees when none of the legal professions was open to them? Some of them worked for advice centres for women or the poor (see Geisel 1997), and some were ready to take the state examination when it became accessible after 1922, while most of them, it has to be assumed, withdrew into the seclusion of family or into non-legal professions or workplaces.[7]

German women gained suffrage in 1918 in the wake of the democratic revolution after World War I and the end of the Bismarck Reich. The right to vote for and be elected to Parliament,[8] however, did not mean that women were considered capable of practicing within the legal profession. They were even excluded from becoming lay judges (*Schöffe* or *Geschworener*). The law amendments necessary for the admission of women to the bar, state offices and the judiciary did not pass Parliament until July 1922. But only a year later, a bill was adopted that allowed married women to be dismissed from civil service (including the judiciary) if their maintenance (usually by a

---

[6] In the second half of the twentieth century there were two exemptions to this procedure. The former German Democratic Republic established a different pathway to the legal professions in the socialist system (see Meador 1986) but retained more or less the same for academics (although the doctoral thesis was called 'dissertation A' and the *Habilitation* thesis 'dissertation B'). In West Germany, during the 1970s and 1980s, some states ran a so-called one-phase legal education (*Einstufige Juristenausbildung*) in which the phase of practical training was integrated into university studies, but these reform models have been abolished since 1982 by federal legislation (see Plett 1986).

[7] See, eg, the figures for Hamburg prior to 1933: 14 women qualified as full-fledged lawyers between 1924 and 1931; three of these took up positions in the social welfare administration and three were admitted to the bar while the remaining eight did not practice law (Deutscher Juristinnenbund 1984, 16, 154).

[8] Actually there were 41 women (9.6 per cent of the total) elected to the Weimar *Nationalversammlung*, the constituent assembly to design and pass the Weimar constitution (see Gerhard 1990, 333).

husband) seemed to be secure.[9] Hence admission to the various legal professions was only a temporary victory. Some women were already dismissed from office during the Weimar Republic (Deutscher Juristinnenbund 1998, 20–4).

The Nazis used this statute as a ready tool for regulating the labour market in the aftermath of the Great Depression and its extremely high unemployment rates. However, the 'more effective' tools for this purpose were the infamous *Gesetz zur Wiederherstellung des Berufsbeamtentums* (Statute for the Restoration of the Professional Civil Service) and *Gesetz über die Zulassung zur Rechtsanwaltschaft* (Statute for Admission to the Bar), both issued as early as 7 April 1933. These decrees[10] openly and directly targeted Jewish citizens and communists and provided, respectively, for compulsory retirement or dismissal from the civil service (including not only government officials, but also school teachers, university professors, physicians and nurses in hospitals, post office employees, etc) and for withdrawal from the bar. The admission of university studies was regulated by the *Reichsgesetz gegen die Überfüllung der Schulen und Hochschulen* (National Act against Overcrowding of Schools and Universities) of 25 April 1933. An executive order of the same day restricted the new enrolment of Jewish students to 1.5 per cent, provided the total enrolment of Jewish students did not exceed 5 per cent. As of 1934, women's new enrolment was restricted to 10 per cent of 15,000—the total limit of new admissions to the universities—whereas first-year women had made up between one fifth to one fourth of students in the late 1920s and early 1930s (Pauwels 1984, 21).

These restrictions were primarily directed against Jewish students. In the draft of the 25 April 1933 act, the word 'overcrowding' had originally been 'domination by foreign influences' (*Überfremdung*), as Huerkamp has pointed out (1994, 103–4). The ratio of Jewish students was traditionally higher than their proportion among the overall population and, surprisingly, among female students even higher than among male students (Huerkamp 1994). Law especially was popular among Jewish women; they made up for 7.1 per cent of all women students, but 15.8 per cent of all women law students in the academic year 1929/30, compared to 3.6 and 11.4 per cent respectively for male students (Huerkamp 1994, 94).

The 10 per cent limit for women students never was strictly implemented, and after remilitarisation and the beginning of World War II had caused

---

[9] *Personalabbauverordnung* of 27 October 1923 (Reichsgesetzblatt [official gazette] 943, 1006); see also Gerhard 1990, 345–8.

[10] It should be kept in mind that all Nazi acts and statutes issued later than 24 March 1933 were in fact governmental orders. The last law in a formal sense was the *Gesetz zur Behebung der Not von Volk und Reich* (Law for the Relief of Plight of the People and the State) of 24 March 1933, by which Parliament (*Reichstag*) disempowered itself.

a sharp decline in student enrolment altogether, the women's share in the body of university students even crossed the 50-per-cent line towards the end of World War II (Pauwels 1984, 95–105). However, when the restriction for women's enrolment was lifted on 9 February 1935 (Pauwels 1984, 29), the regulation had had its intended effect: the number of Jewish male students decreased from 2,698 in summer 1932 to 486 in summer 1934, of Jewish women students from 1,252 to 170 (Huerkamp 1994, 104).

When looking at the popularity of the various disciplines among women students during the Nazi period, law lost most—from 7.1 per cent in winter 1929 to less than 1 per cent after 1936 (Pauwels 1984, 42–4). Though Jacques R Pauwels (1984, 29, 44) cites sources showing that Nazi officials encouraged women to take up jurisprudence, he disregards the fact that from 1936 onwards, women were—irrespective of their marital status— barred from the judiciary and, according to a decision made personally by Hitler in August 1936 (a so-called *Führerentscheidung*) also from admission to the bar. Positions in the administration were still available but only those not requiring an academic degree (see Deutscher Juristinnenbund 1984, 158–69).

All this turned the situation of women lawyers back to how it had been at the beginning of the twentieth century: women could graduate in legal studies but nothing more. Who could possibly build up a collective memory when there were so few, and the few not even in those offices where lawyers usually are? The Women Lawyers Association, which had been founded as early as 1914, was dissolved in 1933. However, it escaped the so-called *Gleichschaltung* (enforced political conformity of all civil society and professional associations) even though not all of its members were anti-Nazis (Deutscher Juristinnenbund 1998, 30). After World War II, West German women lawyers in 1948 established a new association (Deutscher Juristinnenbund 1984, 21–7, 184–93; Pohlhausen 1998), which regarded itself as successor to the earlier Association (Deutscher Juristinnenbund 1998, 31–2), although many of the early members were gone. The collective memory that was built up from then on was restricted to West Germany. The inclusion of East German women lawyers into the collective memory after the German unification in 1990 turned out to be difficult and could only be accomplished for the youngest generation (Deutscher Juristinnenbund 1998, 41–54).

III. IN SEARCH OF THE 'FIRSTS'

In 1996 some colleagues and I thought it might be worthwhile to produce a calendar on our 'ancestors', the very early women lawyers of Germany. This would include the first woman to take the law exams, the first to become a judge, the first to become an attorney-at-law, the first to become a law teacher and so on. This project was also inspired by a very moving novel on the first woman lawyer in a German-speaking country, Emilie Kempin (Hasler 1991). A native Swiss, Kempin had studied at Zurich University, where women were admitted as early as in 1867,[11] and later became important also in the US (Hasler 1991 and 1998; Drachman 1998, 123–6).

When collecting candidates for our calendar it was difficult to find names but even harder to find substantive information about our forerunners. We had learned from a book on women who had acquired their *Habilitation* during the first 50 years after admission to university careers that a certain 'Magdalena Schoch' had been the first in a university law department (Boedeker and Meyer-Plath 1974, 191). But the information on her was rather scant: date and city of birth, emigration in 1933, Dr iur in 1920, *Habilitation* in 1932 and a few publications. None of the special publications on women lawyers had even mentioned Magdalene Schoch. We wanted to include her in the calendar but were not able to find any further information, through conventional methods of research or through the internet; no photo or other picture of her could be obtained, which was indispensable for the calendar project. Therefore, much to our regret, we had to leave her out.[12]

Then in April 1998, I met by chance a historian, Eckart Krause, who was co-editor to a three-volume publication on Hamburg University in the years 1933–45 (Krause, Huber and Fischer 1991). When I disclosed my interest in early women lawyers, he came forward with a narrow file on Schoch that contained even a tiny photograph (see page 354). To illustrate how women are often neglected by (mainstream male) historians, he produced a booklet published in 1969 by Hamburg University's Faculty of Law to celebrate its first 50 years. An appendix contained a list claiming to name all scholars who had received their *Habilitation* at that faculty. Schoch, the very first woman in Germany who qualified at Hamburg University for becoming a law professor, was missing from the list. If nothing else, this clearly indicated that she had ceased to be part of (or had never entered) the collective memory of an institution that set so much store by its traditions.[13] She is

---

[11] Many European countries granted women admission to universities in the 1860s and 1870s (Soden 1997, 618, 621). Zurich University, however, was the most popular place in Europe for women to obtain academic degrees. Rosa Luxemburg is one of these women, who Verein Feministische Wissenschaft (1988) has portrayed, along with many of Luxemburg's contemporaries.

[12] The final product contains 12 memoirs and an introduction (Plett and Diegelmann 1998).

[13] Schoch's absence was shared with two male colleagues: Max Grünhut and Hans Großmann-Doerth. Grünhut, who survived in exile and returned to Hamburg to be buried, is named by Göppinger 1963 (revised and expanded as Göppinger 1990) and also represented in a document about the commemorative ceremony at Bonn University in 1964 (Friesenhahn and Weber 1965), as well as a recently published dissertation (Fontaine 1998).

also missing in other documents on emigrants from Nazi Germany (see Häntzschel 2000, 63).

Krause gave me photocopies of his file, expressing his wish that I do some further research and include her in our calendar as some sort of compensation for the failure of the Hamburg University Law Department. The file contained two manuscripts by Schoch; some newspaper clippings from the 1920s on her activities; a letter to Schoch at her American address written by her successor as director of a special library within the Law Department at Hamburg University in 1952; and her reply to him of the same year. It also contained a handwritten letter by Schoch's mother dated August 1933, expressing her shock to Professor Albrecht Mendelssohn Bartholdy, Schoch's mentor, about his forced retirement and her gratitude regarding the support Mendelssohn Bartholdy had given to 'the widow Schoch and her children, especially to Lena [ie, Magdalene]'. Magdalene Schoch's 1952 letter, written in English, was shown in a 1991 exhibition of Hamburg University on its former members persecuted during the Nazi years (Bottin 1992, 54). No further knowledge on Schoch was available in Hamburg at that time. Although it was unlikely that she was still alive in 1998, Krause did not know for sure that she had died.

From then on I began to track down the course of Magdalene Schoch's life and career. I did not find anything in the catalogue of the Library of Congress, which usually gives the years of birth and death of authors. In June 1998, I received a letter from Krause drawing my attention to an article in a volume on women refugees of the Nazi period (Mecklenburg 1995). The article closed the gap between the years 1937, when Schoch emigrated to the United States, and 1952. It contained information about Schoch's employment at the US Department of Justice. But it still did not reveal whether or when she had died. It gave, however, some references to a special collection at the library of the State University of New York (SUNY) at Albany. At once I wrote to both the US Department of Justice and the Albany library but was not rewarded with prompt replies. Nevertheless, I drafted a memoir of Schoch that had a question mark in the lifespan and ended with the sentence 'After 1952, her trail was lost', which was included in the new edition of the German Women Lawyers Association's publication that celebrated their 50th anniversary in September 1998 (Deutscher Juristinnenbund 1998, 195–6). In the fall of 1998 I finally got in touch with a librarian at SUNY Albany, and she sent me photocopies of the four items they had on file (see Schoch 1940s). These added valuable new details, but again the late years were not covered: none of the documents dated later than 1947.

When preparing this chapter, I returned to the internet once more. After having tried the Library of Congress to no avail, I was successful with the catalogue of the University of Wisconsin library; it had one entry, a publication in 1948—and the years of Schoch's birth and death, 1897 to 1987. At once I sent an email to the library asking about the source of the date of Schoch's death, which was almost forty years after the publication of the book. The next day I received a response, which even contained an obituary for Schoch that disclosed additional information on her professional career in the United States and on her late years (*Washington Post* 1987).

All of this—and the bits I've added in the meantime—is still too little to write a full biography on Magdalene Schoch, yet it is sufficient for a brief memoir of her,[14] the first German woman lawyer who had the stamina to pursue a university career.

IV. M MAGDALENE SCHOCH (1897–1987)

Maria Magdalene Schoch was born on 15 February 1897 in Würzburg, Bavaria, where she grew up and passed her *Abitur* (university entrance exam). She began her university studies in Munich while World War I was still raging. Originally she had intended to become a physician but decided on law and political science after discovering that it would take her much longer to become a doctor. Her father had died early, her brother had been killed in World War I, her mother was not entitled to widow pensions and Magdalene had to support herself through scholarships and jobs outside the university (Hessenauer 2000, 323–4). After having spent one semester in Munich she went back to Würzburg. Notwithstanding her pressing economic situation, she also studied philosophy and was active in the student union. She completed her law studies and was awarded the degree of doctor of law (Dr iur) in 1920. The subject of her thesis was 'The English War Legislation against Enemy Corporations', published in a then-renowned law journal (Schoch 1920).

In 1920 she moved to Hamburg. Albrecht Mendelssohn Bartholdy (1874–1936), a famous professor of international law (see Vagts 1979 and Gantzel-Kress 1985) and supervisor to her dissertation, had given his 'very capable assistant Miss Schoch' a position when he accepted a chair at the newly founded Hamburg University. At first Schoch was a research assistant at the Department for Foreign and International Civil and Procedural Law at Hamburg University. In 1923 Mendelssohn Bartholdy founded the *Institut für Auswärtige Politik* (Institute for Foreign Policy/International Relations), which was to become the first institute for peace research in Germany (Weber 1986, 194). Schoch never belonged formally to the staff of this institute, but the 'Archives for Peace Treaties', which she had established in 1920 and were first housed in the private home of the banker Paul Warburg, became the nucleus of the institute's library (Weber 1986, 212). She regularly wrote book reviews, translated articles and official documents from English,

---

[14] For a fine appraisal of Schoch's life and work, see now Nicolaysen 2006. *Cf* also Krause and Nicolaysen 2008.

French and Italian for the institute's journal *Europäische Gespräche* (European Encounters). She also was the chief editor of the German edition of the 'Proceedings and Awards of the Hague Tribunal for the Interpretation of the Dawes Plan', which she translated, edited and commented upon (Schoch 1927–29).

In 1926 Mendelssohn Bartholdy traveled to the United States for the first time and 'discovered' its legal system as a respectable subject for scholarship. His journey proved to be prolific. He founded the *Gesellschaft der Freunde der Vereinigten Staaten* (Society of Friends of the United States), and became one of its Board members. He inaugurated the bi-lingual journal *Hamburg-Amerika-Post* (since 1931 entitled simply *Amerika-Post*), and assigned the responsibility for editing and publishing to Schoch. The foundation of an America Library, which specialised in American law and political science, followed. On 27 June 1930, the library was formally opened in the presence of high-ranking politicians, officials and foreign guests. Again it was Schoch who was entrusted with the task, and she became the head of the library. In her first annual report she wrote, 'It may be stated with satisfaction that Hamburg University has taken leadership in American law studies amongst the German universities' (Schoch 1931, 3).

Beside her tremendous work load, Schoch also engaged herself outside the academic world. She was cofounder and president of the first German Zonta Club in Hamburg (Hoffmann 2002, 26), a chapter of Zonta International, a worldwide organisation of executives in business and the professions working together to advance the status of women. She was engaged in uniting women against National Socialism, and warned against it at a ralley in Covent Garden in 1932.

In November 1932, Schoch qualified as a university lecturer with a *Habilitation* on 'Klagbarkeit, Prozeßanspruch und Beweis im Licht des internationalen Rechts: Zugleich ein Beitrag zur Lehre von der Qualifikation' (Delimitation of Substance and Procedure in Private International Law) and was appointed *Privatdozentin*[15] for international civil and procedural law, comparative law and civil procedural law. She was the first German woman lawyer to get that far at a German university—something of which she was quite aware—and, after Emilie Kempin, she was the second woman lawyer in a German-speaking country to acquire that qualification altogether. But with the Nazi regime imminent, this achievement, usually the last academic consecration before getting a chair, could not provide this function to Schoch in Germany.[16]

---

[15] Comparable to Associate Professor in the United States.
[16] The generally highly commendable study by Sibylle Quack makes Schoch a full professor (Quack 1995b, 188); but Quack is mistaken in this point (maybe it was wishful thinking).

On 30 January 1933, and only a few weeks after she was appointed *Privatdozentin*, the Nazis came to power. Because of his Jewish descent, Mendelssohn Bartholdy was dismissed from his chair at Hamburg University in September 1933. From his post as Director of the Institute for Foreign Policy (which was established as a state-funded trust and hence formally independent of the University), he resigned in February 1934 before he could be forced to do so (Paußmeyer 1983, 145). Mendelssohn Bartholdy migrated to the United Kingdom in the fall of 1934, where he got a Senior Fellowship at Balliol College, Oxford (Bottin 1992). Schoch herself, who was not threatened by administrative Nazi measures, resigned from all her editorial positions but continued to teach and was listed in the personnel index of Hamburg University in the following years. She hoped, as many others did, that the Nazis' power would not last very long. In 1934 her *Habilitation* was published by the renowned publishers Tauchnitz in Leipzig, and she dedicated it to Mendelssohn Bartholdy. And Magdalene Schoch was granted a scholarship by the Rockefeller Foundation to spend a year in the United States, where she visited several law schools and other institutions.

Upon her return to Germany in October 1935 she had to realise that the Institute for Foreign Policy, where she had worked as lecturer and director of the Law Department, had been 'starved out' and decisively changed by the Nazis after Mendelssohn Bartholdy's dismissal and resignation.[17] She wanted to emigrate immediately but could not raise the high funds needed for leaving the country on such short notice. In November 1936 Mendelssohn Bartholdy died, and Schoch spontaneously decided to attend his funeral in London, in spite of warnings of possible reprisals by the Nazis. None of these materialised, but in summer 1937, she felt that she could not stay any longer in an academic environment where even non-Nazis had joined the Nazi party. She applied for an immigration visa to the United States and wrote a letter of resignation from her University positions, to become effective on 1 November 1937. That allowed the Hamburg University administration to force her to resign the qualification she had acquired through the *Habilitation* as well. On 31 October 1937, she quit Hamburg University and emigrated to the United States.

From 1938 until 1943 Schoch worked as a research associate at Harvard University, where she assisted professors Erwin N Grisweld and Paul Freund in teaching. According to her own account, she 'planned and conducted seminar discussions on selected topics of conflict of laws,

---

[17] The history of the Institut für Auswärtige Politik, including its takeover and instrumentalisation by the Nazis, its continuation after 1945 and the role some academics played both prior to and after 1945, has been subjected to thorough research; see the contributions in Gantzel 1983 and 1986.

with special emphasis on constitutional aspects of conflict of laws in the United States' (Schoch 1946[?], 4) and supervised graduate students. During this period she also edited a book on the German legal school of 'Jurisprudence of Interests' (*Interessenjurisprudenz*) for which she selected, translated and annotated a variety of articles; the book was finally published in 1948.

In August 1943 Schoch gained US citizenship, got leave of absence from Harvard Law School and joined the Office of Economic Warfare (later called Foreign Economic Administration), where she assisted in drafting proposals on the legal foundations and implementation procedures of the Potsdam Agreement for the US military government in Germany. Together with lawyer Ernst Fraenkel, who later became an outstanding political scientist,[18] she wrote an essay entitled 'Extra-territorial Effect of Economic Measures Taken by the Occupying Powers in Germany: Problems of Recognition and Enforcement' (1945). This work, however, hardly received any attention because of the Cold War, which closely followed the defeat of Nazi Germany.

After 1945, Schoch refused to return to Germany, declining an offer of a chair at Hamburg University and stating that she 'would never set foot in [that] institution...' (Schoch 1946[?], 4). In 1952, when the head of the America Library of Hamburg University took unusual private initiative to contact her, she wrote to him (in English) that she thought back to her time in Hamburg without personal bitterness because she had found a very satisfying life and new and interesting fields of work in her 'voluntary exile'.

At the end of 1947 or early in 1948 Schoch moved from Cambridge, Massachusetts to Washington, DC,[19] where she worked for the US Department of Justice. At the time of her retirement in 1966, she was chief of the foreign law section of the Justice Department's Office of Alien Property.

She stayed active with Zonta, becoming President of the Arlington chapter. This activity brought her back to Hamburg, where an Inter-European District conference took place in 1963.[20]

M Magdalene Schoch died on 6 November 1987 of Alzheimer's disease in a nursing home in Arlington, Virginia.

---

[18] Fraenkel (1898–1975) emigrated to the United States in 1938 and returned to Germany in 1951. He was author of the monograph *The Dual State*, an early analysis of the character of Nazi rule, which was first published in 1940 by Oxford University Press, New York, and as *Der Doppelstaat* (a retranslation) by Syndikat, Frankfurt/Main, in 1974. See also Stiefel and Mecklenburg 1991, 88–91.

[19] According to the *Washington Post* obituary, Schoch began working for the Department of Justice as early as 1945. However, the change of address appears only from Schoch (1947[?]) to Schoch (1948[?]).

[20] I owe this piece of information Frau Ada Sieveking, Hamburg. See also Hoffmann 2002, 27–8.

V. WHY WE FORGET

The German Women Lawyers Association admits that a reappraisal of the Jewish women lawyers who could not pursue their legal careers because of the Nazi tyranny still has to be undertaken (Deutscher Juristinnenbund 1998, 30).[21] A comprehensive history is overdue, even more so because the discrimination against these women continued in the Federal Republic of Germany, in particular when it came to compensation claims (so-called *Wiedergutmachungsverfahren*): those who had been married were denied compensation for the loss of their jobs 'because married women could have been dismissed anyway' (see Deutscher Juristinnenbund 1998, 30).

Schoch was not Jewish. She left Nazi Germany because she could not bear to live and work with people who all too quickly and willingly surrendered to the fascist regime, and she was thus excluded from the collective memory of 'her' university for decades. Would it have made a difference if she had not declined the offer made by Hamburg University soon after World War II? Or was this refusal the actual reason for her falling into oblivion? It is hard to tell now. However, when looking at past and current numbers of women in German academia in general and German legal academia in particular, we may assume that the setback during the Nazi period has not yet been made up.[22] Women's inroads into academia during the Weimar Republic had faced such a strong opposition that women academics were not really able to get a stronghold at any institution and had no tradition to relate to after World War II (Wobbe 1994, 46–8).

Both the life of Magdalene Schoch and the search for information about her appear to be exemplary of specific difficulties when dealing with collective memory. Her life story teaches us that expulsions from collective memory can occur easily—and may indeed be taking place constantly. We ought to look at who determines the 'collective' of the collective memory. Legal institutions (and other institutions as well) still have patriarchal traits, such that their collective memory may not be reliable when it comes to the participation of women and their place within the collective memory. This alone makes it difficult for women to accomplish what is necessary to be included. Feminist research, especially during the past decade, has discovered more and more

---

[21] Some names have been mentioned by Göppinger (1963 and 1990), some by Gruchmann (1990), further references in Heinrichs et al (1993); some life stories are included in Stiefel and Mecklenburg (1991), Mecklenburg (1995), and Quack (1995a and 1995b). The forced emigration of law faculty members and its consequences for German legal academia have been described by Höpel 1993 and Breunung 1998. In these articles, however, women do not play a role, since Schoch was the only one meeting the criteria.

[22] Especially when the numbers are compared to, eg, the United States. In 1991, women held only 2.3 per cent of tenured professorships at German university law departments (Rust 1997, 102), while women amounted to 20.4 per cent of professors and associate professors at US Law Schools in 1992–93 (White 1997–98).

women who should play a role in the history of their respective disciplines but do not yet (see, eg, Honegger 1994 and Häntzschel 2000).

Moreover, the life story of Magdalene Schoch demonstrates the difficulty of being remembered in the collective memory of even a distinct group, when opposing political and social forces are at work. The Nazis deprived Jews and political opponents (and members of other groups who were doomed not to fit into the Nazi state) first of their respective professional positions, then of their civic rights, then of their citizenship and, ultimately, of their lives. A few of them were able to immigrate to other countries or survive in hiding. Most of them were deported to concentration camps and murdered. Of those who survived hardly any wanted or were ever able to get back to their countries of origin.

The least we owe them is to bring back as many of them as possible into our collective memories. At least Magdalene Schoch has re-entered the collective memory in various spaces, mostly in Hamburg. In 2006, the refurbished lecture room in the old main building of the University of Hamburg was named after Magadalene Schoch by the President of the University in a ceremonial act (see Krause and Nicolaysen 2008).

REFERENCES

Boedeker, Elisabeth and Meyer-Plath, Maria. 1974. *50 Jahre Habilitation von Frauen in Deutschland*. Göttingen: Verlag Otto Schwartz & Co.

Böhm, Reglindis. 1986. Der Kampf um die Zulassung der Frauen als Rechtsanwältinnen und zum Richteramt: aus historischer Sicht unter Betrachtung gegenwärtiger beschäftigungspolitischer Tendenzen. *Deutsche Richterzeitung* 64: 365–74.

Bottin, Angela (in collaboration with Rainer Nicolaysen). 1992. *Enge Zeit: Spuren Vertriebener und Verfolgter der Hamburger Universität (Katalog der gleichnamigen Ausstellung im Auditorium Maximum, Von-Melle-Park, 22.2. bis 17.5.1991)*. Berlin: Dietrich Reimer.

Breunung, Leonie. 1998. Rechtswissenschaften. In *Handbuch der deutschsprachigen Emigration 1933–1945*, edited by C-D Krohn. Darmstadt: Wissenschaftliche Buchgesellschaft.

Deutscher Juristinnenbund (ed). 1984. *Juristinnen in Deutschland: Eine Dokumentation (1900–1984)*. München: J Schweitzer Verlag.

——. 1998. *Juristinnen in Deutschland: Die Zeit von 1900 bis 1998*. Baden-Baden: Nomos Verlagsgesellschaft.

Drachman, Virginia G. 1998. *Sisters in Law: Women Lawyers in Modern American History*. Cambridge, MA: Harvard University Press.

Fabricius-Brand, Margarete; Berghahn, Sabine and Sudhölter, Kristine (eds). 1982. *Juristinnen: Berichte, Fakten, Interviews*. Berlin-West: Elefanten.

Fontaine, Ulrike. 1998. *Max Grünhut (1893–1964): Leben und wissenschaftliches Wirken eines deutschen Strafrechtlers jüdischer Herkunft*. Frankfurt am Main: Peter Lang.

Fraenkel, Ernst. 1940. *The Dual State*. New York: Oxford University Press.

Fraenkel, Ernst and Magdalena Schoch. 1945. *Extra-Territorial Effect of Economic Measures taken by the Occupying Powers in Germany: Problems of Recognition and Enforcement in Neutral Countries*. Records of the Economic Warfare Section. General Records of the Department of Justice (RG 60) location: 230/31/1/07. Foreign Economic Administration Reports.

———. 1975. *Der Doppelstaat*. Retranslation of *The Dual State*. Frankfurt am Main: Syndikat.

Friesenhahn, Ernst and von Weber, Hellmuth (eds). 1965. *In memoriam Max Grünhut: Reden am 25. Juli 1964 bei der Gedächtnisfeier der Rechts- und Staatswissenschaftlichen Fakultät der Rheinischen Friedrich-Wilhelms-Universität*. Bonn: Hanstein.

Gantzel, Klaus Jürgen (ed). 1983. *Kolonialrechtswissenschaft, Kriegsursachenforschung, Internationale Angelegenheiten: Materialien und Interpretationen zur Geschichte des Instituts für Internationale Angelegenheiten der Universität Hamburg 1923–1983 im Widerstreit der Interessen—herausgegeben aus Anlaß des 60. Jahrestages der Gründung des Instituts für Auswärtige Politik*. Baden-Baden: Nomos.

——— (ed). 1986. *Wissenschaftliche Verantwortung und politische Macht: Zum wissenschaftlichen Umgang mit der Kriegsschuldfrage 1914, mit Versöhnungsdiplomatie und mit dem nationalsozialistischen Großmachtstreben—wissenschaftsgeschichtliche Untersuchungen zum Umfeld und zur Entwicklung des Instituts für Auswärtige Politik Hamburg/Berlin 1923–1945*. Berlin: Reimer.

Gantzel-Kress, Gisela. 1985. Albrecht Mendelssohn Bartholdy: Ein Bürgerhumanist und Versöhnungsdiplomat im Aufbruch der Demokratie in Deutschland. *Zeitschrift des Vereins für Hamburgische Geschichte* 71: 127–43.

Geisel, Beatrix. 1997. *Klasse, Geschlecht und Recht: Vergleichende sozialhistorische Untersuchung der Rechtsberatungspraxis von Frauen- und Arbeiterbewegung (1894–1933)*. Baden-Baden: Nomos.

Gerhard, Ute (in collaboration with Ulla Wischermann). 1990. *Unerhört: Die Geschichte der deutschen Frauenbewegung*. Reinbek bei Hamburg: Rowohlt Taschenbuch Verlag.

Göppinger, Horst. 1963. *Die Verfolgung der Juristen jüdischer Abstammung durch den Nationalsozialismus*. Villingen/Schwarzwald: Ring-Verlag.

———. 1990. *Juristen jüdischer Abstammung im 'Dritten Reich': Entrechtung und Verfolgung*. München: CH Beck.

Gruchmann, Lothar. 1990. *Justiz im Dritten Reich 1933–1940: Anpassung und Unterwerfung in der Ära Gürtner*. München: Oldenbourg.

Häntzschel, Hiltrud. 2000. Die Exilierung der Wissenschaften—weiblich: Zur Dimension der Folgen und zu ihrem Stellenwert in der Emigrationsforschung. In *Barrieren und Karrieren*, edited by E Dickmann and E Schöck-Quinteros (in collaboration with Sigrid Dauks). Berlin: trafo Verlag.

Hasler, Eveline. 1991. *Die Wachsflügelfrau: Die Geschichte der Emily Kempin-Spyri*. Zürich: Nagel & Kimche.

———. 1998. Emily Kempin-Spyri (1853–1901). In *Justitias Töchter*, edited by K Plett and K Diegelmann. Darmstadt: FiT Frauen in der Technik.

Hassels, Angela and Hommerich, Christoph. 1993. *Frauen in der Justiz: Eine empirische Analyse der Berufssituation, Karriereverläufe und Karrierechancen von Richterinnen, Staatsanwältinnen und Rechtspflegerinnen*. Köln: Bundesanzeiger.

Heinrichs, Helmut; Franzki, Harald; Schmatz, Klaus and Stolleis, Michael (eds). 1993. *Deutsche Juristen jüdischer Herkunft*. München: CH Beck.

Hessenauer, Heike. 2000. Studentinnen vor 1939: Eine Fallstudie zur Entwicklung des Frauenstudiums. In *Barrieren und Karrieren*, edited by E Dickmann and E Schöck-Quinteros (in collaboration with Sigrid Dauks). Berlin: trafo Verlag.

Hoffmann, Traute. 2002. *Der erste deutsche ZONTA-Club: Auf den Spuren ungewöhnlicher Frauen*. Hamburg: Dölling & Galitz.

Honegger, Claudia. 1994. Die bittersüße Freiheit der Halbdistanz: Die ersten Soziologinnen im deutschen Sprachraum. In *Denkachsen*, edited by T Wobbe and G Lindemann. Frankfurt am Main: Suhrkamp.

Höpel, Stefan. 1993. Die 'Säuberung' der deutschen Rechtswissenschaft—Ausmaß und Dimensionen der Vertreibung nach 1933. *Kritische Justiz* 26: 438–60.

Huerkamp, Claudia. 1994. Jüdische Akademikerinnen in Deutschland 1900–1938. In *Denkachsen*, edited by T Wobbe and G Lindemann. Frankfurt am Main: Suhrkamp.

Krause, Eckart; Huber, Ludwig; and Fischer, Holger (eds). 1991. *Hochschulalltag im 'Dritten Reich': Die Hamburger Universität 1933–1945*, vols 1–3. Hamburg: Dietrich Reimer Verlag.

Krause, Eckart and Nicolaysen, Rainer (eds). 2008. *Zum Gedenken and Magdalene Schoch (1897–1987): Reden aus Anlass der Benennung des Hörsaals J im Hauptegebäude der Universität Hamburg in Magdalene-Schoch-Hörsaal* Hamburg: Hamburg University Press.

Meador, Daniel John. 1986. *Impressions of Law in East Germany: Legal Education and Legal Systems in the German Democratic Republic*. Charlottesville: University of Virginia Press.

Mecklenburg, Frank. 1995. The Occupation of Women Emigrés: Women Lawyers in the United States. In *Between Sorrow and Strength*, edited by Quack. Cambridge: Cambridge University Press.

Nicolaysen, Rainer. 2006. Für Recht und Gerechtigkeit: Über das couragierte laben der Juristin Magdalene Schoch (1897–1987). In *Zeitschrift des Vereins für Hamburgische Geschichte*, 92: 113–143.

Paußmeyer, Carl H. 1983. Die Grundlagen nationalsozialistischer Völkerrechtstheorie als ideologischer Rahmen für die Geschichte des Instituts für Auswärtige Politik 1933–1945: Die Hamburger Rechtsfakultät im Zeitpunkt des Machtübergangs 1933 bis 1935. In *Kolonialrechtswissenschaft, Kriegsursachenforschung, Internationale Angelegenheiten*, edited by KJ Gantzel. Baden-Baden: Nomos.

Pauwels, Jacques R. 1984. *Women, Nazis and Universities: Female University Students in the Third Reich, 1933–1945*. Westport, CT: Greenwood Press.

Plett, Konstanze. 1986. The Rise and Fall of the Reform in West German Legal Education. In *Materials on the German Traditions in Sociological Jurisprudence and Critique of Law*, edited by K Plett. Madison, WI: Institute for Legal Studies, University of Wisconsin, Madison, Law School.

——. Laudatio für Jutta Limbach aus Anlass der feierlichen Verleihung der Ehrendoktorwürde des Fachbereichs Rechtswissenschaft der Universität Breman. In *Kritische Vierteljahresschrift für Gesetzgebung und Rechtswissenschaft*, 92: 3–11.

Plett, Konstanze and Diegelmann, Karin (with assistance from Sonja Mühlenbruch) (eds). 1998. *Justitias Töchter: Frühen Juristinnen auf der Spur (Wandkalender 1999)*. Darmstadt: FiT Frauen in der Technik.

Pohlhausen, Karola. 1998. Hildegard Gethmann (1903–1988). In *Justitias Töchter*, edited by K Plett and K Diegelmann. Darmstadt: FiT Frauen in der Technik.

Quack, Sibylle (ed). 1995a. *Between Sorrow and Strength: Women Refugees of the Nazi Period*. Cambridge: Cambridge University Press.

——. 1995b. *Zuflucht Amerika: Zur Sozialgeschichte der Emigration deutsch-jüdischer Frauen in die USA 1933–1945*. Bonn: Verlag JHW Dietz Nachfolger.

Rowbotham, Sheila. 1976. *Hidden From History: Rediscovering Women in History from the 17th Century to the Present*. New York: Random House (Vintage Books Edition).

Rust, Ursula. 1997. Zur Situation von Frauen in der juristischen Ausbildung und an den juristischen Fakultäten. In *Juristinnen an den Hochschulen—Frauenrecht in Lehre und Forschung*, edited by U Rust. Baden-Baden: Nomos.

——. 2000. 100 Jahre Frauen in der Rechtswissenschaft: Zur Beteiligung von Juristinnen am wissenschaftlichen Diskurs. In *Barrieren und Karrieren*, edited by E Dickmann and E Schöck-Quinteros (in collaboration with S Dauks). Berlin: trafo Verlag.

Schoch, M Magdalene. 1920. Die englische Kriegsgesetzgebung gegen feindliche Gesell-schaften, insbesondere die Zwangsliquidation durch das Handelsamt nach der Trading with the Enemy (Amendment) Act, 1918. *Rheinische Zeitschrift für Zivil- und Prozessrecht* 10: 323–59.

—— (ed). 1927–29. *Die Entscheidungen des Internationalen Schiedsgerichts zur Auslegung des Dawes-Planes*, vols 1–4. Berlin-Grunewald: Walther Rothschild.

——. 1931. Amerika-Bibliothek und Amerika-Post: Bericht für die Jahresmit-gliederversammlung am 29 Mai 1931. Hamburg: Hamburger Bibliothek für Universitäts-geschichte.

——. 1940s. Papers: 'A Bit about My Career': Fragment; 'Curriculum Vitae' [1942] [Harvard Law School]; 'Curriculum Vitae' [nd] [Harvard Law School]; 'Curriculum Vitae' [nd] [Falls Church, VA]. State University of New York, University at Albany: University Libraries, ME Grenander Department of Special Collections and Archives. (In detail: 1946[?]. A Bit about My Career. State University of New York, University at Albany: University Libraries, ME Grenander Department of Special Collections and Archives; 1947[?]. Curriculum Vitae [Harvard Law School]. State University of New York, University at Albany: University Libraries, ME Grenander Department of Special Collections and Archives; 1948[?]. Curriculum Vitae [Falls Church, VA]. State University of New York, University at Albany: University Libraries, ME Grenander Department of Special Collections and Archives.)

Schoch, M Magdalena (ed). 1948. *The Jurisprudence of Interests: Selected Writings of Max Rümelin [and Others]*. Cambridge, MA: Harvard University Press.

von Soden, Kristine. 1997. Auf dem Weg in die Tempel der Wissenschaft: Zur Durchsetzung des Frauenstudiums im Wilhelminischen Deutschland. In *Frauen in der Geschichte des Rechts*, edited by U Gerhard. München: CH Beck.

Statistisches Bundesamt (ed). 1998. *Im Blickpunkt: Frauen in Deutschland.* Stuttgart: Metzler-Poeschel.

Stiefel, Ernst C and Mecklenburg, Frank (eds). 1991. *Deutsche Juristen im amerikanischen Exil: 1933–1950.* Tübingen: JCB Mohr (Paul Siebeck).

Vagts, Alfred. 1979. Albrecht Mendelssohn Bartholdy: Ein Lebensbild. In *Mendelssohn Studien*, vol 3, edited by C Lowenthal-Hensel and R Elvers. Berlin: Duncker & Humblot.

Verein Feministische Wissenschaft (ed). 1988. *Ebenso neu als kühn: 120 Jahre Frauenstudium an der Universität Zürich.* Zürich: eFeF.

Washington Post. 1987. Magdalene Schoch Dies: Ex-Official at Justice. 12 November, C15.

Weber, Hermann. 1986. Rechtswissenschaft im Dienst der NS-Propaganda: Das Hamburger Institut für Auswärtige Politik und die deutsche Völkerrechtsdoktrin in den Jahren 1933 bis 1945. In *Wissenschaftliche Verantwortung und politische Macht*, edited by KJ Gantzel. Berlin: Reimer.

White, Richard A. 1997–98. Statistical Report on Law School Faculty and Candidates for Law Faculty Positions. *Association of American Law Schools*, available at http://aals.org.cnchost.com/resources_statistical.php

Wobbe, Theresa. 1994. Von Marianne Weber zu Edith Stein: Historische Koordinaten des Zugangs zur Wissenschaft. In *Denkachsen*, edited by T Wobbe and G Lindemann. Frankfurt am Main: Suhrkamp.

Reprint of the photo with permission by: Hamburger Bibliothek für Universitätsgeschichte, Hamburg, Germany.

17

Putting the Nazi Past Behind: Juvenile Justice and Germany's Changing Political Culture

RUTH G HERZ

D URING THE 1990s public discourse on juvenile criminal law and justice, as well as the action in juvenile courts seemed to have become increasingly punitive, especially in relation to foreigners. This corresponded to changes in official political rhetoric regarding foreigners. This chapter sets out to portray and analyse this phenomenon. By exposing the undercurrents of these prevalent attitudes I hope to demonstrate how the discourses, both in politics and in the practice of juvenile courts, reflected the changing political climate in Germany and contributed to the presentation of foreigners as a non-desirable group in society. It seems to be no coincidence that the change dovetailed with Germany's reunification, and it needs to be further contextualised and understood against the backdrop of Germany's Nazi past. It seems indeed to be a shift towards a new nationalism, which tends to overlook the Nazi past and ignore the lessons hitherto learnt from it.

The chapter focuses on the reflection of politics and German history in juvenile justice.[1] It was prompted by the public debate in Germany concerning the National Holocaust Memorial in Berlin, which has been raging for over a decade. On its surface, the debate is confined to remembering the Nazi past. But it is as much a debate about adequate ways of doing so, for example by building memorials, establishing days of commemoration and so on. These actions are one way of remembering and of shaping collective memory, yet it is equally important to explore the ways state institutions remember, even in more or less unconscious ways. This chapter examines whether the routine practices of juvenile justice can be considered a 'site' at which remembering actually takes place. Do memories of the past trickle down into the 'real life' of criminal youth courts in Germany? Is it plausible

---

[1] For an analysis of politics, academic criminologists and 'foreigners' see R Herz (1999).

to assume that in the 1990s juvenile justice, dealing with youth between the ages of 14 to 21, bears any relevance to a period that came to an end more than half a century ago?

To this purpose, I will trace the history of German juvenile court law and then proceed by describing and analysing what has actually happened in criminal juvenile courts since reunification. I then place the courts' actions into broader political context. This context is constituted by public and political discourse, which has clearly stigmatised foreigners. By juxtaposing these discourses it will become possible to explain a certain shift in the treatment of foreigners during the last decade since reunification. In short, taking into account Germany's Nazi legacy, the way justice and politics deal with foreigners today is used here as a litmus test as to whether the lessons from the past have in reality been implemented.

The following case illustrates the actual modus operandi of German courts, in particular juvenile courts, which I am going to scrutinise. The case, which was brought before and dealt with by lower and higher courts in Munich in the summer and fall of 1998, illustrates procedures within the juvenile justice system, the justice system in general and government policy towards young foreigners. Mehmet (not his real name), born in Munich to Turkish immigrants who had lived there for thirty years, had allegedly been involved in criminal activity for quite some time. In 1998 he was sentenced to 12 months in a juvenile prison by a Munich juvenile court on the grounds of robbery and theft committed after reaching the age of criminal responsibility. This sentence is quite harsh for German standards of juvenile justice, in particular when considering that Mehmet had just turned fourteen and thus become legally responsible according to German penal law. Therefore he was at least formally a first-time offender. However, the court certainly could not ignore at about 60 criminal offences that Mehmet had committed before the age of fourteen. Since Mehmet was not a German citizen he was eventually deported to his 'home' country Turkey according to the revised Aliens' Act,[2] disregarding the fact that he had only distant relatives in a remote village in Anatolia.

Mehmet is the offspring of Turks who came to Germany in the 1960s, having been officially encouraged to come there as 'guest-workers'. This group seemed to have been well integrated into German society and remained there even when active recruitment policy was stopped due to widespread economic hardship in the wake of the 'oil crisis' in 1973. However, only very few of them have been naturalised, since German laws of citizenship effectively exclude most of them.[3] Another large group of

---

[2] The Act was repealed on 1 January 2005, and replaced by the Residence Act.

[3] On 1 January 2000 a new citizenship law came into effect. According to this law the required period of residence for foreigners eligible for German citizenship under specific conditions was reduced from 15 to 8 years. Children of such foreigners who have been legal

'foreigners' in Germany are refugees who have sought asylum especially in the wake of the collapse of the communist regimes in Eastern Europe. A third large group of immigrants are the 'Aussiedler', ethnic Germans who immigrated from Poland, Romania and the former Soviet Union and who, in contrast to the former groups, enjoy an unconditional 'right of return' and the immediate acquisition of German citizenship on the basis of their ethnic origin. Nonetheless, their cultural heritage and native languages have made integration difficult.[4]

The case of Mehmet is only one example of the 'moral panic' (Cohen 1973) whereby 'foreigners' are cast as a problem group in German society, connecting them particularly with criminality. The decisions concerning Mehmet became a subject of public debate, especially as this got wrapped up in the federal election campaign of September 1998 and was exploited by electioneering politicians. Representatives of most of the political parties referred to Mehmet's case and backed the court's decision.[5]

I. A 'PROGRESS STORY' OF JUVENILE JUSTICE: FALSE CLAIMS AND CONVENTIONAL NARRATIVES

Before actually looking into the German juvenile court in detail it is necessary to present a brief account of how the conventional 'progress story' of juvenile law and justice is told. The idealistic view of the history of juvenile law and justice begins with the first Youth Court Act in 1923, which was based on reform philosophies of care and education. At the beginning of the twentieth century adolescence became more and more acknowledged as a specific period in life with its own problems and its own needs. The new Act was to provide for this age group through specialised personnel and special procedures, as well as special sanctions and institutions. The Act of 1923 was a page-turner but unfortunately not blessed with longevity. A decade after the Nazis came to power they began tampering with the Act and eventually introduced a new Juvenile Court Act in 1943, which was motivated by the deteriorating situation of young people during the war. This Act replaced the original progressive philosophy with a strictly punitive and

---

residents of Germany no less than 8 years and who are born after 1 January 2000 will be granted dual citizenship. By age 23 they must choose which of their nationalities they wish to keep. For a critique of citizenship laws in Germany, see Canefe 1998.

[4] Obviously many other 'foreigners', in the real sense of the term, live in Germany without being labelled as such. These are for example the large community of Japanese businessmen as well as practically all Western Europeans and North Americans living in Germany.

[5] After he had arrived in Turkey, Mehmet became a TV personality for a short time. He was then allowed back into Germany, and joined his parents. In 2005 he was sentenced to imprisonment for threatening, assaulting and extorting money from his parents. He fled back to Turkey, which resulted in a deportation order. As he did not appeal, it took effect.

Nazi ideology. The worst elements of Nazi ideology were eradicated soon after World War II ended. It is argued that the Act that subsequently came into force in 1953 *grosso modo* returned to the philosophy and spirit of the original Act of 1923. Although it has seen some amendments, practically, it is still in force today.

The claim that Nazi ideology had been eliminated from the Juvenile Court Act of 1953 and that the new version of 1953 more or less reverted to its original 1923 version implies, first, that the 'benign' code was related back to 'benign' pre-war Germany and, second, that this enhances the continuity and normality of the history of Germany's legal institutions. The story obviously fits well with the popular narrative that Germany has learnt its lessons from the Nazi past and distanced itself from it. However, this narrative is only partly true. Habits and loyalties die hard and still prevail. In fact it may be argued that only the very blatant Nazi phraseology has been eliminated from the code (Wolff et al 1997). The permanence of 'Jugendarrest', a short-term custodial sentence of a maximum of four weeks, is an example to the contrary. This sanction was first introduced into German juvenile justice in 1940. It was then hailed as the most important and the most modern national-socialist innovation in this field. Its philosophy was a short but tough treatment for 'redeemable Germanic youth'. The 'Jugendarrest' was not eliminated after the war, and there is hardly any prospect that it may happen in the near future. In this particular case, the myth of removal of Nazi ideology from the Juvenile Court Act is upheld through the false claim that the introduction of 'Jugendarrest' had been considered at various times before the Nazi era and that it had its roots in other legal systems.[6] The initiator of this sanction, Friedrich Schaffstein, who had first propagated it in 1936, became one of the most influential professors of juvenile criminal law after the war and remained in this position well into the 1980s. He is also the author of the most widely used textbook on juvenile criminal law.

The progress story moves on to the next shift in juvenile justice, the so-called 'alternative movement' prompted by developments in North America. In Germany, it took off with a certain time lag in the late 1970s. Community service orders and other strategies, such as outdoor groups and anger-management workshops, were introduced. Social workers were in high demand to implement these programmes. The expressly stated goal of these measures was the reduction of custodial sentences. The movement also gave momentum to victim–offender mediation and programmes of restorative justice, which were introduced in the late 1980s. Essentially such innovations have been welcomed as progressive treatment of adolescents,

---

[6] In recent years the true story of the introduction of Jugendarrest into the Act has been admitted (Pieplow 1998).

based on the philosophy of rationality and on understanding young people, and also in line with developments in other European countries.

Despite these apparent advances, to an insider it is clear that juvenile justice in Germany has undergone a backward shift during the last decade. Official statistics suggest that there is a trend towards more punitive sanctions by adult criminal courts as well as youth courts. Juvenile prisons and pre-trial facilities have never been as crowded in the history of the Federal Republic. Pre-trial detention has increased dramatically since 1989 (Dünkel 1994). The rise of the inmate population in prisons as well as in pre-trial detention centres furthermore shows an increasing over-representation of 'foreigners' and ethnic Germans born in the countries of the former USSR. For example, in the state of Lower-Saxony the foreign population in youth pre-trial detention facilities rose from 27 per cent in 1989 to 68 per cent in 1992 and has been rising since. Over a third of these 'foreigners' are Turks, who were born and have grown up in Germany (Schütze 1993). Lower-Saxony is not exceptional in this regard. In the Cologne pre-trial detention centre, for example, foreigners made up 80 per cent of the inmates in May 1999.[7]

The dramatic over-representation of foreigners in pre-trial detention is not due to the seriousness of the offences allegedly committed. Figures from the pre-trial detention facility in Hameln in Lower-Saxony, for example, show that in most cases the alleged offences were not so serious as to justify pre-trial detention or make it necessary. In fact 65 per cent of all alleged offences committed by foreigners were thefts with no violence involved. It seems that quite a number of inmates would not be in detention if they were Germans (Schütze 1993).

The jurisdiction over pre-trial detention orders usually lies with the lower courts. Extensive use of such orders by the lower courts was formerly corrected by way of appeal to the higher courts. This seems no longer to be the case. In several recent decisions the Frankfurt district court, for example, upheld decisions by lower courts to hold foreigners in pre-trial detention, notwithstanding the fact that they were charged with only minor offences, and custodial sentences were not to be expected (Dünkel 1994).

II. A CASE STUDY OF 'FOREIGNERS' IN A CRIMINAL YOUTH COURT

Although revealing, the sentencing and pre-trial detention figures quoted above do not tell the full story. Statistics often conceal truths about the

---

[7] Ironically, prison officers seem to prefer foreign inmates to their German counterparts, claiming they are less rebellious and demanding ('Jugendkriminalitaet'. *Spiegel*, 22 March 1999).

social world that can be revealed only by narratives. More clear conclusions can be drawn from the following typical case, which took place in June 1999 in the juvenile court of Cologne.[8]

Gregor, a German, and Ahmed, a Turk, both 16 years old, were charged with attempted breaking and entering into a small shop at night in order to steal money out of the till. They were further accused of attempting to steal a compact disc in a department store together with Dragan, a 15-year-old Bosnian boy, and Sabine, a 15-year-old German girl. The four teenagers had attended the same school and therefore knew each other well. Like in the majority of cases brought to the youth court, all the defendants admitted to the charges. Gregor and Ahmed explained their action as a desire for adventure and a need for extra cash. As for the shoplifting, all four teenagers claimed that they were hanging around together after school and happened to stroll into the department store. While there, Sabine mentioned to her friends that she very much desired the CD, so Gregor removed its price tag and handed it to Dragan, who hid it in his pocket while Sabine and Ahmed watched the surroundings to make sure they were not discovered.

The decisions of youth courts in Germany, as in most other similar systems, not only are based on the seriousness of the offences committed, but also take into account the personality of the young offenders and former criminal records. The necessary background information for this sort of consideration is provided by 'social inquiry reports', which in turn are provided by social workers from the youth agency and by further questioning conducted by the judge during trials in court.

The social inquiry report in this case stressed that Gregor was the only son of a German working-class family. His school performance was adequate, and he did not engage in any extra curriculum leisure activities. Gregor's former girlfriend was the mother of his one-year-old baby. At the time of the offences, Gregor had become Sabine's boyfriend. He had a previous criminal record of theft. The judge referred mostly to Gregor's school performance, encouraging him to continue his good work. He did not comment, though, on the fact that Gregor had fathered a baby while still a minor. Nor did the judge comment on the fact that Gregor did not bother to visit the child and had failed to assume any responsibility towards the child's mother. He further ignored Gregor's criminal record.

Ahmed was the youngest of four children of a Turkish family that had been living in Germany for a long time. He was born in Germany, where he had spent all his life. He was the only child still living at home with his parents, as his older siblings had settled with their families in their own

---

[8] I was an observer of this court trial with a group of university students, ie, I and my students were in the audience, for which special permission needs to be obtained for juvenile courts. My observations are based on nearly 30 years of experience as a judge in a juvenile court in Germany.

homes. Ahmed's room was in the basement of his parents' house. His mother looked after his needs, waking him in the mornings and preparing his school lunches before leaving for work as a cleaner. Ahmed did not attend school regularly. The judge started by reproaching Ahmed for truancy, warning him that this would lead to more crime. Throughout the trial, he ignored the fact that Ahmed had no previous criminal record. He stressed that Ahmed should adapt to a German lifestyle, rules and regulations. This seemed to mean attending school regularly, being law-abiding and abstaining from further theft. The judge did not fail to insinuate that Ahmed's parents had been irresponsible in having failed to notice their son's truancy.

Dragan was a refugee from Bosnia who had arrived in Germany with his family several years earlier. He was a conscientious pupil with no criminal record. He had already secured a job that would begin once he finished school. He was also a member of a Bosnian folk-dancing group. The judge approved of Dragan's conscientiousness while commenting favourably on his leisure-time activities.

Sabine appeared to be a sweet and pretty girl who was very popular with the boys in her school. She lived with her German mother, a single parent. She had two older half-siblings, who each had a different father. Her school performance was abominable and deteriorating, about which she provided a flimsy explanation in response to the judge's questions. She told him that when arriving at school in the mornings she was still highly motivated; however, as the mornings wore on she lost interest and could no longer muster up any attention for school matters. The judge accepted this without criticism, also disregarding the fact that she had a previous record of shoplifting.

In passing his sentences the judge sent both Gregor and Ahmed to two weeks' youth custody (Jugendarrest), a sentence at the more severe end of the range of measures provided by German juvenile law. In addition, Ahmed was put on probation for a period of nine months. The judge specified that Ahmed should be put under the control of a male probation officer for 'cultural' reasons and went on to explain this by saying that Turks do not respect women as authorities. Dragan was ordered to do 30 hours of community service work, while Sabine's case was closed with no sanction at all.

Gregor and Ahmed had committed identical offences, yet Gregor was treated more leniently than Ahmed, who had never been to court before. However, this was not the main difference in the judge's interaction with the defendants. Gregor, who had shown no sense of responsibility, as demonstrated by his previous criminal record, and who had never even bothered to visit his child regularly, might very well have been in need of some form of guidance from a social worker; but the judge overlooked this factor altogether. Instead, he only referred to Gregor's school performance, thus implicitly constructing a future for a well integrated grown male. In contrast, Ahmed was constructed as the 'other', as a foreigner. The judge implied that Ahmed belonged to a people who, contrary to Germans, do not respect women as authorities and do not respect the legal and social rules of the country, such as attending school regularly. Actually, there had been nothing especially disturbing about his behaviour. Ahmed had at least not previously broken the rules of the criminal code. Ahmed's parents were made to look as though they had failed in their parental responsibilities, although it is hard to imagine what else his mother could have done to look after her son, considering that she woke him every morning and prepared his school lunch before she went out to work. His parents had apparently done well bringing up their older children, who by then were settled with their own families and homes. Nonetheless Ahmed was portrayed as a 'bad' foreigner who must be placed under the control of a German male probation officer.

In contrast to the portrayal of Ahmed as the 'bad' foreigner, Dragan was portrayed as a 'good' foreigner. The judge emphasised that he liked the way Dragan was an integral member of *his own* foreign community. He could be seen as a folklore 'exhibit', dressed in ethnic clothes and dancing exotic dances. This is the way in which one would like to see foreigners, clearly implying that such good foreigners should eventually find their way back to their home countries. Although Dragan was such a 'model youth', and disregarding the fact that he had no previous record and had been manoeuvred into stealing the CD by Sabine, the judge ordered him to do community service work. Community service work hardly seems justified in this case, given the educative and reintegrative philosophy of youth justice.

It is worth noting that Sabine's case was closed with no rehabilitative sanction at all, despite her family background, her school performance and her previous record, which might well be a cause for concern. Her situation certainly called for a sanction when compared to either Ahmed or Dragan's cases.[9] The judge's attitudes and decisions are all the more out of place considering that both 'foreigners' were exceptionally well integrated into German society.

All in all, contrary to what the bare statistics tell, this trial reveals that the judge's decisions were not especially punitive towards the foreigners. However, it is patently clear that what is going on in the courtroom is rather more subtle. The judge drew on and stressed ethnic differences, evidently treating the 'foreigners' as such during the trial as well as in his sentencing decisions. Nevertheless judges perceive themselves as simply applying the law. Such an attitude allows for more punitive treatment of 'foreigners'

---

[9] Obviously, the judge's decision also involves a component of chivalry and of gender bias, which cannot be adequately dealt with in this chapter.

because of their ties and bonds to society are allegedly weaker than those of German youths. Such judges do not seem to be aware that they are drawing a sharp line between Germans and foreigners.

III. PUBLIC, POLITICAL, AND LEGAL DISCOURSE ABOUT FOREIGNERS

As suggested earlier, the tendency to distinguish between 'Germans' and 'foreigners' as it manifests itself in the court room is linked to public and political discourses. In the mid-1980s, Heiner Geissler, a former Secretary General of the Christian Democratic Party, asked a rhetorical question about the reasons behind the existence of the 'foreigner' category in the federal crime statistics in a TV show (Herz 1999). His attempt to get the category abolished took place before the collapse of the communist regimes of Eastern Europe and the reunification of Germany. Following his election as President of the Federal Republic in May 1999, Johannes Rau thanked the electorate and promised to be 'a president for all Germans and a contact for all those, who without a German passport live and work amongst us' (http://www.bundespraesident. de/-,2.12097/Dankesrede-von-Johannes-Rau-na.htm?global.printview=2). The first quote is an example of German official political rhetoric from the 1980s, when foreigners were not yet marked as undesirable or superfluous, while the second illustrates the changing atmosphere during the last decade, which has emphasised the difference between Germans and non-Germans.

Indeed, between the mid-1980s and the end of the 1990s, public and political discourses about youth crime, juvenile law and justice in Germany had become increasingly punitive. Public discourse focused on the alleged increase in quantity and the more severe offences of young people. 'They rob, they deal, they kill' is just one example of headlines in the media ('Sie rauben, sie dealen, sie töten'. *Stern*, 3 July 1997). Politicians and other moral entrepreneurs called for tougher treatment by youth court judges, whom they labelled 'lenient, lax and lame'. This discourse seems to target youth in general but in fact is directed towards foreigners.

The policy of the coalition government under Chancellor Kohl, which was in power from 1982 to 1998, began openly to point at crime committed by foreigners in the 1990s (Villmow 1999). In August 1997, Manfred Kanther, then Minister of Interior Affairs, warned the public that denial of the over-representation of foreigners in crime statistics would have negative effects on German society, and that legal measures had to be taken. The revised Alien's Act in 1997 provided one response to the problem by allowing deportation of foreigners from Germany to their countries of origin upon receiving custodial sentences for crimes. Further, Kanther demanded harsher treatment of foreigners by the justice system and advocated the implementation of preventive measures such as 'community safety patrols', which should be set up in collaboration between local police, municipalities and citizens. Finally, Kanther asserted that 'the days are over when leftist ideology made us avoid to face the danger which crime poses to society'.[10] Even more striking was the statement by the Christian Democratic Party's committee on crime, issued in the Bundestag (Federal Parliament) in 1995, which alerted German citizens to

> expect the police to do something about crime. It is the responsibility of the police to take action against Vietnamese cigarette smugglers, Albanian thief gangs, African drugtrafficers etc, as well as against the Russian mafia and others... (Pressestelle der CDU/CSU Fraktion im Deutschen Bundestag, quoted in *Frankfurter Allgemeine Zeitung*, 12 August 1995).

In May 2000, the Social Democratic Federal Government introduced special work permits for foreign computer specialists because of the dramatic lack of such professionals in Germany. Candidates were to be recruited from India for a maximum stay of four years. During the election campaign for the parliament of Northrhine-Westfalia in May 2000, the head of the Christian Democratic Party coined the slogan 'Kinder statt Inder', implying that rather than 'importing' foreigners, increasing the birth rate amongst the German population should be encouraged.

This attitude and policy was not confined to the parties in power in Germany before 1998. Social Democratic local governments and their leaders had clearly assumed a similar position. When the Social Democratic Party under Chancellor Gerhard Schröder came to power in September 1998, none of the punitive and restrictive laws introduced by the former government were revised; on the contrary, they became entrenched.

Neither was the stigmatising approach to foreigners and crime restricted to the Federal Government. In 1997, the Police Chief of Cologne—a major city in the west of Germany with a population of one million inhabitants, which had been governed by the Social Democrats for the last 40 years—stated in an interview to the local press:

> [T]he key now is that crime is committed by foreigners, especially because of their over-representation in violent crimes. The foreign population of Cologne is 18 per cent, but foreigners are responsible for 48 per cent of violent crimes committed in Cologne ... The question is, who are these offenders?

Responding to his own question, he went on to say:

> Some foreigners come to our city specifically in order to commit crimes. To those we react harshly and with no compassion. Others are youth who commit robberies and other violent acts who are third-generation unemployed foreigners. They

---

[10] 'Kanther verheißt "eindeutige ausländerrechtliche Antworten"'. *Frankfurter Allgemeine Zeitung*, 20 August 1997.

are frustrated because they have not been successfully integrated into German society. They are caught between two cultures and do not know which way to go. In these cases we want to make serious efforts. These tasks need to be shouldered by all our society (*Kölner Stadt Anzeiger*, 17 September 1997).

One example of such a multi-agency effort initiated in Cologne in 1997 is a 'partnership patrol' of police and citizens in areas populated mainly by poor people, who are mostly foreigners. Another strategy has been the use of new technologies. Closed circuit television (CCTV) cameras have been installed in some areas of the city where many foreigners reside and work (*Kölner Stadt Anzeiger*, 18 September 1997). These 'small-scale' strategies on the community level are not restricted to Cologne. They have been implemented in many regions and cities.

Alongside such practical measures, more restrictive amendments of important federal laws concerning non-Germans have been passed during the last decade. The right to asylum, which was inscribed as a basic human right in the *Grundgesetz*, the German Constitution of 1949, was amended in 1993 through a consensual vote of the large parties in the Bundestag. It is now extremely restricted and practically watered down to exclude a majority of asylum seekers (Art 16, 16a GG). In 1997 the Aliens Act was amended, making deportation of non-German adolescents mandatory if they are sentenced to a prison sentence of at least 2 years, and allowing for deportation even if they are given a lesser sentence (§47 Ausländergesetz).

The political debates reveal how the economic and political conditions of the 1980s have changed during the 1990s since the reunification of Germany and the collapse of the communist regimes of Eastern Europe. In the tranquil economic and political conditions of the 1980s Geissler could comfortably argue that the 'foreigner' category in crime statistics was not an issue and hence should be abolished. During the 1990s and since reunification, however, politicians have felt obliged to react and present solutions to the crime problems that seem so pressing to the public. Doing something about the 'crime question' implies a show of power and effectiveness. The purpose is to uphold the perception that the state is capable of maintaining security, law and order and crime control within its territorial boundaries (Garland 1996). Foreigners' crimes lend themselves to such a message and are thus an easy target for public and political discourse. However, focusing on foreigners' crimes sends the message that life could be much easier if there were fewer foreigners within Germany's territorial boundaries. Forgotten are the days when Turkish immigrants were recognised as an integral part of German society. This discourse now designates foreigners as 'others'. This is done even with best intentions, a case in point being the statement above by President Rau, who is known as a liberal and wanted in fact to express his acceptance of foreigners while he was actually presenting German society as consisting of two different groups. This discourse results in linking foreigners with crime and violence and thus turns them into 'folk devils' (Cohen 1973). They are transformed from a problem population into a dangerous class. Consequently, laws and judicial strategies in courts are designed to exclude foreign minority groups.

Although judges may not generally be markedly tougher on foreigners than on German youth, there is a shift in their behaviour in court. This shift corresponds to the change in the general political climate outside the courtroom. Judges claim to be impartial agents of 'the law' who are little affected by either politics or policies. Judges in Germany do not regard themselves as serving the needs of specific communities. Although they are not oblivious to the pressure exerted on them by the public and through political discourse, they assume that they are not susceptible to it. In a recent study, court judges who had been hearing trials dealing with hate crimes against foreigners were interviewed and asked whether they felt any pressure from the public debates of these issues and cases (Neubacher 1999). They easily waved off such suggestions, insisting that they were strongly committed to the prevailing youth law ideology of understanding and education. They obviously failed to see how profoundly they are affected by the prevailing general political climate, which is then incorporated into their decisions and sentencing.

Analysing data on pre-trial detention decisions, the German criminologist Frieder Dünkel (1994) argues that in times of economic recession and social tension, judges feel that they can resort to pre-trial detention as a means of appeasing the general public. There is, however, a danger that they may then start exploiting this instrument for political rather than strictly legal reasons. He points out that there is no way of relying on the judiciary to stick to 'the law' under such societal conditions. Dünkel does not explain further reasons for such trends in the decision making of judges, failing thus to attribute these changes to wider changes of the political and social climate.

It remains now to be seen how the public discourse permeates into the courtroom and how this influences the judges. Feeley and Simon (1994) argue that criminal justice is profoundly changing. While what they call the 'old penology' was rooted in concern for individuals, the 'new penology' in contrast has a radically different orientation. It is 'actuarial' in its objectives and procedures and is concerned with techniques of identifying, classifying and managing groups according to their assumed levels of dangerousness. It seeks to regulate groups as part of a strategy of general risk and danger management in society. Practices that are not new as such are being used in new ways and thus reinvented. Pre-trial detention, for example, seems to be no longer used in order to assure presence at trial but either as a preventive measure or as summary punishment for any individual with a profile of dangerousness. Consequently, 'foreigners' in Germany, who have been assigned profiles of crime and danger, are subject to extensive pre-trial detention policies, even when the seriousness of such detention reflects neither their crimes nor the actual risk of absconding.

The political and public discourses as described above are seminal in constructing the profile of 'foreigners' as criminal and dangerous. When he campaigned for the position of prime minister of Lower-Saxony in 1997, Schröder, who later became Chancellor, warned that 'Poles are especially active in car thefts, Russians control prostitution in Germany, Southern Europeans and black Africans are drug dealers...' (quoted in *Focus*, 14 January 2008). The new profile of foreigners as dangerous is not confined to the public and political arena but has entered the courtroom. Narratives do more than simply reflect or express existing ideologies: they shape social lives (Ewick and Selby 1995). The narrative of 'the foreigner' thus enters the courtroom not only because it is pervasive in the public discourse. It enters above all because this image of foreigners is promoted and transported by those members of society who are members of the elite in politics and who have the power to shape and legitimise the way foreigners are seen. It is common for judges to identify with this group in society more than with others. When judges in Germany are 'doing justice' they are 'doing ethnicity'. Criminal justice is perhaps not leading but certainly following trends of attitudes, practices and policies towards foreigners. However, criminal justice gives them a particular profile that is a powerful tool in public and political discourse about them, and legitimises changes in policies on all levels.

IV. THE UNDERCURRENT OF GERMANY'S NAZI PAST

The developments discussed above may indeed resemble those presently occurring in other countries where politicians are promoting harsher anti-minority and anti-immigrant policies and introducing laws to make immigration more difficult and deportation easier, and judges are more severe on 'foreigners' (Wacquant 1999). But each country has its unique history, traditions and collective memories. Politics and justice therefore need to be understood in relation to the specific context of political culture. It would be a mistake to assume that apparently similar terms or developments carry corresponding meanings in different contexts. Such an assumption may obscure significant nuances or the fact that terms are heavily burdened with historically and culturally specific connotations.

Germany's Nazi past is not only unique but also constitutive to its present. Post-war Germany has built its legitimacy by claiming to have drawn a clear line between itself and the Nazi period (Olick and Levy 1997). The boundary between past and present is drawn with the help of Germany's 'basic narrative', which in turn consists of many small tales (T Herz 1996). The central element of the basic narrative is the Holocaust, with the tales following several sub-patterns. It basically goes like this: the new Germany started its reconstruction after the war at 'zero hour' ('Stunde Null'); since then it has succeeded in coming to terms with its Nazi past; new democratic institutions have been set up; in the sphere of law and justice, trials were conducted against the Nazi perpetrators; judges and prosecutors, as well as other prominent legal professionals with Nazi pasts were removed from office; and Nazi ideology was removed from the law codes. The 1949 Constitution of the Federal Republic ('basic law' or *Grundgesetz*) incorporated lessons learnt from the past (see Kim Lane Scheppele in this volume). The right to asylum, included in the 'basic rights' of the German constitution and therefore non-amendable, was such a lesson. It was a reaction to the experience of persecuted Jews and others who had been forced to flee to countries where they often had been denied entry. Article 3 of the Constitution, which stipulates that nobody should be discriminated on the grounds of sex, belief, origin or race, is yet another lesson learnt from the past.

What is at the root of new policies on 'foreigners' in contemporary Germany? Notably, the fall of the Berlin wall in 1989 was a starting point for these policies, which certainly coincide with the process of reunification of the two former Germanys. In particular the emergence of widespread racist and xenophobic attitudes can be attributed to the repercussions of reunification as well as the collapse of the Eastern European regimes. The large numbers of refugees who have entered Germany has caused anxiety about economic loss and unemployment, and further about instability and insecurity in neighbourhoods (Heitmeyer 1993). As has been shown above, stigmatisation of foreigners is not restricted to uprooted and unemployed youths. We therefore need to explore other explanations for the change in the political culture in Germany.

One of the changes in German political culture caused by reunification is the general recognition that the post-war period has come to an end. Germany is now a European country like others. This entails a process of normalisation and neutralisation of the past. Reinstating Berlin as the capital of reunified Germany is a defining feature of this trend, which finds its articulation in the debates about the Nazi past. During the 1990s this debate focused on the National Holocaust Memorial in Berlin. Although it was supposed to be a debate about remembering the Nazi past, much of it was about *not* building the memorial at all, or not on such a prominent site, or not only for Jewish victims, etc. The topics and arguments put forward therefore seemed to support a kind of 'relativistic thinking' about the Holocaust and thus became one route toward neutralising and normalising the Nazi past. The final decision in favour of the memorial was larglely related to Germany's preoccupation with its image abroad and its claim to being a 'reliable nation' (Olick 1998). The agreement to build the memorial was finally reached in the very week when the German Federal Parliament and Government moved from Bonn, a city that had established a tradition of peace and integration with the West, to Berlin, a city with strong historical links to power and nationalism. Another recent example of the trend towards normalising and neutralising the Nazi past was the controversy surrounding Martin Walser's speech in October 1998, in which he lamented the ever-present reference to and portrayal of the Holocaust in Germany and claimed that these were counterproductive for the present political culture of Germany. On the surface, these debates apparently deal with the horrors of the Holocaust and about finding adequate forms of remembering it. However, they actually are about overcoming the constraints of the Nazi past. Moreover, since reunification Germany has two competing pasts, and the communist past of the former East Germany may even be replacing the Nazi past (Offe 1993; Olick 1998). At the very least, the former takes the heat off the latter: Germany's problems with its history are now also those of communism and its secret police (see Roger Engelmann in this volume), and much less those of concentration and death camps.

Since reunification, the sharp line of division between the present and the Nazi past, which was a defining characteristic of Germany's political culture, has become increasingly blurred. The dissolution of the boundary line did not begin simultaneously with the reunification of the two former Germanys. Rather it began gradually and slowly during the 1990s. One of the most important contemporary developments since reunification is that the 'basic narrative' of Germany has undergone a shift (T Herz 1996), which has entailed the development of a new nationalism. This nationalism allows for gradually and subtly ignoring or even forgetting the lessons supposedly learnt from the Nazi past (see also Heinz Steinert in this volume). A major consequence is that acceptance and non-acceptance of strangers and foreigners no longer has to be seen against the backdrop of the Nazi period, and the former taboo regarding discrimination of 'others' no longer holds. In this context, the revision of the law of asylum in 1993 cannot be overrated. What began here was a kind of institutional stigmatisation of foreigners that was based on a general parliamentary consensus and opened up the way toward allowing them to be labelled as dangerous and criminal.

Non-German immigrants began to be openly identified as competitors for scarce social goods in the 1990s. Foreigners are now being openly stigmatised whether or not they are actually competitors in the German labour market. In 1999 Otto Schily, the Social Democratic Minister of the Interior, simply declared that 'the boat is full', emphasising the 'insurmountable costs of accommodating foreigners in Germany today' (quoted in Gössner 1999). Not only those who have recently immigrated to Germany but also those who arrived a long time ago have been identified as competitors for scarce social goods (Boers 1996; Offe 1993). In times of social and economic insecurity, being German and belonging to the nation is becoming increasingly important, thus making the political atmosphere conducive to presenting foreigners as 'suitable enemies' (Christie 1986).

When the Berlin Wall came down, former Chancellor Willy Brandt said: 'Now what belongs together must grow together' ('es soll zusammen wachsen was zusammen gehört'). He was thus creating a 'national consciousness' indispensable for the reunification of the two communities that had been divided for more than forty years. United Germany is confronted with the problem of creating a single state. This is done by stressing the notion of a single nation, informed by a common future and a common past. German reunification has therefore emphasised the exclusive content of 'German-ness' at the expense of dealing with the actual diversity in its society. Consequently those who do not and cannot belong are foreigners. They are juxtaposed with the imagined community of Germans as others who shall not be included (Lacey and Zedner 1998).

This is a new nationalism, facilitated by the blurring of the boundary to the Nazi past. However, it is not nationalism of the masses but rather, as Offe (1993) points out, nationalism of the elite. The elite utilise the notion of nation in order to fill the political and ideological vacuum caused by the collapse of the European communist regimes and to overcome economic and social problems. Reunification serves the interests of the country's elite, boosting their economic interest and enhancing their leadership. This new nationalism of the elite both in justice and politics overlooks the Nazi past and ignores the lessons learnt from it. It comes as no surprise that juvenile justice becomes another site where the Nazi past is being put behind.

REFERENCES

Boers, Klaus. 1996. Sozialer Umbruch und Kriminalität in Deutschland. *Monatsschrift für Kriminologie und Strafrechtsreform* 79: 314–37.

Canefe, Nergis. 1998. Citizens versus Permanent Guests: Cultural Memory and Citizenship Laws in a Reunified Germany. *Citizenship Studies* 2: 519–44.

Christie, Nils. 1986. 'Suitable Enemies'. In *Abolition: Towards a Non-repressive Approach to Crime*, edited by H Bianchi and R van Swaaningen. Amsterdam: Free University Press.

Cohen, Stanley. 1973. *Folk Devils and Moral Panics: The Creation of Mods and Rockers*. London: Paladin.

Dünkel, Frieder. 1994. Praxis der Untersuchungshaft in den 90er Jahren— Instrumentalisierung strafprozessualer Zwangsmittel für kriminal- und ausländerpolitische Zwecke? *Strafverteidiger* 14: 610–21.

Ewick, Patricia and Selby, Susan. 1995. Subversive Stories and Hegemonic Tales: Towards a Sociology of Narrative. *Law and Society Review* 29: 197–226.

Feeley, Malcolm and Simon, Jonathan. 1994. Actuarial Justice: The Emerging New Criminal Law. In *The Futures of Criminology*, edited by D Nelken. London: Sage.

Garland, David. 1996. The Limits of the Sovereign State. *The British Journal of Criminology* 36: 445–71.

Gössner, Rolf. 1999. Aufbruch und Erneuerung? *Neue Kriminalpolitik* 11: 9–14.

Heitmeyer, Wilhelm. 1993. Gesellschaftliche Desintegrationsprozesse als Ursachen von fremdenfeindlicher Gewalt und politischer Paralysierung. *Aus Politik und Zeitgeschichte* 43: 3–13.

Herz, Ruth. 1999. Die Kategorie 'Ausländer': Bedarfsforschung für die Kriminalpolitik? *Neue Kriminalpolitik* 11: 20–3.

Herz, Thomas. 1996. Die 'Basiserzählung' und die NS-Vergangenheit, Zur Veränderung der politischen Kultur in Deutschland. In *Gesellschaften im Umbruch, Verhandlungen des 27. Kongresses der deutschen Gesellschaft für Soziologie in Halle an der Saale 1995*, edited by L Clausen. Frankfurt/Main: Campus.

Lacey, Nicola and Zedner, Lucia. 1998. Community in German Criminal Justice: A Significant Absence? *Social and Legal Studies* 7: 7–25.

Neubacher, Frank. 1999. Die fremdenfeindlichen Brandanschläge nach der Vereinigung. *Monatsschrift für Kriminologie und Strafrechtsreform* 82: 1–15.

Offe, Claus. 1993. Wohlstand, Nation, Republik. Aspekte des deutschen Sonderweges vom Sozialismus zum Kapitalismus. In *Der Zusammenbruch der DDR*, edited by H Joas and M Kohli. Frankfurt/Main: Suhrkamp.

Olick, Jeffrey. 1998. What Does It Mean to Normalize the Past? *Social Science History* 22: 547–71.

Olick, Jeffrey and Levy, Daniel. 1997. Collective Memory and Cultural Constraint: Holocaust Myth and Rationality in German Politics. *American Sociological Review* 62: 921–35.

Pieplow, Lukas. 1998. 75 Jahre JGG. *DVJJ-Journal* 9: 210–13.

Schütze, Helmut. 1993. Junge Ausländer im Vollzug der Straf- und Untersuchungshaft. In *Freiheitsentzug bei jungen Straffälligen*, edited by T Trenczek. Bonn: Forum.

Villmow, Bernhard. 1999. Ausländer als Täter und Opfer. *Monatsschrift für Kriminologie und Strafrechtsreform*, Sonderheft 82: 22–9.

Wacquant, Loic. 1999. 'Suitable Enemies': Foreigners and Immigrants in the Prisons of Europe. *Punishment and Society* 1: 215–22.

Wolff, Jörg; Egelkamp, Margareth; and Mulot, Tobias. 1997. *Das Jugendstrafrecht zwischen Nationalsozialismus und Demokratie*. Baden-Baden: Nomos.

Index